ARGUING REVOLUTION

ARGUING REVOLUTION

The Intellectual Left in Postwar France

SUNIL KHILNANI

YALE UNIVERSITY PRESS
NEW HAVEN AND LONDON · 1993

To Rebecca

Set in Meridien by Best-set Typesetter Ltd., Hong Kong
Printed and bound in Great Britain by
Biddles Ltd., Guildford and Kings Lynn

Library of Congress Cataloging-in-Publication Data
Khilnani, Sunil, 1960–
    Arguing revolution: the intellectual left in postwar France/Sunil Khilnani.
        p.   cm.
    Includes bibliographical references and index.
    ISBN 0–300–05745–8
    1. Political science—France.   2. France—Politics and government—1945–   3. Intellectuals–France.   4. Right and left (Political science)   I. Title.
    JA84.F8K5   1993
    320.5'0944—dc20   93–17376
                                                                                    CIP

A catalogue record for this book is available from the British Library.

Contents

Paris est la capitale de la civilisation . . . Et saviez-vous pourquoi Paris est la ville de la civilisation? C'est que Paris est la ville de la révolution.

Victor Hugo, 'Rentrée à Paris', *Actes et Paroles*, III (Paris, 1871).

One would expect people to remember the past and to imagine the future. But in fact, when discoursing or writing about history, they imagine it in terms of their own experience, and when trying to gauge the future they cite supposed analogies from the past: till, by a double process of repetition, they imagine the past and remember the future.

Lewis Namier, 'Symmetry and Repetition', *Conflicts* (London and Basingstoke, 1942).

Preface

This book is intended as a contribution towards understanding the character of political thought and argument in postwar France. But this ambition is lent focus by means of a more specific inquiry, intended to cast light on the extraordinary and recent shift in French intellectual and political taste. Historically, France's intellectuals were always accorded an unusually prominent role in their country's politics: it was through their public arguments that the terms which defined the political community were forged. In the years after the end of the Second World War until the mid-1970s, the arguments of the intellectual Left weighed heavily upon the conduct of French political debate. These arguments loomed not only over the domestic landscape, but also further afield: they came to play a fundamental role in the entire afflatus of Western progressive thought. Parisian fashions, styles of language, and opinions, were transmitted with astonishing rapidity across the globe. Rehoused in vastly different surrounds, the original and very often intensely local obsessions and motivations of these arguments were conveniently effaced; they came to be heard as primarily philosophical in character, as arguments for the Left in general. But it remains impossible to explain the sudden deflation of these forms of argument and thought so long as they are considered purely in internal terms. Nor is it any more helpful to reduce the arguments to indices of extrinsic processes, whether social or economic. Such approaches indolently evade any specification of the character of political thought and argument in France: unable properly to account for the changes that have occurred, they are unable to judge the significance of these changes.

My account is not a social history of the French intellectual Left: it pays attention to social and institutional context only where these are judged to be relevant to its central argument. Nor does it follow the rhythms of conventional history of ideas, systematically reconstructing concepts and debates in their temporal sequence. It is quite explicitly and in the original sense a *biased* book: it proposes a new angle of vision, one which brings certain significant patterns into clearer focus. I do not claim that the numerous existing studies of the French intellectual Left which have identified other concerns or stressed different emphases are mistaken; rather, that it is more useful to view political thought and argument in postwar France in the way suggested here, particularly if we wish to understand why its fundamental premises changed so suddenly, and what the significance of this was.

This book takes the arguments as they were intended to be taken: as *arguments*, advanced and conducted in very particular circumstances, responses to questions raised by the politics of the time. For those on the Left, these arguments centred around the idea of revolution. Intellectuals argued about past revolutions—the French Revolution, the Soviet Revolution, and their relation to one another—, about future revolutions, and about the relation between past and future revolutions. They disputed the political value of revolution, its consequences, and who was to accomplish it. In the historically rich French language of revolutionary politics, they discovered a vocabulary in which to describe the political community, a characterization of France's political identity. And ultimately it was on this terrain, where different conceptions of the political community clashed, that a revolution in the terms of argument was itself effected.

I have benefited from the generosity of several institutions and many people in researching and writing this book. I am grateful to the Studentship Electors of King's College, Cambridge for awarding me a studentship which allowed me to conduct research in Paris. I am enormously grateful too to the Master and Fellows of Christ's College, Cambridge for electing me to a Research Fellowship, which provided me with an excellent environment in which to write an earlier version of this book. I finally completed it while a member of the Department of Politics and Sociology at Birkbeck College, London, and I thank my colleagues there for their patience and support. Personal debts are more numerous. In Paris, Camilla and Valerio Adami were repeatedly the most generous of hosts. I learnt much from conversations with Jean Bazin, Pierre Birnbaum, Cornelius Castoriadis, François Furet, Marcel Gauchet, Pierre Grémion, Pierre Hassner, Claude Lefort, Bernard Manin, Pierre Nora, Pasquale Pasquino, Michel Plon, Jacques Rancière and Jacques Rupnik. For their responses to and comments upon various more primitive versions of the argument, I am very grateful to Perry Anderson, Daniel Bell, Stefan Collini, Vincent Descombes, Peter Dews, Bianca Fontana, Tony Giddens, Keith Hart, Michael Ignatieff, Quentin Skinner, Gareth Stedman Jones and John B. Thompson. I would like also to thank Robert Baldock and his colleagues at Yale University Press, and my copy editor, Susan Haskins. Roy Foster gave me the essay by Namier, from which I take one of the book's epigraphs. My largest debts are to John Dunn, Geoffrey Hawthorn and Tony Judt: their encouragement and criticism has been truly invaluable. Any errors of fact or judgement which persist are of course mine.

PART ONE

CHAPTER ONE

Intellectuals and the Left

I

Nowhere in the West was the collapse of the revolutionary identity of the Left more spectacular than in its original homeland, France. For all of three decades after the end of the Second World War, French intellectuals attached immense importance to the idea of revolution: Marxism, adopted as the modern theory of revolution, gained unparalleled prestige within the intellectual culture as a whole. More completely than in any other Western European country, intellectuals in France revived and pressed into argument the language of revolutionary politics, producing glittering theoretical novelties which came to command the attention of both partisans and critics of the Left across the world.[1] From the mid-1940s to the mid-1970s, Paris stood unchallenged in its claim to possess the most politically radical intellectual class.

This position seemed confirmed in the immediate afterglow of 1968. The events of that year vividly revealed the extent to which the ideal of revolution still nourished the imaginations of the intellectuals of the Left. Marxist theory in its Althusserian interpretation achieved an influence far beyond Louis Althusser's original stronghold, the Ecole Normale Supérieure.[2] It gained unprecedented academic respectability and acceptance (symbolically encapsulated by Althusser's delivery of a lecture to the Société Française de Philosophie in 1968, entitled 'Lénine et la Philosophie').[3] This triumphal entry of theories of revolutionary politics into the sanctuaries of the academic establishment was secured institutionally by the foundation of the University of Vincennes in 1969, with its declared allegiance to Marxist theoretical and political principles. Editions of the Marxist classics and of works devoted to Marxist themes streamed not only from the publishing houses of the French Communist Party and small left-wing publishers like François Maspero and Christian Bourgois, but also from the established bastions of Le Seuil, the Presses Universitaires de France and Gallimard. Theoretical journals belonging, or affiliated, to the Communist Party flourished, publishing work of a far higher intellectual quality than anything produced in earlier decades.[4] *Gauchismes* proliferated in dense abundance: Maoism (for many, the practical counterpart to Althusser's theoretical *chinoiseries*) was writing itself into the history of the French Left as a minor epic, while (on separate trajectories) Trotskyist, anarchist and libertarian currents all enjoyed strong if highly localized revivals. In the broader domain of public opinion, programmes and policies associated with the Left won widespread popular favour,[5] and in the political mainstream the parties of the Left made gains. The newly reconstituted Socialist Party rapidly emerged as a plausible contender for government, and the alliance between the Socialists and the Communists, secured in the Common Programme of 1972, seemed to pose a genuine challenge to the declining Gaullist state. Observers spoke of 'the "marxization" of French culture',[6] and concluded that the French Left had gained for itself the intellectual dominance which all other supporters of the Left in Western Europe had ardently desired in their own countries.

Yet, with prodigious suddenness, everything changed. In the space of a few years, intellectuals abandoned the language of revolutionary politics. By the end of the 1970s, the most vociferous of them were insisting that revolution resulted necessarily in totalitarianism and state-imposed terror. An entire intellectual consensus, founded upon a commitment to rapid and thorough-going social and political change through violent takeover of state power, had dissolved. So substantial was the metamorphosis that one of the most effective international propagators of French radical ideas, Perry Anderson, announced in 1983 that 'Paris is today the capital of European intellectual reaction'.[7] The language of revolutionary politics had deflated helplessly, and Marxism with it. What can explain this reversal in intellectual opinion? Why did it occur? And what did it mean?

The collapse in the intellectual credit of revolutionary politics in France was undoubtedly part of a more general exhaustion of Marxist and socialist thought in the West.[8] But the sheer haste and scale of the decline of the French case was unique. In Italy—the only other Western European country with a comparably developed radical intellectual and political culture—the deflation was less acute: intellectuals there did renege on previous political commitments, but unlike France the shift never reached the proportions of a collective abdication on the part of almost an entire generation. Nor did it veer towards the extremity of the French reaction. And in Britain and the United States, it could be argued that academic radicalism, in the form of Marxist or *marxisant* theories, actually climaxed at the moment when its French counterpart was extinguished.[9] Further, the disengagement of French intellectuals from the hitherto accepted terms of political argument preceded by some years the abrupt fall of the socialist states of Central and Eastern Europe: although it was undoubtedly linked to the unravelling of 'actually existing socialism', it could not be explained simply as a direct reflex of this. The logic of the French collapse lay within France's own political and intellectual history. In this perspective, it appeared still more puzzling: at the very moment when, in 1981, the parties of the Left entered government, they found themselves bereft of the intellectual support which had always been their pride.

This massive shift in the political tastes and affiliations of a sophisticated intellectual culture (one deeply confident of the self-sufficiency and authenticity of its beliefs) raises questions of both intrinsic and general significance. In France, more so than in other Western countries, intellectuals have long been granted—and have held—a prominent public role. Even when at their most arcane, they have self-consciously assumed an audience far wider than their fellow intellectuals: they expect their opinions to be accorded public attention. Participation in public political argument is a trait fundamental to the identity of French intellectuals. This they have manifested by registering their opinions regularly in the public press, by signing their names to petitions, by appearing on political platforms and on television, by leading demonstrations to the Elysée Palace, and at times by distributing newspapers at street corners. This readiness to participate in public life accounts for the efforts of political movements, parties, leaders, the state itself, to cultivate good relations with the intellectuals, to win their support. Even Charles de Gaulle, usually contemptuous, spared Sartre from police arrest. To explain shifts in their political arguments therefore is necessarily to account for a broader dimension of modern France's politics. But these questions also possess a wider significance, extending well beyond the boundaries of France. The political arguments pursued by the French intellectual Left on their own domestic terrain have also played a notable role in the construction of postwar Western radical and progressive thought. The opinions and stringently local concerns of the French intellectual Left, their sometimes byzantine languages and styles, all helped to shape and colour this broader current of thought. The upheaval in the terms of political argument deployed by French intellectuals since the mid-1970s is therefore of direct consequence to understanding the predicament of Western radical thought as whole.

There exists a vast array of studies on postwar French political thought; but none of these captures quite what there is to explain. Two approaches dominate. One adopts an explicitly external view, paying less attention to the thought, and more to the stage upon which it is enacted. Arguments are reduced to what are taken to be their sociological causes. These accounts direct our attention to the distinctive social habitats of academics and intellectuals in Paris, to the institutions that formed and employ these men and women, to the role of the reviews and media, and (more rarely, and vaguely) to the nature of their intended and actual audiences.[10] Shifts in intellectual argument are portrayed as products of changes in forms of social and economic organization: 'modernization', it is claimed, brings ideology to an end.[11] Those exasperated by the unusual instability and volatility that has often typified the political arguments of French intellectuals can be more peremptory still: they insist upon the essential frivolity of the French, the enduring gallic weakness for the excessive rhetorical gesture and the latest fashion.[12] But this is to beg the question, precisely to insert conclusions into premises.

Others, fascinated by the internal intricacies—or irritated by the inconsistencies—of the theories and arguments themselves, have simply taken these theories and arguments on their own professed terms, as ideas and arguments intended not for a specifically French time and place but for the Left in general. Treating these arguments as essentially philosophical in character, they have concentrated on their internal reasoning. The resulting accounts usually take one of three forms. The first extracts selected aspects of fundamentally political arguments, and uses these for its own purposes, generally at blithe variance with the arguments' original intentions.[13] The second reacts polemically to the arguments—perhaps in itself an appropriate response, but invariably a mistimed one.[14] The third group more elaborately stalks imaginary beasts like 'Existential Marxism' or 'Gallic Marxism'.[15] Even the most sophisticated and detailed of these drift generically toward what Richard Rorty has called 'doxography': they 'attempt to impose a problematic on a canon drawn up without reference to that problematic, or, conversely, to impose a canon on a problematic constructed without reference to that canon'.[16] And all evade the fundamental question of why political thinking in postwar France has taken its distinctive form. This explains why such accounts always assume their subject-matter to be unproblematically given or present, existing as a self-specifying and coherent body of thought rather than as a fragmented activity carried out by particular agents in particular circumstances. This assumption is especially inappropriate since what is immediately striking about the history of political thought in postwar France is the paucity of what can properly be called political theory at all: that is, of systematic attempts to causally assess and evaluate the political world, and to suggest how it might be advantageously transformed.[17]

The present study proceeds quite differently. It takes the arguments of some of France's most prominent left-wing intellectuals as they were intended to be taken: as arguments. But equally, in taking them as arguments, it insists that they must be read as contributions to a distinctively French political debate: that they spoke to and were concerned with quite local political preoccupations. It was politics itself that had raised the questions. The forms through which French intellectuals chose to respond to these questions must be read as instances of *arguing*: as intellectual and political actions. To characterize political thinking in this way—as a form of agency within a given context, rather than a reified outcome of social processes—identifies more appropriately just what there is that requires understanding and explanation.[18]

II

Before turning to the central contention of this book, two terms fundamental to its thematic concerns need clarification: the words 'Left' and
'intellectual'. What is the French Left? Obviously no full account can be
given here, but some aspects must be noted. The political sense of the
word 'Left' is of French origin: the term enters political vocabulary after
the French Revolution of 1789, transforming political space by replacing
in suitably egalitarian manner the traditional vertical ordering of God,
king and subject with a horizontal opposition, and becoming immediately 'the anchor term of the political polarity, the one that gives
meaning to its opposite'.[19] Usually opposed in formal and unitary fashion
to the Right (and to a lesser extent, the Centre), the term had to
encompass a wide range of variation. This spectrum broadened constantly, driven by its own internal logic: as if on cue, each successive
generation of the Left in France split away from its predecessor and
parent, and accused it of not being sufficiently 'à gauche'. The continuous scission of the Left in France, the long progression from Opportunism via Radicalism and Socialism to Communism and finally
to the various contestatory *gauchismes*, was not simply the result of
substantive shifts or disagreements over programmes.[20] These splits
came to acquire a decisive and absolute character because they were,
ultimately, disputes about legitimacy: each breakaway element claimed
to incarnate unity, to represent (in the various vocabularies current
at different times) the Nation, the People, the Working Class, or the
Masses. But to establish its distinctive identity each, simultaneously, had
to make itself singular and unlike any other Party or rival on the Left:
precisely less representative. The grip of this paradox, enforced by the
logic of the field, could only be eased by putting yet more rhetorical
vigour into the claim to represent and unify the whole political community. It became in the nature of an absolute and exclusive claim.

Yet, across this differentiated and antagonistic range, fundamental
traits were fully shared.[21] Most immediately, the 'Left' in France designated a kind of culture, one that traced its origins back to the revolutionary decade of 1789–99: it gathered together a set of shared
historical symbols and references which (at certain moments) joined
groups and individuals with otherwise quite diverging purposes. At the
core of this network of allusions (and also at its origin) was the image of
revolution: the promise of boundless and sudden social and political
transformation, so luminously evoked by the legendary *grands soirs*
of the French Revolution. A second shared emphasis was a belief in
centralized political power: the French Left was dominated by consistently statist traditions (there have been few moves to rescue Proudhon
from the drubbing he received at the hands of Marx). Unsurprisingly,

the doctrinal disputes of the Left focused upon questions of political legitimacy rather than on forms of rule: arguments turned on who was to command the powers of the state, who rightfully might claim political authority. (On the questions of what exactly these powers ought to be, how far they should extend, and how exactly their extension beyond their rightful scope might be curbed, the Left in France was decidedly more taciturn.) This obsession with the question of who was *entitled* to rule necessarily raised the issue of identity: what was the authentic political community, who were its true agents or representatives? This was an abiding problem for the Left. Responses generally combined great rhetorical determination with convenient analytical imprecision. Classically, within the Marxist tradition, it was the proletariat who laid rightful claim to state power (even if, at least so the theory said, they were only to exercise such powers temporarily). But in France, a relatively late industrializer, the political Left emerged well before the appearance of the appropriate social category, the French proletariat. It had therefore to forge its insistent language of identity out of more socially plastic oppositions, which could be shaped in salient ways according to political circumstance: us vs. them, patriot vs. traitor, workers vs. parasites, the people vs. the 'two hundred'. The language of proletariat and capitalist was a precarious late graft onto these earlier outgrowths.

At the origin of this imprecision was an obvious ambiguity of scope embodied in the term 'Left'. The Left laid claim to universality: at different times in its history, it stressed the universality of its values, of its forms of agency (the universal class), of the community it promised (the horizon of socialist internationalism). Yet by definition the term remained mired in partiality, referring to a singular component of a larger entity or community that contained its opponent, the 'Right'. How, from the point of view of the Left, was this encompassing community to be conceived, what defined its external boundaries and how did these relate to its internal divisions? What element within this entity could the Left claim to represent? Answers varied across historical periods and situations, but there remained important consistencies. From its origins, the Left in France was closely tied to a specification of the nation. The 'Nation' was the initial response to the revolutionary question of who ought to possess political power. As described by Emmanuel Sieyès, it was composed of the unprivileged 'Third Estate' or 'People', constituting themselves as a political community with powers of agency through one dramatic act of opposition to the privileged estates or monarch.[22] Putatively a principle of unity and universality, there was always a contrary, oppositional, singular and more exclusive meaning written into the term. The battle cry of the revolutionary armies at Valmy—'Vive la Nation'—captured this duality: referring at once to a juridical entity (the sovereign people as opposed to the monarch), and to a territorial, cultural entity (the French nation as opposed to all other nations). The Left and the nation entered proximately into the vocabulary of modern politics, appealing to entirely contrary principles. Sieyès' model of a 'Third Estate' or nation—an imagined alliance of the immense majority against a handful of enemies who perpetually threatened the authentic political community—was inscribed at the core of the Left's imagination and identity. It remained there, impervious to a history of political struggle punctuated by moments of such intensity and violence which might more plausibly have suggested a different balance of social forces, and a different distribution of relevant social identities.[23] Originating in 1789, this image reappeared at critical and temporally distant moments throughout the Left's history, in 1936 as again in the speeches of François Mitterrand during the 1970s.[24] In each case, an identity between legitimate power and the authentic political community was affirmed: any divergence or dissent consequently came to be described as betrayal or treason.

In the century after the French Revolution, however, the term 'nation' drifted from its modern origins on the Left towards the Right. Marx noted the emergence, from 1848 onwards of a 'bourgeois' sense of the word 'national' (akin to 'chauvinist'), and this meaning came to dominate especially, after 1870, amongst those French chafing at the Prussian victory over their country. This more particularist sense of nationalism was defined through the political arguments surrounding the Dreyfus affair. One set of contenders in these disputes sought to dissociate the nation from its links with any transitory political form (especially the Republic), and refused all universalist and cosmopolitan elements: a full-blown anti-Republican, anti-secular ideology of the nationalist Right, claiming to speak for the *pays réel*, was propagated.

This challenge from the Right to the Republican image of the political community pushed the Left to identify itself with (and define itself in terms of) the Republic. This was indeed the programme of Radicalism, with its belief that universal male suffrage practised within the institutional frame of the Republic would eventually secure the supremacy of the whole people over their enemies. Even after the emergence of an industrial proletariat late in the nineteenth century, this commitment was maintained: Jaurèsian socialism simply made the proletariat the leading element of an unified and integral alliance of the whole people, the nation. The continual insecurity of the Third Republic allowed the diverse elements of the Left, at moments of real crisis, to rally to its defence. They could embrace the Republic as the institutional form of the universalist elements of the revolutionary tradition (after all, the Republic might be French, but it was also universal). But equally, at such moments of crisis, the proclaimed universality of the Republic could handily be dissolved into the patriotic appeals of the more singular nation.

At the level of the Left's doctrine, however, such practices had to be made consistent and justified in new ways after 1917. As long as France was unchallenged in its claims to be the historically unique site and vehicle of the universal and universalizing project of revolution, the Republic could be accepted as entitled to represent the political community. But the events in St Petersburg and Moscow during the autumn of 1917 introduced a new conception of revolutionary practice, shifting eastwards the epicentre of revolutionary agency and community. One consequence was to disturb the sense in which the Republic was entitled to represent the political community. Since all the elements of the Left, both republican and socialist, agreed that France's true political identity was specified by terms drawn from the revolutionary tradition, it became possible after 1917 for some on the Left to argue that the contours of the authentic political community extended beyond conventional territorial boundaries. It followed that this political community could not find full representation in national political institutions. Class rather than nation was now seen as the agent of revolution; and, after all, one source of the imaginative power of class was its claim to be a supranational category. It was such claims that directly provoked vigorous and internecine quarrels within the precariously reconciled strands of the French Left: could the French working class, the French revolutionary tradition, or even France itself still claim any privileged role as a revolutionary community and agent, as the vehicle through which universal values might be achieved? These questions, more richly phrased, would cleave and drastically transform the identity of the French Left after 1920, breaking it into Socialist and Communist components. Marxism, enacted in the form of the Leninist Party (itself the proclaimed representative of the revolutionary class) appeared to surpass the indigenous revolutionary tradition and its Republican institutional forms, and to offer an effective alternative to the now apparently spurious claims to universalism on the part of the Republic. The French Communists in particular pressed this argument, directing their doctrinal allegiance beyond the frame of republican politics and towards the new self-proclaimed representative of a universal political community and project, the Soviet Union.

But already during the 1930s and especially after 1945 the disadvantages of putting this argument in too stark a form had become apparent. The resurgence of active controversies over France's own political identity required protagonists to claim that they spoke for the authentic political community or nation: external doctrinal allegiance had to be squared with more recognizably patriotic forms. This reconciliation was achieved through a narrative which linked together the French and the Bolshevik revolutions as moments in a continuous historical progression. In the Communist description, the latter revolution was a continuation of the revolutionary project begun by the Jacobins. True patriotism, commitment to the French political community, required commitment to what was described as the core of the nation's political identity, as specified by the revolutionary tradition; and this, it was further insisted, was now instantiated and represented most fully by the Soviet Union. Thus these dual commitments could be described as mutually reinforcing. This stitching together of universalist and particular vocabularies by means of the thread of revolutionary continuity was to hold attractions after 1945. Marxism and the Communist Party, modern forms of revolutionary universalism, could be fused into a language that specified the true political community.[25] Those who spoke this language could display commitment to the modern form of revolutionary universalism, and could also be described as affirming a kind of patriotism, upholding a specification of the national political community.[26]

A second focus of this book is the figure of the intellectual. Just what is an intellectual? And how have self-conceptions of intellectuals changed in postwar France?[27] There are no uncontentious criteria for what it is to be an intellectual: a term that is at once appraisive and descriptive, and a classic instance of a fundamentally disputed category. But one point that is clear is that to be an intellectual is to share in a collective identity. This collective dimension was manifested in France originally through the political petition, beginning with the famous Dreyfusard *Manifeste des intellectuels* of 1898. A genre of joint authorship, the petition was an important instrument in forming a conception of intellectuals as a collective body with powers of agency.[28] But to be an intellectual is also to desire and pursue the status of a peerless individual, to be surpassingly distinguished. This at least partially accounts for the maniacal concern of all intellectuals for a vocabulary of differentiation and distinction: 'true' intellectuals vs. 'pseudo', 'high' vs. 'low', writers and academics vs. journalists, old vs. young, avant-garde vs. conventional, bourgeois vs. bohemian, left vs. right. Glad to be accorded membership of the intellectual set, most intellectuals are then at pains to distinguish themselves from its other—and it most instances palpably less estimable—members (the *OED* records the usage 'so-called intellectuals' as early as 1898, more or less simultaneously with the first appearance of the noun itself).

The term has a distinctively French sense. As an adjective, it had a long and diffuse history, but the substantive noun first appeared in France during the 1890s, and gained currency during the controversies surrounding the Dreyfus affair at the turn of the century. Studies of its emergence during these years reveal the senses in which it designated a social category, with its own distinct aspirations.[29] But there is a different and more political sense which also emerges at this time, and is of particular relevance here. Forged in the heat of the polemics over the identity of the nation, the term 'intellectual' came to refer to the protagonists in these quarrels. It gained its sense as a self-description in

the course of conflicts over the fundamental political character and
identity of France: over whether this identity was best represented in
the form of the Republic, an institutional form of the universal and
universalizing project begun by the French Revolution, or by a more
local (racial) definition of the nation.

Sociologists and historians commonly ascribe two distinct meanings to
the noun. In a sociological sense, they use it to refer to all those who
produce, diffuse and consume culture: to designate a socio-professional
category or social stratum.[30] But they also employ it as a term of self-
description, intended to place those who so describe themselves in a
particular relation to the rest of society.[31] This second, looser, sense is
essential to the French understanding; the occupational sense leaves out
too much to be of use in the French context. Again, it was the Dreyfus
affair which endowed the term with the sense of a specific chosen
vocation or role, giving the word a political and intentional meaning:
it designated a particular way of acting and intervening in public life.
These senses are succinctly brought together in Régis Debray's description of intellectuals as comprising 'that group socially authorized
to express individual opinions on public affairs independently of the
normal civic procedures to which ordinary citizens are subject'.[32]

What, it might be asked, gives intellectuals the authority to express
their opinions on matters of common concern so publicly and what, still
more importantly, gives them the nerve to expect to be listened to? One
answer is intelligence: intellectual abilities, usually expressed in the
form of literary skills or academic expertise. Another is social standing.
But neither of these, taken together or separately, exhaust the French
case. In France intellectuals have never constituted an 'intellectual
aristocracy', deriving some part of their authority from social background, from their locations in an aristocratic skein of cosmopolitan
salons and country house gatherings.[33] At best they have boasted solidly
bourgeois backgrounds, often decidedly more *déclassé* origins: for many,
embourgeoisement has been the height of ambition.[34] If there are important social criteria of membership, these lie elsewhere: in the intense
geographical concentration of French intellectuals in the Parisian me-
tropole, and in their common educational formation (the Ecole Normale
Supérieure, more recently the Ecole National d'Administration). Neither
has sheer intelligence counted for all. However much it may offend
anglophone fastidiousness, in France a man like Bernard-Henri Lévy
(well-read, unstoppably opinionated and avowedly a non-specialist) is
regarded as an intellectual. Hence, it is possible that some of the figures
and arguments considered in this book, may not—from loftier cognitive
viewpoints—merit the closest attention. But in France, at particular
politically charged moments, these individuals *have mattered*. It is important to ask why this should have been so, and what this term of self-
description has meant to those who have employed it.

The high standing of intellectuals in France has never derived purely from recognition of their creative capacities or their expertise in specific areas of knowledge. Putting it briskly, the position they have been accorded can be seen as a response to a larger problem in the history of post-revolutionary France: that of securing legitimacy in a situation where the title to state power has been continuously and profoundly contested. Intellectuals in France have played a key role in specifying the political community, and have pronounced firmly, in doing so, on the political agencies that may legitimately claim to represent it. The sources of intellectual authority have provoked endless disputes in postwar France: from Sartre via Althusser, Foucault, the *gauchistes* and on to Bourdieu, the authority of the intellectual has been considered from an array of perspectives. Simplifying somewhat, we may note that one important source of authority for intellectuals in the postwar decades was their ability to claim experience of or participation in collective political activity: involvement in the communities of the Resistance, in the often clandestine movements supporting independence in Indo-China and Algeria, in the Leftist sects of 1968, or in the critique of Soviet totalitarianism, have for successive generations of intellectuals provided a resource from which to draw authority for their public pronouncements. In the years immediately after 1945, for instance, many who—purely on grounds of intelligence or intellectual ability— would have counted as intellectuals, able to speak on public matters, were denied such recognition: their political activities during the war, it was widely felt, abrogated their rights to publish and be heard. On the other hand, intellectuals who had participated in the Resistance, or were associated with the Left, could count on being more or less automatically accorded a high status.

III

The conceptions of political community pressed by the Left, and the claims of intellectuals about the validity of such conceptions (claims through which they came to define their own identity and authority), are two principal concerns of this book. They converge in its central argument. After the Liberation (as before), politics posed the questions for intellectuals; they responded through arguments that drew upon the language of revolutionary politics. Chapter Two explains why they did so, showing that the factors which encouraged intellectuals to adopt the language of revolutionary politics derived from pre-war antecedents, and more decisively from the political circumstances at the end of the war. With the restitution of national politics, a key question was how to redefine France's shattered sense of political identity, how to reconceive and re-imagine what the French nation really was. The languages of pre-war republicanism and of the nationalist Right were now comprehensively discredited, effectively unavailable after the war. Gaullism was one powerful answer to this question: but it found few intellectual friends. The Communists offered another powerful response. They showed great determination in equating the revolutionary Left with the nation: attacking the bourgeoisie as 'collaborationist' and anti-national, they asserted their own claim to represent the class which embodied the authentic political community. In promising to renew France and recover its political character, they linked this renewal to the modern version of the revolutionary project, the Soviet Union. Expanding the contours of the political community, they denied any tension between allegiance to Leninist forms of revolutionary politics and the forms of patriotism associated with the French Jacobin tradition. These allegiances, they asserted, reinforced one another (a doctrinal claim which, during the 1970s, would be gleefully accepted by their opponents, and turned against the Communists with devastating effect). Intellectuals were drawn into these arguments: given the linked definitions of political community and intellectual, this was inevitable. They sought a position from which to assert universal claims, yet they were conscious too of the need to describe themselves as members of a particular political community. The terms of the inherited revolutionary tradition held attractions. By adopting Jacobin or more modernist Marxist and Leninist forms of political argument, intellectuals could claim to be doing no more than reminding their fellow countrymen of the true sources of the political character and legitimacy of the modern French nation. There was, of course, no uniformity of response on the part of intellectuals; yet few could entirely ignore the claims of the Communists. Some joined the Party, seeing it as a sovereign counter–state, a microcosm of the authentic political community; others did not. Their arguments also varied.

These variations in intellectual response are examined in the second part of the book. I take two examples: Jean-Paul Sartre and Louis Althusser, the two most prominent intellectuals of the Left in the postwar decades. These chapters are not intended as expositions of the ideas and theories of Sartre and Althusser (there is no dearth of such expositions). Rather, my interest is in what Sartre and Althusser were *doing* in their political arguments, in the significance of their positions. Chapter Three, on Sartre, and Chapter Four, on Althusser, show how each in different but recognizably continuous ways developed the language of revolutionary politics. They pursued different forms of argument: one stressed political engagement, the other theoretical intervention in politics. Remaining outside the Party, Sartre adjusted his arguments constantly; Althusser, from within the Party, tried desperately to maintain a consistent Leninist position. But for each, the language of revolutionary politics was a resource with which to construct both an image of the political community, and of the role of the intellectual in relation to it. They contested the same terrain: Althusser's model of the relations between intellectuals and politics being a direct challenge to Sartre's conception and ultimately displacing it.

The intellectual commitment to the language of revolution reached a dizzy peak in 1968; but it declined sharply in the years after. This collapse is the subject of the third and final part of the book. Chapter Five covers the complicated developments between 1968 and electoral victory of the Left in 1981. The images of community upheld in the conceptions of Communist Party and the Gaullist state, along with the claims of each to be the legitimate representatives of the community, drew increasingly savage and derisive criticism. So too did the views of the relations between intellectuals and politics associated with these conceptions: the model of a specialist technocracy linked to the state, and the Althusserian attempt to redescribe the relations between the intellectual and the Party. Both were the targets of the *gauchistes'* criticism which, in seeking to depose the figure of the intellectual, claimed to enable the true community, the 'masses', to find their direct voice. But the restoration of Gaullist power brought with it disappointments even more severe in their consequences for the far Left than for the Right. The 'masses', the *gauchistes* learned, had no inclination for revolution; while the electoral pact of the Left parties, in the Common Programme, set the Communists and the Socialists in serious pursuit of political power. Worried by the prospect that the parties of the Left, dominated by the Communists, might gain political power, *gauchiste* attacks converged with criticisms from the Right: together, the attack gained a new scope and vehemence. The political consequences of the Soviet Revolution, characterized now in terms of terror and totalitarianism, were reiterated mercilessly. This, the moment of the New Philosophers, saw the most extreme reaction against the conventions of argument hitherto accepted by the intellectual Left. These reversals occurred in parallel with a set of developments in the apparently distinct field of the historiography of the French Revolution. This is the focus of Chapter Six: it was from this somewhat oblique direction that an argument emerged that gave a novel significance to criticisms of revolution. In the absence of a developed political theory, interpretations of the meaning and identity of the French Revolution had served as an all too pliable resource for the political arguments of the French Left: they provided a set of terms with which to evoke the authentic political community and its supposed representatives. These interpretations had been dominated, at least since 1945, by a Jacobin perspective that was comfortably at home with the vision of contemporary politics held by the revolutionary (and especially the Communist) Left. François Furet's intervention in this somewhat stilted discourse, and his comprehensive revision of the dominant interpretation, the 'catéchisme révolutionnaire', had decisive effects. Furet's most rewarding rhetorical move was to accept the link, made at the doctrinal level, between the 1917 Revolution and the Jacobin period of the French Revolution. But where earlier the Communists had vaunted this connection, Furet now proceeded to turn it against its fond admirers. Attacking the heiratic idea of revolution itself, and concentrating in particular on the episode of the Terror, Furet sought to install a new view of the true identity and meaning of the French Revolution. It was not, he insisted, the proleptic figuration of a future Socialist revolution, but the origin of modern democratic politics: at its core was the question of political representation. With this redescription, a new picture of the meaning of France's post—revolutionary history and of its modern political identity could be constructed. France was exceptional not because it was the homeland of the universalist and universalizing projects of modern revolutionary politics, but because it was the birthplace of modern democracy and the Rights of Man.

Furet's argument cast a new set of terms into the arena. Intellectual dispute after 1968, when the critique of centralized political power had been so firmly pressed, had stumbled through a series of efforts to redefine the political community, and to identify the appropriate agencies to represent and act for it. From the *gauchiste* desire for forms of direct or 'pure' democracy, via the invocation of the idea of *autogestion* during the 1970s, to the more timid attempts to voice a French 'social-democracy', and on finally to the efforts during the early 1980s to push forms of economic liberalism, no lasting outcome had been produced. But Furet's characterization of France's political history cast the Republic in a genuinely new light. The 1980s witnessed a new intellectual curiousity in historical and contemporary questions of constitutional and representative politics, set within the frame of the Republic. Critical intellectuals become reconciled to (and with) the Republic. But this was a new Republic: it was no longer the 'absolute' Republic of France's past, one that had hoped to create a dense life of civic participation and to protect the nation's economy from external pressures.[35] To intellectuals, the Republic came to represent a more pluralist and moderate political form, with divided powers, in which positive law was constrained by means of rights upheld by a constitutional court. A circle in the arguments of the French intellectual Left had been turned, a revolution accomplished. The past that could now serve as a model for the future was discovered to be exactly the 'bourgeois' Republic that earlier generations of progressive intellectuals had rejected.

CHAPTER TWO

The Languages of Political Criticism after the Liberation

I

The resumption of national politics after the liberation of Occupied France brought a steep inflation in the rhetoric of political debate. As if to compensate for the defeat of 1940 and the sense of decimated French power, politics was seized upon as a medium through which France might affirm her status and adjust to the postwar world. The restoration of territorial boundaries accentuated the need to invent a new political identity for the nation: no return to the political structures of the pre-war Republic was possible, and the confusions of allegiance produced by Vichy rule had urgently to be resolved. At the centre of the eddying political disputes of the postwar years was the question of France's identity: who exactly constituted the authentic political community, and who rightfully represented it? Intellectuals inevitably were drawn into these quarrels, and it was predominantly through the language of revolutionary politics that they came to address them.

Among the causes conventionally and correctly adduced to explain the attractions of this language to intellectuals, paramount was the unprecedented popularity of the French Communist Party: doctrinally bound to the theory and practice of revolutionary politics, the Party nevertheless competed in elections and between 1945 and 1951 commanded the votes of nearly a third of the French electorate. The rise in the French Party's fortunes was part of a general European pattern; the years immediately following the defeat of Fascist governments seemed, particularly in the countries of Mediterranean Europe, to promise the beginning of sweeping social and institutional improvements.[1] Recent historians of this period soberly remind us that conditions in postwar France were not remotely revolutionary: French beliefs in revolutionary change were always illusory, and at most only piecemeal reforms were likely.[2] But this misses the point of why intellectuals should first have adopted and then persisted with the language of revolutionary politics. The reasons do not lie in the details of a particular social and economic conjuncture, nor for that matter, were they strictly philosophical; they were emphatically political, and their roots lay in France's distinctive political traditions.[3] The language of the Jacobin revolutionary tradition offered intellectuals a powerful and versatile legacy from which to draw

terms to specify the political community.[4] The divisions provoked by
the Vichy regime had shattered the identity of the nation, and new
descriptions of the national political community were needed with some
urgency. Yet, and running against the impulse towards particularist
and exclusive self-definitions, was also a powerful desire to affirm
universalist values and self-conceptions: this, after all, had been precisely
the purpose of the fight against the lethally parochial politics of Fascism.
In France, and only here, these two requirements were not mutually
exclusive; on the contrary, they could be harmonized and actually be
made to reinforce one another. This distinctive solution was a result of
the bequeathed political traditions, especially the language of revolutionary politics, which could be plundered by intellectuals and used
simultaneously to voice a universalist and universalizing form of criticism, as well as to proclaim a credible patriotism. In other European
countries, not heir to a revolutionary tradition, such a conjunction was
comparatively more awkward: in Italy, for instance, the Communist
Left shunned revolutionary or universalist appeals in favour of closer
integration with the traditions of bourgeois republicanism.[5] But in
France, the language of revolutionary politics was promisingly ambivalent: it evoked and established as a critical standard a future, yet-to-be-
created and truly universal community, while simultaneously it could
provide a description of the particular nation, a defensive conception of
the political community in precarious times.

The explanatory clues to the distinctive character of postwar arguments lie in the disorderly and disputatious political and intellectual
currents of the 1920s and '30s, and especially in the numerous contestatory conceptions of community that had begun to challenge the
claims of the Third Republic during its final years.[6] But it was the literal
fracture of the nation's political identity during the war, the scission of
France into territories of German and Vichy rule, that decisively set the
postwar pattern. After the Liberation, the most commanding forms of
political appeal promised both to unite the politically divided nation and
to recover its distinctive identity. Such recuperation could only be
effected, it was widely agreed, through the active construction of a
political community by means of a strong sovereign state. Gaullism and
Communism emerged as the two most elaborate and vocal claims upon
such a state. Both had participated in the Resistance, and both pressed
their title to represent the nation. To intellectuals, however, the Gaullist
version held comparatively less allure. For a start, Gaullism maintained a
haughty indifference towards intellectuals; more damagingly, it was
based upon the consecration of a powerful individual, a military hero,
in a political culture that had come to mistrust military heroes. The
Communists were also of course undeniably besotted with 'Great
Leaders'. But, while they spoke a blatantly populist language, they
solicited intellectual support as a means to secure their claims to

represent the nation. They described themselves as the modern bearers of France's revolutionary essence, and put immense rhetorical vigour into sustaining the equation between the nation and themselves, and with it, France's claim to stand for universal civilization. The equation was drawn in a number of ways. They revived, if only symbolically, the language of revolution, amalgamating older Jacobin cadences (which kept alive the evocative vocabulary of patriot and traitor, betrayal and threat) with more modern Marxist phrases. Equally, a particular histori-ographical account of the French Revolution was developed and in-ducted into political argument. This produced a decisive elision: the project of France's renewal and revival was conflated with that of support for the 'Fatherland' of modern revolutionary politics, the Soviet Union. This revived (and appropriately modified) political equation between the revolutionary Left and the nation held attractions for intel-lectuals. Most decisively of all, the Communists could vaunt their possession of a systematic intellectual doctrine, Marxism, that was committed to theoretical and historical research, and that gave a pivotal position to intellectuals. The Party promised intellectuals the prospect of real political significance. There was, however, no uniformity of intellectual response toward the blandishments of the Party. Many became members, seeing the Party as a sovereign counter-state and society, a microcosmic embodiment of the authentic political community of the French. Others, like Merleau-Ponty and Sartre, engaged in more complex negotiations. But few could entirely resist the force of the equation, or of the Party that claimed to incarnate it.

II

The efforts to re-establish structures of national politics after the liber-ation of Occupied Paris in August 1944 unleashed a deluge of debate. Three questions dominated. The character of France's domestic political reordering obviously commanded attention, but this was considered in parallel with the question of how France might recover a distinctive political identity on the world stage. Intellectuals, meanwhile, confronted with doubts about their own postwar status, came to define and affirm their role by their responses to these larger political questions.

Political dispute immediately zeroed in on the question of who would fill the existing vacuum of political power, and by what title: would there be revival of the political divisions and parties the pre-war Republic, a return to the *mêlée* of groups jostling for control over the powers of a centralized State; or would these be replaced by the young and politically untested organizations of the Resistance?[7] Responses varied according to whether the Resistance was viewed as a 'national insurrection', a virtual revolutionary war against counter-revolutionary enemies (both external and internal), leading to a fundamental transformation of social and political structures, or simply as the expulsion from French territory of an invading enemy, 'les boches'.[8] Underlying these disputes was a deeper uncertainty about the Republic. Most of the groups active in the Resistance were committed to the reassertion and defence of Republican values; yet the Third Republic—the most recent institutional manifestation of these values—was the object of widespread disgust. What, in these circumstances, was the Republic's significance? If André Siegfried could evoke a past sentimental and popular attachment to the Third Republic (a nostalgia he himself shared in), even he recognized that by the 1930s, and especially after 1940, faith in the idea of the Republic was helplessly lapsing.[9]

During the final decades of the Third Republic, the dominant political languages were defined and distinguished by their attitudes towards the Republic. There were, first, those political groups closely identified with and seen as the defenders of the Republic: the Radicals, and the Socialists, who drew upon the intellectual traditions of Durkheimian sociology and Solidarism.[10] Both groups shared a vocabulary based upon the idea of the citizen and citizenship, political individualism, and meritocratic equality. Radicalism was characterized by (and profited from) a deficit of determinate or positively defined political ideas, but in the postwar years this manifest vagueness was intellectually unappealing.[11] During the 1920s and '30s, the vocabularies of Radicalism and Socialism were already under pressure from both Right and Left, from descriptions which analysed the French situation either in terms of national decadence or of class struggle (the sordid spate of political scandals associated with the Third Republic (typified by the Stavisky affair of 1934) gave further edge to such attacks).[12] In response to these rival languages, Republicanism as represented by the Radical party shifted towards the Right, while the Socialists—outflanked by the leftward push of the Communists—found themselves driven towards the political Centre. The Socialists under Léon Blum continued to use the language forged and successfully wielded by Jaurès, which once had reconciled the working class to the democratic traditions embodied in the structures of the Third Republic, but by the mid-1930s, with the migration of working-class support from the Socialists to the Communists, it was clear that this language no longer appealed to its assumed political constituency. The war added to the difficulties of the Socialists. Weakened and riven by internal dissension, they proved unable (in contrast to the Communists) to transform party institutions into effective clandestine Resistance organizations. The relatively low participation of Socialist Party groups in the Resistance seriously weakened their postwar standing; and the attempts by their new leader after the Liberation, Guy Mollet, to revive the Socialists' fortunes by a return to neo-

Guesdist rhetoric was unsuccessful.[13] Too closely identified with the defeated and disgraced Third Republic, the Radicals and Socialists undoubtedly continued after 1945 to play a part in the political bargaining and brokerage of the Fourth Republic, but their intellectual credibility was in shreds.[14] The younger generation of postwar intellectuals were repelled by the perceived timidities of these reformist languages, and of the intellectual modes and models associated with them: the intellectual reputation of men like Alain (Emile Chartier) and Léon Brunschvicg, along with the neo-Kantian philosophies they professed, tumbled after 1945.[15]

Against these, against what were perceived as the representatives of a decaying bourgeois Republic, there emerged during the 1920s and '30s other voices of intellectual and political criticism. Though these differed between themselves over political alignment, together they constituted a 'negative consensus': all repudiated the individualist politics and culture of the bourgeoisie, and parliamentary forms of political representation.[16] Such philippics as Paul Nizan's Les Chiens de Garde was simply one—the most coruscating—of a profusion of attacks directed against the abstraction and idealism of 'bourgeois philosophy' as transmitted in the academic institutions of the Republic; as remedy, they demanded that philosophical knowledge be tied to and based upon 'lived experience'. Parallel themes, expressed differently, could be found in the work of novelists and philosophers.[17] Emmanuel Mounier, founder of the politically eclectic and Catholic review Esprit and theorist of 'Personalisme', proposed a view of intellectual engagement that coincided strikingly with Sartre's postwar formulation,[18] and similar views were expressed by intellectuals who joined the anti-Fascist intellectual movements (such as the Comité de Vigilance des Intellectuels Anti-fascistes), the Popular Front writers, and in starker form amongst the Surrealists and Communists.[19] In each case, intellectuals proclaimed their alignment with a social group or political position, and such affiliation became an index of intellectual credibility. Nizan, for instance, picking up a refrain aired in the nineteenth century by Michelet (and after him by Sartre), asserted that 'the revolutionary philosopher can be effective only if he forms the closest possible ties with the class which is the bearer of the Revolution—that is, only if he identifies completely with this class'.[20] Intellectuals of the Right, like Denis de Rougemont, Thierry Maulnier and Jean-Pierre Maxence echoed these appeals for intellectuals to take a combative social and political role.[21] The general desire was to obtain for intellection a practical efficacy. In the face of these challenges, usually pressed in independent political and intellectual reviews, the authority and prestige of the academic institutions of the Third Republic faltered. This dispersal of intellectual authority across the wider realm of the literate public was confirmed during the Resistance (in the years after 1945, the ability to claim involvement with underground reviews of the

Resistance was a source of intellectual prestige), and was a precondition for the postwar success of reviews like *Les Temps Modernes*.[22]

Among the pre-war criticisms of the Third Republic, one of the most resonant were the polemics pressed by Charles Maurras and the various strands of the nationalist Right, including the Action Française and the extra-parliamentary *Ligues*, comprising Royalist and Catholic groups. The Right had never been particularly fond of the Republic: Maurras had spoken of the Third Republic as the 'anti-France', while for Barrès it was an oligarchy of corrupt politicians.[23] Incessantly damning the corrupt Republic in the name of the nation, Maurrasian nationalism was above all interested in national unity, a unity that it believed had been ruined by the French Revolution. Although it reviled the existing bourgeois order, it rejected the Marxist schema of two dominant classes engaged in conflict, and recurred to an image of a pre-revolutionary society, integrated and heirarchically ordered. Some groups on the Right did describe French politics in terms of class, but they avoided the Marxist schema of two implacably opposed classes, preferring instead a tripartite model that distinguished between the proletariat, the middle classes, and a plutocratic oligarchy made up of the 'two hundred families', agents of anti-national interests.[24] This, the language of French corporatism, which paralleled in some respects the analysis of revisionist socialists like Henri de Man, dominated during the Vichy regime. All on the Right agreed that the fundamental unit of political action was the nation, and its primary agent was the state, dominated by a leader 'who proposed to tear away the disfiguring mask of capitalism, reveal the true face of France, and free it for its civilizing mission among the backward nations'.[25] During the 1930s this position was barely distinguishable from that of Fascism, and it fed comfortably into the doctrines of the Vichy regime. But if the defeat of the Third Republic in 1940 could be taken in any sense as a vindication of the Right's criticisms of Republican decay and misgovernment, the subsequent collaboration with Nazism deprived the political ideas of the Right of any intellectual credibility: after the Liberation, the Right shrank to a residual category, perceived as representative of particular and highly partisan interests rather than of a national political programme, a distasteful specimen of precisely that faction and corruption now invoked, in the postwar years, to explain the *débâcle* of the Third Republic in 1940.

At the end of the war, the language of the old defenders looked distinctly unappealing.[26] The vocabulary of citizenship and rights had already during the 1930s seemed naive, and the tramline progress towards an enlightened liberal solidarist society which this vocabulary assumed and promised now appeared absurdly implausible to intellectuals. Further, the anti-statist predilections of intellectuals such as Alain, chief spokesman for this language, ran directly counter to the virtually unanimous consensus that the renewal of postwar France depended upon the agency of a strong state.[27] But, if there was agreement that defence of the defeated Third Republic was no longer intellectually credible, it was agreed too that the attacks of the Right were indefensible. The nationalist language of Maurras now appeared maliciously self-serving, decadent in the worst sense. In its anti-bourgeois and anti-capitalist emphases it could be seen to possess the requisite realist strains, but it was too insistently parochial. The Vichy regime might possibly have been interpreted as signifying the integration of this language into a particular conception of the national community, but Vichy's defeat demonstrated that this had been an arbitrary and imposed conception, a temporary and deeply wounding betrayal of the rightful nation. The defeat of the Right effectively debarred the counter-revolutionary argument from the postwar political arena. Neither Republicanism in its pre-war form, nor the nationalism of the Right was able to offer intellectually acceptable descriptions of France's postwar political identity.

The revolutionary Left held a more complicated, hazy perspective on the Republic. The Communists, for instance, were notorious and consistent waverers on this subject. From their inception they had been strongly against the Republic: between 1924 and 1926 they had attacked the governing alliance of Republican and Left Parties, the Cartel des gauches, and between 1927 and 1934 they pursued the 'class against class' line, which took them beyond the pale of republican politics.[28] They carried too the stigma of the period between August 1939 and June 1941, when their support for the Nazi-Soviet pact seemed conclusively to demonstrate their subordination to Soviet power, their disregard for and betrayal of the endangered Republic.[29] Yet, equally, they had at times rallied to the defence of the Republic: they had united with the Socialists during the Popular Front years to protect the Republic against the threat of Fascism, and from 1941 onwards they fought in the Resistance.[30] After the Liberation they had participated in coalition governments of the Republic until the onset of the Cold War led to their expulsion in 1947. For all practical purposes, then, the Communists were willing to conform to 'republican discipline', to domesticate their opposition: participation in alliances, coalitions, even in government, was acceptable. But at the level of doctrine, they were unshakeably bound to a view of the Republic as mere 'bourgeois' or 'formal' democracy, a form of class rule quite distant from the 'true' or 'people's' democracy their theory promised. Participation in actual government thus was always liable to description as a form of betrayal, alliance with the class enemy of the true nation. It was an odd doctrinal bind: to sustain their claim to represent the nation, the Communists had to remain outside the very political structures and institutions which, as a Party engaged in political competition, they sought to capture. It was these doctrinal exigencies that led them regularly to stress their identity as a class Party of the proletariat, and to keep their distance from the traditions and habits of bourgeois republicanism (unlike, for instance the Communists in Italy). Their criticism of Republican politics had a genuine edge to it.[31] In France, although Republicanism had claimed to stand for representative democracy and parliamentary elections, there were enough significant exceptions to give this claim a spurious air: the memory of Thiers, Boulanger and Laval, was a sufficient reminder of Republicanism's undemocratic strain. In the years after the Liberation, when words like 'democracy' and 'liberalism' had become impossibly equivocal,[32] those on the Left could announce publicly their support for democracy without necessarily supporting the existing institutions of democratic politics.

But this equivocation over the value of the Republic merely highlighted the need, in the postwar years, to discover positive and stable descriptions of France's political identity. This was reflected in the interest shown in foreign examples as possible models for France: the British Beveridge plan, American policies and Soviet planning all attracted attention.[33] But, if there was a resigned sense that France might have to accept lessons from other countries, French pride ensured that such models would have to be assimilated into and made continuous with the nation's own exemplary past. Here the Communists had a distinctive strategy. They adopted what was (expressed in terms of the French political landscape) an 'ultra-montagne' position. The Communist Party claimed to represent the working class, who in turn embodied the interests of the nation; but the Party directed its ultimate doctrinal allegiance outside the territorial boundaries of the nation since, it claimed, the contours of the true political community did not match the nation's geographical boundaries. The genuine 'homeland' of the working class was the homeland of the socialist and proletarian revolution, the Soviet Union. This intrepid (not to say foolhardy) elision was defended by the Communists, in the face of fierce and continual criticism, until the Party's twilight years in the 1980s. The resources for such a defence derived from the Communists equation of themselves, portrayed as the Party of the revolutionary Left, with the true nation.

From at least the mid-1930, the Communists had begun to make vigorous efforts to describe themselves as the legitimate representatives of the nation. This they did through an appropriation and modification of the forms of Jacobinism. At the level of political practice and policy, developments such as the Franco-Soviet pact of 1935 allowed the Communists to proclaim their commitment to the primacy of national defence, and support for the national government during the Popular Front further encouraged their annexation of the symbols and discourse of patriotism.[34] At the Party Congress held at Villeurbanne in 1936, for instance, the speeches and discussions were dominated by two words: 'Party' and 'France'.[35] Later that year, Party leader Maurice Thorez explained the patriotic turn of the Communists in impeccably Jacobin terms:

> We can say that the Popular Front (and we, the Communists, are part of it for good reason), is in this sense a truly French Front, a Front of the people of France, heirs and sons of the Great Revolution, against the pact of foreign agents, against a modern version of the Treaty of Coblentz. A French Front in the heroic tradition of our people's struggle and liberty, with the strains of the 'Marseillaise' of 1792 mixed in with those of our 'International', under the flag of Valmy and the red flag of the Commune, a Front against anti-French traitors.[36]

Proclaimed by Thorez as the 'heirs of the Jacobins', the Communists revived a political language rooted in the French Revolution. This defined the identity of the nation through its opposition to treacherous enemies, who betrayed 'the People', (or, as it was more commonly designated by the Communists during the 1930s, 'les petits' or 'les travailleurs'; needless to say, none of these terms referred to any precise economic or social category).[37] The Communist press thus consistently attacked the 'bourgeoisie' as a decadent and parasitic class, not truly a part of the nation, and in pursuit of its own interests while blithely betraying those of the nation; the working class and the Party of the working class, on the other hand, were championed as the unique and best defender of the nation.[38] This language relied for its power on its sociological imprecision. The bourgeoisie was loosely conflated with 'les gros' or with 'feudal elements', and the working class with 'le peuple' or 'les petits'.[39] As a language of political identity rather than analysis, it usefully blurred the opposition between the divisive vocabulary of class and the unifying language of nation by eliding the difference between these terms: the nation, properly defined, *was* the People, or the working class.

The equation between the revolutionary Left and the nation also spawned another vocabulary, a counterpart to the protective vocabulary of defending the nation against traitors, and more aggressive and outwardly directed in its form of appeal. This was the language of national mission, of France's universal civilizing role. Such talk too came easily to the Communists. Thus Thorez, speaking at the Party Congress held at Arles in 1937, exalted 'the civilizing role of France in the world' and 'the mission of France'. The Party represented not only a class interest, but the French people: a people charged with a universal civilizing mission. Etienne Fajon, another senior Party figure, concluded the Party Congress held at Gennevilliers in 1939, with this explanation:

> Because our actions are inspired by the most glorious French traditions, because our party is rooted in all those social strata that compose the

French nation, the Party's policies are at one with the cause of France; and it is the voice of France, speaking for human progress, liberty and peace, which has spoken continually here on the platform at Gennevilliers.[40]

During the 1930s, these assertions of France's universal mission typically took the form of a defence of 'civilisation' and 'culture' against the barbarism represented by Fascism. Speaking for the Communists, intellectuals like Paul Vaillant-Couturier affirmed in 1936, that 'we carry on France's traditions. And it is because we carry on France that we wish to save its culture', while Jacques Duclos declared 'the Communists are aware of being the descendants of all those who, across the centuries, have helped humanity forward on the difficult path of civilization'.[41]

After the Liberation, the terms 'nation' and 'nationalism' circulated freely in Communist discourse, and nationalist themes were harmonized with those of internationalism and class struggle.[42] The Communist press was crammed with examples of this elision of nation, class and Party: it became a characteristic and reiterated metaphorical trope, a profitable and easy substitute for actual argument.[43] The effect was to yoke together two languages that proposed divergent political loyalties, and to present them as mutually reinforcing. The Communists hoped to compensate for the potential wobble of such an alliance by entrenching the link between their claim to embody France's hopes of renewal and the revolutionary project of the Soviet Union on a firmer terrain, that of the historiography of the French Revolution. Here, efforts were made to demonstrate the continuities between the French Revolution (especially the Jacobin period) and the Bolshevik Revolution of 1917. The Communists appropriated the interpretations of the French Revolution developed by the historians of the Third Republic, and gave them a new twist: the two revolutions came to be interpreted as moments within a unified continuous narrative. One of the earliest and most strikingly transparent instances of this interpretation was by the historian Albert Mathiez.[44] In 1920 he published a pamphlet entitled *Le Bolchevisme et le jacobinisme*, declaring that he 'would like to show, through a brief analysis, that the analogies between the methods of the Bolsheviks and those of the French Montagnards are not simply superficial, but that there exist between the two strict logical relations'.[45] Both Jacobinism and Bolshevism were united by their aim to bring about universal change.

Jacobinism and Bolshevism are both dictatorships ... two class dictatorships, operating through the same means: Terror, requisition, taxes, and both proposing in the final instance a similar aim, the transformation of society, and not simply of Russian or French society, but of universal society. (pp. 3–4)

The Bolsheviks had simply adapted and perfected the methods and techniques of the Jacobins; they were members of the same political project and community, and henceforth it made no sense to oppose patriotism to internationalism:

> The politicians of our days, who set themselves up as heirs to the Jacobins, vaunt their patriotism by opposing defeatism and the internationalism of the Bolsheviks. The opposition is superficial, it does not stand up to scrutiny . . . Robespierre never renounced class internationalism, to which Lenin himself would have subscribed. (pp. 15–16)

The true revolutionary tradition was universal and internationalist, and to support the Bolsheviks was, for the revolutionary Left in France, to maintain the best Jacobin traditions: 1917 was after all a continuation of the Jacobin project. Mathiez's conclusion was unambivalent:

> The resemblances between the two great crises of 1793 and 1917 which our analysis has revealed are neither superficial nor fortuitous. The Russian revolutionaries freely and closely imitated the French revolutionaries. They are animated by the same spirit. They face the same problems, in an analogous atmosphere. (p. 22)

The Communists seized upon this type of interpretation: it helped, after all, to explain their own identity and role. From this point on, the conviction that there existed an intrinsic relation between the two revolutions became a firm fixture in the discourse of the French Communists and the revolutionary Left.[46]

The idea of a continuity between the two revolutions was eagerly disseminated by the Party after the end of the Second World War. Efforts were made to produce a historiography that embodied the principles of the Party's version of Marxism, and Party historians were charged with securing the Communist claim to be the legitimate heirs to the French revolutionary tradition. The broadly Jacobin emphases of Third Republican revolutionary historiography were appropriated by the Communists, and decorated with more recognizably Marxist terminology. At its barest, this historiographical orthodoxy viewed the French Revolution as a conflict between a declining aristocracy and a bourgeoisie on the ascendant; the result was the installation of bourgeois political rule, a transient point on the grand upward curve of revolution, which ultimately would give political power to the popular masses. Based upon this schema of the Revolution's significance, the Communist view rested on two further presuppositions, and held an important implication: it assumed that the French Revolution inaugurated an historical process whose dynamics and significance was best understood by Marx and, secondly, that after 1917 this dynamic had shifted its location eastward from France to the Soviet Union. This, finally, implied that contemporary politics must be understood as a continuation and part of this extended

historical process. These precepts echoed throughout Communist intellectual and political discourse; they each appeared, for instance, in
a discussion between Communist historians, held in May 1953, on
'Marxism and the History of France'.[47] To Jacques Chambaz, the
class struggle had intensified since the nineteenth century, though its
epicentre had shifted away from France: 'the centre of the revolutionary
movement has been displaced to Russia. Under the leadership of the
Bolshevik Party, socialism has triumphed in the USSR.'[48] Lenin and
Stalin had successfully invented a new model of revolutionary political
agency, more mighty than Blum's petty-bourgeois Socialist Party, or
indeed than anything to be found in France's own revolutionary tradition.
But, nevertheless, France's past history of revolutionary conflict remained a unique and invaluable resource, which continued to determine and illuminate current politics. The collaboration of the bourgeoisie
during Vichy, for instance, was merely the latest manifestation of an
enduring treachery, which extended back to the 1871 Commune and
beyond that to the Revolution itself. Against 'the nationalism of the
bourgeoisie, chauvinist or defeatist according to its own interests',
Chambaz opposed the Jacobin patriotism of the French Communists,
now indissociable from loyalty to the Soviet Union.

> Léon Blum and those like him who, in 1953 as in 1940 and 1871,
> betrayed France through their class interest, did they not speak of the
> 'foreign' nationalist party, thus reviving the calumnies of Versailles?
> Maurice Thorez, loyal to the teaching of Marx, enriched by Lenin and
> Stalin, denounced this calumny. He reminded us of the genuinely
> nationalist politics of the French Communist Party, the sacrifice of its
> militants, the historic role of the Soviet Union and of Generalissimo Stalin
> in the fight against Nazi barbarism, and he concluded: 'Is it not clear
> that the State interests of France and the Soviet Union are not opposed on
> any point? And what worker could forget that the class interests of
> workers of all countries are concordant? What French worker could
> miss the immense significance of the Russian Revolution? Lenin, Stalin
> and the Russian Communists have frequently said, following Marx and
> Engels, that they learnt much from the experience of the Paris Commune.
> And in what way would it be reprehensible for the descendants of the
> Communards to study the rich experience of the Bolsheviks?'[49]

In order to maintain the Jacobin revolutionary tradition, which from
this point of view embodied the core of the nation's identity, Communist
historians were instructed to resist the temptation to adopt 'foreign'
(especially American) methods of research: to succumb would betray
the nation and strengthen the grip of American imperialism.[50] Bourgeois
historians who adopted such methods hoped to subvert 'the inevitable
ascent of Marxism, the theory of the working class, which henceforth
is the vehicle of the national and social aspirations of our people'

(pp. 121–2). Marxism conferred understanding of the true laws of historical development,[51] and Jean Bruhat ended the discussion in sanguine mood:

> 'Where is history going?' What a curious question ... For us, who are endeavouring to be Marxist historians, when one recognizes the objective laws of development of society, one doesn't need to pose such a question. One knows where history is going, one knows where the history of our country is going.[52]

From this perspective, the recovery of France's distinctive political identity was inseparable from a successful renewal of the revolutionary tradition, and this in turn had now to draw its energies through its affiliation with the contemporary instantiation of the universal revolutionary project, the Soviet Union.

The postwar disputes about the character of France's political identity were, essentially, disputes about the community, or communities, for whom French politics could be said to exist. The attempts to construct a distinctive conception of the political community also relied heavily upon the revival, in modified form, of certain claims about France's special role in world history. It was precisely from a position of felt weakness and decline that such claims were made. The theme of national decline, of the loss of the vanguard role bestowed upon France by the Revolution, had a long history, extending back to the 1870s; it became still more explicit after 1918, provoking for instance Paul Valéry's saturnine *Regards sur le monde actuel* (1931). But such disquiet about France's role in world history, and her position relative to other nations became a dominant concern after the Liberation. France was the first of the European nations 'to have been constructed around a self-consciously revolutionary doctrine', and basic to its self-understanding and legitimacy was the conviction that it possessed a universal historical and political role, a civilizing mission.[53] The Jacobin legend of *la grande nation* had deep roots in the political tradition, providing a perpetual resource in periods of turbulence.[54] Strikingly, this self-description acquired resonance in the postwar years—just when it sounded most hollow. The gloomy sense of national eclipse was matched by an impulse to recover grandeur; and the myth of *la grande nation* provided a standard toward which to aim.[55] Trapped in seemingly endemic backwardness, economic, institutional, and intellectual, the French—unlike the other members of the victorious allied triumvirate—felt more painfully a sense of eroded national power and influence.[56] The reality of decline promoted a rhetoric of renewal. Too weak to compete at the level of sheer material and economic power, a customary turn to the political and intellectual domains was contrived: here France could recapture both its singularity and its universal significance. Unsurprisingly, the vocabulary and imagery of past political history was plundered for these purposes, and used to construct a particular version of nationalism.[57]

Nationalism in France refers to at least two distinct traditions: the revolutionary doctrine of a universalist emancipatory mission for France (the tradition of Jacobin patriotism) and, in reaction to this first sense, the inwardly directed racial and ethnic dogmas of Barrès and Maurras.[58] After the Liberation, the reactionary version—celebrated by Fascism and the Vichy regime under Pétain—was abhorred. Yet, if there was a postwar intellectual and political consensus against this form of nationalism, intellectuals were still compelled to speak in the name of some definition of the national community (such a specification was implicit, for example, in the accusations of betrayal and collaboration that surrounded the intellectual purges). The language of nationalism transferred to the heirs of the Resistance movements: to the Gaullists and the Left, especially the Communists.[59] In those European countries where anti-Fascist movements were important during the 1930s, or where war-time Resistance movements had played prominent roles, the commitment to universal rationalist principles could and often did stand in blatant tension to the more parochial nationalist accents of these movements. But in France, uniquely, this was not so. To voice universalist political principles here was, in the context of trying to counter Pétainist and reactionary versions of nationalism, precisely to affirm a distinctive identity of the French nation. To interpret France's identity in terms of its universal mission barely captured the reality of the postwar situation (the late 1940s and the 1950s were, after all, the years of violent repression of independence struggles in Indochina, Madagascar and Algeria), yet it was this interpretation that was adopted—with different inflections—both by the revolutionary Left and by de Gaulle.[60] For all their differences, both the Left and the Right shared the theme of national mission, of France's special destiny.

The variety of interpretations to which nationalist themes could be subject in postwar France was instanced by the Gaullists who, along with the Communists, emerged with special prestige after the Liberation. Both groups described themselves in strongly patriotic and nationalist terms, and both asserted their exclusive title to represent the nation's interests and identity; both, that is, possessed powerful languages of community. In the postwar years, intellectuals could not simply ignore or altogether avoid these vocabularies, but neither were they comfortable with too blatant an invocation of the nation. During the 1930s, those who did not gravitate towards the Right generally rejected patriotic and nationalist languages, in favour of more internationalist forms of anti-Fascism and pacificism. A local definition of socialism was defended by Blum and the Socialists, but by 1938 its intellectual and political appeal had collapsed: the failure of the French government to intervene in Spain, and support for the British policy of appeasement at Munich (both the subject of much criticism by the Communists), were taken as tokens of the Socialists' parochialism. The defeat of Fascism, however, encouraged those who earlier had avoided particularist forms of appeal to move towards a more conventional appeal to the nation: the Gaullism of André Malraux provides perhaps the most notable example of this shift.

For Malraux, there was little doubt that France's special political heritage and destiny was the richest vein from which to seam a new and credible political language. In his analysis, France had entered into a state of decay, its progress and natural mission obstructed by the factious and corrupting presence of the political parties in power, and by the Communists.[61] Against this decaying mess Malraux set *la France réelle*, incarnated by the living principle of Gaullism. Malraux saw well that the Communists were the only other political group with a credible claim to a language of national unity, and thus posed the most serious challenge to Gaullism. The rhetoric of his famous catechism—'what is there today in France? Us, the Communists, and nothing else'—rang true.[62] Gaullism, to Malraux, was a modern reinterpretation of the tradition of revolutionary patriotism forged by Michelet and Péguy. Its natural home was the political Right, and yet Gaullism was peculiar, distinguished from other elements on the French Right by its acceptance of the Revolution: it saw nation and revolution as inseparable. The Left's divisive language of class distorted this tradition, which properly belonged to de Gaulle's party. Gaullism had nothing to do with the provincial accents of the traditional French Right; it was a new political mystique, sustained by the revival of the grand and universalizing claims of Jacobinism:

> The underlying ideology which General de Gaulle opposes to Marxism has been called by him, on many occasions, 'the General Interest'. I remind those with a superficial understanding of fascism that this term is Robespierre's, who was its inventor.[63]

To Malraux's eyes, the Gaullist Rassemblement du Peuple Français was an 'insurrectional movement', which would recover for France a sense of its universal mission. In all these respects, Gaullism shared much with its twin enemy, the Communists: both called for a popular 'rallying' of the People as a means to national unity, both believed that economic renewal depended upon the directive capacities of a strong State, and both spoke for the recovery of national 'grandeur'.[64] This veneration of the nation was precisely the source of the political appeal of Charles de Gaulle, the 'savage embodiment' of national sovereignty, combining in his person a potent mix of Resistance past and the proclaimed will to modernize France.[65] But for most intellectuals, his stress on the decisive and unrestrained authority of the leader raised the spectre of

Bonapartism and Boulangism, while the technocratic and modernizing components of Gaullism seemed too evidently continuous with the aspirations and style of the Vichy regime.[66] And de Gaulle himself of course did little to woo the support of intellectuals. Few, therefore, followed Malraux's path.

It was the doctrinal equations of the Communist Party which held temptations for intellectuals. The Communists possessed a rich and flexible vocabulary to describe the French political community; they maintained an umbilical connection to the Soviet Union, seen as the contemporary instantiation of the universal (and universalist) revolutionary project; and they espoused a revolutionary theory, Marxism, that instructed intellectuals on how they could act effectively while retaining their identity as intellectuals. For more than thirty years after the Liberation, the French Communist Party (itself the product of a disagreement within the French socialist movement over how to respond to the Bolshevik Revolution)[67] although very rarely actually in government, claimed an identity as a kind of sovereign counter-state in relation to which intellectuals of the Left could situate themselves, and fashion their analyses of national and international society. After 1945, the Communists declared themselves to be 'the most national, the most French, the most respectful of the historical traditions and grandeur of the country'.[68] Yet, as observers of the French Communist Party's convolutions often noted, while the Party described itself as 'first, foremost, and most fundamentally French', it also persisted with a special and specially intimate relation with the Soviet Union, and managed with considerable skill 'to defend its politics of friendship with the USSR in terms of the national interest'.[69] An intimacy maintained for three and a half decades, by the late 1970s this had become a fatal embrace.

Linked tightly to these disputes about France's political character were questions concerning the role and authority of the intellectual. Arguments about the authority of intellectuals have a long history in France, and are part of a much broader problem concerning the nature of political authority in a post-revolutionary state.[70] In the postwar years these questions gained a new saliency, expressed in the form of arguments about intellectual commitment, *engagement*. The postwar purges, the execution of Robert Brasillach, the accusations against Paul Nizan, all brought to a critical head longstanding questions of intellectual responsibility and commitment: the murky disputes of the 1930s about the relations between intellectual and political activity now crystalized.[71] In a situation where the destiny and mission of the nation was in doubt, and where the Resistance was the only source of pride in recent national history, the intellectual became a symbol of that destiny and Resistance.[72] From this position, the intellectual had not only a privileged right but a *duty* to speak of national politics.[73] Yet this privilege and duty also raised for intellectuals a fundamental uncertainty about their own identity and authority: it was not obvious for whom, in whose name, they could speak; nor was it clear towards whom their pronouncements were directed, who constituted their audience. Historically a recurrent doubt, particularly at moments when national self-definitions wavered, this question of audience, of the community in relation to whom the intellectual defined and achieved his or her identity and drew authority, was acutely felt in the years after the scissions of the Occupation and Vichy. At stake in the powerful and emotive language of treason and betrayal which predominated during the latter 1940s, employed to identify intellectual and political traitors, was precisely the question of who constituted the proper nation. Those who had betrayed were ostracized from the political community and, in the case of intellectuals, denied the right to publish: they were refused membership of the nation. The Vichy regime, and the division into Vichyite and *Résistant* which it provoked, posed sharply and inescapably the question of what it was to be French, of modern France's original myth of identity and nationhood. This question was etched into the memory of the postwar intellectual and political consciousness through the experience of living in a divided country, a country at war with itself. The core intellectual and political arguments of the postwar years turned on the question of how a unifying sense of national identity and culture could be reconstructed.

The experience of war and resistance delineated in special ways the self-image of French intellectuals, but this conception was also decisively framed by a more enduring historical set. In a tradition stretching from Voltaire to Sartre (by way of Zola, Barrès, and Gide), the intellectual in France performed an important function in articulating national self-definitions, particularly in moments of crisis: as if by a process of metonymy, the pronouncements of the intellectual were heard as the voice of the national consciousness, they spoke the nation's opinion. From this perspective, the heightened tone of a Sartre or the sharp polemics of an Aron become more intelligible. To put it baldly, the rupture and disturbance of the Occupation raised for the French intellectual the problem of finding a position of authority which raised him or her out of the realm of the particular and historically contingent. Away from the crisis-ridden and compromising politics of the postwar republics, the French intellectual aspired to the realm of the universal, from where, as Sartre put it with characteristic immodesty, the 'truth of humanity as a whole' stood revealed. In discovering and establishing such a position the intellectual was in the first instance offering a description of his or her own identity and role. But, in a tradition which internally linked the identity of the intellectual to a sense both of the political and historical value of the nation, and of its destiny, it followed that for the intellectual to describe his or her own identity was also and necessarily to offer a description of what the nation was, or rightfully should be.

III

Politics, as always, raised the questions for intellectuals after the Liberation. The French defeat in 1940 and the subsequent occupation and division of the country had forced intellectuals to recognise their own particular (and hence diminished) places. In their responses to the questions they faced, they were led towards a vocabulary that identified them as at once belonging to yet critical of the political community. The difficulties and opportunities of the new intellectual situation found a rich and succinct expression in Maurice Merleau-Ponty's essay 'La Guerre a eu lieu' ('The War has Taken Place'); published in October 1945, it was his first article for *Les Temps Modernes*.[74] It was to all intents a founding manifesto for the first generation of postwar intellectuals. Merleau-Ponty here described how, before the war, intellectuals of his age had followed an educational path 'in which generations of socialist professors had been trained'.[75] Naïvely believing themselves to be abstract and universal 'consciousnesses naked before the world' (p. 140), his generation imbibed an 'optimistic philosophy, which reduced human society to a sum of consciousnesses always ready for peace and happiness', but which now in retrospect appeared as 'in fact the philosophy of a barely victorious nation, an imagined compensation for the memories of 1914' (p. 139). Oblivious to the relativity of their 'individualism' and 'universalism', at the beginning of the war they continued to 'distinguish Nazis from Germans, to look for the student beneath the lieutenant, the peasant or working man beneath the soldier' (p. 142). So entirely did they separate politics from its national and cultural boundaries that, Merleau-Ponty confessed, 'we did not think there were Jews and Germans but only men, or even consciousnesses' (p. 144). But the experience of the Occupation compelled his generation 'to relearn all the childish behaviour which our education had rid us; we had to ... feel ourselves become not men but 'Frenchmen' beneath their [the German occupiers'] glance' (p. 142). France, they now discovered, 'was a soil to be defended' (p. 140).[76] Raised to think in universal and abstract categories, his generation was startled by the revelation that they belonged (and could take pride in belonging) to a specific cultural and national community, with distinct territorial boundaries. Merleau-Ponty censured the abstractions of the older generation of French academics and intellectuals, 'solitary Cartesians' unable to conceive of themselves as actors in the historical and political world, and whose actions—or rather, inaction—had thus betrayed their country. The pre-war generation of 'socialist professors' consigned their pious thoughts to the pages of intellectual reviews like the *Nouvelle Revue française* and, driven by a wish 'to demobilize consciousness, to return to purely aesthetic problems, to disengage themselves from history...' (p. 152), withdrew to the seclusion of their studies. The reiterated emphasis of the essay, however, was that such a retreat was now impossible: 'one cannot get beyond history and time', nor 'get out of history' (p. 147). 'We have learned history' (p. 150), Merleau-Ponty declared, and the consequence was to 'have unlearned 'pure morality' and learned a kind of vulgar immoralism, which is healthy' (p. 147). It was Marxism's special ability to capture the weight and texture of history that now made it attractive. The essay's crux was his turn to Marxism, 'taken up anew' (p. 148). He distinguished his own understanding of Marxism from pre-war Marxism, which had dismissed politics and ideology as mere appendages of deeper economic and social contradictions. He wrote ironically of those who continued to cling to the ideal of proletarian internationalism even after it had ceased to be a credible position, and who tried to absolve patriotic rebellion 'in the name of the class struggle...yet when liberation came they called it by name, just like everyone else' (p. 148).

Merleau-Ponty rejected both the attitude of the solitary Cartesians and the economistic and internationalist priorities of pre-war Marxism, and proposed a reformulation of these two positions. It is usually, and rightly, noted how he, in common with many others of his generation, claimed for the intellectual a more prominent public role (there was no doubt a certain slyness in presenting this as in fact a demand, placed upon intellectuals by the peculiarities of the historical moment). But equally important, if less noticed and certainly less determinately expressed, was Merleau-Ponty's interest in finding a language of political community adequate to the more public role of the intellectual. There was no ambiguity in his assertion that the ideological and cultural realms—and therefore by implication, intellectuals—would henceforth command a decisive political role. The experience of the Resistance had revealed to intellectuals their capacity for effective action:

> intellectuals least inclined to politics were to be seen in the Resistance. The Resistance was a unique experience for them, which is why they wanted to preserve its spirit in the new French politics because this experience broke away from the famous dilemma of being and doing, which confronts all intellectuals in the face of action. (p. 151)

It followed that the 'political task' (this, Merleau-Ponty had earlier explained, was 'to push things forward in the direction of effective liberty'), was 'not incompatible with any cultural value or literary task' (p. 152). To reconcile the two simply required a recognition that literature and culture were forms of worldly activity and strategy, not 'extramundane techniques'. Once reconciled, the intellectual's public role was assured. If there was one lesson to be drawn from the experience of occupation and resistance, it was to disabuse intellectuals of their belief that they were universal consciousnesses. The fact that during the war so many had used their talents in collusion with the Germans had unmasked this as a myth. Intellectuals, like their fellows, existed as agents within a specific community, and they were obliged to be aware of their intentions and to take responsibility for the consequences of their words. Indeed, words *were* actions.

> We have been led to take upon ourselves and consider as our own not only our intentions—what our actions mean for us—but also the external consequences of these actions, what they mean in a historical context. (p. 145)

The sense that defeat and resistance had created a novel sociality, and given new duties (as also opportunities) to intellectuals was a point widely echoed by others during the 1940s. To Raymond Aron, for instance, it was clear that

> Philosophers, poets, novelists, all feel the tragedy of the fatherland, all discover, with a sort of naïveté when brought face to face with the event, the eternal truth that the writer, even when he professes solitude and distance, lives in a national community and participates in its fate.[77]

More grandiosely, Sartre expressed a similar recognition:

We know that the most intimate of our gestures contributes to the making of history, that the most subjective of our opinions helps to constitute that objective spirit which the future historian will call 'the public spirit of 1945' . . . we exist in history like fish in water, we are acutely conscious of our historical responsibility.[78]

The intellectual had to shake off his self-image as custodian of abstract knowledge, gathered within and validated by the hermetic *Ecoles* and universities of the Third Republic. These, the dimming beacons towards which academics had retreated during the dying years of the Third Republic, were now in the postwar years quite snuffed out.

If intellectuals now had a higher profile in public political life, how might they orient themselves, and what forms of political speech were available to them? Here Merleau-Ponty was at once evasive and canny. In the aftermath of the war, he suggested, the customary rigid opposition between the values of internationalism and nationalism no longer held. On the contrary there now existed excellent pragmatic reasons for fusing the two. The Communists had already tried to bind together these two commitments. But for intellectuals it was a decidedly more tricky manoeuvre. The complications and hesitations involved were conspicuously apparent in Merleau-Ponty's fraught negotiation of the issue:

The ideology of nationalism cannot be classified once and for all as bourgeois: its function in shaping the historical conjunction must be newly appreciated at every moment, and this function may at times be progressive and at other times reactionary. Nationalistic feeling (which is not to say chauvinism) is revolutionary in the France of today and was so in 1940. This does not merely mean that national feeling is in fact opposed to the immediate interest of French capitalism and that, by a pious trick, the Marxists can make it serve their own struggle. It means that the historical conjuncture frees the national reality from the reactionary mortgages which encumbered it and authorizes the proletarian consciousness to integrate it. One might try to argue that in Marxist political thinking the nation can only be a means, never an end, that Marxist patriotism can only be tactical, and that for the Marxist a purgation of morals, for example, serves the ends of revolution, whereas the primary concern of the patriot is, on the contrary, the integration of the movement of the masses into the nation. But even this kind of language is not Marxist. It is the particular attribute of Marxism not to distinguish the means from the end, and, in principle, no system of political thought is less hypocritical and less Machiavellian. It is not a question of abusing the patriots' good faith and leading them where they do not wish to go. Not the Marxist but history transforms nationalist feeling into the will to revolution. It is a question of making the patriots see (and events as well as Marxists undertake to do this) that in a weakened country like France which the movement of history has reduced to a second—rate power, a certain political and economic independence is possible only through a dangerous oscillation or within the framework of a socialist Confederation of States which has no chance of becoming a reality except through revolution. To be a Marxist is not to renounce all differences, to give up one's identity as a Frenchman, a native of Tours or Paris, or to forego individuality in order to blend into the world proletariat. It is indeed to become part of the universal, but without ceasing to be what we are. (pp. 149–50)

The passage might serve as an appropriate epigraph to any account of the postwar position of the intellectual: each rhetorical gesture of certainty was tensed and checked by ambivalence and qualification, the hesitancies of expression capturing symptomatically the ambiguities of period. Intellectuals aspired to wrest for themselves a language that described them as belonging to a specific national community; yet, simultaneously, they sought a certain distance from that community, a position from which to criticize. After all, already, only a few months after the Liberation, politics was returning to its pre-war traits, 'to the time of institutions. The distance between the laws and those to whom they apply is once more apparent' (p. 151).

The need to forge a language that could describe the authentic political community had been the defining purpose of the 'intellectual resistance', which had played a significant symbolic and practical role in the overall activities of the Resistance.[79] In clandestine reviews such as *Les Lettres françaises, Combat,* and in the publications of Les Editions de Minuit, intellectuals enlisted the language of patriotism and betrayal in order construct and defend such a conception of the authentic community. Intellectuals accused of collaboration—men such as Pierre Drieu la Rochelle and Lucien Rebatet—were bitterly denounced as traitors. What they had betrayed, it was most usually alleged, were the political ideals associated with the Revolution: the values set out in the 'Declaration of the Rights of Man and the Citizen'. These universal values provided the kernel of an evocative cultural nationalism, most clearly voiced by organizations such as the Comité National des Ecrivains (CNE), a kind of clandestine Académie française which joined together Communist and non-Communist intellectuals (counted among its members were Louis Aragon, Claude Morgan, François Mauriac, Albert Camus and Jean Paulhan). Though lacking in any official status or powers, it acted as an intellectual tribunal and commanded influence over the intellectual world immediately after the Liberation. In October 1944 it published a 'black list' of writers and intellectuals designated as collaborators and 'collaborationists', men and women accused of placing their literary talents and (still worse) the French language in the service of Fascism.[80]

The language of betrayal and patriotism committed intellectuals to a specification of the nation and the national community. This was arrived at by relapsing to the vocabulary of the nation's revolutionary tradition: here was a language capable of identifying those who properly constituted the nation, and thus of excluding traitors. It named an existing community; but its determinacy was specious, since it also designated a yet-to-be-created community, and so justified political criticism of existing institutional forms. By adopting the terms of the inherited Jacobin tradition, intellectuals could exploit its capacity to identify and resolve present divisions by means of a hypostasized and chronically displaced unity, projected both into the past and into the future. Sartre's discussion of collaboration, reverberating with this language, crisply exemplified this process:

> The collaborator, whether or not he may have the opportunity to reveal himself as such, is an enemy which democratic societies harbour perpetually in their midst. If we want to ensure that he does not survive the war and reappear in other forms, it is not sufficient merely to execute a few traitors. It is necessary, as completely as possible, to achieve the unification of France, that is to say to complete the task begun by the revolution of 1789; and which can only be achieved by a new revolution, a revolution that was attempted in 1830, in 1848, in 1871, and that in each case was followed by a counter-revolution.[81]

The obsessive Jacobin interest in defining friend and enemy, patriot and traitor, and its call to perpetual political vigilance in order to maintain the identity of the authentic nation, was fulsomely displayed here.

But such definitions of the nation's political identity, also embroiled intellectuals in uncomfortable inconsistencies. This was the thrust of Jean Paulhan's criticism of the attitudes of intellectuals towards the postwar purges. Paulhan enjoyed great influence in French intellectual life during the 1920s and 1930s: editor at Gallimard, director and *éminence grise* of the *Nouvelle Revue française* since 1925, patron of André Gide, Paulhan symbolized all that French literary culture stood for (hence Sartre's—temporarily successful—efforts to incorporate him onto the editorial board of *Les Temps Modernes*). His reputation grew still further through his close involvement during the Resistance with *Les Lettres françaises*. His credentials as a defender of true France were impeccable. But he was dismayed by the postwar purges of alleged collaborators, and was determined to reveal the contradictions that surrounded the use by intellectuals of the notions of patriotism and nationalism to condemn their colleagues. This was the intention of *De la paille et du grain* and *Lettre aux directeurs de la Résistance*.[82] The political point of *De la paille et du grain* was obliquely stated. Surveying the current state of the French language, Paulhan lamented the penetration of anglicisms into the language, and praised the use of properly French words.[83] The French language in fact served Paulhan as a metaphor of the condition of France's postwar identity. He deplored the universalizing accents of modern philosophy, which diminished the significance of particular languages and cultures: 'We have a tendency, today, to consider languages (and countries [les patries]) as if they were prisons which one must escape as one can' (p. 12). The parenthetic, easy equivalence between language and 'patrie' led to the question of whether the French language could maintain its integrity in the face of external threats and pressures. The degeneration of the French language was symptomatic of a wider political confusion. The abstracted use of words such as 'patrie', divorced from their cultural context, led intellectuals to betray the very principles they claimed to uphold (p. 57). Paulhan made transparent the ambiguous meanings of such words as 'patrie' and 'nation'. He reacted against those on the Left, who in earlier years had been pacifist, anti-nationalist, internationalist, but who now claimed to speak in the name of patriotism and the nation. By what right, he asked, could they claim this? Paulhan acknowledged that those who had joined the Comité National des Ecrivains—communists, socialists, republicans, conservatives—had done so for similar reasons, 'all guided, I think, by the same love for their country' (p. 59). The Charter of the CNE declared its aim to uphold 'the principles which had carried France to the forefront of nations' (p. 66). But a word such as 'patrie' did not hold a universal signification, common to men of every language. Nor, however, was it an empty word, to be defined according to ideological predilections, as Paulhan claimed the CNE (dominated at the time by the Communist Party) was doing. He cited the examples of Romain Rolland in 1914, and Rimbaud in 1873, both once accused of betraying their country, but now defended by the CNE in the name of 'la patrie'. Still more oddly, before the war men like Julien Benda, Paul Eluard, and Louis Aragon all had dismissed the 'patrie' as repugnant.[84] Yet now these same intellectuals authorized their own self-righteous judgements by appeal to a principle previously rejected. This principle was evident enough:

> C'est la patrie. C'est un peu moins encore: c'est la patrie à l'état brut, avant même la conscience que l'on en prend, avant la volonté que l'on forme de lui appartenir, de l'améliorer, de le défendre. D'un mot, la nation.[85]

The writers accused during the purges were said to have committed crimes against the nation. But, Paulhan insisted, in the pre-war years the roles had been reversed. Nationalist and patriotic themes had been the prerogative of those who now stood accused—Châteaubriant, Maurras, Rebatet, Drieu la Rochelle; these themes had been altogether absent from the discourse of those who now were the accusers.

Paulhan's strictures revealed the deep instability of postwar conceptions of France's political identity. There were multiple ways of defining the national political community and therefore of being patriotic, and more than one way of displaying this: only thus could one explain, for example, the new-found patriotism of men such as Claude Morgan. The explanation for such shifts was pure expediency: 'it's that now it is 1947. In 1940, he [Morgan]—along with Thorez—would have replied to me that a Communist has no country. In 1935, with Aragon, that France is the vermin of the world' (pp. 109–10). Those who now protested their patriotism were in fact political partisans, who distorted the real character and meaning of patriotism.[86] Paulhan's point was to show that patriotism was being incorporated into the political languages and positions of the Left, and was being induced to serve partisan ends. Conversely, it could be inferred from his argument that the political vocabularies of universalist theories such as Marxism were themselves undergoing assimilation and incorporation into the vocabularies of patriotism and nationalism.

If, as Paulhan pointed out, the value of terms like 'patriotism' and 'nationalism' was unstable in the years immediately after the Liberation, the semantics of words such as 'revolution' were equally fluid. In a diffuse way, it designated a political order that promised to resolve and bring to an end the conflicts of the war, which to many had been a battle between revolutionaries of the Left and of the Right. It was precisely the vague, gestural quality of the word that enabled intellectuals in the postwar decades to commit such fierce energy to the defence and propagation of the idea of revolution. Its most determinate sense was overridingly negative: it signified a refusal of the Third Republican and Vichy regimes, rejection of the representative politics of 'bourgeois democracy', capitalism, individualism, and above all antagonism to those who had betrayed France in the cause of Fascism (it was in fact very close to the meanings attached to anti-Fascism).[87] But some elements of this negative sense were common both to the Resistance and to Vichy. The Vichy regime, after all, had described itself as the agent of a *révolution nationale* directed against the Third Republic. Both movements proposed a radical redescription of the French political terrain, both had their origins in the circles of disaffected intellectuals of the 1930s, and both shared common references.[88] Charles Péguy, for instance. First a Dreyfusard and socialist, then a nationalist Republican, invoked by Vichy and the *Résistants*, Péguy's ghostly shadow was invested by all with ambiguous political meanings.[89] The conflation and entanglement of vocabularies provoked a need to draw at least rhetorical distinctions and take positions. This predicament, where political oppositions were asserted only to be helplessly blurred and subverted by the slipperiness of the language which political actors were constrained to use, was registered with customary nuance by Merleau-Ponty:

> In a society in which the proletarian movement called itself the 'National Front' at one point and the conservative mentality labels itself 'Socialist', political thinking and the analysis of events cannot help being very confused. There are no ideas which have not been mutilated; the political position of each of us is not so much defined by a certain number of theses to which we subscribe as by our adherence to one of the two opposing blocs. To be a Communist or a Socialist on the level of ideas no longer means anything definite. We have reached a level of political nominalism of which there is perhaps no other example in French history. The notions of 'Socialist' and 'Communist', to say nothing of the Christian Democrats, will soon be as impossible to define and to communicate in this country, which once prided itself—to take Thibaudet's word for it—on putting a whole view of life into its politics, as the notions of 'Republican' and 'Democrat' are in the United States. Last winter a café waiter attributed the riots during the Brussels uprising to the Fifth Column, went on regretfully about the slowness of the purge, and concluded with the remark, 'The big fish always gets away.' This is how 'patriotic' and 'Marxist' motifs are intertwined in men's minds.[90]

But in the postwar decades, intellectuals were to make a virtue of the necessarily amorphous political vocabulary they inherited. Commitment or opposition to the *idea* of revolution (whatever exactly that might in practice entail; and of course in postwar France, where the promise of revolution receded with each passing year after 1945, very little indeed was entailed in practice), became a crux: to choose wrongly was to be branded a traitor and condemned, at least symbolically, to exclusion from the political community. The language of revolution had a dual utility for intellectuals. It enabled a discourse which clearly belonged to the political traditions of the nation; but this could be finessed, disclosing a more universalist and universalizing form of political appeal, whose scope extended beyond the boundaries of the nation.[91]

The Communists saw the proletariat as the rising and vital principle of the nation, confronting a mouldering bourgeoisie: the proletariat embodied the best and general interest of the nation, and Communist Party manuals and popular textbooks taught such historical 'laws' as that 'in each epoch a rising social class incarnates the true national interest' and 'in every epoch the decadent social class detaches itself from the nation'.[92] When Sartre in 1952 came out in support of the Party, he recycled this language wholesale:

> In France today, the working class is the only one to possess a doctrine, the only one whose 'particularism' is in full harmony with the interests of the nation; a great party represents it, and it is the only one that has made it part of its programme to safeguard democratic institutions, to re-establish national sovereignty and defend peace, the only one concerned with achieving an economic renaissance and increasing spending power, the only which, above all, is alive, which teems with life while the others teem with words.[93]

The proletariat was able to incarnate the authentic interests of the nation but, as a universal class, it could also claim to escape the limitations and particularities of national boundaries.

Seen from within the culture, it was not very surprising that French intellectuals should adopt a language that transposed national politics into a universalist register; historically, this was a perfectly conventional way of carrying on. French intellectual culture had a deep-rooted propensity to conceive of itself in universalist terms. The distinctive character of this self-conception, intimately tied to the French sense of the nation and nationalism, emerges through an obvious but useful comparison with Germany. Herder, an early and chief architect in the construction of the modern German sense of the nation, in his essay *Auch eine Philosophie der Geschichte* (*Another Philosophy of History*: its title and contents were a direct riposte to Voltaire and the ideas of the French Enlightenment) scorned the French Enlightenment notions of a universalizing rationalism and a progressive evolution of civilization.[94] He stressed the cultural diversity of communities, *Volk* or peoples, each expressions of different aspects of humanity: man was irreducibly a socially constructed creature, not an abstract individual endowed with reason.[95] The nation, with its specific textures and tones, was the medium where all those particular cultural attributes which constitute the essence of human being were defined.[96] The French Enlightenment view contrasted starkly. Following Louis Dumont, one might say that in the French view nation possessed no ontological primacy: it was simply the most immediate and empirical approximation of humanity, so that its political problems were seen as contiguous with those of humanity in general. To speak of the nation was thus necessarily to voice universal values and principles. Throughout the nineteenth century, this sense of the French nation as, in Louis Bonaparte's phrase, 'the advanced sentinel and first soldier of civilization', was propagated by a range of writers, quite independently of their political positions. The chord of unblemished confidence which opened Guizot's *Histoire de la civilisation en Europe* ('It is neither an arbitrary nor conventional choice to place France at the centre of this study; on the contrary, it is to place oneself at the centre of civilization itself')[97] was echoed by Quinet ('for good or for ill, for two centuries France's destiny has been to be the dominant organ of civilization')[98] and by Hugo ('the French people have been the missionaries of European civilization . . . at all times and epochs, France has played a considerable role in civilization').[99] It received symphonic orchestration with Jules Michelet, decisive in the formation of a universalist style of nationalist thought and language in France.[100] The defeat of France by Prussia in 1870 introduced discord, but in the call to national renewal and awakening subsequently raised by those such as Taine and Renan, the universalist ambition remained intact, [101] if now modulated by darker themes of decadence.[102] But the colonial doctrine of Jules Ferry brought new vigour to French universalism, and in 1912 the historian Ernest Lavisse could end his primary school manual glibly: 'France is the most just, the most free, the most humane of all countries.'[103]

After 1945, this inherited historical perception seemed cruelly implausible to intellectuals. Belonging to a defeated, compromised, and divided nation and culture, how could they recover authority for themselves, for their pronouncements? Who, if they spoke would listen to them, and why? For Merleau-Ponty, the problem was an opportunity:

> Vichy and the sacrifice of so many French workers made it evident to us that anti-Communism could lead to treason and that the will to revolution could assume responsibility for the nation. Lastly, now that France has clearly ceased to be a power of the first magnitude and national existence seems to depend so strictly upon world imperialisms, our diminished power no longer permits us solemnly to set the drama of worldwide economic organization against the French national fact, as if they were facts of equal weight: our humiliation will perhaps free us of the provinicialism that was so striking in prewar French politics.[104]

This felt need to recover a sense of community by casting a glance elsewhere, outside the nation, this backwards crawl towards the ques-

tion to which nationalism had been an answer, was to become a characteristic response.

Four points of importance emerge from this broad survey. First, there
was a widespread and unshakeable sense that France had emerged from
the war no longer a great power: on this, intellectuals of diverse political
affiliations were agreed. Economically, the nation was clearly under-
developed and backward. Politically, Republican institutions were discredited by the defeat of 1940. Cultural and intellectual life was trapped
in a stifling provincialism. Most importantly, besides economic and institutional rebuilding, robust self-conceptions of the French nation were
needed. The definition of the French political community was in active
dispute, a direct consequence of the dislocation of the national identity
created by the experience of German occupation, the collaboration of
the Vichy government, and the varieties of Resistance movements this
had engendered. The Vichy period had marked the return, in grossly
heightened form, of the fratricidal relations between Left and Right that
had typified France's political history in the long century between the
French Revolution and the First World War. After the defeat of Vichy
and the expulsion of the German presence, the French nation needed
redefinition and reconstitution as a political community.

Second, it was evident that the political languages most able to
address these requirements in clear and resonant terms were those
which could identify an authentic political community, the French
nation, and which could claim to distinguish and protect this from its
enemies and betrayers. For this task, both Charles de Gaulle and the
French Communists showed themselves adept. Both possessed a forceful
accusatory terminology of betrayal, collaboration and corruption. But
both also promised regeneration. The instrument for the progressive
transformation of the nation, they agreed, would be the State, although
they differed over who ought to control this in order to effect such
change. For the Gaullists, it was a new technocratic élite, positioned at
the summits of state power, who would serve as the prime agent of
economic and social modernization. In the Communist view, the French
nation had been betrayed by a decaying bourgeoisie, which continued to
dominate the State and to pursue 'Malthusian' policies that obstructed
any movement toward national modernization. Against this bourgeoisie,
a rhetoric was invoked that borrowed heavily from and in some cases
transposed an earlier pre-industrial political language directed at 'les
gros', owners of landed or commercial capital.[105] The dynamic and
regenerative force for modernization was unquestionably the working
class: 'les travailleurs' or, more inclusively defined, 'le peuple'.[106] The
bourgeoisie was branded anti-national (easier to do after 1944, since so
many of its members had worked with Vichy and the Germans) and in
selfish pursuit of individual interest; it was the proletariat or working

class, with its 'universal' interest, who constituted the authentic representatives of the nation.

Yet—and this was the third important element in the postwar years—it was generally recognized (with chagrin by some) that the French working-class movement now could no longer claim a monopoly over, or even direct access to, the theory and practice of effective revolutionary politics: 1917 had signalled the decisive transfer of revolutionary political energy eastwards, from the French to the Soviet capital. After 1945, access to this could only be through the straitened gates of the French Communist Party. In these years, the French Communists owed their authority both to their Resistance activities, and to their claim to be the national representatives of this new universalist and effective revolutionary politics. Finally, these exigencies and developments had consequences for intellectuals. Faced by the challenge of a political party (the French Communist Party) and a theory (Marxism) which gave a new mapping of the relations between intellectuals and politics, thought and action, intellectuals felt their own independence and authority threatened. It was no longer possible, as for example it had been at certain moments during the nineteenth century, to discover and establish (at least rhetorically) a direct and unmediated relation between the intellectual and the revolutionary agent or class: there was no foothold for a new Michelet, a prophetic Carlylean figure who could summon up and give voice to the People, procuring them for his own purposes. But intellectuals could not abandon politics altogether, and seek their authority from the institutions of the University. They *had* to take a position on contemporary politics; indeed, in the postwar years this imperative was a fundamental part of their own self-description and self-definition. A significant difference in the situation now was the pressure upon intellectuals to mediate their political positions or identity by—and through—a relation with a political party. For those on the Left, this frequently meant the Communist Party which, closely allied to the Soviet Union, claimed uniquely to represent the dynamic principle of national and world history.

PART TWO

CHAPTER THREE

Jean-Paul Sartre: Politics by Procuration

When a society loses its ideology and its system of values as a result of a great upheaval (such as military defeat, or enemy occupation) it often happens that it will—almost without being aware of it—expect its intellectuals to liquidate the old system and recreate a new one. Yet, of course, its intellectuals will not be content simply to replace an outworn ideology with another, just as particularist, that merely facilitates the reconstruction of the same type of society as before. They will attempt to abolish all ideology and to define the historical ends of the exploited classes.

Jean-Paul Sartre, 'A Plea for Intellectuals' (1965),
Between Existentialism and Marxism (London, 1974).

Commitment is action at a distance, politics by procuration, a way of putting ourselves right with the world rather than entering it; and, rather than an art of intervention, it is an art of circumscribing, or preventing intervention.

Maurice Merleau-Ponty, *Les Aventures de la dialectique*
(Paris, 1955).

For at least a generation after the end of the war, Jean-Paul Sartre was the most prolific and flamboyant spokesman of the intellectual Left in France. His image of the intellectual committed to revolutionary politics achieved a dazzling domestic and international prominence, and established itself as an influential self-description for intellectuals of the Left until finally surpassed by the more recondite Althusserian vocabulary of theoretical intervention. Sartre was not in any obvious sense a Marxist, nor did he ever enter the Communist Party, even when its political prestige was at a maximum. And although he decisively framed the terms of intellectual debate for his generation, he never—after the war—held a position in the academic institutions of the State. His conception of intellectual commitment was designed precisely to release the intellectual from the stipulations of either Party or State. But he always remained (by his own avowal) a man of the revolutionary Left; although he often adjusted his political positions (especially with regard to the Party), his commitment to revolution, to the 'seizure of power by violent class struggle', remained the nub of his political imagination.[1] For all his intellectual sensitivity to nuance, Sartre's political vision and rhetoric possessed brutal simplicity. The factious perplexities of French politics were always reduced to a stark conflict between warring principles: these implacable antagonists were, at different times, named as oppressor and oppressed, bourgeois and proletariat, masses and bureaucratic Party or state. The structures of France's Republican politics rendered an alienated image and expression of the true political community, and promised no resolution to this struggle. The wounds of the divided political community could be healed by no other means than revolution: a natural extension of the war, it would bring to an apocalyptic end the great global conflict of the century, between Fascism and Communism. In the vanguard of the postwar intellectual backlash against the bourgeois world, Sartre dismissed its political and intellectual forms as remnants of a tawdry past.

Sartre's ceaseless search for new forms and vocabulary to describe the authentic community was intimately connected to his efforts to justify the role of the intellectual. He conceived of the intellectual in extraordinarily ambitious terms, a promethean figure in pursuit of an encompassing, 'totalizing', knowledge. The authentic intellectual shunned the division of intellectual labour embodied in the academic institutions of the bourgeois Republic: the fragmented knowledge this produced simply reflected and perpetuated the alienations of the bourgeois world. Nor did the authentic intellectual yearn for a bland objectivity or neutrality. Rather, the universal validity of the Sartrean intellectual's totalizing knowledge derived from partisan political engagement and struggle on behalf of the oppressed: whether described as the proletariat, the masses, the People, or (sometimes) the Third World, this category invariably represented a 'concrete universality of negative origins, born of the liquidation of particularisms and the advent of a classless society'.[2] The intellectual aspired to represent this authentic political community, which failed to find representation in the politics of the bourgeois liberal republic. He identified existing political divisions and proposed a theory of revolution, which promised to unify it. He revealed the community to itself.

Sartre was profligate with his intellectual energies, and it is impossible in a single chapter to consider the huge range and volume of his work, which extends across philosophy, fiction, drama, criticism, biography, political essays and journalism.[3] The central tension in his work is conventionally located in the relations between his philosophy and his political writing, and most interpreters aim to show the compatibility of these two aspects of his work, or why they must necessarily diverge.[4] Sartre's own purposes receive purely internal and philosophical defini- tion, with the result that the critical focus is invariably directed at such issues as whether or not he successfully reconciles the division between subject and object, or Existentialism with Marxism, and so on. But I do not intend to foist a systematic pattern on all his political writings, as if they revealed a coherent intellectual project. My interest is specifically in Sartre's conceptions of the intellectual's role, and the intimate con- nection between his view of the intellectual and his efforts to find a language to specify the authentic political community.[5]

Sartre's political writings divide into four distinct periods. After the Liberation and until the early 1950s, he tried to establish for the intellec- tual a political voice independent from either Party or State. In his review *Les Temps Modernes*, the intellectual emerged as best placed to specify the authentic political community, and to lead it to self-recognition. By the early 1950s, this epic conception of the intellectual in direct contact with the political community was faltering. The second period, between 1952 and 1956, were the years of his closest connection with the Communist Party. He turned to the Party, and to the vocabulary of class, as a way of specifying the political community and its repre- sentatives: the role of engaged intellectual was to affirm the identity between class and Party. In the third period, between 1956 and the early 1960s, Sartre harked back to his earlier aspirations: he tried to evolve a philosophical argument that justified the intellectual as the authentic and exclusive custodian of revolutionary politics. His intention, in the *Critique of Dialectical Reason*, was to produce a new vocabulary to describe social solidarities. The argument failed internally. But it was also over- whelmed by external currents, most dramatically by the appearance of Althusser's more modernist redescription of the relations between the intellectual and politics. In the final period, the years after 1968, Sartre partially regained a political position, but with a quite different profile: he now dismissed as forlorn the hope that the intellectual could have access to a 'totalizing' knowledge, or that he could be independent and politically effective. It was a disavowal that converged strikingly with Althusser's own position after 1968.

I

At the end of the war intellectuals faced at least two immediate chal- lenges to their own activity and identity. With the country exercised by the task of economic reconstruction and production, the intellectual had to meet the charge that, in straitened times, he was simply a social parasite with nothing to contribute to the material renewal of his com- munity.[6] The summary purges of writers accused of complicity with

Fascism cast further suspicion on the public role of intellectuals, laying them open to charges of political naiveté, and to injunctions against their further meddling in politics. One response was to strike a pose of withdrawal from politics and the public realm altogether: to recognize, as Paulhan ultimately chose to do, the 'incertitudes of language' or to prefer, with Maurice Blanchot, a 'literature of silence'.[7] This was not Sartre's route. His initial reply to the pressures faced by intellectuals was typically bold and broadside. He delivered a blazing defence of the autonomy of literary and intellectual activity against the exigencies of politics; simultaneously, he championed the intellectual as a decisive political actor in the renewal of postwar France. Sartre bypassed the discredited academic institutions and forms associated with the Third Republican university, and initiated his own bid for intellectual authority in *Les Temps Modernes*. Launched in 1945, it boasted a stellar editorial board: apart from Sartre himself, Raymond Aron, Simone de Beauvoir, Michel Leiris, Maurice Merleau-Ponty, Albert Ollivier, and Jean Paulhan, all served on it at various times.[8] The review's vocation, Simone de Beauvoir recorded, was 'to furnish the postwar [period] with an ideology'. The editorial 'Presentation' of the inaugural issue announced that this would be accomplished through intellectual comment upon and engagement with literally everything: 'we do not wish to miss anything of our times'. The conception of intellectual activity embodied in the review (as in Sartre's own practice) obliterated the boundaries between academic specialisms, in favour of an unremittingly supra-disciplinary approach.

From its inception, *Les Temps Modernes* was Sartre's platform in his campaign to propagate a view of writing that at once guarded its independence and endowed it with a new public importance. 'La Nationalisation de la littérature' was a first gesture towards this end.[9] The essay's title jibed ironically at the country's obsession with economic production: even literature, it seemed, was being dragged into the ambit of the State's economic planning and reconstruction. Toying with the metaphors and language of political economy, Sartre deplored what he called 'literary inflation', a process that debased the aesthetic value of literature into political commentary, converted writers and artists into 'national commodities', and books into newspaper editorials.[10] He bridled against the 'odour of virtue', the air of political correctness, that pervaded intellectual life: it allowed, for instance, the guilt of intellectual collaboration to be assuaged by favouring with undue indulgence the works of writer and intellectuals who resisted. These works eased the injury of betrayal and defeat:

We have discovered with humiliation that in tomorrow's world France will no longer play the role it played in yesterday's ... The decline [*glissement*] of France, which accompanies that of western Europe, is the result of a long evolution . . . We could not easily bear such a brutal revelation: the shame of having lost the battle of 1940, the sorrow of renouncing the exercise of hegemony over Europe, were both joined in our hearts . . . In other words, within the space of five years we have acquired a formidable inferiority complex. The attitude of the masters of the world will hardly help to restore our condition. We rap on the table: we are not heard. We recall our past grandeur: in reply, we are told that it is precisely past. Only in one respect have we surprised the world abroad: its admiration for the vitality of our literature has not ceased.[11]

In these circumstances of eclipsed power, where writing substituted for military and industrial impotence, the writer faced the prospect of being turned into a functionary of the State, becoming thereby a mere propagandist (pp. 50–1). The burden of Sartre's argument was to protect the writer and intellectual from this travesty of his role. But then, in a manner that fully exemplified Sartre's characteristic style of 'radical outthinking', this protective defence of the autonomy of literature metamorphosed into an aggressive gesture of appropriation, that extended the scope of literature so as to encompass the political and historical domain.[12] He did not *deny* the political functions of literature: the writer was not urged towards a 'pure' or disengaged position. Sartre's point, rather, was that the relations between literature and politics were profoundly misunderstood. Rightly construed, the writer possessed an omnipotent political identity, he was 'responsible for everything: wars won or lost, revolts and repressions; he is complicit with the oppressors unless he is the natural ally of the oppressed' (p. 51). This supreme responsibility inevitably presumed a matched capacity of agency, and this allowed Sartre to claim for the writer a status *equal* to that of the politician (p. 52). Yet, by virtue of his critical stance, the writer remained distinguished from (and morally superior to) the politician. This was a stratagem designed to establish for the writer a position at once politically central and oppositional.

The call to intellectual engagement was never a subordination of the intellectual to politics. In its original statement, it implied a defensive position, a way of easing the burden of embarrassment under which the writer apparently laboured: 'we do not wish to be ashamed to write' asserted the launch editorial of *Les Temps Modernes*.[13] The conception of the engaged intellectual that Sartre now propagated was a distinct contrast to his pre-war description of the writer as an isolated individual, pursuing universal values and knowledge through his literary and aesthetic creations. After the war Sartre abandoned this perspective, and asserted that it was exactly the particular 'situation' of the writer, his details of location, which guaranteed him access to universal knowledge. The circumstances of this reversal were well described by Simone de Beauvoir:

The masses were behind the Communist Party; socialism could only triumph through the Party. Furthermore, Sartre was now aware that his connexion with the proletariat entailed a radical reconsideration of his whole existence. He had always supposed the proletariat to be the universal class. But as long as he believed he could attain the absolute by literary creation, his relations to others [être pour autrui] had remained of secondary importance. With his historicity he had discovered his dependence; no more eternity, no more absolute. The universality to which, as a bourgeois intellectual, he aspired could now be bestowed on him only by the men who incarnated it on earth.[14]

The proletariat, graced with a universal historical significance, beckoned to the intellectual, promising him universality in return for his commitment to their cause.

Sartre pursued the question of the writer's status and role most forcefully in *What is Literature?*[15] Literature, it seemed, had no role amidst the utilitarian labours of the postwar world: 'In a society which insists on production, and restricts consumption to what is strictly necessary, the work of literature is evidently gratuitous.'[16] To refute this charge, Sartre developed an historical survey of the changing role of the writer, and connected this to an analysis of contemporary French social and political divisions. It was the very fact of such divisions that offered the writer a chance to recapture his historical role. The split political community, divided between bourgeoisie and the working class, awaited potential unification by a third, independent term: the writer or intellectual, standing apart, but committed to partisan political action. The Sartrean writer created a 'literature of production', designed to 'launch, through all our works, a democratic appeal to the whole of the collectivity' (p. 266/trans. p. 177). Yet, sundered between 'the oppressed classes and the oppressors', the collectivity as a whole remained elusive (ibid.). Just when the writer was promised a role as an effective political actor, his audience seemed to have disappeared: 'at the very moment that we are discovering the importance of *praxis*, at the moment that we are beginning to have some notion of what a *total* literature might be, our public collapses and disappears. We no longer know—literally—for whom to write' (p. 266/p. 178). The first and essential task therefore was to specify anew this public, to define the community for whom he wrote (and whose existence lent purpose and authority to his writing).

Crucial to the success of this was the Sartrean writer's ability to arrogate to himself an exclusive representative function. It was his keen feeling for this that explains the speed with which he assailed his fellow intellectuals if they claimed to speak 'in the name of' others. In the most famous of these scoldings, he berated Albert Camus for claiming to speak 'in the name of . . . poverty . . . [and] . . . in the name of morality'.[17] Mocking Camus' 'paternalist discourse', Sartre disingenuously claimed that he himself 'had never spoken except in my own name' (p. 96), in his *persona* as a philosopher and writer. Yet *What is Literature?* defined the writer as precisely a representative, in both political and aesthetic senses: the writer possessed the capacity to represent figurally, but he was also a political *representative*, who rightfully could speak for others. In particular, the writer represented those who had no voice—the oppressed. 'Who', Sartre asked, 'can *represent* to the government, to the parties, and to the citizens, the means that are being employed [to dupe the masses], if not the writer?'[18] This representative function endowed the writer with authority; but equally, the writer was free both to define the character of his responsibility, and to specify the community to whom it was owed.

The writer did not speak in the name of abstract values, a universal truth or reason, nor did he write for an audience of 'all men'. All literature was historically and culturally rooted, and he scorned the pretensions of those who professed to write for a universal community of auditors (as the writers and academicians who gave their support to the Third Republic had claimed to do). To the question 'for whom does one write?', Sartre replied firmly: 'the writer speaks to his contemporaries, his compatriots, brothers of his race or class' (p. 117/p. 49). The writer was committed to a particular community: he wrote for them, and against their enemies. This recognition of the particular historical and national location of intellectual activity was the common trait of his generation; all who had lived through the events of the 1930s and '40s,

> had understood that we were not citizens of the world, since we could not make ourselves be Swiss, Swedish, or Portuguese. The destiny of our works themselves was tied to a France in danger . . . Brutally reintegrated into history, we were compelled to produce a literature of historicity. (pp. 244–5/pp. 158–9)

Yet, typically, Sartre immediately reversed the sense of his argument. Recognition of their relative and particular location implied no restrictions but in fact gave his generation access to the absolute and universal: 'the war and occupation, by throwing us into a world in fusion, perforce made us rediscover the absolute at the heart of relativity itself' (p. 245/p. 159). Sartre here displayed an intellectual move absorbed through his pre-war interest in phenomenology: a fondness for reversing the significance of ordinary experience, revealing a new meaning by 'making it strange'. The rhetorical force by which Sartre usually achieved such reversals of meaning—virtual *gestalt* changes—has often disarmed his readers and critics, and diverted them from the original scope and point of his writing. Hence the tendency to accept at face value his claims to be addressing universal questions, at the expense of missing the very particular concerns which enabled him to profess a universalist discourse.

Sartre insisted on the local and national peculiarities of the writer's public. Yet his definition of his public as 'a waiting, an emptiness to be filled, *an aspiration,* both figuratively and literally. In a word ... the other' (p. 123/p. 55), could scarcely have been more uncompromisingly abstract and rarefied. The public possessed no constraining powers upon the writer; rather, it awaited its definition. The writer aggressively created his audience, defining it into existence, he wrote for his public (the argument took its force from the ambiguity of the phrase 'to write for': meaning at once a donation and a substitution).[19] But if it might be thought that the writer had partisan or partial interests that, Sartre insisted, was a mistake: although engaged on behalf of the working class, the writer in fact wrote for the 'whole of the collectivity'. Uncannily akin to Marx's proletariat, Sartre's writer incarnated the universal: 'he is writing for everybody and with everybody because the problem which he is trying to solve by means of his own talents is everybody's problem'(p. 257/p. 170).[20]

The experience of the Resistance had disclosed the possibility of a seamless relation between the intellectual and the whole community. Intellectuals who had participated in the Resistance 'addressed themselves in their articles to the whole community' (p. 257/p. 170); they had produced a literature directed at a 'concrete universality' (this he glossed as 'the totality of men living in a given society'). This temporary fusion of writer and the entire community had left the writer with a lingering aspiration to rediscover a public that 'will extend itself to embrace this totality'. Were it now possible, in the postwar years, to revive this 'concrete public' (p. 193/p. 116) so fleetingly present during the Resistance then, 'involved in the same adventure as his readers and situated like them in a society without cleavages, the writer in speaking about them, would be speaking about himself, and in speaking about himself would be speaking about them ... as his situation would be universal, he would express the hopes and anger of all men' (p. 194/ pp. 116–17). Here the core of Sartre's political imagination was revealed: an impossible and impossibly intellectual fantasy of community, a unified collectivity where utterances became interchangeable, continuous, and where the intellectual in speaking for himself took the voice of all. The intellectual incarnated in his person the link between the spiritual and the temporal, and thus abolished any existing political division of labour: he became 'instantly justified in the eyes of everyone'.[21] Politics, and the division of political labour represented by the State, appeared as so many obstructions to the writer's task of holding the revealing mirror of writing up to society: 'it is by means of the book that the members of this society would be able to get their bearings, to see themselves and to see their situation ... literature is in essence the subjectivity of a society in permanent revolution' (p. 196/p. 118). The writer's function was justified by means of this promise of pure transparency, one of the most powerful and beguiling statements of the modern intellectual's desire for empowerment.

More specifically, it was the bourgeoisie who stood in the way of the writer and his utopia of a universal community. Since the mid-nineteenth century a profound chasm had opened up between bourgeois ideology and the requirements of literature; simultaneously, as a result of the introduction of free universal compulsory education, a new, virtual, public began to appear. A choice now loomed: 'what was the writer going to do? Would he choose the masses against the élite, and would he attempt to recreate for his own profit the duality of publics?' (p. 162/p. 88). At first, some did gravitate towards this virtual public, representing it as 'the People'. Sartre's belligerence towards writers who chose in this way—Georges Sand, Victor Hugo, Jules Michelet—, romantics who attached themselves and their destiny to a failed revolution (1848), was tempered by a distinct nostalgia and regret.[22] He conceded Hugo's popularity; and Michelet, after all, was read by 'the People' until 'the success of Marxism pushed him into oblivion' (p. 163/p. 89).

But the abyss between the writer and his true community of readers persisted. Although, as Sartre confessed, he and his fellow intellectuals remained, in 1947, 'the most bourgeois writers in the world' (p. 204/p. 124), it was no longer possible (let alone desirable) for the writer to address himself to a stable bourgeois public. Between the wars, some had tried to discover a new public, and to establish a new relation between writer and audience: the Surrealists, for instance, and in the twilight years of the Third Republic such 'petty-bourgeois' writers as Jacques Prévost, André Chamson, Pierre Bost. But both groups had failed to find a public role for the writer or intellectual. Sartre's readiness to dismiss them as failures was no doubt motivated by his sense that they rivalled his own enterprise. Both were pugnaciously attacked by him. 'It seems', he allowed, 'that [with Surrealism] we have re-encountered that community of interests between intellectuals and the oppressed classes which was the good fortune of the authors of the eighteenth century' (p. 223/p. 141); after all, Surrealism proclaimed itself revolutionary and had allied with the Communist Party. But this was an illusory semblance. Surrealism was essentially negative, exulting in violence as a pure end in itself, rather than seeing it as a means to political power, as the Communists did. Political dilettantes, the Surrealists saw the proletariat as merely an instrumental ally (p. 223/ p. 141), with the result that 'the bourgeois writer's first attempt to reconcile himself with the proletariat remains utopian and abstract because he is not seeking a public but an ally, because he preserves and reinforces the division between the temporal and the spiritual' (p. 224/

p. 142). The Surrealists remained oblivious to the significance of the newly emerged Communist Party. The existence of the Party demanded a new connection between intellectuals and politics: 'the Party [emerges] as a mediator between the middle classes and the proletariat' (p. 225/ p. 143). But the Surrealists, blinded by their ambition to appropriate everything at once, had betrayed themselves to the exigencies of the Party, and of politics.[23]

The *bien-pensant* writers of 'radical-socialist literature' (p. 234/p. 150) likewise failed to establish a satisfactory relation between intellectual activity and politics. These writers, members of 'that class happily baptised 'average'[*moyenne*]' (p. 232/p. 149), intimately associated with the academic institutions of the Third Republic, had tried to furnish their class with a lay morality.

> They all had that strong self-seeking culture which the Third Republic gave its future civil-servants. Thus, almost all of them became civil-servants, administrative officers in the Senate and Chamber, teachers and curators of museums. But, as they came for the most part from modest backgrounds they were not concerned with using their ability to defend bourgeois traditions. They never enjoyed that culture as a *historic* property.[24]

This average class took possession of the universities and educational institutions of the Republic, busying themselves with the ideas and writings of Durkheim, Brunschvicg, Alain. But they failed to create or inculcate a lay ideology, a failure explained 'by the public which they chose for themselves'. They made the mistake of affiliating with the petty-bourgeoisie, a class that 'dreamed rather of mastering itself than of changing the course of the world' (pp. 149, 233). Radicalism, the political ideology of this class and of these writers, 'was the great victim of this war' (p. 234/p. 150). The political choices and judgements of these writers were 'revealed as inadequate for great catastrophes ... [and] ... thus history stole their public from them as it stole voters from the Radical Party' (pp. 234–5/pp. 150–1).

The task of defining the writer's role and of specifying the authentic community for whom he wrote, unresolved by the pre-war generations, possessed a new urgency for Sartre's generation, the men and women who 'began to write after the defeat or shortly before the war' (pp. 151, 235). Sartre set about specifying the authentic community negatively, through unwavering opposition to the bourgeoisie. The characterization of the bourgeoisie he gave in *What is Literature?* was little modified by his later political writings. To Sartre, the European and in particular the French bourgeoisie was losing its distinctive identity, it had collapsed into a 'gelatinous and amorphous aspect' (p. 272/p. 183). Bereft of economic or political power and without a sense of historical mission, its future was sealed: 'the fate of the bourgeoisie was linked to that of European supremacy and colonialism. It is losing its colonies at the

moment when Europe is ceasing to govern its own destiny' (p. 271/
p. 183). It no longer had any ideological convictions, it neither stood for
nor represented anything:

> They [the bourgeoisie] considered wealth as an unjustifiable state of fact;
> they have lost faith. Neither do they retain much confidence in that
> democratic regime which was their pride and which collapsed at the first
> push. But as national socialism in turn collapsed just when they were
> about to rally to it, they no longer believe either in Republic or Dictator-
> ship. Nor in Progress; it was fine when their class was on the way up;
> now that it is declining, they are no longer concerned with the notion; it
> would be heartbreaking for them to think that other men and other
> classes will ensure it. (pp. 273–4/p. 184)

This ideological abdication, the absence of any resources by which to
reconceive the political identity of postwar France, revealed the bourgeoisie as a class of self-interested opportunists. There was nothing to
restrain them from betraying the political community: 'even for those
who judge it in the name of its own principles, it is manifest that the
bourgeoisie has betrayed three times: at Munich, in May '40, and under
the Vichy government' (p. 274/p. 185). The bourgeoisie was the pawn
of foreign powers and influence:

> An object of everybody's solicitude, doped by the USA, by the Church,
> and even by the USSR, at the mercy of the changing fortunes of the
> diplomatic game, the bourgeoisie can neither preserve nor lose its power
> without the concurrence of foreign powers. It is the 'sick man' of con-
> temporary Europe. (p. 273/p. 183)

In decline and alienated from the true political community, the bourgeoisie promised the writer no subvention.

The writer's destiny, Sartre asserted, lay elsewhere: 'it must be said
without hesitation that the fate of literature is bound up with that of
the working class' (p. 277/p. 187). The working class beckoned as a
potential 'revolutionary public', which justified the activity of the writer
and endowed him with authority. Yet this revolutionary public was no
longer directly accessible to the writer or intellectual. The Communist
Party, self-proclaimed representative of the proletariat, intervened between writer and class, restricting access. 'The oppressed class, hemmed
within a Party, tied down by a rigorous ideology, becomes a closed
society: one can no longer communicate with it without an inter-
mediary' (p. 271/p. 182, trans. modified).[25] Flanked on one side by a
declining bourgeoisie and its republican political forms, on the other by
a Party that blocked access to the dynamic and revolutionary element of
the community, what were the intellectual's political prospects? Until
the late 1940s, Sartre clung to the possibility of steering a third, in-

dependent way between the bourgeois Republic and the Party. The writer was the symbolic embodiment of this median position. But this position had to be fought for, captured. Sartre had severed the intellectual from the bourgeoisie; now he proceeded to dispute the revolutionary title of the Communist Party and the Soviet Union. Soviet Russia had muted its revolutionary appeal, 'at the very moment when it was becoming the Mecca of the working classes, Russia saw that it was impossible, on one hand, for her to assume her historical mission and, on the other, to deny it' (p. 278/pp. 187–8). The French Communist Party, ever willing to emulate, had itself become conservative and opportunist, absorbing the traits and the language of its bourgeois enemies: *famille, patrie, religion, moralité* were now Communist virtues.

The intellectual must refuse both the domestic choice between the bourgeoisie or the Communist Party and, as it appeared at the international level, the choice between the USSR and the 'Anglo-Saxon bloc'. Rather, he would be a pioneer of the 'third way', an independent socialist Europe. During these early postwar years, before the onset of the Cold War and while a policy of neutralism seemed a real possibility for France, Sartre's political horizon was that of a unified, neutral group of states with a democratic and collectivist structure, forming a socialist Europe. The prime agents in its construction would be not the old parties and states of Europe, but a popular movement, with radical and independent intellectuals at its helm (this independence extended to the theoretical realm: Marxism at this point had no privileged status for Sartre, and he engaged only superficially with it, producing a critique entirely standard for his time).[26] This conviction that the radical independent intellectual was about to inherit a significant political role was acted out by his involvement with the Rassemblement Démocratique Révolutionnaire (RDR), an organization started early in 1948, and top-heavy with intellectuals of the non-Communist Left. It described itself as revolutionary, and pursued a 'third' way, a neutralist position between the USA and the USSR. The RDR earnestly organized intellectual debates, and called repeatedly for the formation of a directly elected 'Revolutionary People's Assembly', a democratic forum that avoided the institutions of Party politics.[27] The movement failed, both in itself and for Sartre. It drew heavy flak from the Communist Party, to whom it was an agent of Wall Street. Sensing the difficulty of a neutralist position, David Rousset (one of its founders) took it increasingly in a pro-American, anti-Soviet direction. Sartre resigned from the RDR in October 1949.[28] The RDR was no doubt an insignificant blip in the more hectic rhythms of French intellectual activity, but it was a revealing symptom of the hopes harboured by intellectuals about their own political significance as independent actors.

With the dissipation of such hopes, Sartre was cast back to a position of isolation from the putative revolutionary class, and to doubts about how to justify the intellectual's function. The onset of the Cold War had, meanwhile, revived the necessity for stark political choices between friend and enemy. Yet at precisely this important moment of decision, the political profile of Les Temps Modernes began to blur and decline, largely in consequence of Merleau-Ponty's withdrawal as the review's political editor, after the outbreak of the Korean war in June 1950. For five years, he had helped fashion the identity of the review as a voice of the revolutionary Left, but now his own intinerary deviated from that of Sartre. Increasingly secure in institutional positions—he was elected to the Collège de France in 1953—Merleau-Ponty withdrew from his earlier conception of intellectual engagement, and preferred now to distinguish between the roles of the philosopher and the politician.[29] By the mid-1950s, his support was pledged to Pierre Mendès-France's efforts to rejuvenate Republican-Radical politics and the language of meritocratic élites.[30] Sartre had no such comparable institutional base, nor was he sufficiently tempted by the lure of a modernized Radicalism. Caught, as he put it, in the embarrassing position of trying to be a fellow traveller without having been invited on the journey, by 1950 he had become, in André Gorz's somewhat hysterical assessment, 'the most denounced, the most hated man in France'.[31] Faced with the prospect of forfeiting his political identity and voice, Sartre now injected new vigour into securing this. In his own retrospective explanation of his swerve towards the Communist Party, he claimed that it was the example of Merleau-Ponty's earlier writings like Humanism and Terror (1947) which brought him to see the centrality of politics for intellectuals: 'it was time: our epoch required of all men of letters that they produce a dissertation on French politics'.[32] Looking back, Sartre regretted that he had not been revolutionary enough.[33] Yet this self-chastisement was self-excusing. It was hardly true that Sartre had ignored politics in the years between 1945 and 1952; he had struggled to establish the intellectual as an independent voice and authority on politics; and he had now to acknowledge his failure. Unable to justify any such independent position or discourse, he embraced the political line of the Communist Party, if not quite the Party itself.

II

The Communists and Peace is the key to the second phase of Sartre's political trajectory. It appeared in Les Temps Modernes in three parts, between 1952 and 1954, prompted by the events surrounding the demonstrations against the visit to Paris of an American general, Ridgway, and the subsequent arrest of Communist Party deputy leader, Jacques Duclos. The most unambiguous expression of Sartre's support for the Communist Party, it is commonly interpreted as a massive concession on his part. He seemed to acknowledge the impossibility of any direct relation between the intellectual and the revolutionary class; the Party, not the writer, was now invested with symbolic status as the necessary and only possible representative of the 'Proletariat', as the most significant agent of revolutionary politics. But, if the essay was in this respect a concession, it was equally a firm gesture of appropriation. It was published at a time when the Party was in political difficulties and under public attack, at its weakest since the Liberation. Sartre hastened to its rescue at this point, summoning his powers of rhetoric to defend the Party. Ostensibly a justification of the revolutionary claims of the Party, *The Communists and Peace* was without doubt intended as a vindication of the intellectual. It was designed to show how the independent intellectual, situated *outside* the Party, was in fact best placed to demonstrate the Party's status as the necessary representative of the revolutionary intentions of the universal class, the proletariat. Further, the publication of the essay in successive issues of *Les Temps Modernes* reinvigorated the journal's flagging political profile. It was, in short, the most vivid example of the theatrical form and meaning of Sartre's notion of intellectual engagement. His political writings of this period are typically described as 'disingenuous', 'uncritical', and 'embarrassing to recall today', an instance of the coarse subordination of the free-thinking intellectual to the rigid leash of Party discipline.[34] In fact, they were perfectly consonant with his preoccupations.

The circumstantial nature of *The Communists and Peace* was obvious, as were Sartre's purposes: 'the aim of this article is to declare my agreement with the Communists on certain precise and limited subjects, reasoning from my principles and not theirs'.[35] On these subjects, and for his own reasons, Sartre would defend the Party against its bourgeois enemies. The most damaging accusation lodged by the bourgeois political Parties and press against the Party was that it represented no class or community within France; the working class, the bourgeoisie alleged, owed no allegiance to the Party, which it correctly saw as the 'plaything of Moscow', an agent of extra-national forces and interests. Yet, challenged Sartre, the bourgeoisie itself had no contact with or access to the working class; how then could it claim to be so informed about the opinions of the working class, 'what do you know about that? Have you with your own ears heard him [the worker] complain?' (p. 88). Sartre's defence, therefore, was designed to show that, despite all appearances, the Communist Party could not but be the true representative of the proletariat, and the guardian of its revolutionary mission. He produced what by his own admission was a byzantine argument, which proceeded by way of philosophical deduction rather than sociological or empirical demonstration, and whose dénouement revealed the Party as the necessary expression and exact measure of the working class. Sartre's scepticism towards those outside the proletariat who claimed knowledge about it did nothing to deflect him from his own dogmatic conclusion: the Party (and only the Party) had direct communication with the proletariat, and therefore it commanded exclusive knowledge about the desires and interests of the proletariat.

Sartre arrived at his conclusion through four claims. First, he portrayed the French working class as an emasculated entity, demoralized and fatalistic. His characterization of the working class differed fundamentally from views then current among intellectuals outside the Party and on the non-Communist Left. To the syndicalist Left, for instance, the worker was a skilled, fully self-conscious, and politically active being. The working class had no need of a vanguard Party organized along Leninist lines, since it already possessed an articulate revolutionary consciousness, derived directly from its experience. But to Sartre this view expressed a nostalgic wish, since the genre of revolutionary worker celebrated by the syndicalists had been made extinct by the arrival of Taylorism and Fordism.[36] The working class was by no means a self-organizing revolutionary agent. It had neither the ability nor the desire to struggle on its own behalf: 'they [the workers] refused the struggle because they were sure of defeat: the worker had lost confidence in the power of the working class; it seemed that his class had no grip on events and that history was moving on without it' (p. 188). Exhausted and depleted by the levy of production, the working class lacked time or energy to discover a revolutionary political consciousness, or to engage in militant activity (pp. 358–9). The image Sartre conjured of the worker was that of a dull and emaciated spectre, wasted by routine and by the 'Malthusian' policies of the bourgeoisie. Infected by 'the French illness', the 'anaemia of the nation' (p. 249), the French New Proletarian was an enervated thing:

> His exhaustion is the result less of muscular exertion than of continual nervous tension and the constant effort to adapt himself to pre-established norms; at the end of the day, his tiredness sticks to his skin; it remains with him during sleep, and is still there when he awakes; this chronic lassitude becomes second nature, even the way in which he is conscious of his body. It is written on his face, in the way he carries himself, it limits his powers, and makes him in the proper sense of the term, a diminished man. (p. 332)

How could this pathetic figure aspire to independence, to self-conscious (let alone revolutionary) political agency? The proletarian was the victim of the French bourgeoisie, historically committed (ever since 1848 and 1871) to the death and extinction of his class.

This portrayal formed the basis of Sartre's second claim, that the inert community of workers was under imminent threat. The bourgeoisie wished to 'stop history', by arresting the economic development of the

nation. In Germany and in Italy, the bourgeoisie had resorted to the
state-dispensed terrorism of Nazism and Fascism in their efforts to extinguish the working class. But, more sophisticated, the French bourgeoisie conducted a more subdued if (in its effects) equally violent
attrition: it gradually stifled the existence of the working class, through
invisible civil war:

> When the middle classes of the south and the east cried: 'to arms!', the
> French middle classes replied 'Temporize!'; when the foreigner cried 'Loot
> and kill! Massacre!', ours responded 'Underfeed' . . . It was after all simply
> a question of stopping history. Our employers wanted to postpone the
> cataclysm for some decades so that they would have time to die in peace.
> That presented no difficulty provided one was willing to ruin the country.
> (p. 295)

Dominated and encaged by a defeatist anti-national bourgeoisie, the
French worker was excluded from his authentic community. He re-
mained isolated from the dynamism and progress of his Soviet and
Chinese colleagues (pp. 323–4). Yet, despite its lassitude and unwilling-
ness to turn up at political demonstrations called on its behalf, the
French working class remained revolutionary:

> Have they [the working class] moved toward reformism? Not at all
> (p. 182) . . . The French worker retains an exceptional intransigence.
> Perhaps he is not aware that this is Revolution: but how else would you
> describe this irreconcilable violence, this contempt for opportunism, this
> Jacobin tradition, this catastrophism which puts its hopes in disruption
> rather than indefinite progress? (pp. 191–2)

The third of Sartre's claims was that this untapped revolutionary
energy could only be released by the Party, it alone could give shape
to and represent the aspirations of the working class. He tried to sustain
this by producing a piece of logic astonishing in its effrontery. To employ
Sartre's own philosophical language, he had characterized the French
proletariat as pure negation, a nothingness unconscious of itself and
unable to act for itself, an entity constantly on the verge of extinction.
Before it could become a revolutionary political agent, it had first of all
to be defined into existence. Sartre, always scornful of empirical or
sociological definitions of class, saw this as an opportunity for a philosophical demonstration.[37] The proletariat achieved its existence to the
extent that it found representation in the Party. The Party was pure act
and will, pure positivity; it was, in other words, the complete antithesis
of the class it represented. It was impossible both to belong to the class
(embodied by the Party) and to dissent from the Party. To oppose the
Party was to define oneself as outside the working class; and if the
working class as a whole opposed the Party, then it simply ceased to

exist. To those discontented with this definitional bamboozling, Sartre opened his volume of Marx and wagged his finger:

> I would remind them of this phrase of Marx's which they have read, reread, and commented upon a hundred times: 'The proletariat can act as a class only by forming itself into a distinct political party', and I urge them to draw the consequences: whatever they think about the 'Stalinians', even if they deem that the masses are deceiving themselves or are deceived, what could maintain their cohesion, what will assure the effectiveness of their actions if not the Communist Party itself? The 'proletariat formed into a distinct political party': what is that in France, and today, if not all the workers organized by the Communist Party? If the working class wants to detach itself from the Party, there is only one way: to disintegrate into dust.[38]

By failing to appear at the demonstrations called by the Communist Party against the General Ridgway's visit to Paris, the working class had demonstrated and confirmed its own identity as an object of pure passivity, exhausted and politically unselfconscious.[39] So too, the Party was confirmed in its identity as pure act. Both terms were affirmed in their identity, philosophically (and ontologically) justified in their actions.[40] As so often in Sartre's thinking, a practical political difficulty was resolved by philosophical redescription. The intellectual affirmed his own significance by discovering reasons which escaped the actors in the drama. But the brilliant *normalien* never stopped at the obvious question: how could pure act represent pure passivity?

Finally, Sartre turned directly to the question of the boundaries of the genuine political community. The Communist Party appeared to owe ultimate loyalty to the USSR, thus leaving it vulnerable to the charge that it served extrinsic and not national interests. But this, Sartre advised, was simple error. The USSR was qualitatively unlike any other bourgeois nation, with a distinct and historically privileged political identity:

> Historically the opportunity of the proletariat, its 'example' and the source of 'the strength of revolutionary penetration', is the USSR. Besides, it is in itself an historical value to be defended, the first State that, without yet actually realizing socialism, 'contains it in its premises'.[41]

He dismissed the imputation of bellicose intentions to the USSR, and named as hypocrisy the bourgeoisie's claim to speak a 'realistic' discourse. Political 'realism', in the mouth of the French bourgeoisie, was a euphemism for betraying the nation: 'during the war of 1940, those Frenchmen who collaborated with the German army were called realists; today a realist is a Frenchman who believes that the USSR is the devil and who seeks refuge, weeping, in the skirts of America' (p. 98). The anti-Sovietism of the French bourgeoisie was simply an abject counter-

part to its servile pro-Americanism; and this, in turn, was nothing else
but the peacetime continuation of the bourgeoisie's politics of collaboration with Germany during the war. The role of the Soviet Union during
the war had unquestionably secured its title as the universal defender of
the revolutionary politics of the Left, against the threat of revolution
from the Right embodied by German Nazism. With the end of the
war, that threat persisted, though in a new form. America was now
perceived as a new imperial power, seeking to extend its boundaries,
with Germany its European outpost.[42] The allegiance of the French
bourgeoisie was split between its own country, and America (and by
extension, Germany); so too the loyalties of the French working class
were divided between France and the nation which represented them as
a class, the Soviet Union. But in this latter case the effect was benev-
olent, and indeed explained the pacifism of the working class:

> While the other classes project their own society on to the other side of
> the border, but change its value, seeing it as a diabolical image of their
> own society, the worker also sees himself projected there, but possessing
> exactly the same value, since it is the middle class of his own country
> which is the negation of his own class. (p. 110)

Sartre admitted that the emergence of Soviet nationalism complicated
the symmetry, though his argument did nothing to undermine the
Soviet claim that 'the worker has two countries, his own, and the
Republic of Soviet Russia' (p. 111). Within the boundaries of France
itself, the French working class was unable to find representation in the
existing institutions of Republican politics. French society, bourgeois and
proletariat alike, no longer believed in the Republic (p. 140), recognizing
that 'the democratic regime today is nothing more than a façade: all the
real conflicts take place outside it' (p. 142). In this situation of lamed
bourgeois political institutions, the Communist Party had effectively
become the sovereign counter-State of the proletariat, the authentic
representative of the true community. It was able to call on direct
popular support—instanced through demonstrations, strikes and so on–
to 'legitimate its authority' (p. 167) as a revolutionary party. There was
no mistaking the boldness of Sartre's claims: 'the CP has an authority
which resembles that of a government; but since it lacks institutions, its
sovereignty comes directly from the masses themselves' (p. 164). Sartre
would later abandon his faith in the Party, but he always nursed a deep
mistrust of representative politics.

His fundamental point, however, was to confirm that 'the Communists
speak in the name of the proletariat' (p. 163). Now, Sartre fully accepted
the Communist Party view that the proletariat alone embodied the
progressive forces of universal and national history. Any doubts were
obliterated by his driven, climactic, prose, propelled by its obsession to

exclude any possibility of an alternative view (the sense is best conveyed in the original French):

> Dans la France d'aujourd'hui, la classe ouvrière est *la seule* à disposer d'une doctrine, c'est *la seule* dont le 'particularisme' soit en pleine harmonie avec les interêts de la nation; un grand parti la représente et c'est *le seul* qui ait mis à son programme la sauvegarde des institutions démocratiques, le rétablissment de la souveraineté nationale et la défense de la paix, *le seul* qui se préoccupe de la renaissance économique et l'augmentation du pouvoir d'achat, *le seul* enfin qui vive, qui grouille de vie, quand les autres grouillent de vers.[43] (emphasis added)

As the Party of the proletariat, it followed that the Communists represented the progressive, modernizing forces within the nation. Their political actions—such as calling strikes—served not just the interests of the proletariat, but the interests of the nation as a whole, the entire political community. Sartre could therefore conclude in triumph: 'I say that the strike of 4 June served not only the interests of the Communists but those of the proletariat and of the whole nation' (pp. 179–80).

Sartre's endorsement of the Communist Party as the unique agent of revolution and sole representative of the authentic political community drew attack from the non-Communist Left.[44] His response was invariably to challenge the identity of his critics, hoping thus to undermine the validity of what they said. Thus, in his condescending 'Réponse à Claude Lefort', Sartre swiftly moved from substantive argument to *ad hominem* barrage ('You, Lefort, who are you? Where are you?' (p. 19)). Lefort, an unattached, uncommitted intellectual, had no right or title to criticize: 'you have no wish at all to be situated: you would lose knowledge. Your situation would teach you what you are not (you are not Hegel; you are not Marx; nor a worker; nor Absolute Knowledge), and what you are (you are a young French intellectual, remarkably intelligent, who has ideas about Marx as people in 1890 had ideas about women' (p. 34).[45] Intellectuals who criticized the Party spoke from no stable or authorised position, in nobody's name but their own subjectivity. The Communist intellectual, however, was in touch with a different pulse: 'when a Communist makes known the interests or feelings of the proletariat, rightly or wrongly he speaks in the name of the proletariat' (p. 23). Sartre's portrayal of Lefort as without any real connection with the working class, as voicing pure subjectivity, was a perfect model of the manner in which the Communist press constantly sought to spike the guns of its critics. His response to criticism was simply to pull rank: only the Party, and those who supported the Party, had access to revolutionary politics, and so rightfully could claim to speak in the name of the working class. But, for all the orthodoxy of Sartre's position, his support for the Communist Party was quite consistent with his own purposes. The path he had pursued in *What is Literature?* had led him to an impasse: the intellectual was blocked from any immediate connection with the revolutionary class. He had to confront the Party, and affiliate with it. Merleau-Ponty, in his withering critique of Sartre's 'ultra-bolshevism', understood the springs of Sartre's shift well: 'The truth of society or of history is no longer dependent on a specialist of truth, the writer; it is in the gaze of the least-favoured, who is never the writer . . . It is no longer the writer who appeals to the reader's freedom; it is the Party which makes this society.'[46] The terrain remained the same; Sartre had simply retreated in order the better to advance. The intellectual retained the right to specify the true agent of revolutionary politics: 'Yesterday literature was the consciousness of the revolutionary society; today it is the Party which plays this role.'[47]

Until 1956, Sartre actively supported the Communist Party. Early in 1956, for instance, in 'Le Réformisme et les fétiches', he dismissed calls for the Party to adopt a more explicitly reformist strategy, and reiterated that 'carried forward by history, the CP manifests an extraordinary objective intelligence: it is rare for it to make a mistake'; it remained the infallible bearer of revolutionary politics.[48] Stalin's death in 1953, Sartre's voyage to the Soviet Union with Simone de Beauvoir in 1954, and news of Khrushchev report to the Twentieth Congress all served to keep his enthusiasm for the Communists and the Soviet Union high. Although in 1955 two former colleagues, Raymond Aron and Maurice Merleau-Ponty, published books strongly critical of his support for Leninist revolutionary politics,[49] Sartre himself did not seriously question this commitment until after the Soviet invasion of Hungary in November 1956. By then, political circumstances within France had significantly altered. The short-lived Mendès-France government had momentarily revived the credibility of Radicalism as a form of Left politics, and had won intellectual friends.[50] Still more importantly, the Communist Party's decision to support the Mollet government's battle to suppress the Algerian independence struggles cost the Party considerable intellectual support, particularly on the Christian Left.[51] The entry of Soviet tanks into Budapest thus provided Sartre with an opportunity to take advantage of these realignments on the Left. Putting distance between himself and the Communists, he now returned to the more eirenic language of a 'Popular Front' of a 'new type': his declared hope was to create a 'New Left' incorporating the Christian and progressivist Left and the 'dynamic elements' of Radicalism.[52]

The call for a popular front was repeated in 'Le Fantôme de Staline', the most substantial of Sartre's strictly political texts of this third period between 1956 and the early 1960s.[53] Indignant in tone, the essay vowed to show the absence of any moral justification to the Soviet invasion of Hungary. Yet Sartre advanced a strongly evolutionary account, which undermined his stated purpose. Contingent misdemeanours—precisely, politics—were excused by reference to historical progress: Stalinism had fulfilled its historical function and would now be replaced by greater democracy. Claude Lefort, criticizing the 'progressivism' of intellectuals like Sartre, characterized his ambivalence neatly:

> Sartre's texts end up by meaning the contrary of what they claim to mean. Written in order to denounce the action of the USSR and to render justice against the calumnies which the French Communist Party poured on the revolutionaries of Budapest, its ultimate lesson is that nothing which occurred was essential, that the USSR unfortunately succumbed to reflexes of fear, that the Communist Party used detestable methods, that the one must examine its reflexes and the other reform its methods, but that without doubt they incarnate socialism.[54]

Primarily a narrative of events, insofar as the essay contained a political argument it was directed at other, enemy, intellectuals. Sartre did of course also attack those Communist intellectuals who tried to justify the invasion: 'pompous asses', they had altogether missed the meaning of Marxism. This accusation signalled a new twist to his views. In the wake of a widespread intellectual reaction against the Communist Party after 1956, the term 'Marxism' had at this moment suddenly become newly available for appropriation. The crystallization of 'revisionism' as a defensible intellectual position, manifested by the creation of journals such as *Arguments* in 1956, the appearance of Lucien Goldmann's 'Marxist humanist' essays, and the formation of the Parti Socialiste Autonome (later Michel Rocard's Parti Socialiste Unifié), all helped to loosen the hitherto unshakeable grip of the Communist Party on Marxism.[55]

Seizing upon these circumstances of opening and opportunity, between 1957 and 1960 Sartre launched his most aggressive bid to wrest revolutionary politics away from the Party, and to appropriate it for the independent intellectual. The great instance of this was the *Critique of Dialectical Reason* and its companion essay, *Search for a Method*. The *Critique* was substantially a response to Merleau-Ponty's reprimand to Sartre's politics. Since his withdrawal from active involvement with *Les Temps Modernes* in the early 1950s, Merleau-Ponty had increasingly dissented from his own earlier views, and from Sartre's. The distance he had travelled since his original postwar attempts to give the intellectual an active political role, to unite the political and cultural realms, was expressed in his inaugural lecture at the Collège de France in 1953.[56] 'One must be able to withdraw and gain distance in order to become truly engaged, which is, also, always an engagement in truth' (p. 60), Merleau-Ponty now suggested. Philosophy 'limped' rather than strode into action: this was its virtue, and those who insisted on the priority of pure action forgot that it was 'the very detachment of the philosopher [that] assigns to him a certain kind of action among men' (p. 61). The literary and philosophical activities of the intellectual possessed 'an intrinsic value' which could not be replaced by or subordinated to history and politics (p. 56). Merleau-Ponty's break with the precepts that had informed his own work in the 1940s (and that continued to be expressed by *Les Temps Modernes* and Sartre) was eloquently confirmed by his essay, 'Sartre and Ultrabolshevism', the centre-piece of his subtle political testament, *Adventures of the Dialectic* (1955). To Merleau-Ponty, it was apparent that Sartre had misconceived the connection between the intellectual and politics. Sartre had intended his conception of commitment to close the gap between the intellectual and politics; in fact he had simply reproduced it, and with it the division of intellectual and political labour:

> We see proof of this in the fact that Sartre does not end up with a theory of action, that he is obliged to divide the roles between a sympathy limited to pure principles and to certain aspects of action, and an action which itself is completely in-between. Sympathy has meaning only if others move to action.[57]

Sartre, in Merleau-Ponty's view, had failed to show how the intellectual could be an agent at once independent and effective in his own right: he had simply fallen back into the role of an intellectual fellow traveller, a spectator booing or applauding the decisive actions of others. This was a travesty of the intellectual intention that Sartre and Merleau-Ponty had expressed in the early days of their review:

> *Les Temps Modernes* demanded of its founders that they belong to no party or church, because one cannot rethink the whole if one is already bound by a conception of the whole. Commitment was the promise to succeed where the parties had failed; it therefore placed itself outside parties, and a preference or choice in favor of them made no sense at a moment when it was a question recreating principles in contact with fact.[58]

The wish to discover 'all that can be known about history and men' had inspired 'this encyclopedia of situations, this universal inventory that *Les Temps Modernes* undertook' (p. 190). But to Merleau-Ponty it now looked an increasingly forlorn ambition: the gap between the committed intellectual and an obdurate world remained as unbridgeable as ever. In fact, changes in the political world had defeated Sartre's attempts to establish the review as an autonomous intellectual voice on political matters: Sartre's *The Communists and Peace* showed plainly how 'circumstances have transformed his independent criticism into a political line' (p. 192). The original purpose and edge of commitment had been blunted: it had become a politics by procuration, a gestural 'semblance of action' rather than the thing itself (p. 193). It was time, Merleau-Ponty concluded, to 're-examine commitment as Sartre understands it' (p. 193).

Sartre's effort at such reconsideration produced that ragged, garrulous monster of modern philosophy, the *Critique of Dialectical Reason*. It represents the grandest of all French attempts to produce a language of revolutionary politics that escaped the disciplines of the Communist Party and its version of Marxism. In it, Sartre struggled to tame and reconstruct Marxist themes and language into a form that secured for the independent intellectual a commanding political importance. If he succeeded, the intellectual could claim to be the progenitor of a genuine revolutionary politics, exclusively capable of turning philosophy into a means of effective political change, 'an instrument which ferments rotten societies'.[59] Presented as a work of philosophy, the *Critique* was equally a polemical instrument. In *Search For a Method*, the long essay intended to preface the *Critique* (but which grew to the proportions of an autonomous work), Sartre immediately set to work bludgeoning opponents, both real and potential. In particular, he distinguished between true revolutionary intellectuals and their false coin. The arguments of anti-Marxist intellectuals were historical oddities ('a return to pre-Marxism' (p. 7); the Marxist 'revisionism' which intellectuals outside the Communist Party were developing at the time was dismissed as 'either a truism or an absurdity' (p. 7); and alluding to the intellectuals within the Party itself, Sartre was imperiously curt: 'these *relative* men I propose to call "ideologues"' (p. 8). Sartre himself proposed the dialectical method, the construction of a 'dialectical Reason', as the only form adequate to produce a genuine revolutionary politics. All other intellectual approaches, both bourgeois and Marxist, were forms of mystification, unable to grasp reality: 'Today social and historical experience falls outside of Knowledge' (p. 28). His own recovery and reinvigoration of 'lazy Marxism' would transform it from the 'paranoic dream' it had become into 'a social and political weapon'.[60] Dialectical Reason, at the end of the twentieth century, would play a role analogous to that performed by 'analytical Reason' at the end of the eighteenth century (which had permeated and broken down the legitimacy of the *ancien régime*), unleashing once again the Revolution: 'the directed violence of weapons will overthrow privileges which have already been dissolved in Reason'.[61]

Sartre's promise in the *Critique* could scarcely have been trumped: his task, he announced, was to arrive at an answer to the question of 'whether there is any such thing as a Truth of humanity as a whole ['une Vérité de l'Homme']'.[62] This was unmistakably a question in the philosophy of history, and to ask it so starkly in 1960 showed (in equal measure) immense audacity and scant regard for the prevailing division of intellectual labour.[63] But Sartre rightly judged that if he were to secure both the independence and the political importance of the intellectual, only an answer of such scope would suffice. He would have to show that the intellectual possessed a totalizing knowledge: hence the

'attempt to establish that there is one human history, with one truth
and one intelligibility' (p. 69). Such knowledge could ground an ethical
argument, and so justify the claim of the independent intellectual to
possess authentic knowledge about politics, unmediated by the division
of political and intellectual labour implicit, for example, in the institutions of Party or state. Composed at a blistering pace, with the aid of
corydrame and whiskey, during the days of the Algerian crisis and of
General de Gaulle's coup from the Right, the *Critique* saw the fundamental mode of history as violent human struggle under conditions of
scarcity. This is not the place for a discussion of the elaborate panoply of
pleonasms used by Sartre in his chosen battle.[64] The significance of the
argument, however, must be noted. In the *Critique*, Sartre tried to
develop his own vocabulary to describe how individuals could unite to
form a 'true practical community' (p. 680), symbolized most vividly by
the crowd storming the Bastille during the French Revolution, and how
this community could be maintained without hardening into the hier-
archical division of labour common to both the bourgeois state and the
Stalinist Party. But he was unable to show how this moment of revolutionary epiphany could be reproduced over time. The identity of the
political community established in the moment of revolution was unstable, and the 'group-in-fusion' inevitably collapsed back into an inert
mass, dominated by a sovereign figure.

If there were a fundamental truth to human history, this presupposed
a stable historical subject of (and for) whom there could be such a truth.
One symptom of the horrendous difficulties raised by the task of identifying such an historical subject was the rebarbative vocabulary of the
Critique: it was intended to provide an abstract typology of the different
forms of human collectivity or group, and to distinguish the authentic
form of human political community from its inauthentic forms. To
follow his argument here, the involuted language of the *Critique* cannot
be evaded. To Sartre, the false form of human association was epitomized
by the 'series': barely a collectivity at all, this was 'an ensemble each of
whose members is determined in alterity by the other members'.[65] The
electoral politics of representative democracy replicated this alienated
and thin form of political community. Individual members of the series
were brought together to form a 'gathering', a potential 'group', only to
see this potentiality distorted and dispersed by the emergence of the
institutions of government.

> [I]n bourgeois democracies, elections are passive, serial processes. Each
> elector, of course, decides how to vote as Other and through Others; but
> instead of deciding in common and as a united *praxis* with the Others, he
> allows it to be defined inertly and in seriality by opinion. Thus an elected
> assembly represents the gathering *as long as* it has not met . . . .*But as soon
> as* the assembly gets organized, as soon as it constitutes its hierarchy . . .

this very fact of penetrating the gathering with a false totalised unity ('Frenchmen, *your* government... etc.') relegates the gathering to its statute of impotence. France as a totality realises itself outside it through its government: as the free totalisation of the collective which is the nation, the government relieves individuals of the task of determining their inert sociality in a grouping.[66]

Against this, Sartre placed his conception of the 'fused group' or 'fused totality', a collectivity whose members were fraternally united by a common purpose, but which remained free from the hierarchy and division of labour implied by the institutions of government. The fused group had for Sartre a prefigurative quality, it evoked the utopian image of a transparent community. It was not constituted by any pregiven institutional forms, but sprang as a spontaneous response to external threat. The original picture of this authentic community was the image of the crowd assaulting the Bastille in July 1789:

in certain circumstances, a group emerges 'hot' [*à chaud*] and acts where previously there were only gatherings and, through this ephemeral, superficial formation, everyone glimpses new, deeper, but yet-to-be created statutes (the Third Estate as a group from the standpoint of the nation, the class as a group insofar as it produces its apparatuses of unification etc.). Sieyès' question about the Third Estate, which was *nothing* (and therefore a pure multiplicity of inertia, since it existed as nothing) but could be *everything* (that is to say—as certain people then thought, including Sieyès himself, by an abstraction from which, as a liberal bourgeois, he soon recovered—the nation, as a totality permanently reshaping itself, the nation as permanent revolution) shows clearly how through the troubles of 1788−9 and the groups which formed sporadically... the bourgeois even more than the worker in the cities (though work was *really* done by the workers) glimpsed the transition from an ossified, cold world to an Apocalypse. This Apocalypse terrified them; in order to avoid it they would willingly have become accomplices of the aristocracy if only it had been possible. But it was France as the Apocalypse that they discovered through the storming of the Bastille. (pp. 382−3)

For Sartre, the group created by the act of storming the Bastille was '*the sovereign nation*' (p. 363), the true political community. However, at the very moment of its emergence during the French Revolution, this conception of a fused totality was 'combined with the old conception of electoral assemblies' (p. 363). The result was a contradiction that split the ideology both of the Constituent Assembly and its theoretician Sieyès, and that remained unresolved in France's history since the Revolution. This contradiction had become embodied in the state, an institution that enjoyed perfect legitimacy in the eyes of one group (the bourgeoisie), but could claim no such similar legitimacy within the collectivity as a whole. The state 'exists for the sake of the dominant class, but as a practical suppression of class conflicts within the national totalisation' (p. 639). Its contradictory aspect lay in the fact that 'it is a class apparatus pursuing class objectives and, at the same time, positing itself for itself as the sovereign unity of all, that is, as the absolute Other-Being which is the nation' (p. 642).

In the *Critique*, Sartre had to show how a genuine political community, a fused totality, could come into existence and maintain its identity over time. More concretely, he had to show how members of a specific group (the class of workers) could unite and accede to power, coincide with the state, without making use of the distorting institutional mechanisms of the Communist Party or of bourgeois politics (such as electoral competition between parties, parliamentary assemblies, and so on). He had also to identify an internal principle that enabled such a political community to reproduce its identity over time. No short explanation of Sartre's failure to satisfy these demands in the *Critique* is possible. But a fundamental reason was his inability to specify how political and social solidarities could be created and durably maintained. He now avoided the Communist Party's definition of class, and its claim to be the legitimate representative of the universal class, the proletariat, preferring instead to establish his own vocabulary to specify the contours of the universal community and its political representative. But this vocabulary remained highly unstable, and he had constant recourse to the Marxist and Leninist language of class and Party. Sartre resisted the definitions of class found either in the French Syndicalist tradition, or in Marxism.[67] The *Critique* teemed with neologisms intended to describe solidarities, differentiating the authentically revolutionary community from its inauthentic images: 'multiplicity', 'series', 'ensemble', 'group', 'fused group', 'organized group', 'pledged group', 'institution', 'sovereign', and so on. Yet this elaborate typological rigging of social and political identity in the end spun back into a larger narrative generated by an opposition between two antagonistic terms.

For Sartre, the identity of a class was not primarily the result of its structural position within a mode of economic production. Rather, its identity was defined through its mutual antagonism with other classes. It thus, by stipulation, possessed an absolute, non-negotiable identity. This view was evidently indebted to Alexandre Kojève's interpretation of the master-slave dialectic in Hegel's *Phenomenology of Spirit*.[68] Following Kojève, Sartre saw history as struggle between opponents whose very identity derived from the intensity of their antagonism. This philosophical conception had for Sartre a real basis in the peculiarities of French political history. The relations between French bourgeoisie and proletariat were determined by a history of bloody struggle. Since the nineteenth century, the bourgeoisie had practised a form of 'class racism' (p. 758) upon the proletariat, hoping thereby to exterminate it:

In the second half of the nineteenth century, the social policy of the bourgeoisie was aimed entirely at destroying the power (militancy, class consciousness) which it had allowed its erstwhile ally, the working class, to win. Bloodshed provokes hatred, and hatred reinforces hatred: and French employers distinguished themselves from employers in other countries by the peculiar character of their oppression. They sought the death of the working class... [and] with the complicity of other classes [they] practised naked, colonial violence against the producers. (pp. 755–6)

This historical pattern of bloodshed and massacre, once fixed, continued into the present: the contemporary proletariat were 'survivors of the massacre', each of its members a 'son or brother of someone who was massacred in June 1848 or in the Commune' (p. 757). In the twentieth century, the relations between the two classes were frozen in the form of 'civil war and bloody conflict', a result of the 'historical impossibility that either should go back and undo the massacres' (p. 767). The struggle had not ceased, as 'aborting, starving and dividing, the bourgeois class continued the massacre' (p. 784).

The meaning of this apparently irrational violence, quite opaque to the antagonists, was visible only to those who stood outside the immediate conflict: to the revolutionary intellectual. The 'analytical Reason' of bourgeois intellectuals obscured the process of historical advance through struggle, a process at once dialectical in itself, and one which engendered a mode of thought capable of recognizing it as such, namely dialectical Reason. But if bourgeois thought could not grasp this true movement of history, Sartre was equally emphatic that the intellectuals of the Communist Party had no understanding of it. Such understanding was the exclusive possession of the 'theorists of the proletariat', who perceived correctly that practical class conflict also took the form of a 'conflict of rationalities' (p. 802) between analytical and dialectical Reason. These 'theorists of the proletariat' were intellectuals of petty-bourgeois origin who, through sheer power of will and intellect (and in defiance of their social and material situation) betrayed and escaped the determinations of their class, but who equally remained independent from the Communist Party. Sartre admiringly cited the examples of two historians: hero of the intellectual Resistance, Marc Bloch, and doyen of Jacobin revolutionary historiography, Georges Lefebvre.[69] The theorist of the proletariat was able to pierce through bourgeois propaganda and ideology, and provide a totalizing revolutionary knowledge. This explained the proletariat's interest in these men:

the fascination which the proletariat has for petty bourgeois intellectuals—which is not well described by Marx and Marxists—does not derive from particular material interests, but from the fact that the universal is the general material interest of any intellectual and that this universal is realized in potentiality (if not in actuality) by the working

class. The intellectuals, in other words, are products of bourgeois universalism and they *alone* in the bourgeois class are aware of the contradictions
of humanism, that is to say both of its unlimited extension (to all men)
and of its limitations. But if, like Marx, the theorist *produces* a materialist
and dialectical interpretation of History, it is because it is *required* by the
materialist dialectic as a rule for working-class *praxis* as sole foundation of
true (that is to say future) universality. (p. 801)

The struggle against the positivist and atomizing analytical Reason of the
bourgeoisie was conducted at both a practical level (through the efforts
of the proletariat and the socialist countries), and at the level of thought
by the revolutionary intellectual, the theorist of the proletariat. The
intellectual understood that history was the terrain of this struggle,
especially the history of the French Revolution, and that it was nothing
less than contemporary class conflict that lay at stake in disputes about
the Revolution. He understood

why abstract theoretical discussion between historians about particular
events in the French Revolution (atomized crowds with 'ring-leaders', or
totalizing class reactions?) are abstract expressions ... of the deep conflicts between the totalization (proletariat) and the dissolving faculty of
analytical Reason (the action and propaganda of the bourgeoisie).
(p. 802)

But, while the 'theorist of the proletariat' might claim to possess access
to revolutionary consciousness, he remained unable to describe how a
post-revolutionary community which transcended any division of labour
could be reproduced over time. The model of the Leninist Party was
massively inappropriate: the Marxist-Leninist concept of the dictatorship
of the proletariat was an impossible one—'the transformation of class
into an actualised group has never actually occurred, even in revolutionary periods'.[70] The 'group-in-fusion', not the Leninist Party, was the
primary and proper form of revolutionary organization, yet in Sartre's
analysis it inexorably developed into an organized division of labour, an
institution, and thus either fell back into the 'practico-inert', or could
only maintain its unity through the imposed will of a sovereign.[71]

This was the conclusion towards which Sartre was impelled in the
second volume of the *Critique*, abandoned and unpublished during his
lifetime. The theoretical core of the disarrayed reflections of the second
volume was a discussion of the historical fate of the Bolshevik Revolution. Soviet history since 1920 provided the most dazzling example
of a revolutionary 'group-in-fusion' forced to betray its identity, degen-
erating into the dictatorship of a 'sovereign': Stalin. This seemed to
signal the death knell of the hope given birth by the French Revolution,
and nurtured throughout the nineteenth century: the wish for a universal revolutionary theory. Marxism, 'a universalist ideology and practice,

born in the most industrialised European country', had been transformed into the 'historical monstrosity' of 'socialism in one country'. Imported into a backward country and incarnated in a specific territory, it was 'particularised'.[72] It had become the national dogma and *realpolitik* of a single state, and had ceased to be the horizon decorating a universal and presumably stateless society. Yet, simultaneously, the Soviet Union appeared to be the realization of Marxist revolutionary theory, and thus came to secure a dominant position over the varieties of Western Marxism:

> its [Soviet Marxism's] essential character—which was 'the becoming-world of philosophy'—contributed to giving it, in the eyes of all, a new preponderance as *reality lived and perpetually produced by the Soviet masses.* In the name of its own principles, the universalist Marxism subordinated itself to particularist Marxism. (p. 120) [emphasis in original]

Paradoxically, the very success of the Bolshevik Revolution fragmented the universal character of Marxism, subjecting it to the contingencies of history: 'The universal subordinated to singularity and contained within it, directed and transformed according to the transformations of this singular history: this is already, on the theoretical and cultural level, the objective reality of the slogan "socialism in one country"' (p. 120). The destruction of Marxism's unity and dialectical universality left two 'particular universalities' (p. 121). It produced the revolutionary movements of the West (instances of 'abstract universality'), umbilically tied to the Soviet Union. It also engendered Soviet Marxism, an instance of pure particularity that could no longer explain its own history: 'In this sense, the slogan "socialism in one country" was at once the definition of this alienated Marxism, the object rather than the guiding light of History, and at the same time, its first "theoretico-practical" product, the first determination of this rough-hewn (*fruste*) culture' (p. 121). Distaste and contempt dominated Sartre's account of how the 'backward Russians' had assimilated Marxism. Once the insulated and privileged revolutionary discourse of the sophisticated intellectual, Marxism was now available to 'these crude workers, so hastily created, so close to the peasants', who 'transformed Marxism as they absorbed it . . . it was vulgarized even as it refined them' (p. 120). Adopted by these 'mystified peasants', Marxism's universalist purity was corrupted. This erosion and subversion of the universalist scope of Marxism provoked Sartre to cancel his project of a 'totalizing' historical narrative, which he had hoped would explain Stalinism as a 'deviation', a temporary set-back to a larger progressive development. He relinquished too the hope that the intellectual might possess a revolutionary politics of universal scope. Desolation over the fate of world revolution and proletarian internationalism confirmed this: 'No doubt it would not have been thus if a chain of revolutions, by diversifying the incarnations of Marxism, had allowed it to rediscover, by means of new contradictions, a living and concrete universality' (p. 121). No doubt.

III

The truncated *Critique* is witness to the dissipation of Sartre's desire to give a decisive political centrality to the independent committed intellectual. It marked the failure of his efforts to procure for the intellectual a stable political community to whom he could claim commitment, and which could serve to justify his claim to a totalizing, universal theory. Although Sartre remained to the end vehemently opposed both to the representative politics of the bourgeois Republic and to the Communist Party, he treated with increasing scepticism his own earlier hopes to combine intellectual independence with political commitment. In the late 1960s and 1970s, he adopted a self-flagellating anti-intellectualism, and veered towards a crass populism: the intellectual was enjoined to subordinate himself to the 'masses', and denied any right to be considered as an autonomous agent of revolutionary politics.

From the early 1960s onwards, Sartre was also subject to two further lines of criticism, intellectual and political. The first was the criticism pressed by Lévi-Strauss.[73] To Lévi-Strauss, the junction between authenticity and action which Sartre had tried to secure had to be broken. The intellectual who pursued political commitment produced mere subjective truth: he selected, interpreted, and rearranged facts to produce not a truly total history, but rather a 'mystical conception' (p. 256) of history, one adequate as a means towards mobilizing political action, but lacking any universal status. 'In Sartre's system', Lévi-Strauss concluded, 'history plays exactly the part of a myth.'

> [T]he problem raised by the *Critique de la raison dialectique* is reducible to the question: under what conditions is the myth of the French Revolution possible? And I am prepared to grant that the contemporary Frenchman must believe in this myth in order fully to play the part of an historical agent and also that Sartre's analysis admirably extracts the set of formal conditions necessary if this result is to be secured. But it does not follow that his meaning, just because it is the richest (and so most suited to inspire practical action), should be the truest. Here the dialectic turns against itself. This truth is a matter of context, and if we place ourselves outside it—as the man of science is bound to do—what appeared as an experienced truth first becomes confused and finally disappears altogether. The so-called men of the Left still cling to a period of contemporary history which bestowed the blessing of a congruence between practical imperatives and schemes of interpretation. Perhaps this golden age of historical consciousness has already passed.[74]

The politically engaged intellectual, the 'theorist of the proletariat', had no valid claim to universal truths or knowledge. Lévi-Strauss himself adopted a different self-description, 'the man of science', in pursuit of the certitudes of science.[75] This critique of Sartre's proud subjectivity, in favour of an impersonal method that arrogated to itself the status of a science, marked a decisive shift in forms of intellectual self-description and justification. It heralded the ascendancy of structuralism.

Sartre was also censured from an altogether different quarter. After 1956 and the end of the brief partnership between himself and the Communists, Party intellectuals had returned to attacking Sartre: Althusser's entire œuvre was the most considered challenge to him. But the terms and stake of the attack are more easily disclosed by considering another, lesser, instance. In 1966, the Party's intellectual review, La Nouvelle Critique, devoted an issue to Sartre's work, including an essay on his politics by Jean Rony.[76] Rony defended the cardinal role of the Party and the decisive importance of 'Marxist-Leninist science', against Sartre's claim to possess a more authentic understanding of the historical process and of revolutionary politics. The Party was not simply a direct expression of proletarian interests and consciousness (as Sartre, straying into 'theoretical error', had argued in The Communists and Peace). Although the 'rich experience of the Party' was indeed the source of its political wisdom, the Party was fundamentally an autonomous organization, the vehicle of universal scientific knowledge and practice. It exemplified the Leninist precepts of democratic centralism, and played the role of a 'Collective Intellectual'. It maintained a specific division of labour between intellectuals and political leaders: 'intellectuals have their place, they are distinct members, not merely technical collaborators or advisers but members responsible to the whole organization' (p. 125). Intellectuals like Sartre, who remained outside the Party and persevered in their bid to emulate the independent 'classical intellectuals' of the past (Hugo, Zola, Anatole France) now faced a forlorn fate. They ignored the division of labour; yet this division could alone serve to legitimize intellectual activity. These intellectuals lacked contact with a political community or its effective agent, and were responsible to no one; conversely, they had no community in whose name they could speak and claim authority.[77] This was a clear summary of the Party line on intellectuals. At this time, the Communist Party was engaged in re-couping intellectual support, in the wake of the seepages after 1956 and the Algerian war. Its policy was one of mollification, extending hands to potential partners, and Party leader Waldeck Rochet actively solicited the various factions of the Left (including the Christian Left) as well as the 'strata of intellectuals'. The quantative expansion of this category made it important, according to Rony, to gain the support of grands intellectuels like Sartre for the Party—he was a potential exemplar to other, lesser intellectuals.

But Sartre, driven by his obsessive desire to be self-aware and thus always one step ahead of his critics, was himself already in the throes of shedding his identity as 'classical intellectual'. His misgivings about the efficacy of the independent intellectual hardened into a professed self-contempt at his status as a bourgeois intellectual. He ended with a profoundly unsteady view of the intellectual's political role: increasingly (and in contradiction with his continuing labours over Flaubert's arcanum), direct action rather than literature or philosophy, was endorsed as the only proper form of political intervention.[78] He could, on occasion, repeat his plea for a relation of transparency between the intellectual and the political community, which could reassure the intellectual of a decisive political role; but, in the late 1960s and 1970s, his return to the cadences of *What is Literature?* struck hollow. 'A Plea for Intellectuals' took as axiomatic 'that intellectuals cannot receive a mandate from *anyone*': the intellectual retained an absolute autonomy.[79] Yet the 'Plea' itself consisted of a series of injunctions. 'Monstrous product of a monstrous society' (p. 247), the intellectual carried within him the contradictions of his society. Although he aspired to universal knowledge, his petty-bourgeois origins trapped him within 'the particularism of the dominant ideology' (p. 258): 'his consciousness is precisely the opposite of an *overview*' (p. 255). If he wished to understand the society he lived in, and to achieve universality, 'he has only one course open to him and that is to adopt the point of view of its most under-privileged members' (p. 255). Sartre's commands were unambiguous: intellectuals could neither *become* proletarian, nor simply retreat into the institutions of the university, and hope to become 'simple technicians of knowledge at peace with themselves' (p. 258); nor for that matter could they join a mass Party (they would remain perpetually distrusted, always under threat of denunciation as 'corrupt'). The intellectual was therefore ordered to submit to the 'objective intelligence' of the exploited classes, and to adopt their point of view, one which produced a *'popular mode of thought*, which spontaneously views society from its foundations upwards'. He would thus be led to 'abandon what few reformist illusions he has left, and would become a revolutionary' (p. 257). Following this path, he would at once reveal to the exploited classes their own identity and that of their opponents; he would reveal to them their *situation*, and thus fulfil his own vocation. The contortions of Sartre's language must be sampled:

it is at this level that the intellectual can serve the people. Not as a technician of universal knowledge, since he is *situated*, as are the 'under-privileged' classes themselves. But precisely in so far as he is a *singular universal*, since an intellectual achieves self-consciousness by simultaneously discovering his class particularism and his task of universality—which is to contradict and surpass his particularity towards a univer-

salization of the particular, starting from his original particularism...
there is a parallelism between the effort of the intellectual to achieve
universalization and the spontaneous movement of the working class...
His [the intellectual's] task is not to deny his situation but to use his
experience of it to *situate* the working class, and his universalist techniques to illuminate the efforts of the class to achieve universalization. At
this level, the contradiction which produces an intellectual offers him the
means to grasp the historical singularity of the proletariat with universal
methods (historical research, structural analysis, dialectics) and its strivings
towards universalization in their particularity (as they issue from a singular history and preserve it to the very extent that they call for the
incarnation of a revolution).[80]

Yet the identity of the political community that Sartre wished to conjure
in order to fulfil the universalist aspirations of the intellectual had
become impossibly labile: proletariat, working-class, exploited classes,
under-privileged, masses, colonized, third-world—who exactly was
being referred to? In desperation to give some stolidity to these phan-
tasms, Sartre even fastened upon the language of the regional nationalisms of Europe. He endorsed the Basque nationalists' demand for a
revision of territorial boundaries, and called for 'a cultural revolution
which creates socialist man on the basis of his land, his language, and
even his re-emergent customs'.[81] The French intellectual, by supporting
the cause of small nationalisms, was in fact struggling on behalf of
his own authentic political community, itself subject to the 'internal
colonialism' of a state at once bourgeois and Jacobin (clarity on these
matters had never been Sartre's *forte*):

> To listen to the voices of the Basques, the Bretons, the Occitanians, and to
> struggle beside them so they may affirm their concrete singularity, is to
> fight for ourselves as well—to fight as Frenchmen and for the true
> independence of France, which was the first victim of its own centralism.
> For there is a Basque people and a Breton people, but Jacobinism and
> industrialization have liquidated our people. Today there is nothing left
> but the French masses.[82]

After 1968, the 'masses' (and its various Sartrean cognates) held a
superordinate position in his attempt to arrange relations between the
intellectual and politics. His strong nostalgia for the perfect harmony
between intellectuals and the people, the 'organic union' which he
imagined to have existed during the nineteenth century, persisted.[83] But
this, he recognized with equal lucidity, was no longer a real and prac-
ticable possibility. The sense of impotence and frustration that Sartre felt
did not, however, push him towards alignment or accommodation with
either the Party or the bourgeois Republic.[84] Instead, it was transformed into self-contempt for his intellectual identity. The intellectual,

he decided, must 'first of all suppress himself as an intellectual', since 'he remains objectively an enemy of the people'.[85] Sartre admired those young intellectuals who had renounced professional academic careers, and had immersed themselves in the masses (this period, between 1968 and 1972, was the high point of Maoism among intellectuals): 'those who have really changed realize that there is no longer any other way of conceiving universal ends than by forging a direct relationship with those who demand a universal society, i.e. with the masses'.[86] They had discovered the correct means to securing their claims to universality; but this direct relationship was now drastically different from what it had once been. It did 'not mean that they should follow the example of the classical intellectual and "speak" to the proletariat—in short produce a theory that is sustained by the masses in action. This is an attitude that is completely abandoned.'[87] The intellectual was unable to claim priority for his totalizing knowledge or revolutionary theory. He had now simply to place himself at the disposal of the masses: to convert himself into a tool for their authentic speech. This was a retreat into the most philistine and anti-intellectualist of positions, a retreat that would have won the approval of Georges Sorel.[88] There were remarkable analogies between Sartre's dissolution of a previously fought for distinction between thought and action and the trajectory of Louis Althusser. Althusser's starting-point was of course very different. Yet by the late 1960s he too seemed to have given up hope that there might be an attainable position from which the intellectual could be both independent and politically effective.

CHAPTER FOUR

Louis Althusser: The Mystique of Theory

We are absolutely committed to a theoretical destiny.
Louis Althusser, *Lire 'Le Capital'* (Paris, 1965).

The politics of philosophers is what no one practices.
Maurice Merleau-Ponty, *Signes* (Paris, 1960).

The story of Louis Althusser's life, thought and hapless end is one of the most bizarre episodes in modern French intellectual history. Unravelling the twists of his intellectual career is almost as difficult as unpicking the details of his private life, now revealed in a posthumously published confessional autobiography or, as he himself better described it, a 'traumabiography' (ironically for one who authored an implacably impersonal theory of politics, this is his single longest text).[1] A *pied-noir* from Algeria, Althusser was constantly pursued by the anxieties of a marginal man on the make—above all, by the fear of being shown up, discovered as a complete bluffer.[2] This spurred his 'obsession with strategy, with capturing positions', his constant desire to discover and to be seen to possess certain knowledge: his concern with the politics of truth, rather than with politics itself.[3] But, while there may be good reasons to see Althusser's exceeding piety towards theory as rooted in biographical contingencies, his psychic burdens reveal very little about the circumstances in which his arguments gained such renown. My own concerns are with his public intellectual career.

Althusser entered the intellectual and political fray in the early 1960s, when it had become plain that the possibility of dramatic and fundamental social and political change (a possibility that had captured and shaped the imagination of the first postwar intellectual generation) had passed. General de Gaulle's *coup* and the installation of the Fifth Republic gave impetus to hopes of France's modernization, planned and directed by the technical experts of the Commissariat du Plan. Into this newly expanding State technocracy were inducted young academics and researchers (many of whom were post-1956 renegades from the Communist Party), charged with the job of rising above the partisan politics that had so pitted the façade of government during the Fourth

Republic, and committed to using their technical expertise to manage the economy for the benefit of all 'social partners', bourgeois and proletariat alike. The early and mid-1960s witnessed hectic speculation on the future development of French society, and seemed to herald a profound change in the identity of those whose traditional function it was to speculate in this way, the intellectuals. The critical intellectual, attached to revolutionary principles, was, it seemed, mutating into a technocratic manager: on this, both French sociologists like Michel Crozier and external observers like George Lichtheim agreed.

The Communist Party monopoly over revolutionary politics had broken down. The implications of Khrushchev schema of 'convergence' and 'peaceful coexistence' between capitalist and socialist societies (outlined in his speech to the Twentieth Congress of the Soviet Communist Party), the Soviet invasion of Hungary and the French Communists' servile endorsement of this, and, more locally, their surrender to the policies of the Fourth Republic over the conduct of the Algerian struggles, had all decimated the Party's claim to represent genuine and benign revolutionary intentions. It had entered whole-heartedly into the electoral bargains and political manoeuvring of the new Republic, and by 1962 had sealed contractual alliances with the Socialists (SFIO), and even spoke of an alliance between all 'true republicans' (which included the MRP (Mouvement Républicain Populaire), as well as more conservative Radical politicians and business leaders) against Gaullist 'bonapartism'. Intellectuals of the Left therefore looked elsewhere, outside the compass of the Party, in their search for new forms of radical political criticism and involvement. Some gave active support to the Algerian FLN, and momentarily rediscovered the feel of clandestine action reminiscent of the Resistance.[4] Others tried to develop a new cartography of French society and politics. Among those attracted by or affiliated to the small Parti Socialiste Unifié, a language of the 'new working class' emerged. The concerns of these intellectuals remained consonant with those of classical Marxism: they inquired about the size of the proletariat, its relative wealth, and whether it was being displaced by a new group. But their answers—at least in formal expression—were new: the accent was now on different forms of political organization and agency (hence the revival of interest in syndicalism and trade unions), and on broad political alliances in the name of freedom from alienation, a form of appeal that extended to an audience wider than merely the working class. Their terminology blurred the distinction between manual and 'white collar' workers. In addition, the work of the *Arguments* group (especially their empirical studies on class), the persistent polemics of journals such as *Socialisme ou barbarie* against the decay of Marxism into bureaucratic forms, and Sartre's fatiguing efforts to wrest the language of revolutionary politics away from the Communist grip and to recast it, all threatened to rearrange the internal configuration of the intellectual Left. If one political meaning could be given to these qualitatively different and uneven 'revisions' of the inherited vocabulary of revolutionary politics, it was the erosion of the Leninist premise that theory and practice could be united by the medium of a revolutionary working-class movement under Communist Party leadership.

The triumph of a Right committed to 'modernization', doubts about the identity of the intellectual, a dilution of and challenge to the revolutionary identity of the Communist party; these were the central elements of the domestic context in which Louis Althusser began to intervene in intellectual debate. Beginning in 1961 he published a number of articles, mainly in Communist Party journals, culminating with the appearance in 1965 of *Pour Marx* and *Lire 'Le Capital'*. With astonishing rapidity his work captured a central and influential position within French intellectual culture, and then elsewhere.[5] How did this austere, highly abstract body of theoretical work gain such renown as a formulation of revolutionary political practice? A discourse premised on a distinction between 'true' science and 'false' ideology, and which stressed the importance of pedagogic instruction—scientific truth could be appropriated by anyone willing to submit to disciplined study, it had nothing to do with cultural or moral (and hence élitist) modes of transmission—held clear attractions for the rising tide of professional academics produced by the world-wide expansion of the higher education systems of nation-states during the 1960s. But Althusser's arguments have in the first instance to be returned to their French location.

Althusser self-consciously shunned the ethical and normative vocabulary favoured by Sartre, and abjured discussion of immediate politics. In further contrast to his predecessors, he claimed comprehensively to explain the mechanisms of capitalist society by a method that avoided any reference to history. Presented with dour polemical vigour, his approach promised a vocabulary of certainty that both escaped the hesitations and obstinacies of the Party's political line, and resisted the subjective and compromising interests of a personal voice. For Sartre of course it was precisely this individual, intuitive grain of voice that justified and gave authenticity to political speech and judgement. Sartre had raised the question of what it was to *write*, of how the intellectual as a situated individual could find a way of uttering a discourse of universal moral and political truths; Althusser's starting-point was the reverse question, 'what is it to *read*?'.[6] Revolutionary politics was not the expressed self-consciousness of a class—articulated through the imaginative affinities and capacities of the intellectual committed to this class—but rather the articulation of axiomatic and scientific truths contained in texts, with neither truths nor texts being subject to or compromised by their historical location.

The oppositions between Sartre and Althusser are manifold and readily drawn. Sartre's fondness for Hegelian and phenomenological thought, his belief that the early philosophical writings were Marx's greatest legacy, his attempt to formulate Marxism as an history of progressive human self-emancipation, all stand in symmetric contrast to Althusser's rejection of Hegelian styles of thought and language, his conviction that Marxism's revolutionary core lay in Marx's later professedly scientific works, and his declaration that history was a discontinuous 'process without a subject'. Sartre never belonged to the Communist Party, nor was he employed by the academic institutions of the State; Althusser remained a member of the Communist Party for all his effective career, and taught at the most prestigious of French educational institutions, the Ecole Normale Supérieure (ENS). The oppositions between the two could be extended and refined, yet they only possess meaning insofar as they presuppose a common contested ground. This shared terrain is conventionally identified in terms of continuities or discrepancies internal to the philosophical arguments of Sartre and Althusser.[7] This chapter has a different focus. Clearly both men proposed revolution as the solution to France's predicament, a necessity derived in Sartre's case from an account of historical movement, in Althusser's from a proclaimed discovery of scientific truths about capitalist society. However, such a description does not make it apparent why the Althusserian formulation proved so attractive to intellectuals, eclipsing the Sartrean account so completely. Althusserianism scarcely provided a cognitively more incisive or powerful account of French politics. But Althusser *did* provide a powerful redescription of the relations between the intellectual and the political community, and this above all made his work so seductive to intellectuals.

Sartre's defiance of the intellectual and political division of labour sanctioned either by the institutions of the state or the Party, and his desire to install a model of the independent intellectual committed to revolutionary politics, had, by his own acknowledgement, foundered. At a moment when the Sartrean account faltered, and others were becoming available, Althusser provided a compelling redescription of the possible relation between the intellectual and forms of political action. Althusser, unlike Sartre, accepted the division of labour embodied by both University and Party: but he tried, no less ambitiously, to capture the summits of both. The Althusserian project opposed both the technocrats of the Gaullist state and the *apparatchiks* of the Party; it recurred to a conception (whose ancestry could be traced back to Saint-Simon's phantasies) that aspired to produce a counter-technocracy or élite, concerned not with real economic or political problems—the production and allocation of goods, the compromises of electoral politics—but with texts, with ascertaining the scientific principles of revolution, and with refining the élite of a putative revolutionary state. The premise of the

Althusserian project could be described thus: if there could be a science of managing the capitalist state, why not a science of overthrowing it?[8] Yet, like Sartre, Althusser too ended by conceding the ambition of constructing an intellectual system that could both understand practical circumstances and speak decisively about how they might be transformed. Although each started from very different premises, both Sartre and Althusser arrived at peculiarly convergent assessments, especially after 1968, and ended in strongly anti-intellectualist and populist positions.

Althusser's was the most meticulous of intellectual efforts to construct a systematic theory of revolutionary politics, and the sudden ascendency and equally precipitate dissolution of his project raise questions and themes fundamental to the intellectual life of the period. Elaborated when the Communist Party had embarked upon a long period of contraction and stagnation, the Althusserian project did not represent an upsurge of social forces and interests. What were the conditions of its emergence and success? Interpreters have pored over a number of puzzles raised by his work: what, for instance, accounts for Althusser's dogged intellectual opposition towards predecessors most closely identified with his own political aims, an opposition that has been termed a 'paradox'?[9] How can his abstruse 'theoreticism' be squared with his insistence that he was engaged in practical revolutionary politics? How should the alleged 'caesura' between his work before and after 1967 be understood, and what explains the split, double character of his discourse, at once critical and supportive of the Communist Party (for instance, his support for the dissident Maoism of his students, yet his alignment with the Party against the student movements during and after 1968)?[10] Most fundamental of all, why did the author of a sophisticated theory premised on a belief in the desirability of revolution, an argument pursued 'against the grain of the political evolution of the PCF itself', choose nevertheless to remain within and support a Party that was authoritarian, politically inept, and under no possible description engaged in revolutionary politics?[11] Two kinds of solution are usually offered to this central puzzle: one sees it as a temperamental choice, a psychological disposition towards authoritarian structures or, more kindly, simply as sentimentality.[12] The second explains Althusser's adherence to the Party as a strategic or opportunistic decision, designed to maintain for himself a politically effective voice.[13] But in the absence of a firm sense of the significance of the Althusserian episode, such questions defy solution.[14] Althusser's arguments, his pursuit of a pure revolutionary theory, were stratagems devised for particular ends. Understood as purposive acts, it becomes possible to interpret the character of his project, to explain what some critics have described as the 'oddity' of Althusser's 'orthodoxy' and the 'impurity' of his Marxism.[15]

I

Louis Althusser joined the French Communist Party in November 1948, just when Socialist ministers were ordering military force to suppress a miners' strike led by the Communist trade union, the CGT.[16] In October of the same year the NATO accord was signed in Paris, and the Cold War properly begun. Within the Communist Party, discipline tightened: in February 1948, Party ideologue Laurent Casanova produced a report for the Party that prescribed the 'Responsibilities of the Communist intellectual'.[17] This spelt out the wishes of Party leader Maurice Thorez, and instructed Party intellectuals to provide scientific inputs to the proletarian struggle, but to leave political matters to the Party.[18] But the Party was not solely concerned with internal discipline over its existing troops, it was actively recruiting support, and hinted at *rapprochement* with Christian political organizations.[19] Such was the atmosphere at the time of Althusser's adherence to the Party. Before the war, he had been active not in organizations of the Left but in Royalist and Catholic circles.[20] Between 1937 and 1939, at Lyon's Lycée du Parc, Althusser was taught by and formed a close friendship with Jean Guitton, who later held a chair in philosophy at the Sorbonne, and became a chief representative of French Catholic thought. During his time at *khâgne*, Althusser was a militant in the youth wing of the Action Catholique, the Jeunesse Étudiante Chrétienne. His intimate contacts with Guitton, the philosopher Jean Lacroix, and with Catholic groups, all suggest that the Catholic dimension, in particular the enduring influence of Thomist thought, is far more significant than has hitherto been allowed in understanding Althusser's intellectual tastes. This dimension no doubt has special relevance to France, with its long and knotted history of relations between church and state, clerisy and 'lay' functionaries, and to recognize this is to see something about *how* Althusser thought, his intellectual style (though how exactly it bears on *what* he thought is harder to assess).[21] His biographer, Yann Moulier Boutang has noted that 'culturally, Louis Althusser was Catholic, and like one's mother tongue culture is never forgotten but becomes a second and unassignable nature'.[22] If by temperament Althusser was at perfect ease with Catholicism, it was clear that Catholic politics was in some discredit after the Liberation, a consequence of its close links with the Vichy government. Nevertheless, his explicit involvement with Catholicism continued at least until the early 1950s: he did not simply move from Catholic activism to the Communist Party, but continued both associations for some years.[23]

None of Althusser's writings published before the 1960s had an overt political edge to them: they were the work of an academic philosopher, published almost entirely in professional, non-Party journals. During the Fifties, Althusser appeared to accept the allocation of tasks established by Casanova's dispatch: intellectuals were technical experts or cultural creators, whose expertise or creative powers were to be placed at the service of the proletariat, or more precisely, of its political agent, the Party. It was the slowly filtered impact of news of Khrushchev's report in 1956 that gave Communist intellectuals an opportunity to alter the established division of labour between the Party and intellectuals. But if Althusser recognized this as a moment of intellectual opportunity, he was careful also to characterize it as a potential political threat to the Party: without the vigilance of its theoreticians and intellectuals, the Party would succumb to bourgeois ideology and lose its revolutionary identity. 'We were attempting', Althusser wrote in 1975 of his initial manœuvres, 'to give back to Marxist theory . . . something of its status as a theory, a revolutionary theory', and so 'to produce definite effects'.[24]

This attempt was launched from a particular structural position. Althusser was situated at the intersection of two important institutional axes, one political, the other intellectual: the Communist Party and the Ecole Normale Supérieure. This structural location generated considerable power, enhanced by Althusser's self-description of his position within the two institutions: he presented himself as embattled, complicit neither with the orthodoxies of the Party, nor with the conformities of the bourgeois Republic and university. Like Sartre (indeed, like all social critics who succeed in commanding an audience) he was at once situated at the core of the intellectual culture and—at least self-avowedly—at its margins. He was never the 'official philosopher' or watch-dog of the Party (Lucien Sève and Roger Garaudy are more correctly associated with this position), and his relations with the Party were often uneasy if never (as they ultimately were for Sartre) actually impossible.[25] His position at the Ecole Normale, the prestigious core of the highly centralized French educational system, stationed him at the heart of the educational institutions of the State. Established in 1794 by the revolutionary State, the Ecole Normale secured political importance during the Third Republic, preserved this during the Fourth, and only during the second decade of the Fifth Republic did it begin to cede its status to the technocratically oriented Ecole Nationale d'Administration (ENA).[26] Within the Ecole Normale, Althusser's formal designation was not especially senior: '*agrégé répétiteur secrétaire de l'Ecole (Secteur Lettres)*'. But within an institution renowned for its close student and teacher bonds, and for its notorious fraternity of *normaliens*, Althusser held substantial informal powers: as *Caïman*, his duties included, besides the academic instruction of his students, attention to their general well-being (duties comparable to those of an Oxbridge tutor).[27]

Intended primarily for the training and formation of future university and lycée teachers, the Ecole was an important plinth for the Third Republican project of political emancipation through education. It was given the task of producing an intellectual élite for the State or—since Lucien Herr's influential presence—for the political movement which one day would inherit the State: socialism.[28] Jean Jaurès, Edouard Herriot, Léon Blum, all were *normaliens*. During the 1920s and 1930s, the Socialists formed the largest single political group at the Ecole, but this changed after the Liberation. In conformity with a general surge in Communist Party membership, *normaliens* too joined the Party: by the end of the 1940s, about fifteen percent (of a total of 200 students) were members of the Party,[29] forming—along with a significant number of sympathizers who did not actually join the Party[30]—the largest single political group at the Ecole. For most *normaliens*, it was their initial membership in the political organizations of the Communist Party that first introduced them to Marx's writings.[31] To the Party, keen on entering the mainstream, recruitment of this future élite was vital, and in an attempt to maintain levels, (which had dwindled to five percent of *normaliens* in 1956),[32] the Party founded the Union des Eudiants Communistes de France (UECF) in 1957. Dominated by Parisian students, the UECF aimed itself specifically at bourgeois students and young intellectuals; for working-class youth, a separate union was set up, the Union des Jeunesses Communistes de France (UJCF).[33]

The UECF was composed of internal 'cells', representing different academic institutions and, within it, the cell of the Ecole Normale-'lettres', endowed with the greatest intellectual cachet, had by the early 1960s gained an influential position. This group, known as the 'Ulmards',[34] in turn was dominated by the 'cercle d'Ulm', almost all of whose members were Althusser's students. Many attended his seminar on the Young Marx (1964–5), and recalling their names is instructive: amongst others, Pierre Macherey, Roger Establet, Michel Pêcheux, Etienne Balibar, Christian Baudelot, Régis Debray, and Jacques Rancière, joined later by Jacques Bouveresse, Jacques-Alain Miller, and Jean-Claude Milner. Like Kojève thirty years before, Althusser exercised a compelling fascination over his audience, and again as Kojève did for Hegel, Althusser introduced the most prominently situated members of a new intellectual generation to Marx. Althusser's interpretations were influential mainly among circles of young intellectuals, his role was fundamentally pedagogic (few of his contemporaries or elders showed much interest in his reinterpretation of Marx).[35] This highlights an important social dimension to Althusserianism: young adepts of his theories could believe in themselves as ascetic and disciplined intellectual revolutionaries, so distinguishing themselves from the dissolute and bohemian habits of the 'Sartrians' in black turtlenecks prowling the *caves* of Saint-Germain-des-Prés.

How did Althusser himself describe his position and project? Customarily, his writings are situated in relation to two events which decisively altered the landscape of international Communism: Khrushchev's criticism of the 'grave and serious perversions' wrought by the 'Cult of Personality', and the final rupture between the Soviet and Chinese Communist Parties in 1963, which established two rival claims to the legacy of the revolutionary tradition, and dissolved the dream of proletarian internationalism.[36] These two events dominated Althusser's introduction of his own work to 'My English Readers' in October 1967, a preface designed to provide '"bearings" on the philosophical content and ideological significance of this small book'.[37] But for his French readers, Althusser had in March 1965 prefaced his work with another essay, 'Aujourd'hui'.[38] The differing emphases of the two prefaces are not explained by the simple fact that they were written for different audiences, but are equally attributable to a particular political chronology.[39] 'Aujourd'hui' arose from a set of specific preoccupations: a description of the current position of the revolutionary intellectual in France, it was also a programmatic announcement of how this was to be transformed. It made no reference to the Sino-Soviet split.

Like Merleau-Ponty's 'La guerre a eu lieu' and like Sartre's 'Présentation', Althusser's 'Aujourd'hui'—written exactly twenty years later— was a self-conscious reflection on the trajectory of his intellectual generation, and it announced a new beginning. The parallel claims and argumentative strategies of each of these texts are remarkable. Where Merleau-Ponty and Sartre had opposed the idealist and apolitical abstractions of republican philosophy, and had declared the intellectual's commitment to politics, Althusser for his part claimed to break both with the 'dogmatism' and 'pragmatism' of the Stalinist era which had subordinated intellectual activity to the irrational exigencies of the political domain, and with the 'progressivist' model of the relation between intellectuals and revolutionary politics. He invoked Lenin, and proposed a new model: the correct function of the intellectual was as the theoretician of the vanguard Party, indispensable for the discovery and delivery of the correct political 'line', which the Party then simply implemented in its practice.

'Aujourd'hui' described how Althusser, along with other bourgeois and petty-bourgeois students, had become politically radicalized by the events of the 1930s, and above all by the experience of the Second World War. The war revealed the 'existence of classes, of their struggles and aims', and it established the Communist Party as 'the political organization of the working class'.[40] But, by adhering to the Party after the war at the moment of Stalinist domination of the international Communist movement, young intellectuals and philosophers were immediately compelled to silence:

> We were brutally cast into the Party's great political and ideological battles . . . in our philosophical memory it remains the period of intellectuals in arms, hunting out error from all its hiding-places; of the

philosophers we were, without writings of our own ... slicing up the world ... with the pitiless demarcation of class. (p. 22)

Politics, in these years of Lysenko's 'proletarian biology' and the revival of Bogdanov's notion of *Proletkult*, had become the domain of the irrational; philosophy, lost in this arena of 'madness' and 'delirium', was forced into 'dumb embarrassment' (p. 22); and Marxism, instead of being treated as the science it truly was, had degenerated into ideology.

The causes of this dismal situation were, for Althusser, purely intellectual; more precisely, they were the result of pedagogic failures on the part 'of our elders ... those whose responsibility it was to show us the way' (p. 23). The theoretical tradition of Marxism had become a 'dead letter' in France, a victim of the anti-intellectualism of the French revolutionary tradition. Althusser unleashed a merciless assault on the intellectual inheritance of the French workers' movement and its 'stubborn, profound absence of any real theoretical culture'. Heirs to such 'meagre theoretical reserves', Althusser's repeated question was, 'who were our theoreticians?' He recalled the great names of the Marxist tradition, and above all Lenin and the sanction of his principles, to insist with striking obduracy on the inevitable presence and importance of intellectuals:

> The founders of historical and dialectical materialism were intellectuals (Marx and Engels), their theory was developed by intellectuals (Kautsky, Plekhanov, Labriola, Rosa Luxemburg, Lenin, Gramsci). Neither at the beginning, nor long afterwards, could it have been otherwise—it cannot be otherwise, neither now or in the future.[41]

Yet, as though abashed by his arrogation of such importance to the intellectual, Althusser inserted a footnote that apparently qualified and restricted the scope of his claim; but his rhetorical protestations in fact left unaltered the force of the original statement:

> Naturally this term 'intellectuals' denotes a very specific type of intellectual, a type unprecedented in many respects. These are real initiates [*véritables savants*], armed with the most authentic scientific and theoretical culture, forewarned of the crushing reality and manifold mechanisms of all forms of the ruling ideology and constantly on the watch for them, and able in their theoretical practice to borrow—against the stream of all 'accepted truths'—the fertile paths opened up by Marx but bolted and barred by all the reigning prejudices. An undertaking of this nature and this rigour is unthinkable without an unshakeable and lucid confidence in the working class and direct participation in its struggles. (p. 24)

Even the most anti-intellectual and *ouvrièriste* of Party members could acknowledge the virtues of this promethean figure.

Althusser repeated the warnings of Kautsky and Lenin against 'spontaneism' and anarcho-syndicalism, and insisted on the need for 'intellectuals of very high quality'. Why had these appeared in Germany, Russia, Poland and Italy, but never in France? His answer recapitulated in remarkable ways Paul Nizan's polemic, *Les Chiens du garde* (1932). Althusser gave two reasons. First, in France the bourgeoisie, once a revolutionary class, had successfully co-opted the intellectuals by giving them a role to play in the bourgeois revolution (1789), and then by employing them as ideologues of the new bourgeois political forms, allowing them 'a sufficient margin of freedom and illusion to keep them within its authority and under control of its ideology'.[42] Succumbing to the 'forms of bourgeois domination', and thus prone to idealism, reformism and positivism, few French intellectuals felt the 'vital need to seek their salvation at the side of the working class' (p. 25).

Second, Althusser pointed to 'the pitiful history of French philosophy in the 130 years following the Revolution of 1789'.[43] Throughout this period, French philosophy was marked by 'incredible ignorance and lack of culture' (p. 25). The only exception Althusser allowed was, significantly, Auguste Comte: Althusser admired his schematic rationalism and his synthesizing ambitions, and may have recognized something of his own visions in Comte's crazed parleyings with the Jesuits and the Vatican. In consequence, the French Communist Party was 'born into this theoretical vacuum' (p. 26), heir only to 'our sole authentic national tradition, the political tradition'. Politics rushed into this vacuum, edging out theory and philosophy.

> If it was able to attract to itself some famous intellectuals, these were above all great writers, novelists, poets and painters, great natural scientists and also a few first-rate historians and psychologists—and they came primarily for political reasons; but it very rarely attracted men of sufficient philosophical formation to realize that Marxism should not be simply a political doctrine, a 'method' of analysis and action, but also, over and above the rest, the theoretical domain of a fundamental investigation, indispensable not only to the development of the science of society and of the various 'human sciences', but also to that of the natural sciences and philosophy. It was the fate of the French Party to be born and to grow in these conditions: without the heritage and assistance of a national theoretical tradition. (p. 26)

The supremacy of politics and its exigencies left Althusser's generation bereft of any 'true *grands maîtres*' to guide them (thrice in the space of a few sentences, the absence of *maîtres* was lamented), and drove them into a dead end, leaving 'no way out for a philosopher'. Debarred from independent intellectual activity, 'the intellectuals of petty bourgeois origin who came to the Party at this time felt that they had to pay in pure activity, if not in political activism, the imaginary debt they thought they had contracted by not being born proletarians' [trans. altered,

p. 27]. Sympathetically and with a twinge of self-recognition ('we were of his race'), Althusser cited Sartre as an example of a philosopher who felt called upon to redeem this sense of guilt: 'philosophically speaking, our generation sacrificed itself and was sacrificed to political and ideological conflict alone' (p. 27).

Althusser invested great rhetorical force in his fundamental point: for his generation, in the years since 1945, there was no space for independent intellectual activity, outside the political remit and imperatives of the Party. Both Sartre and Aragon had tried (each in very different ways) to secure an alliance between the intellectual and revolutionary politics; but Althusser scorned both the Sartrean and the 'progessivist' models of the relations between the intellectual and the Party. To overcome the 'monstrous philosophical and cultural provincialism' (p. 26) of France, and to escape the stifling spectres of the 'dogmatist night' which had tried to extinguish philosophy (pp. 29–30), Althusser proposed a new model: intellectuals would form a vanguard of politically indispensable theoreticians. This revolutionary intellectual-as-theoretician, subject neither to the ideology of the bourgeois University nor to the stale orthodoxies of the Party, possessed direct and unmediated access to the science of revolution.

II

In order to successfully achieve a position equally distant from both the accumulated political wisdom claimed by the Party and the traditions of bourgeois scholarship maintained by the University, the intellectual would have to find a stable source of authority. Althusser made two distinct claims about the sources of his authority, moving from one to the other at the midpoint of his public career. The first, most forcefully stated in *Pour Marx* (1965) and *Lire 'Le Capital'* (1965), differentiated his own enterprise from cultural or directly political activity, and described it in uncompromising terms as *scientific*. A close (and speculative) reading of Marx's texts, he claimed, yielded all the elements necessary to establish Marxism as the hitherto unrecognized science of society. The details of Althusser's efforts to formulate Marxism as a science are well established.[44] Like any serious bid for intellectual authority, Althusser adopted a strategy at once innovatory and conformist. He enlisted powerful and recognized sources of intellectual patrimony, but channelled these into new disciplinary areas, thereby generating new fields of force. He dispensed with the Hegelian idioms characteristic of French Marxism, rejected as crass and dilettantish misreadings of scientific texts. His own professions of rigour were buttressed by his alignment with and appropriation of the institutionally recognized and respected tradition of

French philosophy of science, as developed by Georges Canguilhem and Gaston Bachelard. Strenuously rationalist (though, at least in Bachelard's case, the possibility of rational progress through discovery of new empirical evidence was allowed for), this approach focused on the formation of scientific concepts, and showed how such concepts were discontinuous with the erratic domain of ordinary knowledge, the domain of 'connaissance commune' wracked by mundane error. Here Althusser also acknowledged his (confessedly larger) debt to Spinoza, the 'effective philosopher' and founder of a properly materialist philosophy, for whom he always nurtured a 'powerful and compromising passion'.[45]

Althusser linked this vocabulary of rational and scientific certitude to that of psychoanalysis and structuralism. His relations with Lacan and Freud were complicated, more strained and fraught than has been generally acknowledged.[46] But he was evidently attracted by the analogies between his own tactics and Lacan's claim to return to a pure intimacy with the founding texts of psychoanalytic science, and by Lacan's attack on 'revisionist' American views of psychoanalysis as essentially a clinical discipline. Structuralism, as developed by Lévi-Strauss and Barthes, offered Althusser a new terminology of precision and, as he put it, a 'language which has already caught on'.[47] This energetic induction of new developments from parallel disciplines into his own expressed a desire for an alliance forged between intellectual leaders—Lacan, Foucault, Lévi-Strauss, Althusser himself—, a union of 'maîtres à penser' who might collectively achieve a revolution in the terms of intellectual debate.

The formulation of Marxist philosophy as a science was part of a larger endeavour to found a 'Theory of the production of knowledges'.[48] What did the wrought intricacies of Althusser's 'Theory of theoretical practice' signify? Although he tried to insulate theory from the exigencies of politics, he was equally determined to show the indispensability of his conception of theory for any correct political practice. Jacques Rancière rightly characterized Althusser's theoretical and political project as based on a fundamental wager, 'that it would be possible to produce a transformation in the politics of the Communist Party through a theoretical effort aimed at restoring Marx's own thought'.[49] Althusser's return to Marx's texts in search of such a theory was not primarily motivated by scholarly or philological interests: the technique of 'symptomatic reading' he developed was quite unconcerned with Marx's writings understood under an intentional description. The return to Marx, and to Marxist theory, was motivated by political intentions. By going back to Marx's own texts, while remaining within the Party, Althusser's strategy was unusual. In accordance with the Party's adoption of a strategy of broad electoral alliances, other Party philosophers, most notably Roger Garaudy, were at this time turning to Hegel and Christian philosophy in order to discover common ground with and to appeal to the traditions of

Social Catholicism.[50] In the late 1950s and early 1960s, intellectuals who were re-reading Marx's own works were generally *outside* the Communist Party. Generically termed 'revisionists', for these intellectuals a return to Marx's early writings, and a reinterpretation of Marxism as a philosophical anthropology, was a way to gain distance from the Marxism of the Party.

Althusser announced the link between the theoretical and political components of his enterprise in his first major text on Marx, 'On The Young Marx': 'il n'est pas de bonne politique sans bonne théorie' ('there can be no good policy without good theory'), he declared.[51] The return to, detour via, theory was never a renunciation of politics; on the contrary, it was nothing less than an attempt to found politics and political action upon solid theoretical and rational bases. Politics, Althusser made clear in his descriptions both of contemporary France and of the Stalinist period in the Soviet Union, was the sphere of the irrational. The years of 'Stalinist dogmatism' had set loose such 'dangerous tendencies' as subjectivism and opportunism, which chased out philosophy and reason. Communist intellectuals became the subject of derision, as 'our enemies flung in our faces the charge that we were merely politicians . . . we failed to offer an objective and public proof of the apodicity of our convictions . . . no one else could see any firm ground beneath our feet—only conviction' (pp. 27–8). To Althusser, 'that new form of "non-rational existence of reason"' (his astonishing circumlocution for Stalinism), was characterized as a dark residue of Russia's obscurantist history, as 'that part of historical "unreason" and of the "inhuman" that the past of the USSR bears within it; terror, repression and dogmatism'. It represented an upsurge of subterranean intellectual currents.[52]

In stark contrast to this, representing the pure embodiment of reason, was 'the revolutionary specificity of Marxist theory': more specifically, revolution represented the only moment of historical and political rationality. The function of theory was to mediate between these two terms, the irrationality of ordinary politics (whether in the forms of bourgeois routines or Stalinist exception) and the rationality of revolution. This conception allowed Althusser to avoid any detailed discussion of the current French political situation, and to locate his proposed solution to its irrationalities elsewhere, in moments of revolutionary political practice staged in other locations. Rancière, Althusser's erstwhile collaborator, then fierce critic, noticed the sleight of hand:

Everything rested on this double relation: if we want to get beyond present politics, trapped as they are by the opposition between dogmatism and opportunism, we must find the solution elsewhere: by discovering the rationality of revolutionary politics in action: that of Lenin in 1917 or Mao in 1937.[53]

But these moments of revolutionary epiphany, always historically and geographically displaced, could only preserve their status as moments of pure rationality if they were treated precisely as theoretical events occurring outside space and time, and not as historical events: hence Althusser's purely theoretical analysis of 1917 in his enormously influential essay 'Contradiction and Overdetermination'.[54]

Althusser's conception of the status of Marxist revolutionary theory was clarified through a dual opposition. This was rooted in a particular historical schema, which possessed continuities with the account given in 'Aujourd'hui' but which he generalized beyond the French situation. On the one hand he declared an antipathy between theory and 'academic philosophy', which for nearly a century 'has buried Marx in the earth of silence, the earth of the cemetery'.[55] On the other hand, theory was also opposed to the consequences which followed from this silence: the vulgarization of Marx's philosophy by the idiom of 'political practice' (p. 32), its reduction to a pragmatic vocabulary which produced 'militant texts' (p. 34) that guided and instructed action (p. 31). These works kept the 'idea of Marx's philosophy' (p. 31) alive, but in a crude and instinctive way: 'I need no other proof of this than that cry of scientific conscience, *Materialism and Empiro-criticism*, and all of Lenin's work.'[56] Ignored by academic philosophy, cheapened by political expediency, the moment had come, Althusser announced, to establish the true status of theory: textual study of Marx's writings would reveal the scientific core of his thought, and secure Marxism's claims to be the universal revolutionary theory. Once established, it would be possible to arrive at a correct 'reading' not only of 'those other practical works of Marxism which are so abundant today', but also of actual political and historical events themselves:

> The same is true of the 'reading' of the still theoretically opaque works of the history of the workers' movement, such as the 'cult of personality' [i.e. Stalinism. S.K.] or the very serious conflict which is our present drama [i.e. the Sino-Soviet split. S.K.]: perhaps this reading will one day be possible on condition that we have correctly identified in the rational works of Marxism the resources for the production of the concepts indispensable to an understanding of the reasons for this unreason. (*Reading 'Capital'*, p. 34)

This elision was characteristic of Althusser and his cohort: text and event were conflated, the revolution in theory would enable the actual political revolution. Theory was utterly privileged, the key to any understanding of the irrationalities of politics.

What was Althusser's conception of theory? He did not define it primarily in relation to practice (as might perhaps have been expected of someone who claimed affiliation with the Marxist tradition). Adducing an argument aimed at both the Party and at 'bourgeois intellectuals' like

Sartre, he denounced the opposition between theory and practice as a false one, 'a play on words':

This dichotomy is merely an ideological myth in which a 'theory of knowledge' reflects many 'interests' other than those of reason: those of the social division of labour . . . and oppression . . . Even when this dichotomy is the servant of a revolutionary vision which exalts the worker's cause, their labour, their sufferings, their struggles and their experience in the undifferentiated proclamation of the primacy of practice, it still remains ideological.[57]

Althusser promised a way out of the 'ideological conception of practice' that reigned supreme over both Marxism, and 'over contemporary philosophy, even over its most honest and generous representatives such as Sartre' (Reading 'Capital', p. 60). This conception engendered a pragmatism blind to the fact that 'it has been possible to apply Marx's theory with success because it is "true"; it is not true because it has been applied with success' (p. 59). Althusser offered a more strenuous but rewarding route: 'by avoiding this market-place of egalitarian practice, or as it has been called in philosophy, of 'praxis', we have won through to a recognition of the fact that there is only one path before us, a narrow path certainly, but an open, or at least openable one' (pp. 60–1). It was this potential foothold for theory, and for the intellectual-as-theoretician, that he was determined to secure.

His conception of theory had four important strands to it. First, he insisted on the autonomy and prior authority of theory: its epistemic foundations lay outside every-day social activity, inaccessible to ordinary social actors. The agents of production, both capitalists and proletarians, existed under conditions of mystification and illusion. One implication of Althusser's severance of the (historically unquestionable) filiation between Marx and Hegel was to subvert a view of the proletariat as the self-consciousness of capitalism (since such a view relied, after all, on the concept of alienation found in Marx's early writings). Theory therefore was not in any sense a reflection or even an expression of the immediate conscious experience of a specific class. In this definition of theory, Althusser was adamant that proletarian consciousness was not a privileged form of understanding, nor did working-class experience of itself yield a revolutionary political practice. Only the theoretician, the intellectual engaged in theoretical practice, had access to revolutionary theory. Further, Althusser's claim to establish Marx's theory as the basis of all science was a challenge to the division of intellectual labour within the University and within the Party (which in this regard mimicked the bourgeois university, reproducing a similar division of specialisms in its relations with intellectuals).[58] A second, closely connected element of Althusser's conception of theory was the assertion that the nature of social reality could not be grasped by the terms and concepts of ordinary language. Quotidian reality would have to be redescribed, a new vocabulary of social ontology created. Thus his insistence on inter-linked and articulated practices, irreducible to a unifying essence; this generated an ontology predicated on a complex structuring of social reality, which remained opaque without the intervening services of theory. His proposed solution to the relation between thought and the real relied, paradoxically, on a 'severance of theory from any real referent'.[59] Third, Althusser attached great importance to pedagogy and education, to 'theoretical formation'. This had obvious attractions to students at the Ecole Normale. Eager to combat the view that intellectual activity was simply a 'reflection' of processes and class positions in the real world, radical students (usually of good bourgeois origins) were particularly sensitive to the charge of élitism. The Althusserian vocabulary was enormously useful in their attempts to refute such charges: they could describe the emphasis on theoretical formation as expressive of a desire for greater democratization. In opposition to the Sartrian model of individual genius and intuition, Althusser offered a scientific theory that could be passed off as potentially available to all militants, whatever their social origins (provided, naturally, that they submitted willingly to the exigencies of 'theoretical formation'):[60]

> It is in fact by means of well-conceived theoretical formation that Com-munist militants—whatever their social origin—can become intellectuals in the strong sense of the term—that is, men and women of science...[61]

It was this conviction that motivated the establishment, by Althusser's students, of the 'Ecole parisienne de formation théorique'. Finally, by affirming the place and authority of theory, Althusser ensured that he was perceived as an upholder of a properly Leninist line: political con-sciousness must be developed by the work of independent theoreticians, and then conveyed to the working class.[62] The working class entrusted this task to the intellectual-theoretician. Althusser, in a letter to Régis Debray in March 1967, explained that

> the struggle poses urgent demands. But it is sometimes...politically urgent to withdraw for a while, and take stock; everything depends on the theoretical work done at that time...I see this as being the duty of all working-class and revolutionary intellectuals. They are entrusted by the people in arms with the guardianship and extension of scientific knowl-edge. They must fulfil this mission with the utmost care.[63]

The proletariat itself was unable to rise to revolutionary political con-sciousness. This had to be formulated elsewhere and then imparted to them, since 'the proletariat was, by itself, incapable of producing the *science* of society, and hence the science of the proletariat's own practice, but was capable only of producing utopian or reformist ideologies of society'.[64]

Althusser's effort to render Marxism its scientific identity was not solely a claim in and about epistemology; it had a distinct political dimension to it. This was revealed, in different ways, by his attack on 'humanism' and 'historicism', and by his essay on 'Problèmes étudiants' (the only text he published concerning a strictly political matter).[65] Althusser's attack on the 'Humanism-historicism' couple, expressed in the slogan 'Marxism is not a Historicism', was central to his enterprise. This deviant historicist interpretation of Marxism had first appeared, he claimed, after 1917, as a protest against the mechanistic Marxism of the Second International and the failure of revolution to spread in Europe. But the costs of this interpretation were severe: Marxism was dethroned from its status as scientific doctrine and treated as a direct and self-conscious expression of an historical subject, the working class, whose destiny it was to emancipate humanity. This 'left-wing' humanism ruled against Lenin's and Kautsky's thesis 'that Marxist theory is produced by a specific theoretical practice, outside the proletariat, and that Marxist theory must be "imported" into the proletariat ', preferring instead a 'spontaneism' that ignored the primacy of the Party and its intel-lectuals.[66] The disastrous consequences of this choice were evinced in the horde of theoretical deformities which it released: 'opportunism', 'reformism', 'revisionism', and 'in a general way the "voluntarism" which deeply marked the period of the dictatorship of the proletariat in the USSR, even in the paradoxical forms of Stalinist dogmatism' (*Reading 'Capital'*, p. 141). It also placed revolutionary intellectuals of bourgeois or petty-bourgeois origins in an impossible situation, forcing them to 'ask themselves, sometimes in genuinely tragic terms, whether they have really a right to be members of a history which is made, as they know or fear, outside them' (p. 142). 'Perhaps this', Althusser suggested, 'is Sartre's profoundest problem':

> It is fully present in his double thesis that Marxism is the 'unsurpassable philosophy of our time', and yet that no literary theory or philosophical work is worth an hour's effort in comparison with the sufferings of a poor wretch reduced by imperialist exploitation to hunger and agony. Caught in this double declaration of faith, on the one hand in an idea of Marxism, on the other in the cause of all the exploited, Sartre reassures himself of the fact that he really does have a role to play ... (*Reading 'Capital'*, p. 142)

Althusser offered his adepts a way out of the dilemma that had en-trapped Sartre. This precisely was the purpose of his 'Theory of theor-etical practice': to provide intellectuals with a self-justifying description of their activity.

While Althusser was careful to defend the autonomy of intellectual activity against challenge from both the Communist and non-Communist Left, he defended himself with equal vigour against the accusation that he was advocating assimilation and incorporation into the academic institutions of the bourgeois state. In this respect, his preoccupations were entirely continuous with those of his predecessors, and in distinguishing Althusser too sharply from what came before, it is easy to miss how elements of his enterprise connected to the 'humanist' notion of commitment he claimed to supersede. His article 'Problèmes étudiants' revealed the extent to which his conception of scientific and theoretical activity was premised upon a doctrine of lay morality and commitment that possessed deep historical roots in France; it continued and displaced the 'progressivist' or 'humanist' account, whether represented by the examples of Sartre or Aragon. Directed at members of the Communist student union (the UECF), 'Problèmes étudiants' proposed a view of the duties and obligations of a revolutionary intellectual which amounted to a doctrine of individual willed commitment to 'a Communist morality', itself conflated with 'the science of Marxism-Leninism'.[67] Such commitment immunized the intellectual against bourgeois ideology, and gave him access to revolutionary science, with all the authority endowed by this.[68]

Althusser's essay on the student problems drew attention to the manner in which his claim to scientific authority was a redescription, in resoundingly modernist terms, of the question that had so dominated the thinking and writing of intellectuals in the 1940s and '50s: the question of the more general significance of intellectual activity, as expressed for instance in Sartre's fervid language of engagement, and his attempt to close the distance between private belief and public action by dissolving their difference. Where Sartre had tried to supersede the existing division of labour, and claimed to bring together in his own person a vision of value, an understanding of things as they were, and a judgement about how they were to be changed, Althusser (who displayed in this respect the more timid temperament of a *boursier* rather than an *héritier*)[69] suggested an apparently more modest course.

'Problèmes étudiants' revealed a close connection between Althusser's science/ideology distinction and his views on the division of labour. Like Marx, he differentiated between the technical and social division of labour. The prime example of the technical division of labour was the University: here, the division of labour functioned primarily to enable the production and transmission of knowledge. The state and its various instruments, meanwhile, was the paradigm of the social division of labour, a system whose function was essentially to ensure the reproduction of classes and class domination. The university, although part of this social division of labour, retained a measure of independence: since it produced and possessed specialist knowledge required by the state, it had to be accorded a degree of freedom. (The hallmark of Althusserian vocabulary, the hair-splitting language of 'relative' or 'semi-autonomy', emerged from a particular political predicament: how could a discourse of revolution, aimed at destroying the state, be uttered from within the core institutions of the state?) This autonomy was under constant threat from the state, which preyed upon the university in its search for new resources: 'the technocracy gluts itself on new ideas and intelligent men' (p. 92). The only way to resist the invasive modernizing technocracy of the Gaullist state was to establish boundaries and take positions, on the side of science against ideology. Instruction in Marxist-Leninist science would guarantee Communist intellectuals recognition as practitioners of science and thus assure them their full independence; thus inoculated, they would be free from pressure or intimidation by the state (a state which, Althusser suggested, practised a kind of intellectual 'Malthusianism', a perpetual decline of standards).[70]

The significance of Althusser's dogged obsession with such questions of demarcation, and his insistence that his own activity be understood as the pursuit of science, is revealed when placed in the context of contemporary accounts about the changed place and status of the intellectual. This was a preoccupation for many in France during the mid-1960s. Apart from Sartre's herculean interpretation of the intellectual as one who would 'miss nothing of his time', a figure endowed with the ability to philosophize upon any and everything, and aside too from Aragon's more puny view of the intellectual who docilely submitted his talents to the requirements of the Party, other new and potential identities for the intellectual were emerging. One new definition had emerged as a consequence of the rapid postwar rise of empirically oriented disciplines like sociology and political economy (both were recognized as university degree disciplines in 1957), and of the close relations established between sociologists, economists and the state.[71] In the view of some, Michel Crozier for instance, the future identity of the intellectual would be that of a technocrat, for whom 'action is no longer a world apart': using imported American techniques,[72] this new intellectual would be incorporated into the management of the state, and would achieve 'the more and more far-reaching appropriation of action by scientific intelligence'.[73] The Gaullist state actively encouraged and solicited this new Saint-Simonian character. New points of contact between administrative and economic managers on the one hand, and researchers and intellectuals on the other, were established,[74] and intellectuals were employed by the State as 'contract workers' on specific research projects (a form of incorporation that became still more prevalent after 1968).[75] Others, although they agreed that the empirical sociologist concerned with policy formation had genuine contact with concrete reality (unlike the armchair philosopher), resisted more critically any assimilation into the structures of the State: a striking example of this attitude was the sociologist Alain Touraine, for whom empirical investigation was simply a direct extension of what remained a basically Sartrean philosophy of commitment.[76] All however, were responding to a general shift away from the disciplines that had traditionally buttressed claims to intellectual authority: literature (as in Sartre's case) and philosophy (as in Althusser's).[77] The shift was clear to Lucien Goldmann, who observed that 'in the intellectual life of Western Europe, and particularly in France, the social sciences (sociology and anthropology) are more and more occupying the ideological place once held by philosophy'.[78] A quite different conception of the new resources intellectuals could draw upon to construct their identities was expressed by the 'anarchistic-democratic' ideas about collective and participative research: these ideas, attacked by Althusser in 'Problèmes étudiants', provided the basis of the future *gauchiste* critique. Althusser, in opposition to all of these, offered for his own part a brilliant re-formulation of the recurrent intellectualist fallacy that errors in the social and political realm were primarily the result of intellectual mistakes. In Althusser's conception, the intellectual was a solitary vanguard theoretician, empowered to 'draw the line' between revolutionary science and bourgeois ideology, and thus in turn able to draw the correct political and policy line for the Party to put into practice.

Each of these competing conceptions of the role of the intellectual assumed quite different mappings of the socio-political world. The model of the intellectual as technocrat or empirical sociologist was associated with a reformist, evolutionary view of society: adepts of this view claimed to detect the formation and growth of a 'new middle class' (based on the image of the American middle class) whose emerging presence would bring stability to the most politically turbulent European nations, Germany and the Latin countries. This technocratic or 'planniste' discourse, predictive and performative as much as descriptive, was a direct counterpart to the Marxist revolutionary schema.[79] Against the technocratic account, intellectuals of the non-Communist Left invented a new social geography, whose central vector was represented by the 'new working class': this term was not used to designate a distinctively new and autonomous group which would take its place along side existing class groups (as the Corporatist discourse of cadres had claimed to do), but rather to describe the transformation of the 'traditional' working class into a new, politically radical class peopled by skilled and literate members.[80] In this perspective, the differences between intellectuals and the working class had decisively narrowed, raising the possibility that each category might potentially merge into the other.[81] This description carried a powerful political resonance: it allowed those who used it to suggest that both the Corporatist-Gaullist and the Communist positions could be seen as 'Third Partyist', reformist, and conservative, seeking a return to the days of Vichy.[82]

The Communist map of the French situation was itself in considerable disarray. By the early 1960s, the Communist Party and its affiliated trade union, the Confédération Générale du Travail (CGT) were forced into a recognition that the forms of political agency described in classical Marxist theory were no longer available nor even primary. New groups, potential allies to the proletariat, would have to be found. Hence the interest in and enthusiasm for cadres, but equally a great unease and confusion about how to define and demarcate this new category in terms of the Marxist lexicon: were they producers or extractors of surplus value (the problem was analagous to that posed by the peasantry for Lenin)? Sociologists affiliated to the Party devoted formidable energy to the definition of boundaries between different class groups, pre-suming thus to identify a guiding political 'line' on the correct relation-ship between the working class and its allies.[83] Yet even at its most rigorously taxonomical, this mode of analysis could only yield a form of electoral, and never a revolutionary, politics.

The political significance and force of Althusser's account is clear, once located in this context. To stem the drift towards electoralism, the dilution of the identity of the classical proletariat, and the possibility that 'de-Stalinization' would be achieved through the revival of a langu-age of democratic rights and civil society (the dread spectre of 'social-democracy'), Althusser advanced a brilliant reformulation of Leninism. That Lenin was a crucial reference in Althusser's work is beyond dis-pute. But the full extent to which his project was premised on Leninist conceptions and distinctions, and the significance of this, is not always appreciated. Some elements must be noted here, others are identified later. By rejecting the significance of the German idealist tradition as guide to the scope and intention of Marx's project, Althusser hoped to align himself with the tradition of Soviet Marxism that had informed Lenin's own thought. The filiations of Lenin's materialist philosophy can be traced, via Plekhanov, to Dietzgen and Engels, and yet further back to Spinoza; this, is one reason for Althusser's odd and fierce attachment to Spinoza. Second, Althusser accepted and developed the theoretical implications of Lenin's strategic distinction between 'trade union con-sciousness' and 'revolutionary class consciousness'. This problematic, with its view of correct consciousness and knowledge imparted to the working class from outside, is one specific to the thought of Lenin rather than Marx. Third, although Althusser launched a painstaking critique of 'historicism' and of conceptions of Marxism that rested on a philosophy of history, his own account presupposed the truth of Lenin's historical judgement that capitalism was prone to cyclical crises, whose cumu-lative effect would be to weaken the bourgeois State and render possible a revolutionary seizure of power.

III

Around 1967–8, Althusser appeared to modify his earlier claims, and to reverse his arguments about the autonomy and priority of Marxist science and theory over politics. The elements of this new position first emerged in a course of lectures on philosophy for scientists given by him at the Ecole Normale, and were further elaborated in a number of articles.[84] In this revised view, philosophy was no longer secured by or beholden to science and scientific authority; rather it was at the disposal of certain *enjeux*, of political stakes and battles. Philosophy was deprived of its specific object—the 'Theory of theoretical practice'—about which it produced 'knowledge'. Instead, it produced 'theses' on various matters, which determined the correct political position and line.[85]

There is no doubt about the magnitude of the swing in Althusser's conception of the status of intellectual activity.[86] But ought Althusser's new position to be understood as a complete break with his earlier argument? Commentators like Elliott, for instance, speak of the 'derailment' of Althusser's project by an ' "external" logic', a result of his excessive enthusiasm for Maoism.[87] It is certainly true that Althusser's inversion of his earlier arguments cannot be satisfactorily explained in terms of the internal logic of his work. (Insofar as his earlier theoretical propositions suggested any narrative or progressive movement at all, this was in the nature of repetition, a kaleidoscopic rearrangement of 'instances', 'practices', and so on: the theoretical still point in a turning world). Elliott's determination to identify this external logic as the baleful influence of the Chinese Cultural Revolution leads him to place great interpretative weight on an unsigned text by Althusser on the Cultural Revolution, published in 1966.[88] But it remains difficult to see much explanatory force in the judgement that Althusser's evacuation of his earlier position was entirely due to his 'indulgence to Maoism'.[89] Althusser's interest in Maoism had specific reasons, and the modifications of his views after 1967–8 are best understood in the light of his relations with the Party. The discussions held at Argenteuil in March 1966, between the Party and Communist intellectuals, are important here. Again, Elliott correctly notes that 'Argenteuil . . . spelt the doom of the autonomy of theory' (p. 191), but he fails to see the implications and significance of this defeat for Althusser's project.

To understand the significance of this defeat, the precise political context of Althusser's shifting intellectual stratagems is relevant. Recalling this also reveals how his abstract formulation of Marxism gained such wide political resonance. The Sino-Soviet split was no doubt important in framing the political circumstances of his intervention. But this fracture in the international Communist movement gained relevance as a result of a more local conflict, between the French Communist Party and factions within the Communist student movement, the UECF. Both these entities—and especially the latter—need in turn to be internally differentiated, and here one is drawn into the interminable but unavoidable 'groupuscular' history of the intellectual and political Left in France during the 1960s. I shall be relatively brief.

Within the Communist student movement, the UECF, the primary division was between the 'reformists' (influenced by the ideas of Togliatti and the Italian Communist Party, and hence known as the 'Italians'), and those who clung to the more uncompromising language of revolutionary politics. The reformist 'Italians' had consistently criticized the Party leadership, especially over the issue of Algerian independence. The most vivid political experience for the generation of French students coming of age in the late 1950s was the Algerian war; apart from anything else, students' minds were concentrated by the prospect of military conscription. The decision by the Communist Party in 1956 to support the Mollet government's demand for special emergency powers to suppress the Algerian independence struggles alienated many students from the Party and encouraged their interest in non-Communist intellectuals like Sartre, who openly supported the battles for Algerian independence. Indeed, a *rapprochement* between Communist students and the non-Communist intellectuals seemed to threaten. The UECF established links with the non-Communist student union, the UNEF.[90] Tensions between the Communist leadership and the Communist students rose when members of the UECF leadership were suspected of being involved in the attempt led by Casanova and Servin to unseat Thorez as party leader in 1961.[91] Finally, at the Sixth Congress of the UECF in 1963, the revisionist programme proposed by the 'Italians' was adopted. It was maintained until 1965, when the Party leadership managed to reassert control over the UECF.

Situated to the Left of the 'Italians' were two groups, the Trotskyists (centred around Alain Krivine's 'Sorbonne-Lettres' cell), and the pro-Chinese, the 'Ulmards' of the Ecole Normale. Both these groups rejected the 'Italians' belief in the possibility of a 'peaceful transition to socialism', and their call for the Party to adopt a 'united class front' strategy reminiscent of the Popular Front era. To the Trotskyists and the pro-Chinese, such strategies threatened to dilute the revolutionary identity and commitment of the Party. The argument came to a head during the campaign for the national presidential elections in 1965. The Communist Party leadership supported the openly pro-NATO Socialist candidate, François Mitterrand. This proved too much to stomach for the Trotskyist students: Krivine's cell publicly criticized the Party for acting like an American stooge, and was promptly expelled in January 1966. The pro-Chinese maintained Party discipline on this matter. But they were to become increasingly dissident over another apparently more esoteric issue: the practical implications of the discussions at Argenteuil held between the members of the Politburo and the Central Committee of the Party on the one hand, and Communist intellectuals on the other.

The significance and consequences of the Argenteuil debates are relevant here (their substance is available elsewhere).[92] Briefly, there were two strands of talk. One was the ambition (expressed in the speech of the new Party leader, Waldeck Rochet) to secure a modern, 'theoretical' basis for the Communist Party's policies of 'de-Stalinization' and its adoption of a 'revisionist' programme. The other was an assault on Althusser, spearheaded by Communist Party philosophers and intellectuals like Garaudy, Lucien Sève, and Michel Simon, and other members of the Central Committee. The discussions of the Central Committee centred principally on the status of theoretical activity and its relation to the practice, politics and policies of the Party: the repeated question was, 'What about practice?' Some have interpreted Argenteuil as a victory for Althusser and his call for independent intellectual and theoretical activity.[93] It is true that the Party did accord a certain recognition to Althusser's position, but this was far from an unequivocal triumph for Althusser. At the time, he registered no public response or opinion on the outcome of the discussions. But for the younger Althusserians of the 'cercle d'Ulm', the conclusions arrived at Argenteuil clearly represented an explicit and aggressive challenge to the Althusserian assertion of the autonomy of theory. In April 1966, the 'Ulmards' counter-attacked, with the publication of a pamphlet, *Faut-il réviser la théorie marxiste-léniniste?*, which mauled the resolutions of the Central Committee in staunchly Althusserian terms,[94] and clarified what the Althusserians perceived as the stake and significance of the debates.

The argument opened with a warning: if Marxism was interpreted as a 'humanist' philosophy, then a series of dangerous consequences threatened the relations between culture and intellectuals, science and revolution. The central target of attack seemed at first sight oddly chosen: it was the poet and novelist Louis Aragon, portrayed as the prime influence on the content of the Party resolution. Aragon represented precisely that old model of the progressivist Communist intellectual that Althusser had worked so hard to abolish: the artist or writer who ceded the priority of his or her intellectual and cultural activity to the political whip of the Party. Aragon's dismal role in the 'Lysenko affair' was recalled, and his aged, outdated, poetic speech satirized.[95] Times had changed, and 'in the new conditions of our epoch' the language of science had now replaced that of literature. The pivot of the argument was a standard Althusserian analogy, which in fact it treated as an identity: political revolution was like revolution in science.

Revolution, like the birth of a science, is a break [*une coupure*] . . . Science is born always out of a rupture with what preceded it. Exactly like revolution. The theoretical world is fundamentally changed, like the world described in the song of the struggling workers. (p. 154)

To bring about the revolution in science and theory, a distinct class of theoreticians was needed. Contrary to the 'humanist' assimilation of different classes into a common subject, the text asserted that 'there exist no "Men"': but capital, the working class, the peasantry, the intellectuals' (p. 152). Aragon, however remained wedded to a view which saw cultural activity as primary, and called for all intellectuals and 'men of culture' to join together in a 'united front' against the monopoly capitalists. To follow the humanist path suggested by Aragon, and to enter into dialogue with non-Communists, spelt the betrayal of theory:

> All those years of struggles and sacrifices . . . simply to hear a poet waste our heritage, the only heritage which we possess and which we will defend to the very end: the treasure of a true theory. (p. 155)

And the consequence of 'the sacrifice of theory' would be to embrace (as intellectuals like Aragon had done) a politics not of revolution but of reformism, of 'social-democracy': the worst possible form of betrayal.

Some months after the publication of this text and its circulation within the UECF, the Communist Party dissolved the Cercle d'Ulm and expelled most of its members. In December 1966, former Ulmards like Jacques Rancière, Robert Linhart, Dominique Lecourt, and Pierre Victor formed another group, the Union des Jeunesses Communistes (Marxistes-Léninistes) (UJC (M-L)). Etienne Balibar and some others, however, followed Althusser's example and remained within the Party. By this time, in China Mao had promulgated the Cultural Revolution. Seized with enthusiasm for this, the UJC (M-L) declared in the pages of the *Cahiers Marxistes-Léninistes* that 'President Mao is the Lenin of our epoch', and promptly aligned itself with the Chinese Cultural Revolution: with the political weight of 800 million behind it, it could attack the Party with renewed confidence. It effectively took over the *Cahiers Marxistes-Léninistes* (set up in December 1964) in December 1966, and devoted the next three issues to the Chinese Cultural Revolution. To the first of these, Althusser contributed an unsigned article, 'Sur la révolution culturelle'. This was the time of his most active interest in Maoism, and his links with his pro-Chinese students who had left the Party remained intact. Yet it was also now that he embarked on a series of concessions to the Party.

There are definite and significant Maoist inflections in Althusser's work, but to explain the 'derailment' of his project as an effect of his interest in Maoism is unconvincing.[96] Althusser was certainly not in any obvious sense a defender of Stalinist politics: on this score, critics like Edward Thompson and Leszek Kolakowski entirely miss the point.[97] But neither did he become a Maoist champion. What Althusser was primarily doing after the Argenteuil confrontation in 1966 was to turn more explicitly and diligently than before to the elaboration and defence of a Leninist line. His interest in Mao and the Chinese Revolution only went so far as his belief that they could be seen as the 'embodiment of Leninist rectitude'.[98] It is evident from his publications after 1966 that Lenin was in fact the central authority to whom Althusser appealed, in order to justify his inversion of the priority of theory over politics. He lavished praise on Lenin in his lectures on *Philosophy and the Spontaneous Philosophy of the Scientists*, and ended the second of these with resounding homage to Lenin: 'suffice to say that without Lenin, and all that we owe him, this course of Philosophy for Scientists would never have been possible'.[99] He was not shy of repeating the point:

> The philosophy which we professed, or more exactly, the position we occupied in philosophy, was not without relation to politics, a certain politics, that of Lenin, to the degree that Lenin's political axioms were able to provide us with reference points for enouncing our Theses on philosophy.[100]

References to Lenin now proliferated. Texts like 'Philosophie comme arme de la révolution' (1968), were suffused with repeated invocations of Lenin,[101] and Althusser used Lenin to encourage and sanction precisely the self-laceration that he had so criticized in Sartre and other petty bourgeois intellectuals.[102] Further evidence of Althusser's Leninism was his lecture to the Société française de Philosophie, entitled 'Lenin and Philosophy'. Finally, one should also take into account his own characterization of his work in 'Elements of Self-Criticism', where he wrote, 'it is not too much to say that what is at stake today, behind the arguments about words, is Leninism' (p. 115). There can no doubt that the authority Althusser invoked for his subordination of theory to politics ('the class struggle') was, before any other, that of Lenin.

Althusser's view of 'philosophy as the class struggle in theory' was closely linked to his interest in and sensitivity to the social origins of revolutionary intellectuals. He reversed his earlier separation between the realm of experience and that of correct theory and the political practice it authorized, and now stressed the difficulties 'petty-bourgeois' intellectuals faced in their struggle to become revolutionaries: unlike the 'proletarians [who] have a "class instinct" which helps them on the way to proletarian "class positions"', the petty-bourgeois intellectual had no such resource.[103] This focus on social origins was itself of good Leninist pedigree.[104] Nevertheless, although the proletariat might be in privileged possession of this revolutionary 'class instinct', it needed the assistance of Party organizations, which inevitably contained a representative dimension: political leaders and intellectuals, not of proletarian origin themselves, would play a role. What was the character of the representative relation btween the Leninist revolutionary Party and the revolutionary class? Three elements of Althusser's views about the relation between class and Party need be noted here. First, his definition of class did not refer to empirical criteria, nor did he give primacy to the subjectively felt sense of belonging to a class. He seemed to offer an innovative and more precise structural definition of class, which did not reduce class to a function of economic factors, but also took account of the political and ideological 'instances'.[105] Second, Althusser claimed to establish an identity between Party and proletariat by means of a theoretical and analytical deduction and not by recourse to a philosophy of history. For Althusser, theory specified the class and its representative; bourgeois ideologies such as 'humanism', which spelt out distinctions between Party, class and workers, only served to disaggregate and disarm the proletariat. It was theory which at once defined the proletariat, and specified who could act for it.[106] Third, and closely connected to the last point, classes were held to exist under conditions of illusion and mystification: left to themselves they were unable to generate a scientific and theoretical analysis of their situation, and indeed, given Althusser's theoretical definition of class, they were precluded even from self-recognition. They only existed to the extent that they had been *theorized* into existence. Given this precarious ontology, the working class could not be expected to develop adequate political consciousness, but required this to be exported to them.[107]

Commitment to the Leninist Party was the cornerstone of Althusser's political views. This is apparent even in those texts which some interpreters cite as instances of a critical break between Althusser and the Party, and of his move towards a more pluralist position; in none of these did Althusser significantly modify his call for a return to a genuinely Leninist vanguard Party. Althusser's commentary 'On the Twenty-Second Congress of the French Communist Party' has been described as a 'nuanced response' towards the policies of the Party.[108] In just exactly what did these nuances consist? Initially concessive, the text apparently endorsed the 'Eurocommunist' turn of the Party, and its abandonment of the concept of the dictatorship of the proletariat. Yet Althusser went on to warn of the extreme dangers of abandoning this concept.[109] He dismissed the possibility of allowing organized 'tendencies' within the Party (at a time when the Parti Socialiste encouraged the formation of intra-party *tendences*, and gained adherents), insisted on 'democratic centralism', and ended with a resolute affirmation of the conception of the Party as the revolutionary vanguard of the working class. Without Party organization, there would be no revolutionary working class, Althusser asserted, and 'if its [the Party's] existence is vital, it is for the struggle of the working class: to provide it with a vanguard organization'.[110] His fundamental criticism of the Party (advanced in impeccably Leninist terms) was that it did not in practice implement the correct 'line', and this because it adopted an incorrect theoretical analysis. Althusser repeated this type of criticism in his last major published political text, *Ce qui ne peut plus durer dans le Parti*.[111] Elliott describes this as 'Althusser's single most powerful text', and endorses Perry Anderson's judgement that it represents 'the most violent oppositional charter ever published within a party in the postwar history of Western Communism'.[112] Written in the bitter aftermath of the breakdown of the Union of the Left (the electoral pact between the Communists and the Socialists), it constituted a stinging criticism of the Communist Party leadership, and of its rapid retreat into a style reminiscent of the years of high Stalinism under Thorez in the 1950s.

But from what point of view was this criticism offered, in the name of what principles did Althusser speak? Once again, Lenin was Althusser's fundamental reference and authority.[113] Once again Althusser admonished the Party for its lack of correct theoretical analyses (in particular, he singled out the 'so-called "theory"' of state monopoly capitalism for attack), and the absence of class analysis: after all, 'before the war, Maurice Thorez still had the courage to present concrete analyses of class relations in France' (not a flicker of worry in invoking Thorez here).[114] And once again Althusser warned of the dangerous consequences that threatened in the absence of such theoretical analysis. Two he noted in particular. First, there was no possibility of explaining the dismal history of the Soviet Revolution, 'the crushing of the middle-classes, the Gulag Archipelago, the repression that still goes on twenty-five years after Stalin's death' (p. 38); and the lack of such explanation made it in turn impossible to allay the fears (which Althusser willingly acknowledged as real) of French voters concerned about the implications of a Communist electoral victory. Second, without such theory and analysis, it was impossible to establish a correct 'line', which the Party might then impart to the 'trusting' (p. 35) militants and working class; and Althusser never wavered in his conviction that 'a party and a line are indispensable in helping the working class to organize as a class—or, which comes to the same thing, to organize its class struggle' (p. 41). Even in 'Unfinished History', an article that registered Althusser's most critical remarks on the Stalin period and which raised fundamental questions ('what social relations today constitute the Soviet social formation' (p. 13)), he lacked the language to—as he put it—'call a spade a spade' (p. 12). Faced with having to explain the Stalin period, Althusser's considered response was: 'Remember Lenin' (p. 8).

IV

The politically disabling consequences of Althusser's attachment to Leninist precepts, in a patently non-revolutionary situation, may be seen in two ways. First, the extent to which it shaped his essay on 'Ideology and Ideological State Apparatuses', the nearest he ever came to a concrete analysis of state and society in contemporary France. This difficult, suggestive, essay is usually and accurately understood as Althusser's theoretical response to the events of 1968. It provoked a great amount of theoretical research on questions of ideology, both within and outside France.[115] It was also subject to powerful theoretical criticism, and attacked for its equivocation between functionalist and voluntarist positions.[116] But, as Althusser's student and associate Michel Pêcheux rightly saw, although the essay 'was read most often and by all sorts of readers as a purely theoretical intervention, to be precise as a functionalist thesis, either in order to reproduce it or condemn it', it was above all a 'political intervention'.[117]

Althusser laid bare the political premise of the essay in his preface to a longer (unpublished) manuscript from which the essay on ideology was excerpted. He claimed there that 'We are entering an era which will witness the triumph of socialism throughout the world . . . the revolution is henceforth on the agenda.'[118] The essay on ideology extracted the determining elements of social change from their usual (Marxist) location in the socio-economic 'base' and dispersed these elements through the political-ideological 'superstructure'. But, although Althusser appeared to start from Gramsci's enabling suggestion that the cultural and political spheres were properly autonomous arenas of effective action, he in fact ended with a 'politically pessimistic' account.[119] His analysis collapsed the distinction between state and civil society (a distinction that Gramsci had seen as fundamental to Western bourgeois democracy), and extended the state into all domains of social life. He dismissed the separation between public and private as a residue of bourgeois ideology, and implied that all state forms—bourgeois-democratic or Fascist alike—used ideology to the same end: to cement social cohesion.[120] The practices of the educational system—Althusser's own sphere of direct action—were described as a mode of transmission which ensured the reproduction of the nation-state.[121] Althusser's conception of the educational system, unlike the Republican conception, did not see it as the site of production for emancipatory or critical discourses. Remarkably, he closed off these sites precisely when, at numerous points in society, French radicals seemed to be finding new forms and methods of opposition.

The 'Ideology' essay did, however, allow one possible form of political agency and action. Indeed the entire political meaning of the essay was intended to identify a unique agent of political change: the Party. If all processes of change were simply trapped by and absorbed within the interstices of the social whole, then the only principle of change must of necessity be an external one. This explains why, for example, Althusser was at such pains to insist on a distinction between 'ISAs' (Ideological State Apparatuses) and the Party. The Communist Party, he noted, was not 'reduced to the role of executor of the bourgeois state, or to the role of Her Majesty's Opposition', and later he clarified that 'I have never written that a political party is an ideological state apparatus'.[122] Althusser justified the necessity and uniquely independent agency of the Leninist Party at a moment when the Communist Party's actions, far from being revolutionary, had failed to meet even the expectations of a reformist Party.[123] Althusser had himself noted a 'contradiction' between his arguments and the strategy of the Party.[124] But to many younger intellectuals, the matter was still more clear-cut: the actions of the Party during and after 1968 confirmed them in their judgement that the Party was a bureaucratic monolith, cast in the image of the Gaullist State it opposed. To these *gauchiste* intellectuals (some, like Rancière, former Althusserians), the terms that to Althusser spelt a contradiction looked more like an identity: they saw Althusser's justifications of the Party as mere sophistry.

A second consequence of Althusser's commitment to Leninist conceptions was manifest in his feeble account of Stalinism. Although his references to the question of Stalinism were invariably oblique, the problem was at the core of his project.[125] Yet he only discussed it explicitly and at some length after 1973; that is, after it had gained prominence through the appearance, most spectacularly in 1968, of Trotskyist, Maoist and anarchist critiques of Stalinism and of the bureaucratic state.[126] Althusser expressed his views on the matter in these circumstances, though—and typically—his own comments were directed not at local French arguments, but at the 'socialist-humanist' position of the British Communist, John Lewis.[127] He termed his own a 'left-wing' critique of Stalinism, distinguished both from the 'rightist' critiques of Togliatti and the Italian Communists (a proto-Eurocommunist account), and from 'humanist' accounts. He studiedly refused to mention existing left-wing critiques, such as Trotskyist or Maoist interpretations (although he absorbed some—though by no means all—elements from the latter view).[128] And he alluded only tangentially to Sartre's attempts to explain Stalinism.

Beyond doubt, Althusser's criticism was delivered in the name of Leninism. His basic analysis of the Stalin period was simple enough. He hoped to establish the conditions of possibility which had enabled Stalin's policies to emerge and dominate in the USSR. These policies represented a 'deviation' from the correct 'line' available in Marx and Lenin, a deviation induced by the interpretation of Marxism propagated by the Second International. This interpretation resulted in the twin defects of 'economism' and 'humanism': the autonomy of the superstructural relations of production was diminished, and the explanatory priority of the forces of production was affirmed; and the emphasis on the proletarian identity of Communism was replaced by a stress on the nation, and the 'people as a whole'. By once again employing terms such as 'economism' and 'humanism' in an explanatory way, Althusser returned to the bounds of the conceptual schema outlined in *Reading*

'*Capital*': Stalinism was described as an intellectual error, a *theoretical straying*. More precisely, the 'Stalinian deviation' was identified as a profoundly anti-intellectualist position, one infected by bourgeois ideology. Althusser's account contained two obvious weaknesses. First, it was unable to give a precise definition of the theoretical object it claimed to analyse: in tautologous fashion, it defined the 'deviation' by using the tactic of 'drawing a line' between friend and enemy, proletarian revolutionary and bourgeois ideologue. The 'Stalinian deviation' represented the infiltration of enemy thought into the bastions of revolutionary theory. The purpose of all philosophical activity, Althusser announced in 1968, was to fulfil this manichean task:

> A single word sums up the master function of philosophical practice: 'to draw a dividing line' between the true ideas and the false ideas. Lenin's words . . . But the same words sum up one of the essential operations in the direction of the practice of class struggle: 'to draw a dividing line' between the antagonistic classes. Between our class friends and our class enemies . . . It is the same word. A theoretical dividing line between true and false ideas. A political dividing line between the people (the proletariat and its allies) and the people's enemies.[129]

In this conception, the 'Stalinian deviation' represented a swerve onto the wrong side of the line: the fact of its historical existence did not raise questions about to what extent their might be continuities between this deviation and the Leninist line. Relying on Leninism to criticize Stalinism, Althusser never entertained the possibility of continuities, causal or otherwise, between the two positions.[130] Another flaw in the Althusserian critique of Stalinism, only briefly noted here, is that it itself employed forms of explanation that it identified as characteristic of the 'Stalinian deviation', namely economism and voluntarism.[131]

Stalinism and the historical experience of the Soviet Revolution posed a more fundamental theoretical question: how did a revolutionary doctrine whose intention was emancipatory end up serving as an ideological justification for an oppressive State, (was there something inherent to the theory which lent itself to this outcome)?[132] Since Althusser had chosen to consider the question of Stalinism at a purely theoretical level, he might have been expected to address this question. His pronouncements were not, however, particularly subtle: Marxism, he concluded, was politically labile.

> As astonishing as this may seem . . . Marxism itself can, in certain circumstances, be considered and treated as, even practised as a bourgeois point of view. Not only by 'armchair Marxists', who reduce it to academic bourgeois sociology, and who are never anything but 'functionaries of the dominant ideology'—but also by sections of the Labour Movement, and their leaders.[133]

In 'Unfinished History', he returned to the point, asking 'have Marxist philosophers forgotten what Marx said about dialectics, that it could become one thing or the other, could either become "critical and revolutionary" or play the role of "glorifying the existing state of affairs"?'.[134]

Now what, according to Althusser, determined in any particular case which identity Marxism adopted? This, he suggested, was a function of the relations which existed at any given time between Marxist philosophy and practice: between, that is, intellectuals and the Party. Althusser's introduction to Dominique Lecourt's book on the Lysenko affair explained this 'decay of philosophy into a practical ideology' by reference to precisely such a schema of relations between intellectuals, Party, and State.[135] According to Althusser, the ' official' explanation of Lysenkoism saw it as 'a folly abetted by State intervention', prevalent in past Soviet history, but now ceased. Other issues, such as the question of the 'social stratum of "intellectuals" involved by this State ideology which bound them . . . to the State', and the question of the deviation in political line which reduced theory to ideology, such questions were passed over in 'official silence'.[136] The effect of this silence was to perpetuate Marxist philosophy in its 'dominant version', a 'vulgar', orthodox form 'which excels in "glorifying the existing state of affairs"' ', a version which 'serves the existing political practices too well to be allowed to disappear: they "need" it'. The Party subjugated philosophy, they forced it 'play their servant, not to say their maid-of-all-work'. The Party thus 'suffered the loss of many intellectuals', the very intellectuals capable of achieving the necessary rectification in philosophy and theory, which in turn would have allowed the correct 'line' to be drawn and hence spared the revolution from the 'Stalinian deviation'. Instead, intellectuals, in the USSR as in France, were in thrall to the dominant version of dialectical materialism and the theory of the 'two sciences':

> the aim was both to unite them [the intellectuals] and to subjugate them. Intellectuals—it is an effect of the existing division of labour—are particularly sensitive to theoretical and philosophical questions. They already have plenty of prejudices against the party of communism, and when the attempt is made, in the name of criticism and revolution, to win them over to a theoretical fraud, to a philosophy which 'glorifies the existing state of affairs', then there is no need to be surprised when they keep, wherever they can (in the West, of course), their distance. Nor must you be astonished that it proves difficult even to pose correctly, let alone solve the 'irritating question' of the relations between the party and the intellectuals.[137]

The Althusserian argument had turned full circle. Althusser recurred to the terms and analysis employed more than a decade earlier, in 'Aujourd'hui': the only way out of Stalinist 'dogmatism' was to accord intellectual activity a correct status, to give it autonomy and priority.

There were undoubted shifts in Althusser's argument, but it is the overall continuity of his preoccupations that is most remarkable.[138] He returned to these throughout his public career, and in particular he always insisted on the need for a Leninist party, and on the necessity for intellectuals to assume a vanguard position. Intellectuals were able to 'draw the line' in both senses: distinguish between revolutionary science and bourgeois ideology, and on the basis of this distinction determine the correct forms of political action. But Althusser's account did not emerge from substantive political argument, it was emphatically a theoretical account, and hence it persistently faced the difficulty of entering the political arena as a mobilizing language. In the immediate postwar years, it was easier for intellectuals like Sartre to resolve this problem: the Resistance vocabulary of patriot and traitor could be invoked, and this could be conflated with the terminology of revolutionary Jacobinism, with such categories as 'people' and enemy. Althusser too searched for a divisive language of friend and enemy: this, above all, was the great utility of Maoism. But the identity of politically mobilizing terms such as 'friend' and 'enemy' lost sharpness in situations of comparative political stability: only in exceptional situations, moments of revolution, war and occupation, did they retain their starkness. A great deal of the utility of the language of Maoism, or of support for the Vietnamese FNL against the USA, derived from their power to infuse new life into this language of division and mobilization.[139] Hence too, the effort of sheer will on the part of some (former Althusserians and *gauchistes*), to revive during the late 1960s and early 1970s the language of the war-time Resistance in France: the creation of a 'Nouvelle Résistance Populaire', directed against the 'Fascist' Gaullist state which was 'occupying' the country, and also against the Communist Party, seen as complicit in this 'occupation'.[140]

But the identities of such mobilizing terms were fading. The Maoists were 'going to the people', and discovering that in many cases this mythic category was after all uninterested in the revolutionary apocalypse. Younger intellectuals employed on government 'contract' research projects, gained new channels of access to the state.[141] In a situation of economic growth, with higher levels of consumption than ever before, elements in French society were discovering new and differentiated terms of self-definition. The emergence of what were broadly described as 'social movements', offered terms for the construction of new categories of political identity, categories that seemed to possess an immediacy and authenticity endowed by practice and lived experience. In these circumstances, forms of political language which conceived of society in unitary terms slipped into decline. Both the Communist and the Gaullist discourses found their universalizing languages losing appeal. By the mid-1970s, Althusser's reformulation of Leninism had lost its attractions. Although many of those involved in radical politics during 1968 and after ostensibly employed Leninist conceptions, in fact the premises of the Leninist argument were undermined. Quite different mappings of the French situation were now developed: these rejected the central Leninist duality and schema of action, which continued to believe that the vanguard Party, representing the proletariat, would capture the bourgeois state, and so empower the proletariat. In the analysis which followed from this Leninist conception, the students of 1968 were dismissed as 'petty-bourgeois fragments' whose actions had obscured the real divisions and conflicts. This justified the Party's refusal to become involved in their protests and action, and lost it any credibility as the Party of revolution. After 1968, it became a commonplace to associate the Party with the Gaullist state, and to subject both to new anti-statist critical languages, drawn from anarchist, libertarian and other traditions.

PART THREE

CHAPTER FIVE

Revolution Exorcised: 1968–1981

> The whole society totters, drunk with its discovery of the possibility of a revolution, which only seems so miraculously original because it is the most classical of all.
>
> André Glucksmann, *Stratège et révolution* (Paris, 1968).

> The very desirability of the Revolution is the problem today.
>
> Michel Foucault (1972), *Politics, Philosophy and Culture: Interviews and Other Writings 1977–84* (London, 1988).

The 'long decade' between the revolutionary efflorescence of May 1968 and the Socialist Party's election to government in 1981 produced the most dramatic and decisive realignment in the political affiliations of French intellectuals that has occurred in recent times. The wave of dissent that in the late 1960s disturbed existing political routines across the globe, established Paris as the world capital of political radicalism: the idea of revolution there found new and glittering life. But within a few years the bubble of revolutionary rhetoric had deflated helplessly, and by the end of the 1970s intellectual opinion had shifted sharply away from revolutionary politics. The Communist Party relinquished any remaining political command over the intellectuals (thereby confirming a trend begun in the early 1960s), and for the first time intellectuals broadcast *en masse* their bitter disillusion not just with the Soviet regime and the Communist Party, but with Marxism and Left politics in general. With the entry of the Socialist Party into government (talking still of a 'rupture' with capitalism), the shift in intellectual mood was confirmed: the idea of revolution, now twinned to that of totalitarianism, was set in menacing opposition to democratic politics. This is paradoxical. Why should one of the consequences of 1968 have been an abrupt rejection of revolution, followed by a move away from Left politics altogether, and what did this break between the intellectuals and revolutionary politics signify? Did it signify a drift towards a hard political conservatism, an attempt to construct a liberal political theory, or a more generalized retreat from public politics altogether?

The 'events' of 1968 and the intellectual changes that followed are enshrouded in legend. There is an obvious but important respect in which 1968 was an event made by (and for) intellectuals: they participated in great numbers, and produced a torrent of interpretation and speculation about the significance of their activities (it would not be unjust to see 1968 as an interpretation in search of an event). The dominant intellectual sense of the period was the massive reaction against all forms of centrally organized political authority—whether in the form of the self-proclaimed revolutionary Party or the bourgeois State—and the image of a unified community this assumed. But France, where existing political traditions were all strongly centralizing, persistently lacked available forms to express such criticism (political dissent was invariably described by terms such as 'reactionary', 'anti-national', 'collaborationist', and so on). As so often before, the political argument was projected elsewhere: the critique of the revolutionary idea took the form of a critical re-evaluation of twentieth-century revolutionary societies, a re-evaluation which culminated in a virulent attack on the 1917 Soviet Revolution and its consequences.

Domestically, one consequence of the upheavals of 1968 was to splinter once-unified political identities: on the Left, the appearance of numerous *gauchiste* groups helped to erode Communist dominance, on the Right, Gaullism began rapidly to drift apart. The senses of political community and national identity that had been precariously negotiated after Vichy and the end of the war began now to blur, and this was perceived at once with anxiety and a sense of opportunity to define anew. The 1970s heralded the beginning of a major transformation in available and plausible self-conceptions of the nation's identity. The decline of the Gaullist language of national mission and destiny, and the attempt by the Communists to redefine themselves, by trimming their conception of political value to a less universal and more circumscribed geographical and cultural location, were each part of this mutation. There were perfectly real pressures acting upon these two conceptions, pressures which arose from the constraints of the international economy on the actions of the French state. It had become clear by the late 1970s that not even 'France's best economist', Raymond Barre, could continue to run the economy as if it were an autarkic unit. The language of 'external constraints' undermined the notion of a sovereign national plan: even Keynesian policies—let alone state planning—were beginning to lose plausibility as a way of effective control over an economy closely tied to an evidently international system (even if in just what sense this might constitute a 'system' remained somewhat conceptually opaque). The idea of a sovereign national state, self-sufficient, representative and instrument of the people's will, began to look unlikely.[1]

If there were causes, there were also reasons. The rejection of available forms of political agency compelled intellectuals to construct new self-understandings of their identity, and of the forms and capacities of agency available to them. This precisely was the significance of the *gauchiste* episode. *Gauchisme* turned most spectacularly against the Althusserian model of intellectual activity. The *gauchistes* preserved revolution as a political value and goal; but they were adamant that it could not be achieved by a Party organized along Leninist precepts. Their stress on spontaneous and libertarian forms of organization, their anti-Sovietism (encouraged by reading Chinese polemics against the Soviet Union), and their sense that the French Communists had become mere servitors of the Gaullist state, all were instances of their view that the Communist Party was a bureaucratic and grotesquely inappropriate instrument for bringing about revolutionary change in France. The Communist Party, meanwhile, had itself moved some distance from Leninist ideals: it talked more easily of the parliamentary road to political power, and began to take notice of the ingenious efforts of Italian and Spanish Communists to pass off 'Eurocommunism' as a major theoretical innovation in the Marxist tradition. Within the Party, as in its public pronouncements, revolution as a value was diminished (in 1976, at the twenty-second Party Congress, the concept of the 'dictatorship of the proletariat' was officially dropped from the Party's programme and theoretical menu: much to the chagrin of certain Althusserians), and the Communists condemned the *gauchiste* advocacy of revolution as naïve, nothing more than a petty-bourgeois diversion of the working class from its authentic interests.[2] Yet the model of the authoritarian Party was reaffirmed as the proper form of political agency, and the problem of Stalinism (a problem which many—and not only outside the Party—were coming to recognize as of direct relevance to the internal structure and functioning of the Party) elicited no serious comment.

The disparate senses of the *gauchiste* and Communist arguments—the former retaining the value of revolution, but abolishing the agency of the Party; the latter partially effacing the value of revolution, but stubbornly clinging to the model of the authoritarian Party—were aligned and given a new sense by a series of arguments that emerged in the late 1970s. The most notoriously unstable moment in the intellectual disengagement with the vocabulary of revolutionary politics was represented by the self-proclaimed 'New Philosophers', former *gauchistes* who took history to be little more than the playing out of ideas, and to whom the Marxist conception of revolution inevitably resulted in terror and violence administered by the State. Trumpeting arguments appropriated from Popper, Talmon and Arendt (each had until that point received little attention in France), the New Philosophers asserted the impossibility of revolutionary innocence: there was no lost treasure to recover. This ferociously negative argument—anti-Statist, anti-totalitarian, anti-Soviet—gained wide diffusion. The obsessional centre of their reflections was the notion of 'totalitarianism', a term which by the late 1970s had elsewhere passed through various cycles of intellectual and political currency.[3] But in France, it was appropriated by intellectuals in a distinctive and local way: it was used to interrogate France's own history, and was linked to the idea of revolution, the idea which held such a constitutive role in modern France's political identity. A direct continuity between modern totalitarianism and the period of Jacobin Terror was asserted, and the term came to signify at once an actual episode of the French Revolution and a threatening legacy, manifested by the history of the Soviet Revolution after 1917. These attacks gained momentum when joined to and by another argument from an apparently quite distinct field: the academic historiography of the French Revolution. The conceptually more acute arguments of historians like François Furet drained the idea of revolution of its coherence and value, and yoked it to a politics not of democratic emancipation but of totalitarianism and terror. Furet's reassessment of the significance of France's postrevolutionary history (in the light of the consequences of twentieth-century revolutions), and his rejection of the encompassing explanatory grid of Marxism in favour of a more Tocquevillean position, made current a new political vocabulary. It was this revaluation of the terms which constituted the French nation's identity that gave a crucial historical imprimatur to the furies of the New Philosophers, and successfully transformed the terms of political argument.

The uncertainly poised domestic political situation gave these intellectual exchanges a wider resonance. The electoral campaigns of 1977 and 1978, for municipal and legislative seats, had lost their routine air, and the parties of both Right and Left claimed that these elections presented the people with a decisive choice about France's future political identity: the Socialists and Communists promised a decisive 'rupture' with capitalism, while Giscard d'Estaing and the parties of the Right broadcast dark warnings of a totalitarian future if the Left won the elections.[4] With the economy—under Giscard's presidency—stubbornly in recession, the parties of the Left seemed set fair for electoral victory. Yet they had fallen to squabbling amongst themselves, throwing at each other accusations of 'social-democratic' and reformist betrayal. The intellectual response to this bemusing return on the part of the Communists (and some Socialists) to the hardline language of a 'rupture with state capitalism' and the promised installation of a socialist economy, crystallized around the notion of totalitarianism. In previous decades, intellectuals of the Left had been willing to give the Soviet Revolution some (variously measured) positive value; but henceforth the term most frequently employed by intellectuals of the Left to describe the Soviet Union was 'totalitarian'. This effect was a decisive revaluation of the idea of revolution.

I

For roughly five decades after the Bolshevik Revolution, the otherwise quarrelsome members of the French Left largely concurred over the existence of a special kinship between 1789 and 1917: both revolutions formed part of a larger but unified process of historical development. It was precisely this association that served as a protective shield against any profound criticism of the Soviet Revolution and its consequences. During the 1970s, however, the value attached to the Soviet Union suffered quite spectacular deflation in both public and intellectual opinion.[5] Intellectuals of the Left condemned with increasingly unreserved confidence the Soviet revolutionary experience, and by the end of the decade an unprecedented virulence laced their pronouncements. Such criticism—while perfectly expected from the Right—had in previous decades been taboo for those who wished to be identified with the Left. And since the French Left's own identity had, after 1917, been decisively defined through its relation to the Bolshevik Revolution and its legacies, this altered and newly critical perception inevitably held wider implications. Any explanation of this shift must register, even if briefly, the position held by the Soviet Union in the political imagination of the French Left in earlier decades. These perspectives on the Soviet Union were decisively coloured by the new critical vocabulary that emerged in France in the mid-1970s, centred around the term 'totalitarianism'. In itself the term possessed little analytical merit, but in the French intellectual *milieu* it gained a special significance, and joined together different critical strands into a new configuration. The clearest instance of this was the manner in which a number of intellectuals—of differing political persuasions—gained new prominence during the 1970s: Cornelius Castoriadis, Claude Lefort, and Raymond Aron each attracted attention in large measure because of what they had to say about totalitarianism.

Well before the 1917 Revolution, Russia had been an object of fascination for France's 'men of letters': Voltaire envied its enlightened progress (though, he warned, this threatened to outpace France herself), to Tocqueville it presaged an image of an authoritarian political future, while Michelet's ventriloquist imagination had Russia declare, 'Je suis le socialisme.'[6] At the end of the nineteenth century, men like Lucien Herr picked up on thoughts such as Michelet's and transposed them into more professionalized settings: writing in the shadow of France's defeat at the hands of Germany in 1870, Herr for instance saw Russia and the Russian intelligentsia as the legitimate heirs to the philosophies of Hegel and Marx.[7] But this enduring French interest in Russia's political and historical significance gained a new focus and impetus after the Bolshevik Revolution of 1917, an event which profoundly disturbed western European conceptions of historical progress and development.[8] There is a large literature on the impact of the October Revolution upon the intellectual and political imagination on inter-war Europe,[9] and much of it is focused on France, not least because the Bolshevik Revolution acted so directly to split the French Left at Tours in 1920. For the main political parties of the French Left, their perception of the Soviet Union was fundamentally set in the two decades after 1917, and in fact there was notably little departure from this interpretative pattern after the end of the Second World War, or indeed until the 1970s. Dissident or critical positions gained little intellectual or political credibility.

The Bolshevik Revolution was immediately interpreted in terms drawn from its French predecessor, and a kinship between the two events was unhesitatingly declared. Reviving divisions whose origins lay in the revolutionary decade of the 1790s, it is clear that the French Left from the very outset 'became identified with sympathy towards the new Soviet government, while the French Right stood for policies of intervention and non-recognition'.[10] But the Left possessed no unified perspective. Each faction within the Left understood the Bolshevik Revolution as a re-enactment of its own preferred episode of French Revolutionary history: to liberals it was a modern 1789; to Jacobin democrats it seemed to realize the hopes of 1792; while for the Socialists it was a replay of the Paris Commune.[11] There was agreement, however, that 1917 was fundamentally a further episode in the historical process begun in 1789: it was through this filiation that it revealed its proper historical meaning. To all on the Left, the Bolshevik Revolution fuelled hope for the possibility of a renewal of the revolution in France, conceived of in the classical terms of Jaurès and Pelloutier. The Jaurèsian synthesis, blending a selective form of Marxist socialist analysis and a belief in final goals with a conviction that it was the territorial boundaries of the French Republic that provided the appropriate framework for political advance, reigned supreme (because unchallenged) before 1920; but after the scission at Tours, it ceased to dominate.

The fracture of the French Left into Socialist and Communist components hardened attitudes that undoubtedly differed in broad emphasis; but neither Socialists nor Communists produced any particularly acute analyses of the Bolshevik Revolution and its effects, and the attitudes of both were firmly constrained by doctrinal considerations. Until as recently as the 1980s, Socialist views of the Soviet Union had progressed little beyond the terms employed by Léon Blum in his perorations against Bolshevism at the Congress of Tours in 1920.[12] Blum's critique of Bolshevism was unambiguously in the name of a French, national tradition of socialism.[13] It was essentially a moral critique, and although subsequently during the inter-war years some Socialists did try to extend Blum's pieties into more detailed and historically based criticisms of the Soviet regime, these exercises ceased with the rise of the extreme Right in France and the threat of Fascism abroad.[14] The Communist-Socialist pact in July 1935 effectively silenced all Socialist debate about the significance of the Soviet experience for the Left's politics: any such discussion was seen as a threat to Left unity. Thus, for instance, the fact that the Moscow Trials occurred after the signing of the Franco-Soviet Pact in May 1935, and roughly coincided with the Popular Front government (June 1936 to March 1938), decisively determined the extent to which the Trials were reported and treated in the French press. In particular, the left-wing press made very little effort to explain them,[15] and those on the Left who did try to consider critically the events in the Soviet Union found themselves excluded from the mainstream of left-wing debate.[16] Contrary to the rigid doctrinal positions, of the Left, the French Right employed a quite different and more plastic standard of judgement. Although generally consistently anti-Soviet, it was more concerned with *realpolitik*: a major reason for this more pragmatic approach was the fact that the Right more usually held governmental power, and consequently had cause to devise a workable foreign policy.[17] In the period after the Second World War, this pragmatism was manifest in the importance Gaullist foreign policy attached to *détente* with the Soviet Union, as a way of counterbalancing good relations with the United States and Germany, and hence of preserving France's independence. Whereas the Left invariably stressed qualitative differences between the Soviet model and its western counterparts, and celebrated its status as a landmark on the path to socialism, the Right on the contrary tended to emphasize the interdependence (especially economic) between the socialist and capitalist nations.[18]

Communist embarrassment at the Hitler-Stalin Pact was removed by the subsequent role of the Soviet Union in the defeat of Nazism. This allowed French Communists after 1945 to claim that to support the Soviet Union was now the best (and only) way of displaying genuine patriotism; above all, such support removed the suspicion of having overtly or even tacitly supported collaboration with the Nazis and the Vichy regime.[19] After the Liberation, the Communist evaluation of the Soviet Union dominated the perceptions of the French Left, and seemed to intellectuals a more realistic appraisal than the moralizings of Blum and the Socialists. On this, men of such different intellectual and political tastes as Aragon and Merleau-Ponty could agree. For intellectuals of the Left, the image of the Soviet Union was refracted through and dominated by 'progressivist' culture (itself in large part beholden to the Communist line). In this view, the Soviet Union was the home of world socialism, and demanded support because of 'the determining role of the USSR in the forward march of the world'.[20] Naturally, there were qualifications to this view. The suppression of the Hungarian uprising in 1956 had some impact upon intellectual circles, though less in France than elsewhere, and arguably less than Khrushchev's 1956 Report. Khrushchev's doctrinal adjustments promised intellectuals a new perspective: it blurred the idea of Soviet Communism as a decisive historical

alternative to Western capitalism, and substituted instead the hope
of a convergence between the two systems. In the revised schema
now favoured by some ('revisionist') intellectuals, gradual social change
promoted by the expanding industrialization and rationalization of
Soviet life was seen as the key to transformation of the political system.[21]
But the invasion of Czechoslovakia by the Soviet military in 1968 scup-
pered this view: it no longer appeared that the Soviet Union would
gradually be assimilated into the larger European political culture;
on the contrary, Europe now seemed threatened by Soviet military
aggression.[22] The political pragmatism that revisionism had encouraged
was abandoned, provoking diverse intellectual responses. Some, like
Althusser, had already withdrawn into the adamantine abstractions of
theory, into an intellectual discourse that achieved distance from (but
remained in parallel to, and travelled in the same direction as) the
official discourse of the Communist Party. Others, the *gauchistes* and
Maoists, were in no doubt about their contempt for the Soviet regime.
But few saw it as possessing a decisive significance for the desirability
and possibility of revolutionary politics as such, and the deformities
of Soviet Communism could be exculpated by the peculiarities of its
circumstances, leaving the value of revolution in pristine condition.
Until the 1970s, criticism of the Soviet Union conformed to an etiquette
that implied a community of shared conceptions and projects. This
was irreparably shattered by the French publication of Solzhenitsyn's
L'Archipel du goulag in 1974, which vividly introduced a new, radical
(but non-communist) generation of intellectuals to some of the realities
of the Stalinist period.[23]

   This revaluation of the Soviet Revolution was accomplished by means
of a terminological bludgeon, 'totalitarianism', and in the 1970s, especially after the publication in French of Solzhenitsyn's work, discussions of the Soviet regime increasingly and invariably centred around
this term. Viewed from afar, this is an odd turn of events, and raises the
question of why French intellectuals should have so avidly retrieved
this hardly *recherché* term. To suppose that this was merely a belated
reheating of Cold War ideology obscures a more complicated picture. In
France in the 1970s, the term was used with greatest force by those who
described themselves as Left radicals and critics, not ideologues of the
Right: it became the rallying point for 'la gauche anti-totalitaire' or, as it
was also known, 'la deuxième gauche'. The term entered the political
talk of intellectuals in the latter half of the 1970s from quite opposed
points on the political spectrum, and there are at least two distinct
moments to its entry into French political and intellectual debate. Totalitarianism had been a term current in the writings of an older generation
of intellectuals, but it gained a new value in the mid-1970s through
the performances of the New Philosophers. The older discourse itself
contained two strands of criticism. One had its origins in the critique—

developed in the 1940s and 1950s by Cornelius Castoriadis, Claude Lefort, and the *Socialisme ou barbarie* group—of the totalitarian and bureaucratic consequences of the Soviet Revolution. But this was a critique launched from the Left, in the name of authentic revolution, and this was precisely what made it attractive to the *gauchistes* in the late 1960s, who adopted it as their own.[24] The other strand of criticism, elaborated by Raymond Aron, did not espouse a 'true' revolutionary position, but was uttered in the name of liberal democratic values. Aron first advanced this argument in the late 1930s, and developed it (under different intellectual influences) in the 1950s.[25] Aron of course execrated the 1968 *gauchistes*, and they in turn reviled him. Strikingly, however, both these strands of criticism, the anti-totalitarian revolutionary critique of Lefort and Castoriadis and the Aronian account, each based on vastly disparate and politically opposed premises, jointly came to prominence in the 1970s; they converged in turn with the more histrionic assault on totalitarianism led by those ex-*gauchistes* who called themselves the 'New Philosophers'. This constituted the second moment of totalitarianism's trajectory in French political argument, and what was anyway an analytically shapeless and elastic term was now further stretched through the infusion of personal experience. It was the political ambivalence of the term, its radical pedigree, which first made it attractive to intellectuals after 1968, and which allowed the New Philosophers to exploit it to such political effect.

In the late 1940s and 1950s, Castoriadis and Lefort, like Aron, pursued a strongly anti-Soviet line, but unlike Aron they located themselves amongst the small and relatively marginalized Trotskyist and revolutionary groups that constituted the non-Communist Left. Nevertheless, they were uneasily situated on the French Left, whose orthodoxies they had always criticized. In 1949, they founded the journal *Socialisme ou barbarie*, and published a series of analyses of the Soviet regime, Stalinism, bureaucracy, and totalitarianism.[26] Time and again they said what few on the Left could bring themselves to say: that to support the Soviet Union was in fact to be anti-revolutionary.[27] Contrary to the situation in Britain, where the much more immediately (and differently) felt effect of writers like Koestler and Orwell made it perfectly reasonable, if by no means mandatory, to reject the Soviet Union as a political model and yet continue to remain on the Left, in France it was not until the 1970s that such a position became intellectually and politically sustainable. There did of course exist a longstanding tradition on the French Left critical of the Soviet regime: beginning in the 1920s, an extensive range of memoirs, *exposés* and analyses which arraigned Soviet communism was published. Some were the work of Trotskyists like Victor Serge or of those such as Boris Souvarine, influenced by Trotsky's analyses of Soviet history; but Social Catholics like Simone Weil, writers like André Gide, and historians like Elie Halévy, along with men like

Pierre Pascal and Manès Sperber must also be included in this critical tradition, as must critics like Georges Bataille, who already in 1933 was drawing parallels between Nazism and Soviet communism.[28] To explain why the various strands of this tradition were largely unheard for so long would require a very differentiated set of reasons, but the reasons for the revival of interest in this critical tradition help also to explain the renewed fortunes of men such as Aron, Castoriadis and Lefort.

The prominence secured by these three in French intellectual life at the end of the 1970s and the early 1980s was an index of the shift in political mood, since the substance of what they said was largely continuous with what they had been arguing for the past thirty years. Castoriadis' work began to gain prominence after 1968, especially among the *gauchiste* left, but he was propelled into the sphere of public debate by the publication in 1980 of his *Devant la guerre*. This was received as an exercise in the *realpolitik* of Soviet and American nuclear strategy by, unusually, a man of the Left. Suddenly after years on the margins of intellectual debate (until the 1970s, his political articles under published under pseudonyms for fear of endangering his émigré status in France), Castoriadis found himself ranked amongst the top level of French experts on the Soviet Union, his work the subject of heated debate.[29] Similarly Lefort, after a series of significant yet largely unremarked-upon works, published in 1976 a study of Solzhenitsyn's *L'Archipel du goulag*, followed by a number of articles analysing the problem of totalitarianism and its relation to revolution and democracy and, by the late 1970s, his public identity had been transformed from an obscure Left-wing critic to that of a major political philosopher.[30] Some idea of the distinctiveness of his position can be gleaned from the fact that he was one of the very few Left intellectuals with a serious interest in Tocqueville (it would be revealing to construct a typology of French intellectuals in terms of which of them was reading and writing about Tocqueville during these years).[31] Raymond Aron had always recommended Tocqueville, and now Tocqueville was to become *the* thinker against Marxism, and what was understood as its political reality, totalitarianism.

In the 1950s Aron had refused altogether the progressivist and Marxist philosophies of history, in favour of theories of modernization and industrialization drawn from American social science (theories which, in opposition to the prevailing mood, argued for a growing convergence rather than a qualitative and underlying difference between the societies of East and West).[32] Aron was never a negligible figure, yet his career veered between contrasting periods of recognition and oblivion. In the late 1940s and the 1950s, he was attacked by the Left and largely ignored by the Gaullist Right. When, in 1956, he described the Budapest uprising as the 'first anti-totalitarian revolution', he was loudly derided.[33] In the early 1960s, with the French discovery of American social science,[34] he enjoyed a brief honeymoon, but his hyperbolic response to the events of May 1968 allowed his critics to label him as a reactionary and pushed him to the edges of the intellectual landscape.[35] But, in the late 1970s, Aron gained a special prominence: the French suddenly discovered that they had in their midst a major thinker on such subjects as international relations, war and totalitarianism. Aron maintained throughout his career a consistency of purpose unusual amongst most other French intellectuals, and it is therefore surprising how rapidly intellectual opinion transformed 'Aron le réac' into 'Aron le sage'.

One explanation of Aron's relatively peripheral intellectual position during the 1960s and the early 1970s sees it as a consequence of the rise to dominance of structuralism. Structuralism, François Furet has suggested, took root primarily amongst intellectuals of the Left, usually former Marxists (in the broad sense of the term).[36] It allowed disillusioned radicals to conduct an ambivalent relationship with Marxism and Left politics, and so to distance themselves from liberal critiques of Marxism: adopting structuralist tenets displayed a commitment to intellectual rigour, without compelling direct political involvement. To summarize Furet's argument a touch brusquely, Lévi-Strauss triumphed over Aron, the liberal and empirical critique of Marxism lost to a hyper-rationalist and systematic general theory of Man. There is something to this explanation, though for it be really illuminating it would need to go further, and account for the decline in turn of structuralism. About this extremely complex episode in French intellectual life, little can be said here.[37] But there is a clear sense in which the decline of structuralism was brought on by purely intellectual motives, since it was no longer yielding intellectually satisfying results: 'it embraced everything, but explained nothing'.[38] The objects of intellectual attention also began to shift. Structuralism had its origins in literary and textual analysis. French intellectual life conventionally accorded centrality to literature, and structuralism represented an aspiration to universalism, adapted to an idea of culture as expressed essentially in literary form: structuralist theory was a way of generating a universal theory out of culturally very specific material, a national literature. The moment of structuralism's decline, consequently, was linked intimately to the decline of the social and cultural importance of literature, itself hastened by the waning tradition of great French writers (think, for instance, of Sartre's decline— and not merely physical—during the 1970s). The two areas of inquiry that structuralism evaded—politics and history—now gained a renewed importance. This change was manifest in the manner in which the work of writers from the Soviet Union and Eastern Europe was received and assimilated in France. The warm reception extended to writers like Solzhenitsyn (and later, to Milan Kundera) was in large part because they filled a vacuum created by the departure of indigenous literary talent. But in France these writers were read not primarily as authors of novels and fictions, but as historical chroniclers, indeed at times as political philosophers and sages.

A second explanation of Aron's new prominence would be to see it as a consequence of a battle within German philosophy, conducted on French intellectual territory. German philosophy had decisively shaped modern French thought since at least the 1930s, when intellectuals of Aron's generation resorted to it as a way of putting distance between themselves and the prevailing academic orthodoxy, represented on the one hand by the neo-Kantian rationalism of Boutroux and Brunschvicg, on the other by the Durkheimian positivism of Bouglé.[39] Some, most famously Sartre (whose sensitivity to all that was contesting neo-Kantian thought in Germany was matched only by his aggressive appropriation of it), were attracted to German philosophy because it offered a form of dissent from and opposition to the political and academic establishment. Sartre, who freely admitted that his interest in German philosophy, and in particular in phenomenology, was sparked by Aron,[40] followed in 1932 Aron's lead to Berlin to continue his studies on Husserl and Heidegger. What resulted, Sartrian existentialism, was a *bricolage* of Husserl, Heidegger, and Kojève's interpretation of Hegel (gathered second-hand by Sartre from his acquaintances who attended Kojève's lectures at the Ecole des Hautes Etudes in 1933).[41] Aron, in sharp contrast, was attracted to German philosophy not because it promised a contestatory or revolutionary mode of thought; if anything, his voyage to Germany in 1931 conformed faithfully to the demands of neo-kantian Republicanism. Academics during the Third Republic displayed great curiosity for Germany and German thought, and Aron's interest in German philosophy and sociology was founded upon strict philological and scholarly scruples.[42] He wanted to establish a thorough and soundly based neo-Kantianism, and his favoured thinker was Weber, not Husserl.[43] The underlying divergence in the motivations of Sartre and Aron surfaced clearly after 1945: 'Sartrism' (and Merleau-Ponty, at least until his break with Sartre in 1955, was associated with this position), intellectually bolstered by its cavalier incorporation of Husserl, Heidegger, and most importantly Hegel, became the dominant philosophical form through which to oppose the academic philosophy of the university.[44] Aron's neo-Kantian interpretation of Weber was buried by the dominance of the Sartrian interpretation of German philosophy. It is possible to see French philosophy of the 1960s as a radicalization of elements within this Sartrian interpretation, resulting in what has been described as a radical 'anti-humanism'.[45] Aron became an important touchstone for those who subsequently reacted to this interpretation of German philosophy, and who turned with renewed interest to Weber and Kant; during the 1980s the Aronian interpretation of German philosophy dominated in France.[46]

Finally, a less determinate but nevertheless significant dimension to any explanation of Aron's late prominence in French intellectual life lies in the international and domestic political context. In circumstances where national foreign policy had traditionally been defined by a strong presidential will, France in the mid-1970s was still adjusting to post-Gaullism, with no clear view about how the imperatives of foreign policy were to be defined.[47] The situation was made more acute by the major shift in international relations then under way. America's defeat in Vietnam appeared to signal the waning of American global influence, while conversely, Soviet influence seemed to be on the ascent: the havoc in Cambodia, and the presence of Soviet arms and officers on the African continent, were taken as evidence of this. In circumstances of international change and uncertainty, Aron—seen from within the confines of a remarkably inward-looking intellectual culture—seemed to embody a more cosmopolitan vision and tone. He was conversant with European thought, familiar with American and Keynesian economics, and he had written extensively on subjects such as international relations, defence strategy, and totalitarianism, topics unfamiliar to most French intellectuals, schooled in the manners of parochial polemic.[48] By the beginning of the 1980s, Aron was triumphantly enthroned at the centre of French intellectual attention: the journal he had helped found in 1978, *Commentaire* (its identity was defined by its 'anti-totalitarian' positions), had quickly established itself as an important arena for non-Left intellectual debate, and in 1980 *Le Spectateur engagé* was published, a collection of conversations between Aron and two young journalists. This became a best-seller, later a television series, and was followed in 1983 by his *Mémoires*, the publishing event of the Parisian *rentrée* in 1983.

The writings of Castoriadis, Lefort and Aron were important conduits in channelling the mounting intellectual criticism of the Soviet Revolution and its totalitarian outcome, but it was a younger generation of intellectuals, some of whom had participated in the anti-Gaullist and anti-Communist radicalism of 1968, who burst the dam. *La Nouvelle Philosophie* was the title chosen by Bernard-Henri Lévy for a collection of essays by himself and 'a few friends' (these included Michel Le Bris, Guy Lardreau, Christian Jambet, André Glucksmann and Philippe Nemo).[49] What explained the emergence and success of these men, what was it about the situation after 1968 that enabled former *gauchistes* to move, less than ten years later, sharply to the Right of the political spectrum? And what was the significance of this episode? The writings of the New Philosophers were pervaded by a penitential mode. For them, the explanation of Soviet terror and totalitarianism lay not in the peculiar backwardness of Russian society, nor even in a revival of indigenous forms of tsarist absolutism, but instead in the very idea of Enlightenment Reason, a product of the French eighteenth century. If the political ideas of Paris had once been the hope of humankind, they were now just as decisively a cause for despair: 'The miseries of the world are sometimes of French origin', André Glucksmann announced in 1977 ('for example', he tried to explain, 'the Khmer Rouge leaders who are responsible for

one or two million dead were often educated in France').[50] As if to
emphasize this sensed responsibility, the New Philosophers produced a
train of self-confessional memoirs chronicling the political trajectory of
their generation.[51] These memoirs converged with the appearance of a
number of autobiographical works by an older generation of former
Communists (Emmanuel Le Roy Ladurie, Pierre Daix, Jean Rony and
others), all marked by a renunciation of previously held political beliefs
and affiliations.[52] Almost without exception, these confessions and
memoirs left their subjects entrenched in Right-wing positions (although
it must be recognized that the New Philosophers invariably insisted that
they were writing from a position on the Left). All displayed a recurrent
and common trope in French political discourse of this period: the
shedding of previous blindness and a return to vision, to cognitive
experience. One way of interpreting this stream of 'confessional' literature is to see it (as many French commentators themselves have done)
in terms of a functionalist sociology of belief: political ideologies like
Communism appear as a formal substitute for religious passions, religion
and politics become communicating vessels.[53]

This confessional drift is better understood, however, as symptomatic
of the difficulties French intellectuals have faced in developing and
sustaining criticisms of centralized political power that did not end up
as simplistic forms of anti-statism. There are at least two dimensions
relevant to understanding the obstacles facing this type of criticism in
France, and recalling them reveals why the term totalitarianism became
such a political talisman for intellectuals during the 1970s. The first,
an effect of the Second World War, was the continued importance
attached to the display of a visibly anti-Fascist position. After the defeat
of Fascism, in an atmosphere thick with accusations of collaboration and
betrayal, anti-Fascism was most easily displayed by support for the
Soviet Union. In this context, the anti-Soviet and revolutionary critique
made by those such as Castoriadis and Lefort could not gain much
force. The writings of the New Philosophers fell squarely within the
boundaries of the French understanding of intellectual commitment, a
specific and highly moralistic conception of the intellectual. This conception was first stated in its modern form by Julien Benda, and then
(with a different political accent) by Paul Nizan in his acerbic commentary on the philosophers and intellectuals of the Third Republic.[54]
From this view, 'le clerc ne trahit jamais', regardless of whether it was a
universal truth or class to which his loyalty was pledged. The obverse of
this notion of intellectual commitment was that of intellectual betrayal.
It is from within this matrix of ideas and values that the powerful
and emotive language of treason and collaboration, so pervasive in the
intellectual battles of the postwar years, drew sustenance. In the con-
fused aftermath of Vichy France and the experience of occupation, the
elision between intellectual and political activity, and the association

between political treason and intellectual betrayal were both confirmed as fundamental traits within the French intellectual imagination. The political effects were potent. After the war, mechanisms of compensation emerged, whereby collaboration with Nazism was punished by rewarding support for the Soviet Union.[55] This unequal forgiveness is one of the more evident reasons why the term 'totalitarianism'—closely linked with the Nazi and Fascist regimes—could not be aired in the critical discourse of the revolutionary Left.[56] In the 1940s and '50s it was impossible for intellectuals on the Left to suggest comparisons between the Soviet and Nazi regimes, particularly given the Communist Party's record as the 'Party of Resistance' and the Soviet Union's role in the war (as Edgar Morin averred in his *Autocritique*, the halo of Stalingrad served to blind an entire generation to the demerits of Stalin).[57] This reluctance to adopt anti-Communist positions existed across the spectrum of French intellectual opinion, with Catholic intellectuals like Emmanuel Mounier, for instance, agreeing that 'anti-communism . . . is . . . the necessary and sufficient catalyst for a revival of Fascism'.[58]

But deeper historical reasons can be found in the tenuousness of the democratic perspective in France. Beneath the veneer of a Republican political regime, the idea and practices of representative democracy in modern France were under continuous threat from the authoritarianism of both Left and Right.[59] This fragility of democratic politics was a direct result of the enduring inability of those who opposed or criticized existing political power to conceive of such opposition and criticism within the existing political system or framework: an inability that was founded upon a deep-seated mistrust of the theory and practice of representative democracy.[60] Further, the absence of a developed critical discourse of civil rights, rights enjoyed by members of an heterogeneous and plural civil society, meant that those who criticized the state in the name of democratic or liberal principles were customarily identified as belonging on the Right, and hence in the postwar period possessed sparse intellectual credibility. In such circumstances, the arguments of the liberal and non-Communist Left lacked conviction. Unable to align itself with either the Left or the Right in France (both of whom viewed it with sentiments ranging from suspicion to repugnance), French liberalism was disabled by the absence of a well-founded tradition of rights discourse, and by a feeble conceptualization of the relations between civil society and the modern state.[61] Indeed, this is the prime reason why the French have turned so avidly to American political philosophers like Rawls and Nozick.[62] The New Philosophers certainly did not bring a liberal voice to French political argument; but their analytical and historical indiscretions did help to create conditions which enabled the revival of liberal political theory in France during the 1980s.

The weakness of liberal and social-democratic intellectual traditions (which might have contributed to a more credible if prosaic understanding of the political complexities facing postwar France) are made apparent by the belated recognition which French intellectuals accorded to the achievements of General de Gaulle. De Gaulle's success was not ideological: in its form, and to some extent in its reality, Gaullism was marked by an authoritarian strain (its opponents of course went further, even to the point of seeing Gaullism as an incipient totalitarianism: the Communists, for example, tried repeatedly to label de Gaulle as a Fascist—the most serious political insult in postwar France).[63] But de Gaulle's 1958 Constitution did secure for France its first effective democratic regime, in the shape of the political and legal institutions of the Fifth Republic: after 1958, helped by the end of the colonial wars, and sustained economic expansion, France experienced a decade of unusual political stability. At the time this passed unnoticed, but with the benefit of hindsight the 1968 revolt can be seen not simply as a revolt against Gaullism *tout court*, but rather as the outcome of two contradictory processes: the setting in place of institutions which allowed a measure of democratic politics (under considerably more stable conditions than before) by a leader who simultaneously maintained an ideological form typical of the traditional authoritarian Right. (Although the existence of such an ideological form was not exclusive to Gaullism— the reaction amongst the younger generation against the Communist Party in 1968 in large part derived from similar motivations.)[64] That the rupture between de Gaulle and those who revolted against him in 1968 was perhaps not so profound after all can be deduced from the fascination he now exerts on the generation who were involved in the 'events' of 1968.[65] French *gauchisme* was in many respects more efficacious than its other European counterparts in large part because French society had become more permeable to such ideas, a result precisely of the processes of democratic institutionalization initiated by de Gaulle. All explanations of the intellectual drift away from the Left during the 1970s must, however, return to 1968, and to the changed forms of intellectual identity and political action which this made available. The New Philosophers all had their origins here.

II

Some have interpreted May 1968 as the 'beginning of a new radicalism emerging . . . in opposition to advanced capitalism', but the subsequent history of political thinking in France has confirmed such judgements as somewhat wide-eyed.[66] If, conversely, to have seen it as the last universalist 'psychodrama' of the French nation was to favour too narrow an optic, it is nevertheless clear that there was a fair measure of deception as to its significance.[67] Of the many available interpretations, one that attained popularity saw the events of 1968 as manifestations of an impulse towards individualism: political passions and interests were displaced into private and narcissistic forms of activity.[68] It is indeed true that many who were disappointed by the sequel to May 1968 did drift away from the arena of directly public politics and towards an interest in the individual and private. This turn towards a philosophical and political concern with the individual was an important mutation in an intellectual tradition that had often been strongly anti-individualist (this shared emphasis united thinkers as dissimilar as Althusser, Braudel and Lévi-Strauss).[69]

The manner in which psychoanalysis was embraced by radical intellectuals can be situated in terms of this movement, and is sometimes adduced as symptomatic evidence of a more glacial shift towards the individual and private sphere. With the re-establishment of Gaullist power in the early 1970s, many *gauchistes* turned away from the disappointments of politics towards the theoretical *topoi of* Jacques Lacan's reworking of Freudian psychoanalysis.[70] Unlike in America, where psychoanalysis was adopted as a specific technique in the repertory of the medical establishment, a clinical discipline, in France psychoanalysis (in its Lacanian form) was translated into terms which gave it the lustre of a revolutionary theory, a way of changing the world: 'using Lacanian psychoanalytic discourse as a referent served to legitimate political discourse'.[71] The move towards psychoanalysis enabled simultaneously a disengagement from radical political action and the maintenance of a position that displayed all the vestiges of intellectual and even social subversion.[72] Pursuing this, one reason sometimes suggested to explain why France, unlike Germany and Italy during the 1970s and '80s, was spared the experience of terrorism was the disengagement of many political radicals from militant politics, in favour of the battleground of the psychoanalytic couch and its associated practices.[73] There were certainly some who at the time saw it in these terms: to one faculty member, commenting in 1972 on increased government funding for the Department of Psychoanalysis at the newly-established University of Vincennes, it was evident that 'that's just the government paying us off for keeping marxist troublemakers preoccupied with their unconscious'.[74]

But, and more tangibly, the significance of 1968 lies in the high prominence it gave to processes that dissolved the inherited languages of revolutionary politics, especially in their Jacobin form. There were two dimensions to this, and both acted to undermine the premises of revolutionary politics and the conceptions of agency and causality this assumed. The events of 1968 evidently spelt a break with the statist, Jacobin programme of postwar economic and social reconstruction begun in 1945. The bulk of intellectual criticism was directed against the images of community implied by both the Gaullist and the Communist programs. The Gaullist aspiration of a unified France in sovereign control of its destiny, guided into modernity by a strong technocratic state in possession of a managerial élite who saw themselves as engaged in a 'universal mission', was subject to devastating criticism. So too was the Communist vision of a vanguard Party leading a unified working class along tramlines which extended into a future Communist society. The once-rallying ideas of unity, reconstruction and modernization, all of which held appeal in the aftermath of the Resistance struggles, and which remained central to both Gaullist and Communist discourse, now lost their intellectual charms. This attack on the conceptions of community and project embodied in the dominant political languages also reduced the attractions of the institutions charged with upholding these definitions of the community's identity: the state and the Party. The characteristic *gauchiste* language was strongly anti-state and anti-Party, engaged in a general critique of institutions.

These criticisms of the Gaullist and Communist images of political community raised all the old questions about the intellectual's identity and function. The *gauchistes* agreed that authentic intellectuals must refuse membership of or affiliation with the institutions of state or Party, since both represented false or partial communities, and both reproduced an illegitimate division of labour. The search for a new vocabulary to describe the relation between intellectual criticism and political action produced one solution, powerful for a time, which denied the intellectual any special attributes or priority, and aspired to establish a direct and unmediated contact between the intellectual and 'the people'. (Sartre's brief reappearance on the public stage after 1968 is explained by the fact that he symbolized a defiance of the division of intellectual and political labour). The new terms of intellectual self-description that became available after 1968 rejected the available forms of self-definition, all of which had assumed a corporate and unitary identity for intellectuals, and assumed too that intellectuals were the legitimate representatives either of certain universal values, or of scientific truths, or of a class. But this new description was short-lived. By the mid-1970s, the fragments produced by the critique of the 'intellectual' or 'philosopher' and his sources of authority had been recomposed: the intellectual or philosopher re-emerged as a unified subject (although now a collective rather than individual one), once again endowed with authority. Thus the emergence of the New Philosophers. That the New Philosophers could, in the mid-1970s, present themselves as a kind of corporate intellectual body, an avant-garde speaking in the name of universal principles and of the oppressed masses, was a measure of the failure of the new critical descriptions that had momentarily appeared after 1968.[75] This recuperation was most prominently manifested by the career of Michel Foucault, who although he ostensibly subverted conventional notions of the intellectual, by the late 1970s had become an intellectual guru, and a central (if often subliminal) reference for the New Philosophers.

The vivisection of the figure of the intellectual was an effect of three different strands of criticism (aimed at three different models or types of intellectual activity), which converged in the late 1960s. The first, shared in common across the broad spectrum of the intellectual Left, was directed against the technocratic modernizers and planners of the Gaullist state. There was consensus among intellectuals of the Left that the processes of modernization and the proliferation amongst the French population of a 'consumer culture' imported from America threatened to dilute the revolutionary identity of the working class; equally there was agreement that economists or social scientists who claimed to produce 'value-neutral' theories about these processes (for example, the theorists of 'industrial society') were bourgeois apologists or treacherous reformists. But if there was agreement that this conception of the intellectual as a functionary of the Republic was a travesty of the intellectual's *métier*, there was considerable disagreement about how this fate could be avoided. One answer was embodied in the model of the 'progressive' intellectual: represented in its pure form by figures like Aragon, progressive intellectuals combined a political identity, given by their membership of the Communist Party, with public careers as cultural and literary figures, or even with successful careers in the academic institutions of the state. The commitment to revolution was asserted by metaphorical means: the arena of dramatic change was displaced from politics and economics to culture. The intellectual volunteered to serve and take instructions from the Party of the working class, and hoped to bring about social and political change through literary, artistic and educational activity, limited always to his or her own field of expertise.[76] A second line of criticism that emerged in the late 1960s attacked both Gaullist and progressivist conceptions. The progressivist model had been effectively wounded by the two-pronged Althusserian attack on the ideology of 'humanism' and on the University, an attack which described both as fundamentally instruments of bourgeois mystification. Commitment to the revolutionary idea was now properly displayed by 'relatively autonomous' intellectuals, engaged in the perfection of a theory which was explicitly divorced from experience. The self-confounding nature of the Althusserian project (it undermined the authority of the university from *within* the university, just as it criticized the Party from *within* the Party itself), was seized upon and exploited by the *gauchistes*, who now in turn introduced a third line of criticism. Calling the Althusserian bluff, they attacked the Party, the academic institutions of the state, and the Althusserian model of correct intellectual activity.

The ruin of the progressivist and Althusserian models provoked initially a return to revolutionary first principles: if, it was claimed, an alliance directed against the coercive powers of the state could be struck between workers, peasants and intellectuals, this would in turn combine with the anti-imperialist struggles in the Third World and together would overthrow the capitalist state and world system. This was apparently a return to Leninism, though the *gauchistes* vehemently rejected any dependence upon the model of the Soviet Communism. Jacques Sauvageot, a student activist, explained in 1968 that 'we no longer speak of 'soviets', because the word is out of fashion [*démodé*]': the preferred word was *autogestion*, a term with special charms because it could be connected to *French* traditions of revolutionary and libertarian socialism.[77] Interest in non-Western revolutionary movements such as the Vietnamese FNL was rooted in the sense that such struggles renewed for intellectuals their contact with real and effective revolutionary movements, which fell outside the ambit of the Soviet version. To Alain Geismar and his associates, for example, the revolutions in China, Cuba and Vietnam were all revolutions against the model of Soviet Communism, and suggested a way of returning to France her revolutionary destiny.[78] This deceptive quality to the proclaimed internationalism of *gauchisme* is often overlooked, but nowhere was it more blatantly manifest than in the writings of André Glucksmann, self-appointed strategist of the *gauchiste* campaigns. To Glucksmann, the significance of the political crisis of 1968 lay in the opportunity it provided for France to repossess her revolutionary heritage, to reassert her role as prime mover and vanguard of world revolution. If the Soviet Revolution had temporarily usurped this role, this was now about to be remedied:

> A revolution in Paris would very shortly bring chain reactions in Western Europe (Rome, Athens, Madrid, etc.) as well as in Eastern Europe (Warsaw) . . . A socialist revolution in France will unleash the tempest step by step . . . a people's revolution in France promises further revolutions of various types, in Eastern Europe and threatens to spread to Russia itself.[79]

France stood poised to shake off the burdens of French and Soviet communism and recover her authentic revolutionary vigour and identity. 'The Communist leadership defends two monopolies,' Glucksmann continued, 'its own—the monopoly it exercises at home by proclaiming itself the only revolutionary force; and the monopoly in Europe of the USSR conceived as the "fatherland" of socialism and as a privileged model of the socialist state.' The new French revolution would destroy this monopoly and unleash a revolution 'tous azimuts', of 'world scope'.[80]

The varieties of *gauchisme* all aimed to forge a new image of France's authentic political community. Viewed from this perspective, it is easier to account for the dogged efforts of the *gauchistes* to move France into a situation of political exception or crisis, their odd talk of civil war, and their call to 'resist' the 'occupying forces' of the 'Fascist' Gaullist state.

'Patrons, c'est la guerre', declared the Maoist *Cause du Peuple*, 'Vive la
Nouvelle Résistance Populaire!'[81] The rhetorical evocation of exceptional
situations was of course a standard strategy for defining community, and
promised a vocabulary for determining who was included and who
excluded, who was trustworthy and who threatening. But the practical
effects of this vocabulary were ironic, and produced an atomization of
the various Leftist groups, leading them to turn against themselves.
Between 1968 and 1972 (the year predicted for the commencement of
the new French revolution),[82] *gauchiste* intentions were enacted in a
variety of practical forms. Vigorous efforts were made to break down the
existing division between mental and manual labour, and to establish
new relations between the intellectual and the 'masses'.[83] The intellectual was commanded henceforth to abjure his or her right to speak in
the name of the masses and to choose silence instead, thus allowing the
masses to speak for themselves. Following Mao's precepts, the Maoists
of the Gauche Prolétarienne called on all intellectuals to 'dismount from
their steeds' and to go forth to 'the people' (a more shapeless category
than the 'proletariat', which Glucksmann had dismissed as a fiction of
Marxist theory): correct and powerful ideas were those of the masses,
not those propagated by the academic purveyors of theory or by the
political parties. What made Maoism so compelling was its suggestion
that revolutionary theory could be made directly available to the masses,
avoiding the monopoly claimed both by the Communist Party manuals
and the specialists of theory. This was the time of *normalien* populism,
of *établissement*: *normaliens* like Christian Riss and Robert Linhart gave
up academic careers, and chose instead to work in industrial factories.[84]
Other practical manifestations of *gauchisme* were the efforts to establish
alternative and independent information networks, and to make these
available for the use of groups newly identified as politically important.
The Gauche Prolétarienne began publishing *La Cause du Peuple* in 1970;
in May 1970, the first issue of the feminist journal *L'Idiot international*
appeared; in February 1971 Michel Foucault announced the formation of
the 'Groupe d'information sur les prisons', designed to enable prisoners
to communicate between themselves.[85] But the most insistent feature of
gauchiste criticism was its utter rejection of given institutional forms:
the University, the Party, the family, were all dismissed. With the exception of the tightly organized Trotskyists (centred around Alain Krivine),
the other *gauchiste* groups pointedly refused both the rigid organizational
structures and the theoretical or pedagogical work often associated with
Left intellectual groups, preferring the feel of 'factory and struggle committees' or clandestine groups like the 'Nouvelle Résistance Populaire':
they rejected forms of Party structure or Party membership cards (heresy
to Leninists). More often than not they defined their own identity
through pure opposition, by means of a usefully imprecise vocabulary of
the 'enemy', which could be used to describe anything from a factory

patron to the police and police informers: all were agents of the bourgeois state. Some of the groups that emerged joined together quite disparate individuals, and their informal character is not surprising: apart from Sartre's own odd coupling with young Maoists, other groups such as 'Secours Rouge' (set up to defend leaders of the Gauche Prolétarienne) clubbed together former Resistance and pre-war activists (like Charles Tillon and Jean Chaintron), with young leftists, and with members of an older generation of protesters against the Algerian war. It was never likely that these loose political compacts would become enduring organizations.

In the years after 1968, the fragmentation of the Left into the splinters of *gauchisme* was matched by pulverization of the collective subject known as the 'intellectual'. The basic split among the intellectuals was between the academic mandarins, the *universitaires* who sought in conventional fashion to pursue professional academic careers within the state's academic institutions and who usually maintained affiliations with a political Party (the Communists and, increasingly after 1971, the Socialists); and the *gauchistes* who (at least initially) refused academic careers, and rejected altogether the mainstream parties of the Left. But the *gauchistes* were themselves divided between more radical voices who proclaimed the death of the traditional intellectual and demanded a dissolution of the intellectual's identity through immersion in the 'masses', and those to the 'right' of this extreme position, who aimed to put into practice the Althusserian line of 'the class struggle in theory': the theoretical text was the arena of battle for these intellectuals.[86]

By 'going to the people', the *gauchistes* hoped to deny their own (usually bourgeois) origins, to forget their professional destiny within France's academic institutions. Yet these anti-intellectualist strains had, to say the least, ambivalent consequences for the identity of the intellectual.[87] Although *gauchiste* anti-intellectualism seemed intent on eliminating the intellectual as a distinct social identity, so dissolving with drastic finality the old theme of the intellectual cut off from life, paradoxically it yielded new resources for intellectual self-description, which served precisely to affirm the intellectual's special identity. By listening to the people's speech, the *gauchistes* asserted, the intellectual would gain access to and master a 'new reality':

> To the extent that the proletariat and the popular masses raise their head, attack the employers and denounce their crimes, a different reality is revealed to intellectuals, one from which they are radically cut off. And the more this new reality, made from blood, tears and struggles, is recognized, the more acute becomes the contradictory position of the intellectual. The essential aspects of reality escape him while, in the consciousness he has of his own function, he is the one who masters and comprehends reality. That is why whenever he rebels against lies, for justice and for

freedom of expression, he is necessarily obliged to place himself *at the service of the masses, that is to say at the service of reality, of the truth* [emphasis added]. For the intellectual, the masses are the future, and to unite with them is to discover the road to genuine democracy.[88]

The intellectual was hereby provided with a new source of authority. Where earlier Sartre had tried to secure his intellectual authority by invoking the weighty presence of the true political community, the oppressed (and later, in the *Critique*, by appeal to a philosophical understanding of the movement of history), and where Althusser had rested his claim to authority on his promise of science and Theory, the *gauchiste* intellectual hoped to combine these two claims. Armed with theory, and in direct spontaneous contact with the People—a genuine concrete universal—, the *gauchiste* intellectual was made the beneficiary of two sources of authority: a technical or disciplinary specialism (gained through academic training), and personal experience gathered through activity as a militant in contact with the people, the authentic political community.

It was this new possibility of unmediated contact with a putative collective political agent that excited Sartre, and pulled him back into the political arena in 1970, to protest against the suppression of *La Cause du Peuple* (with a Parisian sense of appropriate dress he had—before taking to the pavements to hawk the paper—'given up ties and regular suits since 1968').[89] His contacts with Maoist intellectuals and participation in their activities was no mere passing fad, but extended from 1970 until 1974, and he frequently acted as *de facto* editor of *La Cause du Peuple* (and used his influence at *Le Nouvel Observateur* to promote the interests of the Maoist paper to a wider audience).[90] Interviewed in September 1970, he declared that the old-style classical intellectual was now promised the possibility of escape from his permanent condition of 'bad faith', if only he adopted the new intellectual trend set by the Maoists; if, that is, he entered into direct contact with the masses who embodied 'universal society'.[91] Here was precisely that unity of universal form (the intellectual) and particular content (the masses) which, in the 1950s, Sartre had recognized as an impossibility because of the presence of a third, intervening term: the Communist Party. Sartre now literally silenced his old intellectual identity as the leader of a political avant-garde, and appeared at such events as the Lens Tribunal, organized by *La Cause du Peuple*, not in order to speak, but simply as a silent and symbolic bulwark against the state, his mere presence granting the people their right to speak. The intellectual no longer spoke for or represented the people, but acted as an instrumental protector of popular speech.[92]

The arena of intellectual activity had shifted away from the Party Committee room or the University seminar, and to the 'popular tribunal'.

This *gauchiste* creation, was designed to resist the state's justice, and to militate against the judicial procedures and penalities which at this time were being exercised upon the Maoists.[93] At such tribunals, reminiscent of revolutionary situations and more especially of the forms of 'popular justice' employed against collaborators after the Liberation, intellectuals were called upon to testify on the basis of their technical knowledge (for example, engineers were called in as witnesses at the Lens Tribunal, which followed a mining accident there), and decisions were reached through majority voting, which voiced the 'people's will'. The popular tribunals hoped to dissolve the 'bourgeois' concepts of 'justice' and 'truth', and to unmask what had been subsumed under these terms as an infinity of local struggles, conducted against and within institutions whose purpose was none other than domination. These issues were high on Foucault's intellectual agenda during the early 1970s, and they implied a new representation of intellectual authority and power. This was expressed in the form of the dialogue, held between intellectuals, or preferably between intellectual and militant.[94]

The dialogue held in 1972 between Foucault and Deleuze was a chief instance of this mode.[95] Both men simultaneously attacked the standard conception of theory and conventional definitions of the intellectual. Foucault, himself deeply ambivalent about whether he should 'act outside or inside the University', had earlier urged his interlocutors to 'reject all forms of general discourse. This need for theory is still part of the system we reject'.[96] According to Deleuze, on the other hand, the upheavals of 1968 created the possibility of a new relationship between theory and practice. Theory was now to be reconceived as local and fragmentary,

> a system of relays within a larger sphere, within a multiplicity of parts that are both theoretical and practical. A theorising intellectual, for us, is no longer a subject, a representing or representative consciousness. Those who act and struggle are no longer represented, either by a group or union that appropriates the right to stand as their conscience. Who speaks and acts? It is always a multiplicity, even within the person who speaks and acts. All of us are 'groupuscules'.[97]

This refusal of the principle and possibility of political and intellectual representation was echoed by Foucault's celebration of the authenticity of immediate experience. For him, the lesson of the events of May 1968 was that

> the intellectual discovered that the masses no longer need him to gain knowledge: they know perfectly well, without illusion; they know far better than he and they are certainly capable of expressing themselves. But there exists a system of power which blocks, prohibits, and invalidates this discourse and this knowledge, a power not only found in the manifest

authority of censorship, but one which profoundly and subtly penetrates an entire societal network. Intellectuals are themselves agents of this system of power—the idea of their responsibility for 'consciousness' and discourse forms part of the system. (p. 207)

From this recognition of 'the indignity of speaking for others', Deleuze drew the 'theoretical fact that only those directly concerned can speak in a practical way on their own behalf' (p. 209). It was a view expressed with equal (and equally disabling) indignation by other intellectuals (Roland Barthes, for instance, in one of the numerous diagnoses of teacher-student relations that appeared in the early 1970s, went so far as to urge intellectuals and teachers to 'a yet more stringent call to silence, to a renunciation of speech in the face of its innate authoritarianism').[98]

Foucault, in response to 'the political opening created around those years [1968]', was engaged during the 1970s in manœuvres that had important consequences. He ostentatiously abandoned the pursuit of Hegelian conceptions of progressive historical meaning, in favour of the perpetually suspicious disposition of Nietzschean genealogy ('what does this person want, who says . . .'), and turned against the existing models of intellectual radicalism. Here, his links with such groups as the Maoists served him well, allowing him to claim radical credentials and an anti-bourgeois position, while releasing him from any hesitations in his public criticisms of radical intellectuals like Sartre and Althusser. Sartre's *Critique of Dialectical Reason* he dismissed as 'the last work of the nineteenth century', the 'magnificent and pathetic effort of a nineteenth-century man to think the twentieth century'. About Althusser—a personal friend—he was more polite, but his drift was unmistakable. Of Althusser's favourite intellectual pastime, for instance, Foucault offered this judgement: 'I believe the problem does not consist in drawing the line between that in a discourse which falls under the category of scientificity or truth, and that which comes under some other category but in seeing historically how effects of truth are produced within discourses which are themselves neither true nor false.'[99] These attacks, like his criticisms of the 'universal intellectual', undermined the earlier Sartrean and Althusserian languages of intellectual self-description and self-justification.[100] But if Foucault appeared to subvert the identity of the intellectual as a privileged representative with a special vocation, this was mere conjuring, for in the very act of destroying the conventional notion of the intellectual as a distinct figure with a public 'role', Foucault defined and established a new function for the intellectual.[101] By preserving the term 'intellectual', and by introducing the new term 'power', a fertile opposition was maintained, from which could be generated a new language of self-description. The intellectual now no longer 'represented', say, the consciousness of a class engaged in struggle, nor was he a purveyor of revolutionary science and truths: he was indifferent as between bourgeois or proletarian consciousness, or truths. Instead, the intellectual was defined by his relation to 'power', a conceptually much more plastic notion. The counterpart to this critique of 'representation' was the affirmation of a multiplicity of 'powers', of dispersed and local struggles. The masses, of course, knew all about (because they experienced) these power struggles; yet power itself remained a 'secret' to the masses. Thus Foucault, with recovered authority, could ask rhetorically, 'the question of power remains a total enigma. Who exercises power? And in what sphere?'[102] Here, once again, was a role for the intellectual. His or her function now was to unearth this secret, to make this enigma speak. Foucault, driven by an ambition to displace the earlier models of intellectuals and politics, presented his own analysis of truth and power precisely as a novel way of conceiving the political role of the intellectual:

> It is necessary to think of the political problems of intellectuals not in terms of 'science' and 'ideology', but in terms of 'truth' and 'power'. And thus the question of the professionalization of intellectuals and the division between intellectuals and manual labour can be envisaged in a new way.[103]

The vocabulary was more modern, but the questions were uniform with those of earlier generations of the postwar period.

These intellectual reconfigurations drew the sting of some of the more radical aspects of the *gauchiste* attack, and were a necessary precondition for the emergence of the New Philosophers.[104] But it was more directly political developments and disappointments that decisively altered the temper of Leftist intellectuals. The actions of the *gauchistes* had been motivated by the expectation that revolution was a real and imminent possibility in France, and some even went so far as to predict a specific apocalyptic year, 1972. In fact, 1972 saw a collapse of this imagined revolutionary horizon. The working class showed itself to be uninterested in militant action. It did not, as *gauchiste* intellectuals had fondly hoped, rise in open revolt when one of tis members, the young Maoist Pierre Overney, was shot dead in February 1972 by a Renault factory watchman, and indeed one of the ironic and unintended effects of 'going to the people' was the discovery that most were not particularly interested in revolutionary politics.[105] Political events further fed the disaffection of the *gauchistes*. In June 1972 the Socialist and Communist leaderships signed the Common Programme.[106] This had the support of the *universitaires*, the academics with Party affiliations, but for the *gauchistes* it raised the threatening possibility that the 'institutional' Left might gain power. In the legislative elections of March 1973, the united Left made significant gains, the Socialists winning 102 seats and the Communists 73. Caught between fear and disappointment, the Gauche Prolétarienne dissolved itself in 1973 (the last issue of *La Cause du Peuple* appeared on

13 September 1973). And in June 1974, the first volume of the French translation of Solzhenitsyn's *L'Archipel du goulag* appeared. The career of André Glucksmann instanced most strikingly the direction now taken by many former Leftists. In response to Solzhenitsyn's work, Glucksmann published *La Cuisinière et le mangeur d'hommes* in 1975.[107] Reading the writings of Solzhenitsyn and the Russian dissidents was, he announced with a typically narcissistic twist of mind, a form of self-knowledge for French and Western intellectuals: 'the Russian dissidents can in this respect help us to know ourselves better' (p. 11). Glucksmann defined his identity as an intellectual in the terms advanced by the *gauchistes* and endorsed by Foucault. The intellectual would simply listen and encourage, and thus confirm his renunciation of a discourse of special authority or power: 'to listen to Lip or tortured Russia requires greater modesty. That is to say, democracy' (p. 11). Yet, although Glucksmann chastised Sartre's political positions, the intellectual strategy of the essay was a return to that of the classical, 'old-style' Sartrean intellectual, who claimed to speak in the name of and for the 'pleb' or the oppressed people. The substance of the New Philosophers' work and filiations are discussed elsewhere.[108] Their importance for present purposes lies in their efforts to establish a new description of the intellectual as a 'dissident', unaligned with political parties and situated outside the state, and able to speak directly in the name of what Glucksmann termed the 'pleb', a figure hardly less allegorical than Sartre's 'worker' or Althusser's 'masses'.[109]

Why was the characteristic discursive style of the New Philosophers— an odd mixture of celebrated spontaneous rebellion, proclaimed subjectivity, anti-rationalism, and religious imagery, all breathlessly delivered through a confessional grille—taken seriously as a way of speaking about political matters? (Some sense of the renown of the New Philosophers is conveyed by the fact that even the Socialist Party Manifesto thought them worth a mention).[110] Unlike Sartre, who used his review, *Les Temps Modernes*, to spread his message, and unlike Althusser, who presided over the *thurnes* (seminar rooms) of the Ecole Normale Supérieure, the New Philosophers made use of new mediatic forms. From the 1960s onwards, the position of intellectuals in the broader French social structure significantly changed. This was very largely the result of the economic development France experienced during the *trentes glorieuses*, part of the great postwar upswing of capitalist expansion in the western world that engendered higher levels of consumption, and massive expansion in the areas of cultural production and diffusion.[111] Young intellectuals embarked on professional careers which—in conventional Marxist (and indeed in Althusserian) analysis— would have been viewed as functional positions for the reproduction of the state's ideological domination of society. The development of new cultural institutions and forms, which linked the University to the media, made available to intellectuals a greater diversity of career paths than had existed previously (*Apostrophes*, the launch-pad for all 'media intellectuals', received its first television broadcast in January 1975). These newly ramified networks of diffusion were a vital facility for the propagation of the New Philosophers' views, and helped to smooth the otherwise awkward passage from street militant to columnist for *Le Figaro*. The message of the New Philosophers, however, cannot be entirely explained by reference to the structural location from where they spoke: rather, it was a direct response to the political situation in the late 1970s. Recalling this situation reveals both how their concerns were continuous with those of the *gauchistes*, and how their political views converged with and gained impetus from the arguments put about by other intellectual circuits, all worried by the prospect of an electoral victory by the parties of the Left.

Paradoxically, the major political disappointment for the *gauchistes* in the years after 1968 came not from the reinstallation of Gaullist government, but from the Left: the signing in June 1972 of the Common Programme, which sealed an electoral pact between the Socialist and the Communist Parties.[112] With the government of the Right terminally enfeebled, the political initiative seemed to pass to the parties of the Left, and the prospect of actually having Communists in government (even if they now claimed to be 'Eurocommunists') hastened the abandonment of extreme-Left politics. By 1978, the events of a decade earlier were commemorated by a series of writings that chronicled the trajectory of the *gauchistes*, the '1968 generation', and described their drift away from the mainstream Left.[113] The break between intellectuals and the political Left was encouraged by a generational struggle. Intellectual shifts in France, as anywhere, have a definite oedipal dimension, and generational strife has often been a significant incitement (though, needless to say, recognition of this point reveals nothing about the content of such shifts).[114] The young militants of 1968 were the first postwar generation whom the Communist Party were unable to incorporate within Party organizations. This generation, shaped by the experience of participation in the struggles against colonialism in Algeria and (more vicariously) in Vietnam, and singularly unimpressed by the Party's mortgage on its Resistance past, felt nothing but contempt for their Communist elders. The generational distance was manifest in the contrasting attitudes each took towards the anti-colonial independence struggles: where many Communist student groups had called for the unconditional victory of the Algerian and Vietnamese independence movements (the Trotskyist JCR launched in 1966 the slogan 'FNL [Vietnam Liberation Front] Vaincra', which the Party judged 'gauchiste'), older Communists (and the Party leadership) spoke merely of a negotiated peace.[115]

Superimposed upon these generational tensions was a rivalry whose sources lay in a very French stratification. This could be described as a contest between the 'low intelligentsia' (constituted by the professional teachers employed by the French educational system) and the 'high intelligentsia' (the traditional intellectuals, 'those authorized to express individual opinions on public matters').[116] Ever since 1906, professional academics and teachers had provided an important constituency of support for the French socialist movement; during the 1970s, at the very moment when this now much expanded strata affirmed their support for the renewed Socialist Party,[117] intellectuals such as Foucault abandoned explicit support for the Left, and even Sartre finally admitted in 1977 that he had for some years past ceased to believe in Marxism.[118] But, if there was a perceptible trace of snobbery here, and while generational frictions did matter, the real impetus for the intellectual break with left-wing politics came from the possibility that the Parties of the Left might be elected into office. This break occurred before the legislative elections in the spring of 1978, at a point when the Left seemed set for electoral success. Although the Common Programme broke down in 1977, Left intellectuals still feared that even if the Socialists did emerge as the largest single Left party (as it in fact did, for the first time since 1936), a Left government would remain dominated in important ways by the Communists.[119]

The mood of intellectual anxiety was revealed in two essays written at the time, both by long-standing critics of the French Communist Party and of the Soviet regime. The first, by Cornelius Castoriadis, was a scathing attack on the French Left, and loudly forewarned of the consequences if the Left were to gain political power.[120] Castoriadis' premise was that 'the internal logic of the Left is the logic of bureaucratic centralization', and he dismissed the Communist Party's 'evolution' towards Eurocommunism as a rhetorical sham, since, he claimed, it remained 'a politically totalitarian bureaucratic Apparatus' still in the pocket of the Soviet Union.[121] He concluded that 'one can no longer exclude . . . the possibility of an evolution wherein the Stalinists, successful in their infatuation with social protest movements and in provoking a split in the Socialist Party, attempt to seize power for themselves and in alliance with the CERES',[122] and that thus 'we must speak of the ever-present risk constituted by the existence of the totalitarian Apparatus of the PCF, as well as the reinforcement of this risk by the tendencies in the PS'.[123] A second and converging text, which also spelt a break between the intellectuals and the Left parties, was an analysis of the political situation by Castoriadis' one-time colleague, Claude Lefort.[124] Lefort acknowledged that the success of New Philosophers like Bernard-Henri Lévy was an index of a fresh political sensibility amongst intellectuals of the Left, which expressed a realization among the *gauchistes*—Trotskyists, Maoists, and others—that their aspirations had no chance of fulfilment under a government of the Left, since 'a government of the Left can *accelerate* [emphasis added] the process of state bureaucratization'. Lefort

cautioned that even though the Socialists might now command more
electoral support than the Communists, it would be mistaken to conclude that the Communists would accept a politically subordinate role
in the formation of a Left government. The Communist Party commanded an extremely well organized party apparatus (which the Socialists lacked) and the major trade unions such as the Confédération
Générale du Travail remained Communist, or Communist-dominated.
The Communists would therefore assume a major role in any Left
government. For Lefort, the 1978 elections were not merely about a
change in the party of government, and he warned that 'at stake in
these elections is not only the government, but the regime'.[125] This was
Lefort's most serious charge: that the Union of the Left was a Trojan
horse.[126] 'Marchais displays the liberal face of Brezhnev's socialism,
Mitterrand the liberal face of Marchais' socialism' (p. 142). The Socialists,
like their Communist allies, were blind to 'the novel, massive, most
enigmatic and challenging event of our epoch: the birth and worldwide
expansion of totalitarianism under the flag of Communism'.[127] The only
way to confront this question, Lefort concluded, was to break entirely
with Marxism and develop a philosophy of 'radical democracy'.[128]

The main political parties of the French Left could no longer count on
the support of the intellectuals after the spring of 1978, and from then
on the abyss between the parties of the Left and the intellectuals grew
until, by 1983, this had become a topic of public debate.[129] Recognition
of this break was delayed, largely a result of the confusions created
by the ambiguity with which established intellectuals like Sartre and
Foucault responded towards the upstart New Philosophers. They were
dismissive of the intellectual credentials of the New Philosophers, but
they did not attack the political significance and implications of their
message.[130] In fact, there was a tacit agreement on this score. And
politically, what the New Philosophers were broadcasting broke political
and intellectual taboos in postwar France. In a vigorous polemic against
the Communists, they used the notion of totalitarianism to draw an
explicit equivalence between the political regimes of Hitler and Stalin.
This, the moment of totalitarianism's re-entry into the vocabulary of
French political debate, coincided with a precise political juncture: the
expected electoral victory of the Left (it is worth remembering that at
this time Mitterrand was not averse to quoting Marx and Engels in his
speeches).[131] It is fair to say that if the Left had not appeared near
to political power, it is extremely unlikely that the New Philosophers
would have gained their phenomenal (if momentary) success.

That the New Philosophers did introduce a sudden decompression
into the hermeticism of the French Left was confirmed by the subsequent wreckage of French Marxism.[132] But if their ambition was to
produce a political theory, then they failed miserably. The intellectual
career of André Glucksmann—by far the most interesting and complex

of the New Philosophers—oscillated between a form of political realism characteristic of the hawkish hard Right, and an anti-statism based on a faith in populism.[133] All of the figures associated with the New Philosophy operated with a naïve conception of power and, relying on the hope of a popular revolt against political domination (for all their novelty, they were old-fashioned enough to follow the established principles of the French Left when faced with the problem of political power: the answer was to be found outside the political field, in the social body), ended up with an anti-statism as utopian as the best statist ambitions.[134] The threnodies of the New Philosophers found their greatest echo, however, not in political theory but in other intellectual disciplines, especially anthropology. Pierre Clastres' anti-statist theories, for instance, based on his studies of societies without states lent a wider anthropological focus to the often wayward parochialism of the New Philosophers.[135] During the mid-1970s, Clastres was associated with Lefort and Castoriadis and with the younger generation of intellectuals centred around the reviews *Libre* (founded in May 1977) and *Textures*. *Libre* (its title presaged the coming interest in liberal and libertarian thought), ran for only a few years, but its particular combination of philosophy and ethnology helped to lessen the importance of *Les Temps Modernes* (which until then had served as a link between these two disciplines). Clastres' attack on the use of Marxist concepts in anthropological work was particularly resonant, since the discipline of anthropology had been so influenced by the Marxist approaches of Godelier and Althusser.[136] The work of Clastres and the *Libre* group was a perfect instance of the displacement of political thinking into other academic disciplines and specialist vocabularies, an example of how 'some ethnographers . . . like the philosophers, proceed by way of Amazonia to speak of Stalinism, thus projecting the shadow of our own terrors and phantasies onto a magnified image of others, and placing anthropology inside our own history'.[137]

III

By the late 1970s, the umbilical attachment of intellectuals to the vocabulary of revolution was broken. The New Philosophers had played a role in this, but the fragments out of which a new political vocabulary could be formed were to be found elsewhere. Relevant here were the arguments of two groups: what was called 'la deuxième gauche' (comprising the *autogestionnaire* and Rocardian currents of the Socialist Party, along with intellectuals associated with the Catholic trade unions), and 'Le Front anti-totalitaire'. The latter was a chimerical conjunction of intellectuals and political reviews, which included Castoriadis, Lefort, and Edgar Morin, as well as François Furet and the group of intellectuals centred around Aron (and involved with reviews like *Commentaire* or the more right-wing *Contrepoint*), and the Catholic Left, whose most influential voice was the review *Esprit*. All would find a voice in *Le Débat*, which quickly established itself as the most influential Parisian intellectual review of the 1980s.

These otherwise dissimilar individuals and groups were united by an interest in the problem of 'actually existing socialism' as found in the Soviet Union and eastern Europe, and in the implications of this for the Left in western capitalist democracies. Their attention was focused by two issues: the question of the Gulag, so palpably raised by Solzhenitsyn, and the issue of the intellectual freedom of the East European dissidents. Unlike the debates of the 1950s, when the very existence of Soviet labour camps was doubted,[138] it was now widely accepted that the Soviet Union did have such camps: the disagreement turned on the implications of this for appraisals of the Soviet regime's character (was it similar in form to a Latin American dictatorship? Or did it possess a special political logic of its own, which placed it qualitatively apart?). Was it, as the Communists insisted, 'un pays pas comme les autres'? The influx of intellectual dissidents from eastern Europe (from Czechoslovakia after 1968 and from the Soviet Union and other Socialist countries during the 1970s), placed at the centre of French intellectual life the question of human rights and democratic freedoms.[139] In some sense the discovery of, and sudden interest in, these questions equalled in its abstraction the anti-statist posturings of the New Philosophers. As Castoriadis put it in 1978 'simply to denounce totalitarianism and defend the Rights of Man is certainly very important . . . but it does not constitute a politics'.[140] Some went further, and saw the obsession with human rights as a smokescreen which obscured the issues French intellectuals had really to think hard about:

> Let us not be fooled: the rights of man can be nothing more than a way of avoiding—by naming and putting to one side—all those questions which stem from the collapse of the societal project forged during the course of a century and a half of the workers' movement.[141]

But, while the intellectuals now took very seriously the questions raised by political dissidence in the socialist societies, in France the political parties of both Left and Right persisted with an obstinately ambivalent posture towards the Soviet Union. In June 1977, President Giscard D'Estaing entertained Soviet Party Secretary Leonid Brezhnev at a state banquet to which leading French intellectuals had been invited. None, however, attended: Sartre and Foucault, for instance, were to be found at an alternative gathering held the same evening for Soviet dissidents such as Leonid Plyusch.[142] The political parties of the Left were even more compromised. In the early 1970s, western European Communist parties, spearheaded by the Spanish and Italians, inflated the notion of 'Eurocommunism' as a doctrinal *cordon sanitaire* against Soviet Communism. In a reversal of earlier policy, the French Communists moved—relatively late in the short lifespan of the Eurocommunist doctrine (in 1975, during the Portuguese crisis)—towards the line of the Spanish and Italian Communists. As a result the Communist Party began to take a more critical line than ever before towards the Soviet Union: in November 1975, for instance, the Party daily, *L'Humanité*, criticized psychiatric internment for political purposes in the Soviet Union, and at its twenty-second Congress in 1976 the Party abandoned the concept of the dictatorship of the proletariat. The substantive political content of Eurocommunism was unsurprisingly vague, but it was the declared attitudes towards the Prague Spring of 1968 and its subsequent suppression by the Soviet Union that were viewed by intellectuals as the most revealing test of the political intentions of the various national versions of Eurocommunism. Customarily, the French Communists were studiedly ambivalent on both matters.[143] They had tentatively adopted a more critical tone in their discussions of the Soviet Union, and in particular of the Stalinist period. In 1978, for instance, a group of Party historians and political scientists published *L'URSS et nous* which tried to establish a theoretical basis for a distance between the French Communists and the Soviet model.[144] The study was primarily a description and rejection of the Stalinist terror (at an explanatory level, it simply invoked the old thesis of Russian 'backwardness'); yet it did—and this was new—criticize the monopolization of power by the Soviet Party, and did so in the name of greater pluralism and democracy. Lenin, however, escaped any criticism. But such critical flickers were soon extinguished, as the Communist Party leadership recurred to its well-worn language: in early 1979, Georges Marchais began to speak of the 'globally positive balance-sheet' of the Soviet Union and its allies; in the summer of 1979 he emphasized the achievements of the Soviet system, and in January 1980 he appeared on television to affirm his Party's support and approval for the Soviet invasion of Afghanistan.[145]

These were disastrous moves, given that the attentions of the French intellectuals were now focused on the Soviet Union, and that, as Jorge Semprun noted, 'today the touchstone of any Left thought is its attitude towards the Soviet Union'.[146] A significant and visible intellectual index of evaluations of the Soviet Union was displayed by responses to Solzhenitsyn. On this issue, the Communist Party diverged little from the Soviet line. The Party press dismissed Solzhenitsyn's work as part of a general conspiracy to discredit the Soviet Union. The Soviet Union was not in fact practising systematic political repression, and dissidence was the work of a few isolated writers, within a system whose general tendency was indeed towards democracy. More specifically, the French Communists alleged that the attention given to Russian dissidents was a concerted tactic by the Right to ruin the French Left's electoral chances.

These chances had come to rely, since 1972, on the Common Programme, agreed by the Communists and the Socialists. The agreement
in fact also acted as a constraint on the Socialists. Some weeks before
the French translation of the *Gulag* was published, François Mitterrand
expressed agreement with the Communist view that the Soviet Union
was moving towards democracy when he wrote that 'for my part, I am
persuaded that what is most important is not what Solzhenitsyn says,
but the fact that he is able to say it'.[147]

The differing reactions towards the problem of the Gulag displayed by,
on the one hand, the Socialists and Communists, and on the other, the
intellectuals, was a good measure of the chasm that separated them. The
Socialists did condemn the Gulag (they had by now dropped the earlier
discourse of special pleading for the particular conditions of the Soviet
Union), but they condemned it in terms of infractions against human
rights (that is, they likened it to the repression of the South American
dictatorships). The Socialists were happiest, however, not to discuss the
question at all. They justified this silence on two grounds: that it was an
irrelevance—French Socialism (à la Jaurès, Guesde and Blum) was a
tradition historically distinct from Soviet or even German Marxism, and
thus the question of the Gulag had no special implication for French
politics; and that it was an impertinence, introduced into the national
debate by a Right bent on splitting the popular unity of the Left. 'We
cannot consider the societies of the East as "socialist" societies', the
Socialist Party Manifesto declared, and therefore 'the Socialists have no
self-criticism to make.'[148] They could not have more totally misjudged
the intellectual mood. For the intellectuals, the question of the Gulag
and its relation to the idea of the Revolution had gained a massive
centrality. At a time when the French Socialists, newly in office, were
appointing committees to prepare celebrations for the bicentenary of
the Revolution in 1989 (here was another chance to affirm modern
France's founding myth, its universal mission), French intellectuals concluded that if France were indeed Mitterrand's much vaunted pluralist
democracy, then this was a consequence less of the Revolution than of
the Restoration, which had immunized France against the dangers of
totalitarianism.[149] As one commentator described it, it was not possible
to imagine a greater conflict of mentalities than that between those who
studied the symbolism of revolutionary statues, and those who were
placing roses at the feet of these statues,[150] the intellectuals who were
analysing the mythic character of the Revolution, and the politicians
who were, precisely, mythologizing it.[151] It was on the terrain of the
historiography of the French Revolution, that inexhaustible patrimony
of France's modern political identity, that a decisive argument was
advanced, which established a new political vocabulary to describe both
the nation's identity and the place of its intellectuals.

CHAPTER SIX

The Revolution is over: François Furet and the Historians' Challenge

The history of the French Revolution is . . . always more or less an introduction to an understanding of the political wisdom of the French.
Claude Mazauric, *Sur la Révolution français* (Paris, 1970).

The frontiers of French identity are not spatial . . . but temporal.
Jean-Pierre Rioux, 'Twentieth Century Historiography: Clio in a Phrygian Bonnet', in J. Howorth and G. Ross (eds), *Contemporary France* (London, 1987).

The whole problem of revolutions is to bring them to a close.
François Furet, 'Une Révolution sans révolution?',
Le Nouvel Observateur, 28 February 1986.

In arguing about revolutions, intellectuals in France have been engaged in disputes about differing conceptions of the nation's identity. This is most apparent in the controversies surrounding their own Revolution of 1789: these often arcane disagreements have never been purely academic in significance, but have involved conflicting definitions of the political community, and of the agencies that may legitimately re-present the community. The historiography of the French Revolution is notoriously—indeed necessarily—susceptible to shifting political taste and, since so much of the terminology of modern French political debate is descended directly from the revolutionary decade of the 1790s, it is hardly a matter of surprise that the history of the Revolution is available in counter-revolutionary, Republican, Socialist and Communist guises.[1] Yet political concerns did not simply shape historical writing on the Revolution; the writing of this history in turn has served as a medium of political theory. This was particularly true for the intellectual culture of the French Left, which lacked or avoided any elaborated language of political theory, partly as a consequence of institutional arrange-ments (in France the discipline of 'science politique' was a creation of the Right, and remained closely associated with the academic disciplines of 'Droit' and the 'sciences juridiques').[2] Republicans, Socialists, Com-munists, even the *gauchistes* (with their fondness for the Paris Commune of 1871) tended to do their political thinking in other forms and vocabu-laries and in particular they resorted a terminology drawn from the long history of French revolutionary politics, from 1789 to the late nineteenth century. Revolutionary historiography was an inexhaustible source of exemplary tales, both inspirational and cautionary. In the absence of a discourse which described differentiated rights and the institutional arrangements needed to secure and enforce such rights, the vacuum was filled by an historical legend of political emancipation and development whose starting-point was the Revolution of 1789.

The significance of François Furet's aggressive reinterpretation of the French Revolution rests upon the fact that the intellectual Left's political imagination has been dominated by revolutionary historiography. Furet's attack, apparently little more than a routine professional skirmish within academic historiography, had far greater scope, and was motivated by a lucid sense that shifting the terms of historical understanding would have directly political consequences. His arguments against the idea of revolution, against the Jacobin and Bolshevik views of political representation, and against the schema of historical development assumed by intellectuals of the Left, together aspired to undermine the credibility of revolutionary politics. And in doing this, Furet advanced new terms to appraise the meaning of France's post-revolutionary history, along with a new definition of the nation's political identity. His initial target was what he labelled 'le catéchisme révolutionnaire', an accumulation of Jacobin and Marxist pieties about the identity and significance of the French Revolution. The analytic focus of this 'catechism' was directed towards revealing an underlying and determinate matrix of social causality that would demonstrate why the Revolution (understood as a set of political adjustments to more primary social and economic disjunctions) must repeat itself, in formally similar, if substantively different, shape. But to Furet, this analytic focus distorted altogether both the causation and the true meaning of the Revolution, and even more damagingly it deformed understandings of modern politics. His own dominant themes derived from a return to older questions, which had preoccupied the writers of the Thermidorian period, the *Doctrinaires*, and Tocqueville: how could the Revolution be brought to its conclusion, terminated? Why did the Revolution 'begin well but turn out badly'? What was the character of the Terror and how did it relate to what preceded it? This recovery of questions first raised immediately after 1789, by thinkers who in large part accepted the Revolution but who wrote before the rise of revolutionary socialism, highlighted Furet's determination to construct a form of political thinking that was in no way counter- or anti-revolutionary, but which abandoned the conviction that revolution continued to be a persisting possibility in the French situation. In short, it heralded a novel project in postwar intellectual life: the attempt to create a distinctively French political liberalism.

Furet's argument was part of the more general drift away from revolutionary politics which occurred in French intellectual life in the mid-1970s; but, quite unusually, his own position connected what had often been a rather abstract critique of the idea of revolution to more substantive questions in French history. His assault on this notion took the form of a critique of Jacobinism: in his view, the Jacobin conception of revolution and revolutionary power contained all the essential characteristics of modern revolutionary politics, and therefore to show the incoherence of one was to demolish the credentials of the other. He engaged quite self-consciously in polemical battle with his contemporaries and beyond them with the entire tradition of academic historiography, and made explicit his intentions: to avoid any fussy tinkering with the given machinery of historiographical dispute, and to install a wholly new conception of the Revolution, a new appraisal of its meaning and significance. His ambitions extended yet further: fully recognizing the ways in which the modern concept of revolution was shaped by a particular understanding of the French Revolution, Furet's critical barrage was directed against 'the exorbitant privilege assigned to the idea of revolution' itself.[3]

A complex mesh of intellectual and political interests motivated Furet's arguments, and these are best recovered by considering the targets he attacked. Here, the academic history of the French Revolution is undoubtedly the most important context for situating his work. He pursued his purposes by means of a number of not always consistent arguments, and tracing these arguments and inconsistencies help to focus upon his political intentions. There are at least three separate moments to his project: his initial and unsuccessful bid, made in the mid-1960s, to modify conceptions of the French Revolution; the far more resonant critique of the idea of revolution made in the late 1970s, in quite different political circumstances; and the elaboration of his claims during the 1980s, culminating in his triumphant domination of the bicentennial interpretations of the Revolution and its meaning for France's history.

I

Furet's approach was distinguished by a deep sensitivity towards both the historiography of the French Revolution and his own situation within this tradition of understanding.[4] This interest was manifest in, for instance, his desire to discover a new ancestry for his own interpretations: a loose genealogy that over the years has grown to include Tocqueville, Cochin, Quinet, Michelet, Burke, Constant, Guizot.[5] None of them professional academic historians, their views were largely ignored by the 'revolutionary catechism', the tradition cultivated by

Aulard, Mathiez, Lefebvre and Soboul. Furet's work was consistently motivated by strong antagonism towards the professionalization of the history of the Revolution, and especially towards the monopoly over correct knowledge of the Revolution claimed by the university. The claim to a scientific, positivist understanding of the Revolution was of course fundamental to the self-understanding of the Third Republic. The Third Republican university had separated history from philosophy, and refused all general philosophies of history, preferring instead to institute a clear division of intellectual labour:

> In becoming an academic specialty the history of the Revolution became both more professionalized and more narrow. Scholarship was supposed to extend the range of knowledge and limit that of interpretation. It claimed the certainty of science and narrowed the scope of debate and disagreement ... the new course in revolutionary history gave the professor privileged rights to exploit the domain ... In every possible way it sought guarantees against excess.[6]

Tamed by the university, the Revolution was harnessed to explicit political ends. Established as a monument around which the nation was urged to rally in defence of the Republic, it was declared, in Clemenceau's famous phrase, to be 'un bloc', an indivisible unity that could not be questioned without doubting the integrity of the Republic itself.

A new breed of clerics, the academic historians, were installed to secure this self-justifying political legend of the Third Republic, a task which in Furet's account they were only too eager to fulfil. Alphonse Aulard (1849–1928), appointed in 1886 to the first permanent chair in the History of the French Revolution at the Sorbonne (he occupied it for thirty-six years), perfected a fusion of Comte and Michelet, designed to establish on a scientific historical basis the view that 1789 had founded a new secular and humanitarian religion, which embodied the principle of modern progress.[7] By endowing the history of the nation with universal significance, Aulard fulfilled the specific political purpose of history as a discipline within the 'Ecole laïque': to provide a source of moral and patriotic indoctrination.[8] The official Republican orthodoxy was of course challenged and criticized by both the Left and the Right. The confusions introduced by the Dreyfus affair, for instance, had given the Right an opportunity to proclaim themselves as the true defenders of 'la patrie',[9] while on the Left the socialist and solidarist movements also disputed the Republic's claim to represent the revolutionary nation. But, partly in response to the turn-of-the-century challenge from the Right, Jaurès integrated the socialists into the Republican fold: in his formulation of Marxism in evolutionary terms, the Republic (and its myth of self-legitimation) could be embraced because it contained in embryo the principles of a future socialist society. Jaurès—in Furet's eyes, 'the last writer, the last "amateur" to deal with the Revolution'—successfully reconciled the socialist movement and Third Republican traditions through his story of the French Republic's political evolution towards socialism, a development whose point of origin was the diverse events of the revolutionary years between 1789–93 (though Jaurès was careful to excise the Babouvist moment from this narrative, an episode so important to Guesde and Vaillant and symbolically revived after the Commune). For Jaurès, the Revolution and its legacy of principles, institutions, and ideology, held out the promised of a yet-to-be achieved socialism. The present Republic affirmed the authenticity of this un-folding process, but by definition it was a transient form:

> We consider the French Revolution to be an immense and admirably fertile event; but it is not, in our view, a conclusive fact, one that makes subsequent history simply an unfurling of its consequences. The French Revolution prepared indirectly the accession of the proletariat. It achieved the two conditions essential for socialism: democracy and capitalism. But it was, in essence, the political accession of the bourgeoisie.[10]

Jaurès traced an evolution and progress whose dynamic principles were national, and potential conflicts between his strongly gallocentric per-spective and his evident pacifism and internationalism were ignored. This synthetic account, which brought together the universalizing claims of socialist politics with the peculiarities of national history, was widely accepted by the Left. It was relegated and superseded not by intellectual argument and refutation, but by political events: the 1914–18 War, and above all the Bolshevik Revolution of 1917. The Jaurèsian claim that the true promise of the Revolution lay at some point in France's future now had to confront and make sense of a new fact: the Bolshevik Revolution declared itself to be precisely that proletarian revolution which, in the Jaurèsian account, the French Revolution had prefigured, and which by rights should have occurred in France.

For Furet, from this point the understanding of the Revolution veered badly off course. Albert Mathiez (1874–1932), who in 1922 succeeded Aulard to the Sorbonne chair,[11] was a prime villain in this story. We have seen already how Mathiez integrated the French and Bolshevik Revolutions within a single continuous narrative. To Furet, the effects of this association were disastrous: 'Ever since Mathiez the ghost of the Russian Revolution has haunted the history of the French Revolution, and a Communist vulgate has supplanted Aulard's republican version . . . After him, the discourse on the French Revolution contained between the lines a second discourse on the Soviet Revolution.'[12] The result was the installation of an interpretation which at once arrogated to itself scientific validity and conveyed a blatantly political message. The academic orthodoxy that was enshrined, the 'social interpretation', was 'based not only on Marxism but on a democratic sensitivity to the common folk, the forgotten of history'.[13] The emphasis on social and

economic history, and on classes, combined with the ambition to develop
a scientific understanding, helped during the inter-war years to establish
points of contact with the *Annales* school; but the study of the French
Revolution became 'commonly dominated after 1917 by the Leninist
version of Marxism', and was thus made 'even less capable of blazing a
trail toward a "scientific" interpretation'.[14] The social interpretation
focused above all on the social causes and conflicts of the Revolution,
and devoted much effort to narrating and celebrating revolutionary
events; but it stayed largely oblivious to its consequences. It 'enabled
historians to ignore the enigma that had so intrigued liberals—and
Marx along with them—a century before, that of the contrast between
the results of the Revolution and its unfolding'.[15] No attempt was made
to explain the diversity of political forms of government which emerged
in the century after the 1789 Revolution, nor to address the problem
of nineteenth-century France's persistent political instability (if the
Revolution confirmed the accession to political power of the bourgeoisie,
why was this not reflected in stable bourgeois political forms?). Most
damagingly of all, in Furet's opinion, the revolutionary Terror was
explained away, as a mere effect of contingent circumstances, and
its relation to the revolutionary process was left unexamined: after
all, devotees of the social interpretation could assert that 'the Soviet
experience had demonstrated the necessity of the dictatorship and the
Terror'.[16]

After the end of the Second World War, the 'social interpretation'
congealed in the hands of historians associated with the Communist
Party. The Party was committed to developing its own politically inflected historiography, and it put great effort into attracting historians to
the cause: during the 1940s and 1950s, an array of young historians,
later to distinguish themselves, passed through its ranks, including
Emmanuel Le Roy Ladurie, François Furet, Denis Richet, Jacques
Chambaz, Robert Bonnaud, Alain Besançon, Jacques Ozouf, Maurice
Agulhon, Annie Kriegel, Maxim Rodinson, and Albert Soboul.[17] Interest
in the research and study of revolution was encouraged, and the French
Revolution in particular attracted attention.[18] The historians were
charged with securing the Communist claim to be the legitimate heirs to
the French revolutionary tradition, and with modernizing the Jacobin
interpretation. This had received its most convincing and sophisticated
formulation in the work of Georges Lefebvre (1874–1959). Lefebvre
decisively shifted historical attention to the social dimension of the
Revolution, understood within a progressive schema. An admirer of
Guesde and Jaurès, in the late 1920s and 1930s he moved close to
Marxism. He had friendly contacts with the intellectuals grouped around
the 'Cercle de la Russie Neuve', and declared himself in agreement with
historical materialism.[19] Lefebvre's researches into the peasantry during
the Revolution conformed to a general interest during the 1930s in the

social aspects of the Revolution (as instanced by, for example, Maurice Dommanget's studies on Babouvism).[20] He succeeded Philippe Sagnac to the Sorbonne chair in 1937, and the major statement of his interpretation, *Quatre-vingt-neuf*, was published in 1939 as part of the Third Republic's commemoration of the 150th anniversary of the Revolution. Suppressed by the Vichy regime, it emerged after 1945 as the dominant interpretation of the Revolution's significance, and remained 'unchallenged for the best part of twenty years after it appeared'.[21] Lefebvre's was a bemusingly erudite treatment of the processes that apparently produced the revolutionary events of 1789, and drew extensively on Ernest Labrousse's monumental researches on the correlations between eighteenth-century price fluctuations and political discontent. At the analytic core of his account lay the concept of bourgeois revolution, understood within a perspective that saw class struggle as the principal motive force in history. Lefebvre never employed a consistently Marxist framework or terminology (in the way that his student Albert Soboul did), yet he could hardly have been unaware that he was applying the concept of bourgeois revolution to the study of late eighteenth-century France in a context where the concept's political centrality to Marxism and to the Communist movement was being affirmed.[22] Outside France, Lefebvre's work was welcomed, and interest fastened on his scholarship and sense of nuance; the political circumstances which helped to define his intentions, his Jacobin political principles set within a Marxist schema of historical progress, were all but disregarded.[23] Lefebvre's narrative distinguished between the progressive and emancipatory protagonists of the Revolution, and those who had tried to restrain and divert the true course of the Revolution. Several factors conspired to make his the dominant interpretation after 1945. His work received no real challenge from the institutionally powerful *Annales* school of historians. Although the *Annales* historians employed a recognizably Marxist notion of economic determination, they forsook political narrative history in favour of discovering (in ultra-materialist fashion) the geographical and demographic determinants of 'la longue durée'. Further, Lefebvre's identification of an historical subject, a social class, charged with bringing about the Revolution, fitted very well with the Communist view of historical development. And, finally, it provided a way of identifying revolutionary patriots and counter-revolutionary traitors, at a time when such forms of identification were crucial to the task of constituting postwar France as a unified political community.

Albert Soboul's work stood as a coda to Lefebvre's researches.[24] Soboul worked tirelessly to refine the purity of the canon of orthodox interpretation, and his writing constantly echoed with calls for its defence. For Soboul, propagation of revolutionary political wisdom was a task entrusted to loyal 'sons' of 'our universal mother' ('notre mère à tous'), the Revolution. Soboul continually reminded younger historians of their duty to defend the purity of the canon, and warned them that in studying the Revolution,

> they should remain faithful to the line which certain people, seeking to be denigratory, call the 'Jacobin' historiography of the Revolution: a term which we do not challenge, since—as our master Georges Lefebvre taught us—we understand it to mean fidelity and devotion to the cause of the people... Let us put it more exactly: the progressivist tradition of revolutionary historiography, from Michelet to Lefebvre, by way of Jaurès, Aulard, and Mathiez... the only one which in its principle orientation was and remains scientific.[25]

Perhaps even more than his actual scholarship, Soboul's ultimate and most important contribution lay in his indefatigable efforts to popularize the Jacobin and progressivist interpretation of the Revolution, and aside from his academic works, much of his energy was devoted to producing popular manuals on the Revolution, all part of the 'relentless effusion' of his work.[26]

II

Furet's targets and opponents were perfectly tangible, and unmistakably identified. What forms did his opposition take, by what means did he pursue his purposes and intentions? Intensely political by temperament, it is not surprising that his own views often varied since he first began advancing them in the early 1960s.[27] So too the broader impact and success of his arguments varied according to shifts in the political climate. What began as a contribution to a debate between academic historians, confined to the pages of professional journals, culminated by the time of the bicentennial in an encompassing reconceptualization of France's modern history: 1789 was identified as the origin and source of modern democratic culture, not a proleptic figuration of the socialist revolution. Furet's judiciously timed interventions successfully broke the monopoly of the 'authorized' interpreters of the Revolution, and returned arguments about its significance to the broader arena of public intellectual debate. In his interpretation, the Revolution continued to be an inexhaustible source of political wisdom for the French: but no longer because it provided examples or promises of how to continue or commence the Revolution anew. Rather, for Furet the Revolution raised the fundamental questions of political modernity, above all the problem of democracy under modern conditions: 'What is there to unify a society if it defines itself by what belongs only to individuals?'[28] Furet had carefully to negotiate his political positions: in criticizing the Jacobin and Marxist interpretations, he had to avoid the accusation that his position was counter-revolutionary (this was especially so during the 1980s, which saw the revival of right-wing and counter-revolutionary accounts of the Revolution).[29] Furet's stated desire, 'terminer la Révolution', to bring it to a close, was quite distinct from the Right's slogan, 'Pour en finir avec la Révolution' ('to have done with the Revolution').[30] All of his work was united by this political intention to capture a long-abandoned space in the historiography of the Revolution (and more generally in French politics), between 'la rhétorique contre-révolutionnaire' and 'la tradition jacobine'.

Furet's polemic against existing orthodoxies about the Revolution was inaugurated relatively unspectacularly in 1965, with the publication of a two-volume narrative history of the Revolution, authored jointly with Denis Richet.[31] Until then, the Jacobin interpretation had received little serious challenge. Daniel Guérin's Trotskyist studies certainly opposed the orthodox interpretation on many points, but Guérin was not a professional academic, and (since in these matters institutional positions counted for much) it was easy for professionals like Lefebvre to discredit his claims.[32] The Communists, sensing a political threat, also countered Guérin. Soboul, goaded by the Party, defended Robespierre and the Jacobin line against the Trotskyist argument.[33] But it was a younger generation of historians, several of whom were members of the Communist Party but all of whom had left by the late 1950s, who over the next three decades decisively unravelled the Jacobin orthodoxies: historians like Agulhon, Richet, Pierre Nora, and Furet (the latter three kin by marriage). Furet (who already in the early 1950s had engaged in polemics with Soboul)[34] was the most persistent, and pressed the attack farthest.

Furet and Richet's most controversial interpretative strategem in *La Révolution française* was to question the belief that the Revolution must be understood as, in Clemenceau's remark, a 'bloc': that is, that the various phases of the revolutionary period could be 'telescoped' into a single event, that possessed a unitary historical cause and meaning. To Furet, this view was simply a political prejudice, fed by 'la pensée socialiste d'obédience marxiste'.[35] It implied a crude determinism, which reduced complex political processes to the mere foam upon supposedly deeper social and economic currents. Furet and Richet insisted on the need to distinguish three 'revolutions', none of which necessarily entailed any of the others. The first, the period of liberal constitutional reform between 1789 and 1791, could not be explained as the outcome of a social conflict between a decaying feudal class and a proud and rising bourgeoisie: rather, its origins lay in the ideological realm. The second, the period of Jacobin government and Terror between 10 August 1792 and Thermidor (July 1794), represented a *dérapage* of the initial liberal revolution. This 'skidding off course' of the Revolution could hardly be construed as an interlude of popular democracy where

the most advanced social elements, the *sans-culottes*, temporarily sa-
voured power (as Soboul's interpretation urged). It was the product of
heightened political antagonisms, not of worsening conflict between
social classes. In narrating the events of this period, Furet and Richet
portrayed the *sans-culottes* as pawns of the new élite of bourgeois and
formerly noble property-owners, who dispensed with them after
Thermidor. The third period saw the Revolution returning, after
Thermidor, to its original course: it signalled 'le retour du réel'. But it
also brought with it a gradual 'depoliticization' of society, which once
again returned political debate and decision to the élites, and provided
Bonaparte with a situation ripe for exploitation.

This account was starkly contrary to the orthodoxy defended by Communist historians. Although it was given no explicit political twist, the
responses it elicited from Communist historians revealed the stakes of
the dispute. Reacting to the political sub-text of their work one Party
historian, Claude Mazauric (he was later to become secretary to Party
leader Georges Marchais), noted that

> Their allusions, explicit and more frequently implicit, to the Bolsheviks, to
> the contemporary history of the USSR and of the Communist parties,
> and to socialist and Marxist historiography, are sufficiently numerous to
> ensure that nobody can be accused of being unfair by pointing out that
> their [i.e. Furet's and Richet's] hostile prejudices have led them on in just
> the way they accuse others of being led.[36]

Furet and Richet's position, Mazauric ruled, was anti-Marxist, based on
a thorough intellectual 'revisionism'. At the theoretical level, it refused
to acknowledge dialectical materialism as the objective science of history
(here Mazauric adduced Althusser's *Lénine et la philosophie* as proof of
dialectical materialism's scientific status); more specifically within the
field of revolutionary historiography, it ignored the 'fertile hypotheses
and discoveries' embodied in the great line extending from Jaurès
through Mathiez and Lefebvre to Soboul.[37] But 'revisionism' had also a
directly political sense, which Mazauric exploited in order to assert
a series of equivalences. Revisionism meant anti-Communism; and
adopting his best commissarial tone, Mazauric judged that this in turn
meant a

> parti pris antipopulaire ... [and] ... Enfin, dérive du parti pris pré-
> cédent ... de parti pris antinational, lequel à son tour conduit à l'instruction
> d'un véritable procès en dépréciation de la période patriotique, c'est-à-
> dire jacobine, de la Révolution française.[38]

The mode of argumentation had altered little.[39]

These political disputes were given further edge by an institutional
conflict, apparent in Furet's decision to pursue his polemic in the
pages of the journal, *Annales: Economies, Sociétés, Civilisations*. In 1971 he

published there 'Le Catéchisme révolutionnaire': the title captured well the aggressive political content of the piece. Conventionally, the *Annales historiques de la Révolution française*, edited by Soboul and associated with the Sorbonne, had monopolized scholarly opinion about the Revolution. *Annales: ESC* was not the obvious place for Furet to publish an article on the historiography of the Revolution. A journal which enjoyed international prestige, with contributions mainly from professional academics, its agenda was largely set by its magisterial editor, Fernand Braudel.[40] It had certainly published research on the French Revolution, but it was essentially uninterested in 'histoire événementiel', in narrative history (precisely the predominant form taken by accounts of the French Revolution), and its main focus was on long-term historical regularities and constraints.[41] It located the identity of French history in geographical and demographic factors, and not in France's distinctive political trajectory. It had no prominent political profile (it stood broadly on the non-Communist Left), although intellectually it was one of the most innovative in its field in France. But more importantly, *Annales: ESC* was closely linked to an institutional nexus which was an active rival to the Sorbonne: founded in 1947 with the help of American funds (a fact that allowed Soboul and his colleagues to accuse it of serving as a bridgehead of American ideological and political influence), it was the 'house' journal of the 'VIe section' of the Ecole Pratique (in 1975 this became the Ecole des Hautes Etudes en Sciences Sociales). By inducting *Annales: ESC* into his battle with the orthodox interpretation, Furet successfully mobilized substantial intellectual *cachet*; he also initiated a decisive shift. Gradually over the next decade, polite intellectual opinion on the Revolution was no longer formed by or to be found in the pages of the journal founded by Mathiez and now controlled by Soboul, the *Annales historiques de la Révolution française*; the *Annales: ESC* usurped this role. In the *Annales: ESC*, the work of historians like Emmanuel Le Roy Ladurie could be found, which located the Revolution in the long rhythms of the eighteenth century, and helped to produce a picture of the Revolution drastically different from that found in the epic narratives cherished by Lefebvre and Soboul. Michel Vovelle noticed well the change that was occurring in perceptions of the Revolution: the new interpretation challenged 'the notion of rapid mutation and change in history: in short, the idea of Revolution'.[42]

Construed in its most ambitious form, Furet's attack on the revolutionary catechism hoped to wipe away a century of historiographical shibboleths. But in 1971 Furet had only a vague sense of what might replace this. Mazauric, in his defence of the orthodox interpretation of the Revolution as a bourgeois one, had made clear that revisionism jeopardized not only the work of 'progressivist or Marxist historians' like Jaurès, Mathiez, Lefebvre and their disciples, but more threateningly still it signified a scepticism about Marx himself: 'Any challenge to the interpretation of the French Revolution as a bourgeois revolution is equally a challenge to Marx himself, and to all Marxists'.[43] This accusation might come from the side of the Communist Party, but in the post-1968 climate of political radicalism, a much wider constituency could feel sympathy with it. Furet had therefore to defend himself against the charge that he was betraying Marx and the heritage of Marxism. To this end, he employed a standard strategy of Left intellectual criticism (no different from that used by, for example, Sartre, Althusser, or some *gauchistes*): he distinguished carefully between Marx's own understanding and analysis of the Revolution (acknowledged as sophisticated and worthy of attention) and the 'simplified and simplistic Marxism' employed by Communist historians. Furet's adversary was not Marxism itself (so he claimed), but what he variously termed 'the Mazaurico-Soboulian vulgate' or 'the Lenino-populist vulgate', a mix of 'Jacobinism and Leninism'. Yet the weakness of Furet's position at this stage remained his lack of a defined alternative intellectual or political standpoint: Tocqueville, for instance, a fundamental resource in his later work, appeared only in a footnote. And the analysis of Augustin Cochin, central to Furet's later critique of Jacobinism, did not figure at all. The task of constructing an alternative historiographical tradition—a task that was to dominate Furet's work during the 1980s—had not yet begun.

By the late 1970s, the political implications of Furet's argument began to resonate much further than the confines of academic debate. This was the result of at least two developments. Within academic historiography, the intellectual claims and foundations of the orthodox interpretation were challenged and weakened, although ironically the challenge came from those who claimed a more radical reading of Marx. Younger Marxist historians like Régine Robin and Michel Grenon opposed both the revisionist and orthodox interpretations, and alleged that neither had properly understood Marx. They adopted and developed Althusserian verities, to provide a more differentiated typology of the pre- and post-revolutionary bourgeoisie, and a conceptually more layered account of the processes of revolutionary transition.[44] This attack on the Marxist credentials of Soboul and others offered support from an unexpected quarter for Furet, who had made a similar analytic point (with a vastly different political meaning).[45] Far more important, however, were the changes in the political atmosphere: in 1975 Solzhenitsyn's *Le Archipel du Goulag* was published, selling 600,000 copies of the first volume in the first year, 175,000 of the second volume. The inconclusive drift of *gauchiste* politics now fetched up, and the fragments of the intellectual Left were pressed into new alliances against a common enemy. The themes of totalitarianism and terror, and their relation to revolution invaded the agenda of intellectual debate.[46] The revival of the electoral hopes of the Left and, in response to this, the stridencies of the New Philosophers, staked out a highly charged political space. This was a moment of opportunity, seized by Furet without vacillation. He published in 1978 *Penser la Révolution française*, a collection of articles (some previously published) with a new introductory essay whose title captured the tone and import of the book: 'The Revolution is Over'. It was a small, even slight book: neither a continuous narrative nor a monograph, it did not conform to the accepted and conventional generic categories for studies of the Revolution.[47] It differed also from Furet's own earlier work both in form and content. He renounced with a flourish the conventions of narrative structure, and made explicit the conceptual models and analytic questions which informed his interpretation. The primacy of ideological and political forms of explanation, as against social and economic ones, was asserted, and from this perspective, the Revolution's several episodes were reassessed. Earlier, Furet and Richet, in Tocquevillean mode, had stressed the continuities between the pre- and post- revolutionary periods. Thermidor, for example received little attention in 1965; but in 1978, Thermidor became a conceptually pivotal if explanatorily weak moment in Furet's account, and was seen now as the symbolic 'revenge of society' upon Jacobin ideology. The Jacobin ideology, in particular the modes in which it represented power, now attracted Furet's attention. Earlier, the period of Jacobin rule and Terror had been characterized as a 'dérapage', a moment when the Revolution 'skidded off course'; now, the rule of Terror was analysed as the necessary and inevitable fate of any revolutionary politics. And now, in 1978, Furet could declare—with a hitherto unavailable *frisson*—that the analysis of Jacobinism unveiled the very essence of revolutionary politics, an essence whose modern manifestation was Soviet totalitarianism. Furet's political cards were frankly revealed.

Indeed, *Penser la Révolution française* noted the difficulty—particularly acute for French historians—of maintaining any intellectual and political distance from arguments about the Revolution. As the founding moment of the modern French nation, the Revolution remained a shining beacon of political identification, and to all except counter-revolutionaries it signified a rupture with the past, and the promise of a glorious future. But there were costs to this continued political over-investment in the Revolution. All who wrote about it were trapped within the categories employed by the revolutionaries themselves; they vicariously participated in its re-enactment. Instead of producing cool analysis, the writing of the Revolution's history was used an opportunity to perpetually commemorate the nation's original foundation.[48] This continuing 'closeness' of the Revolution meant that it constantly fed into and was overlaid with contemporary political passions. Thus for the nineteenth-century socialists, the Revolution symbolized the beginning of a process whose end-point would be a future socialist revolution, and therefore all disputes about the Revolution were arguments about France's socialist future. But the Soviet Revolution hijacked this narrative, and set it on a different course. This dislocation was made apparent by the curious turn taken by the historiography of the Revolution after 1945. With the defeat of Fascism and the effacement of the counter-revolutionary perspective from French politics, one might have expected arguments about the French Revolution to subside into the pool of 'dead' historical subjects. On the contrary, it was assigned a new political significance, and served as a battleground for disputes about the Soviet Union and Communism. Because of the divisive nature of the event and the subsequent history it had produced, Furet was sceptical of the possibility of 'scholarly' or objective accounts of the Revolution: 'No Frenchman living in the second half of the twentieth century can perceive the French Revolution from the outside. One cannot practise ethnology on so familiar a landscape.'[49] Nevertheless, he urged the need for some intellectual distance, and indeed this was now possible, he claimed, because the Revolution was, in Lévi-Strauss's phrase, 'cooling off'. One could get outside and beyond agent descriptions of the event, the 'mode of personal identification' that Michelet had so vividly practised.[50] According to Furet, two conditions had made this possible. The first was obvious, the inherent mutability of historical knowledge. But more important was the new political situation, brought about by 'the contradictions between the myth of revolution and the societies that have experienced it'. This had fundamentally altered the terms appropriate to understanding the identity and significance of the Revolution (and indeed of all subsequent revolutions).[51]

The polemical crux of the essay lay here. The Communists after the Liberation had vaunted the description of 1917 as the continuation of 1789; the time had come to turn this against them:

> In 1920, Mathiez justified Bolshevik violence by the French precedent, in the name of comparable circumstances. Today the Gulag is leading to a rethinking of the Terror precisely because the two undertakings are seen as identical.[52]

As obdurately as Mathiez had done in 1920, Furet insisted that 'the two revolutions remain connected'; but now he switched the evaluative signs. Solzhenitsyn had revealed political oppression, symbolized by the Gulag, to be the essence of revolutionary politics, and once this was recognized 'the Russian example was bound to turn around, like a boomerang, to strike its French "origin"'.[53] And, as Furet made clear in his journalistic writing, this 'boomerang effect' struck not only at the canon of historiography, but at Marx and Marxism too: 'Marx, today, can no longer escape his legacy, and the boomerang effect is all the more powerful for having been delayed for so long.'[54] Furet's wager was clear. Ten years after the abortive political events of 1968, he aimed now to abolish 'the exorbitant privilege assigned to the idea of revolution'.[55] He dismissed all definitions of revolution as the expression of conscious intentions formed by socio-economic determinants, and chose instead a strikingly formal definition. The Revolution represented a vacant space, a 'power vacuum that was filled by a rush of new forces'.

> The Revolution was the historical space that separated two powers, the embodiment of the idea that history is shaped by human action rather than by the combination of existing institutions and forces.[56]

It was a vacuum structured by and around a political ideology, Jacobinism, which according to Furet set the formal pattern of all subsequent revolutionary politics. He developed a brilliant analysis of Jacobinism, which emptied it of all social content, and characterized it as a discursive system, a way of representing and legitimating power.[57]

The analysis played on several registers. The most readily identifiable was that of revolutionary historiography. Here he outlined an account whose novelty rested on two moves. The first was to recover the work of Augustin Cochin (1876–1916). A man of the political Right, Cochin was entirely absent from the Republican and Communist canons. Most of his work was published posthumously during the 1920s, and consisted of a series of studies on the revolutionary 'Sociétés de pensée' of the 1790s. For Cochin, Jacobinism was not the product of masonic conspiracies,[58] nor could the Jacobin Terror be explained as the result either of conflicting socio-economic interests, military contingencies, or individual megalomania. Jacobinism was essentially an instrument for the creation of a community of unanimous belief. It did this through the form of the Jacobin clubs, microcosmic societies governed by well-articulated rules. To become a member of this 'philosophical society', one had to divest oneself of individual and social distinctions: membership was strictly a matter of ideas held in common. The Jacobin clubs were intended not as forms of political agency or representation (as was the purpose of, for example, guilds and occupational corporations), but rather as mechanisms to produce consensus and agreement. According to Cochin this conception of 'pure democracy' became generalized to society as a whole at the end of the eighteenth century, and entered into confrontation with the 'corporative' conception of social organization typical of the Ancien Régime, which saw legitimate power as vested in a nation constituted of stratified *corps*, each with different entitlements to express their opinions. Furet discovered in Cochin's sociological analysis 'a theory of politics and theory of ideology', which revealed the propensities of modern revolutionary politics. He used Cochin's analysis to lend weight to his claim that important features of the twentieth-century revolutionary party, such as the Bolshevik Party, could be traced back, via the Jacobin clubs, to the 'Sociétés de Pensée' of the eighteenth-century Enlightenment:

It becomes clear that he [Cochin] put his finger on a central feature, not only of the French Revolution but of what it shared with later revolutions, if one realises that he described in advance many traits of Lenin's Bolshevism.[59]

Furet's appropriation of Cochin's argument was motivated by a directly political intention: to show that the Jacobin Terror was an intrinsic part of the revolutionary process, not a circumstantial effect. Intended in this way, Furet's reconstruction of Cochin was hardly very faithful to Cochin's actual writings.[60] Furet's second move was to insert Cochin's static sociological analysis into a schema of historical and political development derived from Tocqueville. Like Cochin's, Tocqueville's interpretation of the French Revolution had received little attention from those who explained the Revolution as an outcome of conflict between social classes.[61] Furet fully endorsed Tocqueville's anti-climactic view that the Revolution was best understood as a moment in the continuous and long-term development of the French state and of democratic political forms, and not as the violent eruption of a social struggle, pregnant with universal historical significance. This perspective promised a new genealogy, which linked the French Revolution to the more strictly political and 'democratic revolutions' of seventeenth-century England and eighteenth-century America, and thus belied any imputed relation between the French and the Soviet Revolutions.[62]

Furet secured the intellectual credibility of his argument by skilfully interweaving into this first historiographical key a second, more allusive and intellectually resonant register. The unnamed references and inter-locutors in his analysis were well judged for Paris in the late 1970s.[63] Take for instance his argument that the Revolution 'ushered in a world where mental representations of power governed all actions, and where a network of signs completely dominated political life'.[64] To justify this claim, he examined Jacobinism as a discursive system, a language through which political power was constituted and represented. Furet here referred in a loose but identifiable way to Foucault's work. According to Furet, the Jacobin revolutionaries did not wield 'power in the normal sense', that is, executive or administrative power (what Foucault in his work termed 'juridical power'); instead, they operated with 'a specific idea of power'.[65] By a process of simple inversion, the Jacobin discourse disassociated power from its usual and customary location in the institutions of the Ancien Régime, and assigned it to 'the people'. This category of 'the people', fundamental to Jacobin ideology, was curiously shapeless, 'an amorphous mass of the well-intentioned'.[66] It existed in the form of ' "opinion", constructed in language. Power was made identical with language:

> Language was substituted for power, for it was the sole guarantee that power would belong only to the people, that is, to nobody . . . Once it had become power, opinion had to be at one with the people. (p. 48)

For Furet, 'not only did power come to reside in the word . . . but also power was always at stake in the conflict between words'.[67] Like Foucault's power/knowledge, Furet's power/opinion had no stable site: it continually dispersed itself into omnipresent effects, transforming itself into '"opinion", an entity that was nowhere and yet already everywhere . . . power had dissolved itself in the people'.[68] The notion of the 'people', in Furet's argument (like the subject in Foucault) became the shadowy effect and product of power. It was, to use the signature phrase of this intellectual style, 'de-centred':

> The 'people' was not a datum or concept that reflected existing society. Rather, it was the Revolution's claim to legitimacy, its very definition as it were; for henceforth all power, all political endeavour revolved around that founding principle, which it was nevertheless impossible to embody. (p. 51)

Convergent with Foucault's critique of the categories of class and economic interests,[69] Furet's claim that the category of 'the people' was simply an ideological construct was a deft way of changing the subject: it allowed him to avoid entirely the need to elaborate a critique of the social interpretation, since 'that type of interpretation is irrelevant to the problem at hand'.[70] In this sonorous description, the Revolution was no longer portrayed as fundamentally a struggle between social interests, but as a conflict of languages: 'the Revolution replaced the conflict of interests for power with a competition of discourses for the appropriation of legitimacy'.[71] Given Furet's argument about the internal continuities between Jacobinism and Bolshevism, his audience could hardly fail to draw the implications that this analysis of the Jacobin category of 'the people' held for the idea of the proletariat.[72] The Foucauldian elements and tone of Furet's analysis of Jacobin revolutionary ideology helped to find him a wider audience, especially among younger Leftist intellectuals who were beginning to voice misgivings about the idea of revolution.

This conception of revolutionary politics as an imaginary discourse of power led Furet to drastically revise Robespierre's role during the period of revolutionary Terror. Robespierre was an icon of Republican and then Communist historiography, both of which 'explained Robespierre's public role by his moral virtues', and discovered in the details of his biography and character a symbol of the Revolution's meaning.[73] In Furet's treatment, however, Robespierre emerged not as an autonomous political agent but the product of a political language: the great and visionary leader of the Revolution, hero to Mathiez and to Communist historiography, was transformed into the mere 'mouthpiece of its purest and most tragic discourse'.[74] Alluding to Foucault's work on the technologies of total incarceration, Furet reduced Robespierre to an automaton:

> Robespierre was not a minister; his function was one of 'surveillance'. He watched over the consensus, sniffing out the slightest deviance. But then

ideology is not a matter of thinking . . . it spoke, or rather expressed itself, through its spokesman and above all through the machine. So the Revolution was not so much an action as a language, and it was in relation to this language, the locus of consensus, that the ideological machine established differences among men.[75]

The Terror over which Robespierre presided was not the contingent product of his subjective response to external circumstances; on the contrary, it was a necessary and inevitable consequence of the discursive representation of power which lay at the core of the Revolution. Robespierre simply brought to the fore the implicit logic of Jacobin ideology, he made manifest 'the truth . . . that the Terror was an integral part of revolutionary ideology' (p. 62).

If Foucault's shadowy presence pervaded Furet's text, others too made more fitful appearances. In his discussion of Rousseau's theory of sovereignty and representation, there were hints of Derrida's critique of Rousseau's theory of representation,[76] and more significantly, in his use of the idea of the 'imaginaire démocratique du pouvior' [trans. as 'imaginary discourse on power' (p. 54)], Furet invoked the work of Castoriadis and Lefort.[77] He acknowledged that his analysis was indebted to discussions in Pierre Nora's seminar at the Ecole des Hautes Etudes en Sciences Sociales in 1977; and in particular to Marcel Gauchet and Laurent Theis (Gauchet stood at this point as an important intellectual conduit between different disciplinary and institutional networks: a student of Claude Lefort at Caen, he collaborated with Lefort and Castoriadis on the review *Libre*). These allusions each highlight the location of Furet's work at a crucial juncture in the intellectual field, which linked argument within academic history to very contemporary political realignments. In Furet's work, historical revisionism and political theory fused to form a powerful combination. Clearly therefore, Furet's claim that ideological debate over the Revolution could henceforth be dropped should be treated with scepticism.[78] It was some part of his cunning to make this claim in a text which was precisely and firmly within the genre of revolutionary historiography as political theory (by other means). Furet's revision of understandings of the Revolution functioned and succeeded by transgressing the intellectual and political boundaries conventionally demarcated by monographic and narrative accounts of the Revolution. He took what had become a rather monotonous and academic debate, but which had always embodied crucial political stakes, and recomposed it in an intellectually richer and more attractive key. But to this double register he added a third, explicitly political, key. This was defined by his journalistic affiliations with reviews such as *Le Nouvel Observateur* and *Commentaire*, and later *Le Débat*. Thus in 1975, as the Communist Party declared Solzhenitsyn a 'reactionary writer', and the Socialists (anxious to preserve the unity of the Common Programme) acquiesced in this verdict, it was *Le Nouvel Observateur* that championed Solzhenitsyn's case.[79] And, reviewing his work in *Le Nouvel Observateur*, it was Furet who declared Solzhenitsyn 'one of our greatest contemporaries, the man who has ensured that Soviet Russia, an essential part of the universal, has been brought within the realm of history and of reason. There will be a before—and an after—Solzhenitsyn'.[80] Bernard-Henri Lévy, the svengali of the New Philosophers, had with similar hyperbole described Solzhenitsyn as 'the Dante of our age'.

Furet's political intentions in part converged with those of the New Philosophers, but his arguments carried greater intellectual weight. Unlike the New Philosophers, he did not hope to discredit the idea of revolution by opposing it to a celebration of irrationalist spontaneity. His strategy was more oblique. He redefined the identity and meaning of the French Revolution by re-framing it within a new historical schema. France's post-revolutionary history was a gradual political evolution way from the absolutist state, and towards stable democratic forms that provided equality as a political principle; it was not the unfolding of a social process, convulsed by moments of revolutionary reorganization of systems of property ownership and appropriation. From this Tocquevillean perspective, the French Revolution retained its position as a founding and universal event, but was now described as the inventor of modern democratic political culture.[81] The fundamental question it posed was not—as Marx had urged—that of how the Revolution could be started anew, but that of how the Revolution could be brought to a close, concluded: how it could institutionalize itself in stable democratic forms?

III

The ramifications of Furet's argument surfaced clearly during the 1980s, against the background of two sets of political changes, national and international. The effacement of both Communism and Gaullism (in its original proud form) as effective challengers to state power had placed government firmly in the hands of the Socialist Party. Promising, on its election in 1981, a dramatic 'rupture' with capitalism and the initiation of systematic state intervention to redistribute the balance of opportunities within France, in fact the Socialist government found itself committed to both the constitutional limitation and administrative decentralization of the French state's capacities, and (after 1983) to the principle of a market economy and private property. Meanwhile, those twentieth-century regimes created by the triumph of socialist revolutions began to unravel, culminating in an historic conjunction that could not fail to generate an imaginative charge: the bicentennial of the French

Revolution was commemorated in 1989 by the dissolution of revolutionary politics, precisely that which was supposed to have been the French Revolution's greatest legacy.

Furet's work during the 1980s took three directions. The historiography of the Revolution continued to receive detailed attention, as he pursued his reconstruction of alternative traditions of understanding the mixed inheritance of the Revolution. He published a study of Edgar Quinet's interpretation of Jacobinism and of the Christian filiations of revolutionary ideology, which praised Quinet's ability to pose basic questions of philosophical history rather than merely approving or denigrating different phases of the Revolution. Marx was also a subject of reappraisal and, while Furet endorsed the young Marx's view of the Revolution as the 'genesis of the modern democratic state', the point of his account was to show that once Marx came to rely on the explanatory framework of historical materialism, he was forced to pose the problems of the Revolution and its subsequent course in forms that defied solution.[82] By making the Revolution 'a political event determined by economic and social evolution, by the development of social forces', Marx was unable to answer the central problem: 'what explains the extraordinary diversity of forms of state manifested by the French Revolution, if the civil society that supported it remained the same?'[83] To correctly understand the Revolution, Furet again insisted, Marx had to be set aside. In addition to these works of historiographical criticism, he initiated and presided over the publication of a number of collaborative volumes which confirmed the interpretative shift he had begun. Here, his concerns were as much with matters of political theory as with history, and he showed a very presentist sense of what was important to understand about the Revolution.[84] Together with more established figures, Furet marshalled a team of younger intellectuals whose interests fully reflected the turn that had occurred in French political argument, away from questions of socialism and towards questions of democracy. Contributions from Pierre Rosanvallon, Luc Ferry, Marcel Gauchet, Bernard Manin, Philippe Raynaud, and Alain Renaut could be found beside those by members of Furet's own generation: Mona Ozouf, Pierre Nora, Denis Richet, Jean Starobinski, Pierre Manent, Maurice Agulhon, Alain Besançon and Claude Lefort. All concurred with the definition of the French Revolution as 'the birth of democracy'. This, 'the basis of its strangeness', had escaped all interpretations that defined the Revolution as 'the emergence of the bourgeoisie into the national political arena', and that thus drastically minimized the sense in which the Revolution had ruptured Europe's political imagination. A third flank in Furet's push to install a new political consensus amongst intellectuals was defined by his writings on contemporary politics. Here, in a series of articles and essays, he claimed to detect the emergence of a more homogeneous, politically moderate and centrist France, no longer riven by revolutionary cleavages. The Republic had won general acceptance, but its purposes were now seen more minimally than in earlier conceptions. This was a more pluralist Republic, designed to uphold individual human rights (against positive law, if necessary), and not the 'one and indivisible Republic' which aspired both to protect the nation from the international economy (as it had done during the Third Republican 'synthesis' of the late nineteenth century) and to regenerate through a programme of civic education a richer sense of citizenship, based on models of the ancient polis.

During the 1980s, Furet's work obviously had a significant impact in the field of academic history of the French Revolution, as the interpretative claims and assertions put forward in *Penser la Révolution française* were filled out by the researches of an array of historians and political theorists. But his arguments now infiltrated farther afield, and altered the terms of political argument employed by intellectuals, just as they affected conceptions of France's political identity and intellectual self-conceptions. By reconceptualizing the Revolution through a return to fundamental questions about its identity and meaning (what was it, when it did it begin and end, and what was its significance for subsequent politics?), Furet drew attention to the unavoidable role of political values and judgements in the study of the Revolution, and opened debate about the Revolution to intellectual perspectives other than those of professional historians or scholars.

Furet himself ventured strong answers to these questions, but he also conceded their inevitable open-endedness: a fact that underlined the Revolution's intensely political character. By jettisoning the explanatory framework (common to Marxist and to liberal interpretations) which traced the causal origins of the Revolution to social conflicts, the result was to create a much less definite sense of what the Revolution actually was. No longer the surface expression of subterranean social processes, the Revolution emerged in the portrayal of Furet and his collaborators more as a series of political disputes, practices and actions made by agents with frequently diverging purposes. But if the Revolution was no longer the 'bloc' or indivisible unity enshrined in the Left's historiography, there was nevertheless for Furet a unifying sense to the various episodes of the Revolution. This was manifest in 1789 itself, especially in the weeks between the elections to the Estates General and the October Days of 1789: 'a very brief expanse of time and yet the most important in French history, during which everything there was to say about the new principles was said'.[85] Nothing, it was boldly insisted, should be allowed to obstruct recognition of 'the intellectual unity of a Revolution founded on the Rights of Man'. The subsequent political history of France, indeed of 'modern political culture' was centred on the construction and consolidation of stable democratic structures that could secure such rights. The significance of post-revolutionary history therefore lay in the attempts to construct constitutional representative democracy as a form of limited government that ensured the protection of a sphere of rights to private enjoyment—what Benjamin Constant had termed 'modern liberty'.

At a more general level, Furet engaged in a comprehensive redrawing of the relations between the social and political dimensions. Marxism claimed to possess a firm model of these relations: the concept of revolution functioned as an instrument that removed disparities between the social and the political realms, bringing them into alignment. But in undermining this model, Furet redirected attention towards the concept of representation as a way of reconnecting the two realms: 'the problem of political representation stood at the heart of the French Revolution'.[86] For Furet, constitutional representative democracy, the 'bourgeois liberal republic', was not a transient form to be superseded by a more transparent 'direct' democracy: rather it was the safe haven towards which the French Revolution had made its tortuous way in the two centuries since 1789.[87] This view of France's political development, hardly less teleological than the perspectives it rejected, was most clearly expressed in an essay that surveyed the French political scene after the election in 1988 of François Mitterrand to a second term in office. Furet interpreted the unique 'cohabitation' of a Socialist president with a prime minister of the Right as a sign that democratic politics had ultimately come of age in France: with the universal acceptance of the political institutions and constitutional settlement of the Fifth Republic, the fiercely partisan political disputes of the past had finally subsided. The 'spectacular peculiarity' of France's political identity, its perpetually unstable state forms (constantly under challenge from the Jacobin Left and Catholic Right) had been transformed into the routines of constitutional representative democracy. The achievement of a synthesis that had been pursued since 1789, in the form of 'a Constitution in which the executive power reconciled the Old Regime and the Revolution' also signalled a deep mutation in conceptions of the nation's identity. Previously, this had been constructed around an historical legend begun by the Revolution:

> habituated to seeing the universal in the particular, the history of the world in that of their own nation . . . the originality of the French was to write the political civilization of their country, unique insofar as it was national, in a universal register: the exceptional was not what separated it from other nations, but on the contrary that which made it exemplary, constituted it as a model.[88]

The demise of this faith in the exceptional destiny of the French nation—a conviction that had been shared both by de Gaulle and the Communists—had eroded the belief in the sovereign power of the nation-state, and engendered a widespread disinvestment of passion from national political debate and dispute.[89] The nation ceased to be the relevant sphere for the creation of political identity: this was now displaced, on the one hand towards the realm of private individual activity, on the other (and more tentatively) towards the construction of a new political space, Europe.[90]

Furet's insistence on seeing the French Revolution as a fundamentally *political* episode, which required explanation in political terms, recovered a dimension of human agency and indeterminacy glaringly absent from those earlier interpretations that inserted the Revolution into a linear and progressive schema of world historical development. But, and in contradiction with his recognition of agency and indeterminacy, Furet himself also proposed an alternative schema, a cumulative historical context that could be made to yield criteria for assessing the significance of the Revolution. For Furet, the Revolution signified the 'birth of modern political culture', of modern democracy. It was this fact that endowed post-revolutionary history with its significance. This contradiction in his argument derived from the tension between his analytic and his political purposes. It was above all his political purposes which gave unity to his work, and motivated his pursuit of the twin themes of how the Revolution could be brought to a close, and of the complex but necessary relation between the 'democratic revolution' of 1789 and the Terror.[91] These were old and deeply political themes, coeval with the Revolution itself, subjects familiar to Edmund Burke, Benjamin Constant, Germaine de Staël and Joseph de Maistre among others.[92] Why, two hundred years later, was Furet able to press these questions with such effect? The character of his success is best seen by separating three distinct issues, all elided in his claim that the Revolution had now finally come to its conclusion. First was the severely practical question of how the Revolution could be 'stopped'; but equally significant was the issue of whether in fact it had stopped at long last (also a question of practical judgement); and, thirdly, the much more explanatorily ambitious question of *why* the Revolution had indeed at long last stopped. On the first and last of these matters, Furet had no especially distinctive answer. But it was his unhesitating judgement on the second question, and the rhetorical force with which he expressed this, that ensured that his argument struck home. Any clear-headed reading of the political history of the late twentieth century would force the conclusion that the classical revolutionary model—derived from the experience of the French Revolution—had disintegrated (to explain why, however, would require being able to explain modern politics as whole). Furet's skill was to provide an interpretative framework that absorbed this historical experience into the mainstream of French intellectual debate: the effect was to revolutionize the political agenda and terms of argument of the intellectual Left.

Furet's argument pointed a way out of the impasse created by the virulent intellectual reaction of the late 1970s, towards something which looked more recognizably like a French 'Left-liberal' position, a French social-democracy: previously, and certainly in the period since 1945, an undefined space on the French intellectual landscape. The heroes of this newly emerging tradition of French political liberalism were those thinkers in Restoration France who tried to work through the implications of the French Revolution and of Rousseau before the rise of Socialism—figures like Constant, Guizot, and Madame de Staël, who were neither counter-revolutionaries nor believed that society could be constructed entirely anew from rational first principles, who admitted popular sovereignty, but felt urgently the need to develop institutional forms to limit it. Political philosophers like Benjamin Constant were already at the beginning of the nineteenth century refusing to view the Revolution as an indivisible monolith, and played off 1789 against 1793, the Rights of Man against the logic of citizenship. With some pride, French intellectuals during the 1980s embarked upon the recovery of an indigenous and original tradition of political philosophers, beginning with Montesquieu in the eighteenth century, and extending through the liberals of the Restoration period to Tocqueville.[93] This return to national thinkers may be seen as a form of compensation for the embarrassment of modern French philosophy which, with the exception of Henri Bergson, exists under the shadow of German philosophy (from Victor Cousin to Jacques Derrida, the history of French philosophy is the history of the importation and transposition of German philosophy). Furet's recognition that 'it is the Revolution that holds the title-deeds to the nation's legitimacy', his sense that it stood at the centre of French political representations, enabled him to change something fundamental by changing conceptions of the Revolution.

Epilogue

After having for so long been relegated as an ancestor of Bolshevism, political democracy has become its hope; it was its past, now it is its future.

François Furet, in F. Furet, J. Julliard and P. Rosanvallon, *La République du centre* (Paris, 1988).

For a political culture habituated to exceptionally passionate conflict and intemperate polemic, the years of the Mitterrand presidency appeared embarrassingly banal. Stability, continuity, and the 'cohabitation' of a prime minister of the Right with a Socialist president, all seemed to have brought to an end the era of France's 'exceptionalism'. Political instability, after all, was the one undeniably enduring legacy of the French Revolution: beginning in 1789, the French tried an array of political systems and regimes, which included constitutional monarchies, emergency committees and dictatorships, five Republics, Empires, as well as hybrid forms such as Vichy. Each specified the political community in various ways, and tried by differing means to legitimate its authority over the community. Drawing upon (and frequently conflating) the languages of nation, race and class, each definition claimed for itself a self-evidence and solidity that was invariably challengeable and challenged. It was not economic capabilities that came to be the defining trait of France's identity (as, periodically, they did in the German case), nor was the political community defined to the same extent as in Britain by military and commercial prowess, or by religion.[1] Revolutionary culture and, paradoxically, the political instability it generated became the defining traits of French identity. Politics emerged as the medium through which the community was defined. Hence the French state's characteristic focus on culture: this was the domain where it could strive most vigorously to produce the nation, to maintain fictively a homogeneous body that it could claim to represent and act for.[2] Hence too the centrality of the intellectuals, since it fell to them to argue and defend definitions of the nation, to focus doubts and disputes into a self-portrait of the political community. The intimate link between, on the one hand, arguments about the proper French community and, on the other, intellectual self-understandings signals the political centrality of intellectuals in France, and points towards how they acquired and maintained their mystique: the mere fact of their continuous existence, the constant murmur of their high-pitched and recondite arguments, functioned as a site of national memory, a legacy through which the community, by its adoration and homage, could in uneasy times remind itself of its identity and continuity.[3] For their part, France's intellectuals did not stint in their provision of national self-portraits: from Michelet, via the Dreyfusards, and onwards after the Second World War to Sartre and Braudel, they made this their welcome task.[4]

Instability has been matched by unevenness: the continuously awkward conjunction in French political and intellectual history of the avant-garde and the backward, the cosmopolitan and the parochial, the liberal and the authoritarian, the sophisticated and the crude. Nowhere has this persistent sense of *décalage*, of lag and asynchrony, been more vividly instanced than in the relationship between revolution and democracy. The French Revolution ringingly described itself as the bearer of democratic rights and liberties; the values of rights, political representation, and elections were all affirmed early in France. But the Revolution—and the Left it created—proved to be the best enemy of these values.[5] Democracy in its constitutional representative form—the only form in which inhabitants of the modern political world are ever likely to be durably acquainted with it—remained in quite fundamental respects unpractised, untheorized, and unloved in France.[6] To the intellectual Left, constitutional representative democracy, 'bourgeois' or 'formal' democracy, was a contemptible and mystifying illusion; only beginning in the late 1970s did it gradually come to be accepted as a political form in its own right, and not merely an illicit simulation of 'true', direct, or revolutionary democracy. To properly explain the lag between the affirmation of constitutional and democratic political values and their enshrinement in institutional practices would of course require a fully textured history of post-revolutionary France, but the (at best) insouciance of the intellectual Left towards elections, constitutions, and the forms of political representation itself constitutes a fundamental part of any such explanation.[7]

The language of rights, for instance, figured early and prominently in the French Revolution; but whereas in America and England it was invoked and acted as a check upon political power, in France it served to legitimate the creation of new forms of sovereign political power (forms which, by appropriating this critical language, deprived those who sought to protect themselves against the excesses of this new power of a crucial weapon).[8] The Revolution, and the state it engendered, claimed for itself a representative identity, it incarnated the nation: as the legitimate upholder and enactor of the rights of the nation, 'the people', it claimed sovereign power and authority over its population. Individual rights were subordinated to the state, and any potential for pluralism was dissipated by laws promulgated and acts performed in the name of the people as a whole. The dimension of individual agency seeped away from the concept of rights, as the language came to be wielded in the service of a paternalist and often authoritarian consequentialism. The example of elections and representative democracy tells a similar story. Although ushered in by the revolutionary era, and accepted in principle by the Left, in fact the most significant opposition to elections and the institutions and practices of representative democracy was to be found on the Left (an attitude summed up by Sartre's lapidary dismissal, 'élections, piège à cons'). In conformity with the general tenor of the political culture, those on the Left retained a commitment to political rationalism (embodied most usually for them in the form of a benign revolutionary party; for the Right, in a technocratic state), and both Left and Right came to harbour a deep distrust of representative politics and democratic decision-making procedures.[9]

For the Left, revolution was the instrument whereby the disjunctions between the social and the political, society and the state, would be rationally reconciled and harmonized. The language of revolution became a way of welding together potential diversity into a unitary image of political community, with state or party as its legitimate representative and agency. The Revolution had bequeathed to the French Left a vocabulary that stressed unity and identity, not diversity and pluralism: it claimed to unite the political community, and to act for it against its enemies. It proposed a seamless connection between society and state. But this tight conjunction has become an object of suspicion in France, the result of a dawning sense that the distance between state and society must be structured and represented, not effaced. This shift in the principal political question which inspires intellectual inquiry in late twentieth-century France has been well caught by Pierre Rosanvallon: the central dilemma of modern politics, he writes, is that 'the separation between the political system and civil society is a condition of individual liberty, yet this productive separation is permanently in danger of being transformed into a negative distance'.[10] The fascination with the phantasia of revolution has yielded place to an interest in the forms and practices of political representation.

All unitary images of the political community and its representatives came under attack in the late 1960s, and the evanescence of the value of revolution was an unforeseen effect of this period. Characterizing broadly, two lines of intellectual criticism emerged after 1968, the *gauchiste* and the 'reformist'. Despite their opposing political colours and uneven styles and strategies, they shared common opponents.[11] Both were deeply critical of the claim, advanced separately by the Gaullist state and its opposing *frère semblable* the Communist Party, that each exclusively possessed the proper description of the authentic political community and thus could legitimately represent it. The *gauchiste*

criticism brought together two distinct strands: those intellectuals who
desired a return to the pristine idea of revolution (the Maoists, the
Trotskyists and the Althusserians), and those (such as Henri Lefebvre,
Cornelius Castoriadis, André Gorz and Guy Debord) who confronted the
revolutionary ideal with the consequences of the spectacular growth of
the economy in the postwar decades, growth which had produced an
apparently pacified and distinctly unrevolutionary consumer society.
The reformist criticism, on the other hand, emerged from the liberal and
republican political clubs of the 1960s and from the work of 'critical
technocrats' like Michel Crozier.[12] Like the *gauchistes*, these intellectuals
and politicians were worried by the political effects of the centralized
state's efforts to modernize society which, they held, 'de-politicized'
society as it weakened civic meanings and loosened social bonds and
cohesion. Both reformists and *gauchistes* agreed that this was as much
the responsibility of swelling consumerism as of the expansion of the
bureaucratic welfare state. Both agreed too on the need for change
(the *gauchiste* slogan, subsequently taken up by the Socialist Party, was
'changer la vie'; the reformists, naturally more measured, were content
with 'changer la société') and on the imperative that this be initiated not
from above, by state or Party, but by what came to be called 'civil
society'. Both converged in their criticism of state-centred, Jacobin,
conceptions of value, agency and possibility. But if both the Gaullist
definition of the political community and that of its Communist chal-
lenger were faltering, what could substitute as a way of giving identity
to the French political community and its legitimate representative? The
problem was made more acute by the new representation of power and
agency which the *gauchiste* and reformist critiques shared: both dispersed
power across the social field, abandoned pyramidal models that located
it at a specific point or attributed it to an identifiable agent, and proposed a conception of power that transformed it into an effect of the
totality of social relations.[13] In these circumstances, the classical model
of revolution and its associated languages began to look redundant.

Several responses, each abortive, emerged. One centred around the
notion of *autogestion*, a term launched on a meteorically bright and brief
career by some elements of the intellectual Left, with the wish that it
might illuminate a distinctively French path towards socialism.[14] The
theme of *autogestion* had entered French intellectual debate in the 1950s
through the *Socialisme ou barbarie* group, but by the time it invaded the
political language of the intellectuals and of the Socialists in the early
1970s, it had been kneaded into an infinitely plastic idea, prompting one
observer to conclude that the idea remained just that: a discursive object
lacking any practical content, an ideology used to rationalize a political
position.[15] This is undoubtedly correct. Espoused by the Socialists, *autogestion* enjoyed the same magical encompassing quality as the idea
of communism once possessed for Marx: 'It is the ideal of socialism:

extended to the whole of society, *autogestion* signifies the end of exploitation, the disappearance of antagonistic classes, the abolition of wage-
labour, the achievement of democracy.'[16] More prosaically, what it in
fact represented was a wish for a new definition of democratic socialism;
that it did not represent anything more than an aspiration is apparent
from the relative ease with which Michel Rocard—the politician who
(along with Edmond Maire) did most to convert the Socialists to the
idea—dropped it (in favour of the much less socialist-sounding term,
'autonomy').[17] But those of more acute hearing could discern through
all this a struggle to pronounce the words 'social democracy'. The question of social democracy in France has been the site of a deeply emotive
if not very frank discussion.[18] In an environment in which doctrinal
purity was exigent upon those wishing to display enduring commitment
to a national historical project (that begun by the Revolution of 1789),
to speak of social democracy was indeed to be named a renegade.[19]
Symptomatic of this fear was the cunning interplay between various
factions within the Socialist Party, each seeking to label the other as
social democratic. To Jean-Pierre Chévènement and the CERES current,
for instance, Rocard was no part of the French Left at all—with his
'populist neo-liberal political economy', Rocard belonged to the *gauche
américaine*.[20] Rocard for his part produced a critique of social-democracy
which dismissed it as too bound to economic imperatives, and as too
statist and collectivist.[21] If the notion of *autogestion* proved too vague,
and if the social-democratic route was obstructed, a third possible response was to turn to the language of liberalism.[22] In the French ecom-
omic situation, however, the (at least rhetorical) invocation of the laws
of the free market as a way of best governing the economic arrange-
ments of the community appeared weak. Some sought to preserve the
attractions of the liberal account by distinguishing between economic
liberalism and political liberalism.[23] But, in a country where historically
the state had played a leading role in defining and constituting the
community, liberalism even conceived of simply as a vocabulary of
individual political rights and liberties yielded too thin a description of
community.

A fourth strategy, at once surprising, obvious, and politically ambiguous, was to recur to the idea of the Republic. The rift between intellectuals of the Left and the Republic, so marked during the heyday of
revolutionary politics in the postwar decades, was startlingly healed:
modern republicanism rallied intellectuals of the Left, and the Republic
became an institution towards which they could feel allegiance. As
an idea, the Republic in France has several distinct aspects. On the
one hand it is tenaciously defended by those like Claude Nicolet, upholder of the influential and basically Third Republican tradition of
'Mendèsisme'.[24] But the resurgence of interest in the Republic also
answered to other questions and interests. It camouflaged an attempt to

conceive a social-democratic regime, at a moment when the welfare state was in crisis and the unions in disarray.[25] It offered an institutional (and symbolic) form with which intellectuals of the Left could align in order to criticize the state and praise the market economy, without conflating themselves with the neo-liberals or the Right. For those who sought to divest themselves of statist connotations (the CERES group, for example) it provided a means to break with their Marxist or Communist pasts. For Mitterrand, meanwhile, it was a chance to broaden his electoral appeal and renew his claim to stand for democratic political rights.[26] To Jean-Pierre Chévènement, the new-found rhetoric of the Republic served a clear purpose:

> Between the market and socialism, there is place for something else: the Republic. Our task at the end of the twentieth century is not to invent socialism in the colours of liberalism. It is to *revive the Republic*, that French model of democracy... Why the Republic?, I am asked. The answer, I confess, is simple: because Long Live France!... France, in order to carry the message of democracy to the world, to give meaning to Europe... has need for the cohesion given by the belief in a project for its people.[27]

But if this unashamedly transparent statement is most politely viewed as the efforts of a professional politician to secure a quick political fix, it symptomatically laid bare how the idea of the Republic had come to stand for a 'synthèse à la française', representing a mid-path between the American minimal state and the Soviet totalitarian state.

The idea of the Republic has in this way served as a prism for refocusing the question of France's political identity: unable to believe in themselves as the universal Republic, the French are nevertheless trying to discover a unique—if now unmistakably local—political form through which to define their identity. This change in the available descriptions of the nation's identity[28]—evinced as much by Mitterrand's embrace of the idea of Europe as by debates about citizenship and nationality in France—was paralleled by a deflation in intellectuals' self-conceptions of their role.[29] But the conception of the Republic that has captured the attention of intellectuals is one quite different from the classical French idea of the Republic, as elaborated for instance during the Third Republic. It is a new, liberal and democratic Republic, not the traditional 'one and indivisible' Republic: sovereign power is no longer seen as its essential attribute. Intellectuals have moved towards an understanding of the Republic as a framework for the conduct of democratic politics, a framework that renounces any conception of a substantive *bien commun*, and that distrusts rationalist claims to be able to design and construct a trustworthy domestic enforcer of the right and the good. French intellectuals have had to modify their conception of what government is *for*, its purpose. Democratic politics is not the enactment of the right or the good, but the constant effort to protect from the worse; and it is the capacity of constitutional representative democracy to moderate the effects of concentrated power which holds attractions. This new Republic is closer in conception to the idea of a *Rechtsstaat*. And yet, the greater the degree to which the Republic is conceived of in terms similar to the liberal democratic regimes of America and Britain, the more difficult it becomes to see just what is distinctively French about it. If the Rights of Man and democracy are seen as the most valuable residue of the French Revolution and constitutive of France's modern political identity, then France's own history and contribution becomes less unique: on these matters, there is after all much to be learnt from the American and English experiences, and indeed French scholarship has of late become more interested than even before in trying to incorporate this experience into its own reflections.[30] Finally, the turn to the idea of the Republic has become possible because it is no longer compulsory to take the Revolution as a 'bloc', so collapsing its political meaning into its social aspect.[31] This encouraged a recognition that the fundamental revolutionary values—liberty, equality, fraternity—represent a desire for a more just political order, a political order not reducible to any particular arrangement of property rights and distribution within a society. It follows that the most important political legacy of the Revolution was its fleeting ability to give institutional form to the modern desire for political justice. The outlines of that form were traced in the constitutional politics that flourished briefly in the months between the 'Declaration of the Rights of Man and the Citizen' and the promulgation of the Committee of Public Safety.[32] Seen in this context, the turn to republican and constitutional theory is the most significant development in modern French political thinking.[33]

At a moment when interpretative orthodoxies about the French Revolution have collapsed—a moment that therefore signifies a great disturbance in the political languages available to intellectuals of the Left—, the Republic promises a potentially stable platform upon which to secure political consensus. Unmistakably an acquisition of the Revolution, the Republic is able also to contain elements that are recognizably of the *ancien régime* (for example, the conception of executive power described in the Constitution of the present Republic). Interest in the idea of the Republic represents a desire within French intellectual and political culture to divest itself of the universalist meanings— previously so vaunted—of French national history: 'France has brought to a close her political theatre of the exceptional, and she has returned to the common rights and customs of the other democracies.'[34] With the acknowledgement that the truth of the French Revolution was not to be found in the outcome of the Soviet Revolution, nor in the Jacobin tradition kept alive by the counter-state for so long represented by the Communist Party, a specific historical narrative about France's universal and revolutionary destiny was terminated.

Yet there is irony in the new-found interest of French intellectuals for the institutions of democratic politics conducted within a national frame, for constitutions and rights. With typical bad timing, French intellectuals have embraced the value of the Republic at the very moment when national politics, and the capacities of agency given to a national *demos* and its representatives, are ceding their importance to larger communities and frameworks. Conversion to a belief in the value of constitutional representative democracy has not brought with it any more lucid understanding of precisely what causal mechanisms are required to deliver the benefits which this political form promises. The European Community is exactly a response to fears about the continuing causal efficacy—especially economic—of the nation state, and it has successfully invested great decision-making capacities in the hands of a supra-national professional bureaucracy, quite removed from the day-to-day political pressures of the desires and interests of those members of the national *demos* who do happen to be able to get themselves represented. The most forceful argument against the integration of a sovereign nation-state into the European community—that this gives immense powers to professionals who stand in a more tenuous relation of responsibility to a national *demos* than incumbents of national state office claim to do—is an argument that in France (unlike in Britain) has been infrequently made. The role of Brussels, or of the Bundesbank, in constraining the desires and capacities of agency of the French *demos* has been accepted with little demur by French politicians and intellectuals (excepting of course Le Pen, the Communist rump, and—as always—the farmers). Through such shifts, national politics have been defused of some of their charge; but whether this will continue, or whether national politics will be reinvested with passions and become a crucible in which exclusive identities are forged, will significantly depend on the success with which a new conception of political community, a redefinition of its contours and content, can be created. In this task—with which they ought to feel perfectly familiar—France's intellectuals should doubtless find themselves with a role to play.

Notes

CHAPTER ONE

1   Cf P. Anderson, 1983, p. 32: 'In the three decades or so after the Liberation, France came to enjoy a cosmopolitan paramountcy in the general Marxist universe that recalls in its own way something of the French ascendency in the epoch of the Enlightenment.' For reiterations of this judgement, see, for example, M. Kelly, 1982, p. 1: 'Nationally and internationally, French Marxists have played a crucial role in the social and political changes of the past century. For almost half that time, their practical importance has been complemented by a theoretical contribution of equally remarkable proportions' (cf also p. 225). Even those more critical in their evaluation of this now lapsed emphasis in French thought agree on its importance: cf T. Judt, 1986, p. 170: 'since 1945, there is no doubt that it is in France that theoretical discussion around problems in and of Marxism have been liveliest'. For local corroboration of this view, see M. Foucault, 1988, p. 41.

2   This influence was felt across a spectrum of disciplines: for example, in political sociology, there was the work of Nicos Poulantzas; in anthropology, that of Maurice Godelier, Emmanuel Terray and Pierre-Philippe Rey; in urban sociology, Mañuel Castells; in linguistics, Michel Pêcheux; in philosophy, Dominique Lecourt, Etienne Balibar and Georges Labica; in literary criticism, Pierre Macherey. Others like Régis Debray and Charles Bettelheim also borrowed from Althusser. For a loving survey of the Althusserian afflatus, see R.P. Resch, 1992.

3   Cf F. Châtelet, 1979, p. 246: 'Today, Althusserianism has become a constitutive part of the university ideology in France: it is the mode of existence of academically respectable Marxism.'

4   Cf P. Bandopadhyay, 1972, pp. 129–57.

5   For indications of this support, see SOFRES, 1969, nos 1–2 and SOFRES, 1976, nos 3–4.

6   D. Lindenberg, 1975, p. 20.

7   P. Anderson, 1983, p. 32. Compare F. Bourricaud, 1986, p. 11; and V. Descombes, 1980, pp. 129 and 132. This assessment was widely and repeatedly echoed across the range of French journals and reviews: for random examples, see P. Ducasset, Après-Demain (February 1981), p. 6; P.-M. de la Gorce, 'Le Recul de grandes espérances révolutionnaires', Le Monde Diplomatique (May 1984); E. Morin, 1986, pp. 72–84; F. Furet, 1986d, pp. 114–15.

8   For a powerful view on this question, but from a determinedly external position, see J. Dunn, 1984; compare P. Anderson, 1983.

9   Ibid., pp. 24–7. The emergence

of analytical Marxism, and the rise of cultural studies are symptomatic of this. On the influence of Marxism upon recent American sociology, see F. Chazel, 1986, pp. 319–42. Almost all the English figures interviewed in R. Fraser, 1988, continued to describe themselves as in some sense Marxists (unlike their French counterparts). See also M. Rustin, 1980, pp. 63–89.

10 From a large literature, see esp. R. Boudon, 1980, and idem, 1981, pp. 465–80; F. Bourricaud, 1980; R. Debray, 1979b, trans. 1981; P. Bourdieu, 1988; J.-F. Sirinelli, 1988.

11 See, for instance, R. Aron, 1955b; D. Bell, 1964. Also F. Furet, 'Les Intellectuels français et le structuralisme', in 1982.

12 For native examples, see: J.-P. Aron, 1984; F. de Negroni, 1985; S. Quadrupanni, 1983; H. Hamon and P. Rotman, 1981; P. Bourdieu, 1988, pp. 265–70.

This form of 'explanation' has become second nature for many. Thus what one commentator describes as 'The nightmarish inversion of many of the concepts developed on the intellectual Left over the years, now suddenly turned against their advocates', is put down to the 'trendy forms' and 'faddish aspects' of '(fashion-conscious) intellectuals': see K. Reader, 1987, p. 20; P. Bourdieu, 1986c, pp. 36 and 38, and G. Elliott, 1988, p. 11. 'Paris', we are told, 'has always been a fertile ground for pseudo-discoveries of a cultural kind. The intensity of the debates to which they give rise is often no substitute for either depth or durability', and intellectuals there display a persistent, if regrettable, French taste for 'la vulgarisation culturelle': see M. Vaughan, 'La Nouvelle Droite: Cultural power and poli-

tical influence', 1986, pp. 93–103.

Compare also the remarks cited by R. Aron, 1955b, trans. 1957, p. xiii (attributed to John Bowle): 'It is one of the most depressing aspects of the brilliant French culture that opinions so fundamentally silly should command so much prestige'; and N. Chomsky, personal correspondence (June 1985): 'I've always found the general atmosphere in Paris to be extremely irrational. Whatever one says or writes has to pass through the prism of current fad, whatever it is. Some years ago, it was one or another form of what George Lichtheim once called "Marxistical babytalk". Now it is equally idiotic Reaganite lunacies.' See also M. Aymé, 1945, where the politics of both the Left and Right are seen as being exposed to the 'ravages de la littérature', pp. 161–2. The literary dimension of French intellectual life is stressed in recent studies: see S. Turkle, 1979; M. Bowie, 1987. The criticism of French intellectuals as being too literary is of course coterminous with their first appearance on the political stage: cf the imprecations of Edmund Burke, *Reflections on the Revolution in France* (London, 1790); and later, Alexis de Tocqueville, *L'Ancien régime et la Révolution* (Paris, 1856). More recently, and with differing political intent, a similar perspective is adopted in G. Lukács, *The Destruction of Reason* (1954), trans. by P. Palmer (London, 1980); J. Habermas, 1987; and P. Dews, 1987. Although the latter two are considerably more distinguished accounts than that of Lukács', they share comparable strategies of explanation.

13 See, for example, S. Lukes, 1985.

14 See, for example, the accounts

of Sartre, Althusser and Foucault in R. Scruton, 1985; for a polemic from a quite different political persuasion, see P. Delwit and J.-M. Dewaele, 1984, pp. 324–48.

15 M. Poster, 1975; A. Hirsh, 1981; M. Kelly, 1982. For a more general account, see R. Pierce, 1966.

16 R. Rorty, 1984, p. 62. Thus Poster, 1975, p. vii, claims to show 'the relationship between Marxism and existentialism as the dominant theme in recent French social thought'; Hirsh, 1981, p. xi, tells us that the 'main theme' of 'French new Left theory' is 'focused on the project of discovering egalitarian solutions to the problems of alienation and bureaucracy in advanced industrial society' (see also p. 17); Kelly, 1982, finds the guiding thread for his study in the attempts to develop a 'materialist dialectics'. More cogently, P. Anderson, 1983, has argued that the 'master-problem' of contemporary French thought, common to both Marxists and their opponents, has been 'the nature of the relationships between structure and subject in human history and society' (p. 33).

17 Cf M.-A. Macciocchi, 1974, p. 259: 'Political thought in France is impoverished . . . even among those intellectuals most rigorous in their studies, it is very rare to find political thinkers, that is to say men . . . who are capable of sticking to the reality of their own country and their own times.'

18 For arguments which I take to secure this point, see J. Dunn, 1968, pp. 85–104; Q. Skinner, 1969, pp. 3–53.

19 J.A. Laponce, 1981, p. 43.

20 Cf C. Nicolet, 1982, p. 185.

21 For a fuller discussion, see O. Duhamel, 1980, pp. 8–29; and T. Judt, 1986, pp. 1–23.

22 See P. Pasquino, 1989, pp. 309–33.

23 See A. Bergounioux and B. Manin, 1980, pp. 45–53.

24 Cf L. Blum, Le Populaire, 5 April 1936: 'One must end the oligarchy of a handful of individuals who hold the nation to ransom, who betray and oppress the mass of citizens'; and F. Mitterrand, 'Présentation', Programme socialiste et Programme commun de gouvernement (Paris, 1972), p. 9: 'It [the Socialist Party] does not seek the approval of the privileged, of exploiters and profiteers. There can be no pact between it and the enemies of the people. But the workers, the peasants, the cadres, the technicians, the engineers—almost the entire tertiary sector—all are subject to the same oppression. And the middle classes have for their part learned that the power of the monopolies is built on their ruin . . . all therefore seek to free themselves from the grip of Big Capital. By such means a true class front is constituted between the workers, one which transcends their differences.'

25 Cf G. Lichtheim, 1966, p. 10: 'it is often forgotten that Marxism has been the major link between the French and the Russian Revolutions'.

26 On this aspect of French particularism, see the helpful discussion in T. Todorov, 1989a, esp. p. 5. The argument of these paragraphs is elaborated in the next chapter.

27 For some French observations on the problem, see R. Aron, 1955b, trans. 1957. Cf 'Les Intellectuels dans la société française contemporaine', Revue française de science politique, vol. 9, no. 4 (1959), in particular the articles by R. Rémond, and L. Bodin and J. Touchard; L. Bodin, 1964; R.

Debray, 1979b; P. Ory and J.-F. Sirinelli, 1986.

28 See J.-F. Sirinelli, 1990.

29 On the entry of the term into the French language at the time of the Dreyfus affair, see V. Brombert, 1960, pp. 20–40; and T. Field, 1976, pp. 159–67. See also the studies of C. Charle: especially 1990, and 1977, pp. 240–64. For the appearance and senses of the term in English, see P.A. Allen, 1986, pp. 342–58, and S. Collini, 1991, 'Introduction'.

30 This type of definition is equally common both to those working in the tradition of American social science and in the Marxist tradition: compare, for example, S.M. Lipset, 1963a; L. Coser, 1965; and M. Löwy, 1979.

31 Ory and Sirinelli, 1986, p. 10; and *cf* Sartre, 'Plaidoyer pour les intellectuels', in 1947–76, *Situations VIII* (1972).

32 R. Debray, 1979b, trans. 1981, p. 32.

33 For the claim that this is true of the English case, see the genealogy traced by N. Annan, 1955.

34 An aspect of French intellectual sensibility well caught by Flaubert: 'je soutiens (et ceci pour moi doit être un dogme pratique dans la vie d'artiste) qu'il faut faire dans son existence deux parts: vivre en bourgeois et penser en demi-dieu' (I am convinced (and for me this must be practical dogma for an artist's life) that it is necessary to divide one's existence in two: to live like a bourgeois and to think like a demi-god). G. Flaubert, Letter to Louise Colet (21 August 1853) in *Correspondance*, ed. J. Bruneau (Paris, 1980), vol. 2, p. 402. Quoted in C. Charle, 1990, p. 19.

35 See O. Rudelle, 1982.

CHAPTER TWO

1 *Cf* T. Judt (ed.), 1989.

2 The literature is reviewed in F. Bloch-Lainé and J. Bouvier, 1986, and R. Kuisel, 1981.

3 *Cf* M. Poster, 1975.

4 On the discourse and ideology of Jacobinism, see F. Fehér, 1987, esp. chap. 4; L. Loubère, 1959, pp. 415–31; and L. Jaume, 1989.

5 D. Travis, 1989, pp. 80–109.

6 On these currents, see D. Lindenberg, 1990.

7 R. Rémond, 1976, pp. 815–34.

8 *Cf* J. Paulhan, 1952. Paulhan here pointed out that while the intellectuals spoke of 'les Nazis', ordinary Frenchmen spoke of 'les Allemands' or 'les boches'.

9 A. Siegfried, 1956, p. 60; see also pp. 62–73. On the declining legitimacy of the Republic, see P. Bernard and H. Dubief, 1985.

10 On the close association between Radicalism and the Republic, *cf* Bernard and Dubief, 1985, p. 201: 'It had been the vocation of the Radicals to govern France under the Third Republic since 1900.' On the temporary flowering of solidarism at the close of the nineteenth century, see the articles by J. Hayward, 1959, pp. 261–84; 1961, pp. 19–48, and 1963, pp. 1–17.

11 On this vagueness of Radical ideas, see F. de Tarr, 1961, pp. 1–13. On the tenuous attachment of Radicalism to parliamentary politics, see D. Bardonnet, 1960; C. Nicolet, 1957; S. Bernstein, 1980.

12 See Bernard and Dubief, 1985; J. Jackson, 1988.

13 M. Sadoun, 1978, pp. 459–87 and 1982; but see also D. Mayer, 1968. On Mollet's neo-Guesdism, see B. D. Graham, 1947.

14 This was to change temporarily during the mid-1950s, when the new leader of the Radical Party,

Pierre Mendès–France, succeeded in winning the support of a number of intellectuals. See F. Bédarida and J.-P. Rioux (eds), 1985.

15 Thus Sartre, for example, attacked the Radical opposition between the citizen and state power, an opposition elaborated in the inter-war years through Alain's anti-statism. See J.-P. Sartre, 'Présentation', *Les Temps Modernes*, vol. 1, no. 1 (1945) repr. in 1947–76, *Situations* II (1948); also M. Merleau-Ponty, 1955, trans. 1973, pp. 3–4, and idem, 1960, trans. 1964, p. 348. On the intellectual reaction against the neo-Kantian assumptions of Third Republican philosophy, see V. Descombes, 1980, chap. 1.

16 J. Wilkinson, 1981, p. 7. See also, J.-L. Loubet del Bayle, 1969, and D. Lindenberg, 1990. For contemporary examples of such critical attacks, see E. Berl, 1929; A. Bonnard, 1935.

17 See, for example, the novels of A. Malraux, and *cf* V. Brombert, 1960, chap. 9. For philosophical expression of this mood, see J. Wahl, 1932.

18 See E. Mounier, 1961–3, vol. I, pp. 526, and 128. On some of the political implications of 'Personalisme', see T. Judt, 1992, esp. chap. 4.

19 A. Bergounioux, 1983–4, pp. 8–18. More specifically, on the anti-Fascist front, see H. Lottman, 1982; On the Popular Front, J. Jackson, 1988, pp. 85–145; on the Surrealists, R. Short, 1966, pp. 3–25, and A. Thirion, 1975; on the Marxists, D. Tartakowsky, 1979, pp. 30–40.

20 P. Nizan, 1932, trans. 1971, p. 138. Compare J. Michelet, 'Une année au Collège de France', *Œuvres complètes* (Paris, 1877), p. 535: 'Que peut le savant sans le peuple et le peuple sans le savant? Rien. Il faut que tous deux coopérent à l'action sociale.' Quoted in C. Charle, 1990, p. 24.

21 J.-L. Loubet del Bayle, 1969, esp. pp. 323ff.

22 The sense that intellectuals had an active role to play in the life of the wider community was encouraged by the formation of a new type of audience during the 1930s. Increased levels of higher education—a result of the educational priorities of the Third Republic—helped to produce a new, anonymous reading public, which in turn promoted the growing autonomy of the literary field. Replacing the salons of the Parisian bourgeoisie and the seminar rooms of the university, this audience allowed the emergence of a new type of intellectual, relatively free from rhw pressures of direct patronage, with potential access to intellectual and political reviews and so able to address a wider audience than hitherto. This was the moment of journals like the *Nouvelle Revue française*, as well as the beginning of the era of the great publishing houses founded by men such as Bernard Grasset and Gaston Gallimard. A greater movement between the worlds of the university and academy and that of writers and intellectuals became possible, as instanced in the trajectories of Rolland, Jules Romain, Giraudoux and Nizan. On these developments: see J. Lough, 1978, pp. 377–90; also G. Boillat, 1974; P. Assouline, 1984.

23 On the hostility of the French Right towards the Third Republic, see W.D. Irvine, 1974, pp. 534–62. For an account of the attitude of the intellectuals, see M. Curtis, 1959.

24 On the formulation during the 1930s of a new representation of society as divided into three

rather than two distinct groups (in part, an attempt to incorporate and absorb the more threatening Marxist analysis that described society as consisting essentially of two monolithically opposed blocs), see L. Boltanski, 1987, p. 37ff. Also G. Lichtheim, 1966, pp. 34–51.

25 E. Weber, 1962b, pp. 273–307, at p. 286.

26 The widespread and utter rejection of the Third Republic was made clear by the referendum of October 1945, when 96.4% of the votes cast were against any return to the constitutional arrangements of the Third Republic, or to the pre-war political system. See J.-P. Rioux, 1987, on the 'overwhelming rejection of the Third Republic, a regime too closely associated with the defeat of 1940' (p. 59).

27 For Alain's views on the tyrannical character of power, and the need to restrain the government and state, see 1926.

28 See J.-N. Jeanneney, 1977. On the French Communist Party during the 'Third Period' see P. Robrieux, 1980, vol. 1.

29 On this key and highly sensitive period in PCF historiography, see S. Courtois, 1980, and L. Taylor, 1989, pp. 53–79.

30 See J. Jackson, 1988.

31 This sense that existing institutions of 'formal' democracy were merely a front for 'bourgeois liberalism' permeated the immediate postwar writings of Sartre and Merleau-Ponty, and many others. Compare Sartre's comments in 'Les Communistes et la paix': 'The democratic regime today is nothing but a façade; all the real conflicts take place outside it' (in 1947–76, *Situations* VI, 1964, p. 142); and Merleau-Ponty (1947), 1980 edn., esp. pp. 39–79. This view was summed up in Sartre's (later) phrase, 'élections, piège à

cons'. In a sense this was quite right: so partial were some of the electoral systems devised after 1945 that in 1958 the Gaullists needed only 17.7% of the vote to gain 40.4% of the parliamentary seats, while the Communists required 19% to gather a mere 2.2% of the seats.

32 *Cf* M. Merleau-Ponty: 'We have reached a state of political nominalism of which there is perhaps no other example in French history', 'For the Sake of Truth' (originally published in *Les Temps Modernes*, no. 4, 1946), in 1948, trans. 1964, p. 160.

33 For a good reconstruction of the post-Liberation 'search for a new national mystique', see A. Shennan, 1989.

34 *Cf* P. Bernard and H. Dubief, 1985, pp. 295–6: 'The Communists turned back to Blanquism, the most chauvinistic strand in French socialism. The spirit of Jacobinism prevailed right up to the war. It was as if a long-suppressed patriotism burst out with extraordinary force, with immense satisfaction and relief to the militant rank and file, happy to leave their isolation.' On the Franco-Soviet Pact see M. Mourin, 1967.

35 *Cf* R. Gallisot, 1981, pp. 27–55.

36 M. Thorez, speech 6 August, 1936, quoted in ibid., pp. 40–1.

37 *Cf* P. Birnbaum, 1979, pp. 40–5; also Gallisot, 1981, p. 32.

38 The Communist press was saturated with this language. Some random examples taken from the late 1930s: *L'Humanité* (29 April 1938): 'They [the bourgeoisie] sabotage the national economy without the least consideration of the country's interest'; *L'Humanité* (22 March 1938): 'They [the bourgeoisie] attack the working class, without whom there would be no one to defend the nation.'

39 For extensive documentation of this conflation, see P. Birnbaum, 1979. It was clearly and famously exemplified in Maurice Thorez's 'main tendue' speech; *cf* L. Bodin and J. Touchard, 1961, p. 52.

40 Quoted in R. Gallisot, 1981. See also H. Lefebvre, 1937, and J. Bruhat's review of it in *L'Humanité* (17 December 1937).

41 Quoted in P. Bénéton, 1975, pp. 109–10. During the Resistance period, this stress on revolutionary patriotism was a central feature of Communist language: see H.R. Kedward, 1978, esp. pp. 55–60 and chap. 7.

42 R. Gallisot, 1981, p. 31.

43 J. Berlioz, 'Europe, nation, internationalisme', *Les Cahiers du Communisme* (July 1949), pp. 820–1: 'The idea of the nation, from its origin, was linked with the idea of democratic progress, until it was hijacked by Big Capital, which then used it for its own reactionary purposes. In the present epoch, this link has been rediscovered: the working class is the true vehicle of the national project, which can only be achieved through the development of proletarian internationalism. [...] the national question and the social question are the same. The combatants of the French Revolution of 1789 were called patriots, in opposition to the traitors of Coblentz, who formed an alien cosmopolitan network ... we are struggling for the reconquest of French independence because it will help our people and weaken the camp of imperialism, which will in turn help other peoples. Thus we remain on the terrain of class, the only solid terrain: that of the liberation of the whole nation through the liberation of the proletariat.' See also G. Cogniot, *Réalité de la nation* (Paris, 1950), and idem., 'Classe

ouvrière et nation', *Les Cahiers du Communisme* (October 1945), p. 24: 'Today, because of social and economic evolution, the working class has become the leader of the modern Third Estate: it is the vital element of the nation and it alone can emancipate the nation from those modern privileged persons who, like those of 1789, are a burden on the nation although they are not part of it. The working class is identified with the nation to the extent that it is called upon to achieve the unification of France.' Quoted in B. Legendre, 1980, pp. 130–1.

44 Aulard had drawn a parallel between the French Revolution and the Russian Revolution of March 1917 in a pamphlet written at the request of the French government, 'La Révolution française et la Révolution russe. Lettre aux citoyens de la libre Russie.' This was delivered as an address to the Ligue des Droits de l'Homme in April 1917. See H. Rollin, 1931, vol. 1, pp. 55–6.

45 A. Mathiez, 1920a, p. 3.

46 Frossard, in his speech at Tours in 1920, alluded to Mathiez's study, and extended the analogy which described the Bolshevik Revolution as a continuation of the emancipatory process begun in 1789–93. The speech is reprinted in A. Kriegel, 1964b, see esp. p. 62. See also R. Wohl, 1966. Wohl rightly observes that 'though no one seemed to notice it, an important corner had been turned: the mystique of the Russian Revolution had become a weapon in the internal politics of the French working-class movement' (p. 86).

47 This was part of a series of discussions held to mark the seventieth anniversary of Marx's death. They were published in

La Pensée, no. 51 (1953), pp. 109–43.

48 J. Chambaz *et al.*, 1953, p. 111.

49 Ibid., p. 119.

50 Ibid., p. 121. This was an attack on French sociologists (such as Georges Friedmann) who were trying to provide answers to the question of what exactly had happened to the French working class in the decade after 1945. They attempted to do so by focusing on two themes: the apparent fusion of interests between the working class and the lower middle classes; and the changing links between the working class and the sphere of technical production.

51 This claim, authorized here by reference to Stalin's *Economic Problems of Socialism in the USSR*, was stated in a language whose continuities with the Althusserian discourse of the 1960s are noteworthy: 'Marxism is not true because it is successful. It is successful because it is true. Historical materialism is not a vulgar philosophy of history, it is the ensemble of discoveries that founds the scientific study of societies' (*La Pensée*, no. 51, 1953, p. 122).

52 Ibid., p. 140.

53 T. Judt, 1986, p. 6.

54 *Cf* J. Godechot, 1958, 2nd edn., 1983, pp. 535–6: 'This image of the *"grande nation"*, upholder of the rights of man, champion of the people's right to self-determination, creator of the modern state, unified, indivisible and centralized, remained henceforth in the memory of men. It was by reference to this memory that one came to judge the politics of France, not only during the epoch of the Directory, but even in our own times ... whether it wishes so or not, France remains bound by those tacit obligations contracted, between 1789 and 1799, by the *"grande nation"*; it is charged with a mission, and if it betrays this it cannot be excused.'

55 See S. Bernstein and R. Frank, (esp. p. 263), both in J. Becker and F. Knipping (eds), 1986.

56 P. Melandri and M. Vaisse, 'France: from Powerlessness to the Search for Influence' and P. Ory, 'Introduction to an Era of Doubt. Cultural Reflections of 'French Power', around the year 1948', both in ibid. See also J.-B. Duroselle, 'Changes in French Foreign Policy since 1945', in S. Hoffmann *et al.*, 1963, pp. 305–58. For an account of one of the 'Big Three', Britain, see P. Addison, *The Road to 1945* (London, 1977).

57 *Cf* S. Hoffmann, 1961, pp. 28–63, at p. 43: 'Because of the defeat and later reaction against Vichy there occurred a kind of rediscovery of France and of the French by the French.'

58 On this 'internationalist' aspect of French nationalism, C.J.H. Hayes, 1930, is still useful. That French nationalism was a political doctrine, a set of ideas, rather than a reflection of the real organization or belief-systems of the vast rural areas of France has been persuasively argued by historians like Theodore Zeldin and Eugen Weber. *Cf* E. Weber, 1976, p. 493: 'the nation [was] not ... a given reality but ... a work-in-progress, a model of something at once to be built and to be treated for political reasons as already in existence'.

59 See H.R. Kedward, 1982, pp. 175–92, at p. 189: 'A central dynamic of the years 1940–44 is the growing claim of Resistance individuals and movements on the very language and imagery which the ideological Pétainists believed was inalienably theirs.'

60 *Cf* Charles de Gaulle: 'France must fulfill her mission as a world power. We are every-

where in the world. There is no corner of the earth, where, at a given time, men do not look to us and ask what France says. It is a great responsibility to be France, the humanizing power par excellence', (speech at Bordeaux, 15 April 1961), quoted in Duroselle, 'Changes in French Foreign Policy since 1945', in S. Hoffmann *et al.*, 1963, p. 352. In a sense, de Gaulle was right: France had maintained its colonial empire longer than most other European nations, and had insisted on a global geo-political presence (with military and naval bases in the Pacific, Guyana, the Indian Ocean, the North Pole, etc.). But this was a fictive power, the limits of which were clearly marked by the end of the Algerian war in 1962, and the return to France of around one million *pieds-noirs*. Compare R. Aron, 1960, p. 148: 'General de Gaulle ordered France to play a role commensurate not with her means but with his own conception of grandeur.' For a study of de Gaulle's conception of France's role in world politics, see P. Cerny, 1980. Cerny notes that 'the French conception of France's mission or vocation takes on a cultural function akin to that played by the Constitution in American political culture or the monarchy in Britain' (p. 31); for further illumination of this comparative aspect, see the comments in D. Cannadine, 1984, p. 156–7.

61 See A. Malraux, 1952; and A. Malraux and J. Burnham, 1948. On Malraux's Gaullist nationalism, see J. Mossuz-Lavau, 1982, esp. pp. 95–121.

62 A. Malraux, *Le Rassemblement*, no. 96 (19 February 1949).

63 Speech, 2 July 1947, quoted in J. Mossuz-Lavau, 1982, p. 136.

64 The similarity has often been noted: *cf* P. Birnbaum, 1979, p. 83; and R. Aron, 1955b, trans. 1957, p. x: 'Gaullists and socialists unite around the slogan of national independence. Does this slogan stem from the integral nationalism of Maurras or from Jacobin patriotism?' On de Gaulle's political vocabulary, and the prevalence of terms which symbolized unity, see J.-M. Cotteret and R. Moreau, 1969.

65 J. Lacouture, 1984–6, trans. 1990, vol. 1, p. 468. On the character of de Gaulle's nationalism, see J. Touchard, 1978, esp. pp. 299–300.

66 *Cf* R. Paxton, 1972, pp. 259–73.

67 On the split of the French Left at the Congress of Tours in 1920, and the origins of the French Communist Party, see A. Kriegel, 1964a, and 1964b; also P. Robrieux, 1980–4, esp. vol. 1; and R. Wohl, 1966. All the documents and texts pertaining to the Congress of Tours are collected in J. Charles *et al.*, 1980. On the impact of the Tours split on the French Socialists, see T. Judt, 1976.

68 M. Cachin, *L'Humanité* (13 November 1946), quoted in I.M. Wall, 1983, p. 46.

69 Ibid., pp. 3 and 4. There is a large literature on relations between the French Communists and the Soviet Union, and the Communist International. See in particular: A. Rieber, 1964; F. Fejtö, 1987; A.E. Stiefbold, 1977; L. Marcou, 1977; J. Friend, 1982, pp. 212–35; and G. Lavau, 1982, pp. 189–210.

70 *Cf* R. Koselleck, 1988. In postrevolutionary France, the arguments received a new definition during the Third Republic, especially at the time of the Dreyfus affair. See, for example, E. Durkheim, 1898, 1969, pp. 14–30. Also C. Delhorbe, 1932;

C. Charle, 1985.

71 *Cf* J. Benda, 1927, and Paul Nizan, 1932, trans. 1971.

72 *Cf* A. Siegfried, 1956, pp. 119–20: 'Regardless of the extreme diversity of the Maquis and the Resistance groups, all were informed by the political spirit of the Resistance. This was a patriotic mystique, in the sense of the republican 'patriots' of the Revolution, although the desired Republic bore no resemblance to that of the Third Republic but was founded upon a mystique of total social renovation, and borrowed instinctively from the vocabulary of the Apocalypse. The prophetic spirit came naturally to the Resistor, as it had in the past to the persecuted of the Cevennes. It was not, therefore, merely a case of resisting: it was necessary to prepare a new regime for the moment when the totalitarian Babylon would be overthrown: all of which makes clear that, in the minds of its leaders, the Resistance would not come to an end with the Liberation.'

73 For comparisons with Germany and Italy, see J. Wilkinson, 1981.

74 Reprinted in M. Merleau-Ponty, 1948, trans. 1964.

75 Ibid., p. 139. Further page references are given in the main text.

76 *Cf* S. Hoffmann, 1961, pp. 28–63. As Hoffmann pointed out, the Vichy period saw the division and fragmentation of France into more administrative zones and separate realms than at any time since the Revolution. Hoffmann noted the sociological consequences of this, but there were also intellectual effects: a new sense of France as a geographical territory whose unity had been fractured and violated. See F.

Braudel, 'Introduction', vol. 1, 1988.

77 R. Aron, 1945, p. 91, originally in *La France Libre* (15 June 1941).

78 J.-P. Sartre, 'La Nationalisation de la littérature', (1945), in 1947–76, *Situations* II (1948), pp. 40–1.

79 See J. Wilkinson, 1981, pp. 42–50.

80 On the intellectual purges, see H. Lottmann, 1985; Robert Aron, 1975, vol. 3; P. Assouline, 1985; T. Judt, 1992, chaps 3 and 4.

81 Sartre, 'Qu'est-ce qu'un collaborateur?' (1945), in 1947–76, *Situations* III (1949), p. 60.

82 J. Paulhan, 1948.

83 Ibid., pp. 9–11. Further references given in main text.

84 Paulhan quoted extensively from these three writers, and from the responses of their colleagues, to demonstrate that they had in fact taken recognizably 'anti-national positions' during the 1930s.

85 Ibid., pp. 99–100. 'It is the fatherland. Still less: it is the fatherland in its raw state, before one is even conscious of it, before one even formulates the will to belong to it, to improve it, to defend it. In a word, it is the nation.'

86 Paulhan defined real patriotism as the bringing together of two senses of the word: the Fascist 'patrie charnelle', which only considered interests, and the democratic 'patrie spirituelle', which considered the liberty of its citizens: 'When M. Bardèche (who is a Fascist) speaks of France, what does he show us? Streets, harvests, a French peasant seated at a long table, an old woman queuing for milk... But when Julien Benda (who is a democrat) speaks, it is a question of French truth, French

justice . . . It seems to me that the conclusion which forces itself upon any normal mind is that M. Bardèche and M. Benda are each a good part of what it is to be a patriot. It would be sufficient to combine each to arrive at a complete Frenchman. . . . The problem for all of us lies here: how to be Bàrdeche and Benda at the same time? How to love with the same affection France in her spiritual and fleshly aspects ['la France charnelle et la France spirituelle']? How to cease being a partisan and become a patriot?' (pp. 169–71). See also J. Bersani (ed.), 1976, esp. the papers by T. Ferenczi, 'Jean Paulhan et le discours politique', and F. Grover, 'Jean Paulhan et la politique'.

87   In the Resistance press and journals, 'Fascism' was taken generically and inclusively to mean the Vichy regime, the capitalist system, the German Occupation, and every aspect of collaboration. See H.R. Kedward, 1982, p. 156.

88   On this critique, shared both by Fascists and Left revolutionaries, and on the numerous crossovers between the two, see Z. Sternhell, 1986; P. Burrin, 1986; and more generally, D. Lindenberg, 1990. For a case-study, see D. Wolf, 1969. For a detailed study of the common languages in the German context, see J.-P. Faye, 1972.

89   The Resistance valued Péguy for his 'intransigent and revolutionary patriotism'; a special collection of his writings edited by the Communist Gabriel Péri was published by Les Editions de Minuit, *Péguy-Péri* (1944).

90   Merleau-Ponty, 1948, trans. 1964, pp. 159–60.

91   This elision of class with nation was made more easy as a conse-quence of the popular resistance to Fascism. Even conservative intellectuals like François Mauriac noted that 'Only the working class in its entirety remained loyal to France at the moment of its desecration'; F. Mauriac (pseudonym 'Forez'), 1944, p. 19.

92   *Cours Elémentaire du parti: la Nation* (November 1945), in the series published by the Party, *Ecole élémentaire du PCF*.

93   'Les communistes et la paix' 1952–4, repr. in *Situations* VI, 1964, p. 259. Antibourgeois perorations were not, however, confined to Communist language; they could be found also in journals like *Esprit*, at this time fully endorsing revolutionary politics. See, for instance, G. Sérapha, 'Le Problème politique français, 1789–1944', *Esprit*, no. 105 (1944): 'L'élimination de la bourgeoisie française des postes de commande sociaux est une mésure de salut spirituel et national.'

94   *Auch eine Philosophie der Geschichte* (1774). And *cf* Voltaire, *Philosophie de l'histoire* (1765).

95   *Cf* L. Dumont, 1985, p. 507:'"I am human by nature, and French by accident" is set in opposition to "I am essentially a German, and I am human thanks to my qualities as a German".' For this contrast put differently, see J. Plamenatz, 1973, pp. 23–36. For the classic statement of the specific difference of German thought as regards other western European thought, see E. Troeltsch 'The Ideas of Natural Law and Humanity in World Politics', appendix I in O. Gierke, *Natural Law and the Theory of Society*, 2 vols, trans. by E. Barker (Cambridge, 1934). See also F. Meinecke, *Cosmopolitanism and the National State*, trans. by

R.B. Kimber (Princeton, 1970), chap. 1.

96 Cf L. Dumont, 1986a, pp. 130–1: '...The French liberals, as the Revolutionaries before them, seem to have thought that constituting European and other peoples into nations would be enough to solve all problems and ensure peace. In the last analysis, they conceived the nation only as a framework for the emancipation of the individual, the latter being the alpha and omega of all political problems...Therefore, while the French were content with juxtaposing nations as so many fragments of mankind, the Germans, acknowledging the individuality of each nation, were preoccupied in *ordering* the nations within mankind in relation to their value—or their might...The Germans saw themselves, and tried to impose themselves, as superior *qua* Germans, while the French consciously postulated only the superiority of the universalist culture, but identified with it so naively that they looked on themselves as the educators of mankind'. See also Dumont, 1985, esp. p. 507.

97 Guizot, 1828, p. 5.

98 *De l'Allemagne et de la Révolution* (Paris, 1832), quoted in R.A. Lochore, 1935, p. 74.

99 *La Pologne* (Paris, 1846), quoted in Lochore, p. 51.

100 See, for example, Michelet, *Le Peuple* (Paris, 1846). *Cf* Edmund Wilson's description of Michelet's nationalism: 'Though his organic conception of history enabled him to see humanity as a whole, he was in the habit of thinking of it and dealing with it in terms of its components: nations. He had, however, a special version of nationalism which enabled him, in the case of France, to identify the 'patrie' exclusively with the revolutionary tradition. In the name of the Revolution she had been chosen to lead and enlighten the world.' (1968, p. 38).

101 E. Renan, 1871 and 1882; H. Taine, 1889.

102 See K. Swaart, 1964. On Ferry, R. Girardet, 1973, and F. Furet (ed.), 1985.

103 *Histoire de France* (Paris, 1912), quoted in P. Nora, 1962, pp. 73–106, at p. 104.

104 'Autour de Marxisme', 1946, reprinted in 1948, trans. 1964, p. 110.

105 On the historical roots of this language, see W. Sewell, 1980.

106 On the oscillation in Communist terminology between *peuple, ouvrier*, and *travailleur*, and the adoption of a language of unity and virtue as opposed to that of divisive particular interests, *cf* T. Judt, 1986, pp. 108–9.

CHAPTER THREE

1 'Itinerary of a Thought', in 1974, p. 59.

2 'A Plea for Intellectuals', in 1974, p. 256.

3 For bibliographies of Sartre's work, see M. Contat and M. Rybalka, 1970, 1971, and 1979; and F. Lapointe, 1975.

4 See, by way of example, W.L. McBride, 1991; P. Chiodi, 1976; M. Poster, 1979; R. Aronson, 1981; M. Jay, 1984, chap. 11.

5 I have restricted the discussion in this chapter to what I take to be the key writings in which Sartre publicly declared his political purposes. Another possible approach would be to study the way his writing was *received*. This is, of course, particularly relevant for assessing the significance and meaning of Sartre's writings published in his review *Les Temps Modernes*. This is an area that still requires research,

but see H. Davies, 1987.

6 On the insistent government propaganda campaign calling for increased production, *cf* J.-P. Rioux, 1987, chap. 5. This suggests one dimension for understanding Sartre's later enthusiasm for Maoism. See S.M. Lipset, 1963b, for a discussion of newly independent post-colonial states, where a similar discourse on the superfluity of intellectual and literary activity prevailed.

7 Georges Bataille is another case in point; on this form of intellectual response, see J.-M. Besnier, 1988.

8 On the review, and on Sartre's role in it, the best study is A. Boschetti, 1985; *cf* H. Davies, 1987.

9 'La Nationalisation de la littérature', *Les Temps Modernes*, no. 1, 1945; reprinted in 1947–76, *Situations* II, 1948, pp. 33–53. Further references are given in the main text.

10 Sartre was continually exercised by this distinction, which embodies a long-standing tension in French intellectual life between the literary author and the 'social-political' writer, symbolized by the figures of Flaubert and Zola respectively. On this, see Barthes, 'Ecrivains et écrivants', in 1964; and for an argument that this distinction and tension fundamentally defines twentieth-century French intellectual life, see Stoekl, 1992.

11 *Situations* II, pp. 48–9.

12 On this 'Heideggerian' strategy, see Bourdieu, 1980, pp. 11–12.

13 'Présentation' (1945), *Situations* II, p. 11.

14 de Beauvoir, 1968, pp. 14–15.

15 'Qu'est-ce que la littérature?', *Les Temps Modernes* (March 1947), reprinted in *Situations* II, p. 267. Subsequent quotations are given in the main text.

16 Ibid., p. 261 in Sartre (1948; trans. 1967) p. 173; see also pp. 259–60/pp. 171–2. *Cf* Sartre's description of how writers saw themselves during the Resistance: 'those among us [writers and intellectuals] who worked in the Resistance in their capacity as specialists could not ignore the fact that the doctors, engineers, sailors, were doing a much more important job' (p. 258/p. 170).

17 'Réponse à Albert Camus', 1952, in 1947–76, *Situations* IV, 1964, pp. 93 and 96. On these polemics, see Judt, 1992.

18 'Qu'est-ce que la littérature?', *Situations* II, p. 309; *What is Literature?*, 1967, p. 214.

19 On Sartre's excessive generosity as a form of aggression, see Davies, 1987, pp. 159–60.

20 Compare Sartre's description of the proletariat: 'He is trying to free himself, and by the same token, to free all men from oppression forever' (p. 276/p. 186).

21 *Cf* p. 195/p. 117: 'It is quite evident that in such a society, there would be nothing which would even remotely recall the separation of the temporal and the spiritual'; and p. 168/pp. 93–4, where Sartre assailed the severance of this link. The quotation in the text is from Merleau-Ponty, 1955, trans. 1973, p. 200.

22 '... the People were much more the subject of certain of their works than their chosen public', was Sartre's judgement (p. 162/p. 89).

23 Sartre's phrase to describe the Surrealists' ambition was 's'approprier tout à la fois'; a phrase that roundly captures Sartre's own ambition. The vehemence Sartre reserved for his attack on Surrealism stemmed in part from a recognition of his own strategies in theirs.

24 Sartre, 1948, trans. 1967, p. 147.

25 *Cf* p. 277/p. 187: 'Unhappily, these men, to whom we *must*

speak are separated from us by an iron curtain in our own country: they will not hear a word we shall say to them. The majority of the proletariat, strait-jacketed by a single party, encircled by a propaganda which isolates it, forms a closed society without doors or windows. There is only one way of access, a very narrow one, the Communist Party', and p. 287/196: 'It is true that today one can hardly reach the working class if not through the Party.'

26 'Matérialisme et révolution', reprinted in 1947–76, *Situations* III, 1949; trans. in Sartre, 1955.

27 The fullest statement of the movement's intentions were presented in the *Entretiens sur la politique* held between Sartre, David Rousset, and Gerard Rosenthal, and first printed in *Les Temps Modernes* in 1948. Subsequently published by Gallimard (1949), it went through at least twenty editions in the first couple of years. See also the 'Manifesto' of the Rassemblement, reprinted in Contat and Rybalka, 1970, pp. 194–9. For a summary account of the RDR episode, see Burnier, 1966, pp. 63–75.

28 For Sartre's own account of this episode, see his 'Merleau-Ponty vivant', *Situations* IV, 1964, pp. 223–5.

29 For a representative statement of his earlier view, see Merleau-Ponty, 'Foi et bonne Foi', *Les Temps Modernes*, no. 5 (1946), reprinted in 1948, trans. 1964, p. 179: 'The intellectual who refuses his commitments on the pretext that his function is to see all sides is in fact contriving to live a pleasant life under the guise of obeying a vocation. He resolves to avoid all resolutions and to supply strong reasons to those weak in conviction. He who is not with me is against

me. Not being a Communist is being anti-Communist.' And compare *Eloge de la philosophie* (Paris, 1953). See also K. Whiteside, 1988, p. 235.

30 It should not be supposed that Merleau-Ponty's support for Mendès-France was the result of a heightened understanding of the French political situation: he declared his support at the very moment when popular support for the Mendèsist party was slackening; see G. Invitto, 1971, p. 106.

31 Sartre, 'Merleau-Ponty vivant', *Situations* IV, p. 221. And *cf* de Beauvoir, 1968, pp. 140–1.

32 'Merleau-Ponty vivant', *Situations* IV, p. 217.

33 Ibid., p. 220: 'It is a fact that we had forgotten the class struggle.'

34 *Cf* Aronson, 1980. For typical examples of critical reaction to the languages of nationalism and patriotism which appear in Sartre's political writings of this period, *cf* Gleicher, 1982, who writes of 'touching and surprisingly nationalistic' elements in Sartre's writing. Numerous examples of this criticial vocabulary and response could be adduced.

35 'Les Communistes et la paix', *Les Temps Modernes*, 1952–4, reprinted in 1947–76, *Situations* VI, 1964, p. 168; trans., 1969.

36 Sartre's understanding of the anarcho-syndicalist tradition seems largely to have been derived from his reading of Michel Collinet: see, for example, M. Collinet, 1948.

37 Sartre dismissed in a paragraph the definitions of class pursued in the work of Bukharin, Sorokin, Gurvitch, and Halbwachs. See *Les Communistes et la paix*, pp. 201–2.

38 Ibid., p. 195; *cf* also pp. 249–50, 207 and 252.

39 Merleau-Ponty, 1955, trans. 1973, pointed out how in Sartre's

political language the masses were repeatedly represented through feminine metaphors: they appear as women, 'daignent se soumettre, elles attendent d'être forcées, d'être prises' (they condescend to submit, wait to be forced, to be taken) (1955, p. 218).

40 Compare ibid., pp. 107–8.

41 Les Communistes et la paix, p. 92. Sartre elaborated this reasoning, and went on to ascribe it to Lenin (p. 93); but he adopted it for his own. He conceded that the identification between the Soviet Union and the revolutionary cause could never be complete. But such an identification could only be shown to be actually false if it could be proved, first, that the Soviet leadership no longer believed in the Revolution; and, second, that the Revolution had reached a stalemate. Even if true, neither of these propositions could at this point in history be proved. Sartre's rationalization here was identical to Althusser's later.

42 If Sartre's political attitude towards America was 'anti-American', it is nevertheless true that he was fascinated by American culture, literature and films. See M. Granjon, 'Sartre, Beauvoir, Aron: An Ambiguous Affair', in D. Lacorne, J. Rupnik and M.-F. Toinet (eds), 1990, pp. 116–33.

43 'Les Communists et la paix', Situations VI, p. 259; translation: 'In France today, the working class alone possesses a doctrine, its 'particularism' alone is in full harmony with the interests of the nation; a great party represents it and it alone has made it its programme to safeguard democratic institutions, to re-establish national sovereignty and to defend peace, it alone is concerned with economic renaissance and an increase in

purchasing power, finally, it alone lives, is teeming with life, while the others teem with words.'

44 Cf C. Lefort, 1953, pp. 1541–70.

45 For details of this debate, and for Merleau-Ponty's defence of Lefort, which became a devastating attack on Sartre, see K. Whiteside, 1988, esp. chap. 8; B. Cooper, 1979; and M. Poster, 1975, chap. 5.

46 Merleau-Ponty, 'Sartre and Ultra-Bolshevism', in 1955, trans. 1973, p. 157.

47 Ibid., p. 158.

48 'Le Réformisme et les fétiches', 1956 reprinted in 1947–76, Situations VII, 1965, p. 110. See also in the same volume his criticism of the Trotskyist Pierre Naville, 'Réponse à Pierre Naville'(1956).

49 Aron, L'Opium des intellectuels (1955b); Merleau-Ponty, Les Aventures de la dialectique (1955).

50 'Mendésisme' was in the main a movement amongst and for intellectuals. See Sirinelli, 'Les Intellectuels et Pierre Mendès-France: un phénomène de génération?', in F. Bédarida and J.-P. Rioux (eds), 1985.

51 See Sorum, 1977.

52 Cf the interview given by Sartre to L'Express (at this time a supporter of Mendès-France), excerpted in Contat and Rybalka, 1970, pp. 304–6.

53 'Le Fântome de Staline' (1956), reprinted in 1947–76, Situations VII, 1965, pp. 290 and 292.

54 Lefort, 1958, reprinted in 1971, pp. 260–84, at p. 271. Cf R. Aronson, 1980, p. 231, who noted that Sartre's 'analysis unveiled one necessity after another...as he presented them, the facts all spoke in favour of the Soviet invasion'.

55 See, for instance, Delannoi, 1982.

56 Merleau-Ponty, 1953, trans. 1963.

57 Merleau-Ponty, 1955, trans. 1973, p. 189.
58 Ibid., p. 190.
59 Sartre, 1968, p. 6.
60 Ibid., pp. 53 and 5.
61 Ibid., p. 6; cf Sartre, 1960, trans. 1991, vol. 1, p. 823: 'We are now facing the same difficulty which confronted analytical Reason at the end of eighteenth century, when it became necessary to prove its legitimacy.'
62 Ibid., vol. 1, p. 822. Cf p. 52: 'we are trying to establish the *Truth of History*'.
63 Cf Sartre's disarming disclaimer: 'I am far from believing that the isolated effort of an individual can provide a satisfactory answer—even a partial one—to so vast a question, a question which engages with the totality of History . . . if as would be best, this discussion is carried on collectively in working groups, then I shall be satisfied', *Critique*, 1991, vol. 1, pp. 40–1. Sartre's ultimate failure to complete the projected second volume of the *Critique* can be explained by the ambition of his original conception. Cf Contat and Rybalka, 1979, p. 340: 'Sartre was interrupted when he realized that the elaboration of the second volume—which, it may be recalled, was supposed to reach the level of concrete history—required a sum of readings and historical research representing the work of a life-time for a philosopher, or for a group of researchers, the work of many years.'
64 For internal explications, see W. Desan, 1965; P. Chiodi, 1976; M. Poster, 1979; F. Jameson, 1971, chap. 4; A. Gorz, 1977.
65 This is the definition given in the glossary appended to the English translation of the *Critique*, vol. 1, p. 829.
66 *Critique*, 1991, vol. 1, pp. 351–2. Cf 'Elections: A Trap for Fools' (1973) in 1978, p. 203: 'Only the parties, which were originally groups—though more or less bureaucratic and serialized—can be considered to have a modicum of power. In this case it would be necessary to reverse the classic formula, and when a party says "Choose Me"!' understand it to mean not that the voters would delegate their sovereignty, but that, refusing to unite in a group to obtain sovereignty, they would appoint one or several of the political communities already formed, in order to extend the power they have to the national limits. No party will be able to represent the series of citizens, because every party draws its power from itself, from its communal structure. In any case the series in its powerlessnes cannot delegate any authority.'
67 Cf Poster, 1979, p. 72.
68 Kojève, 1969.
69 *Critique*, 1991, vol. 1, p. 804. See also Sartre's praise for André Gorz's autobiographical account of his struggles to betray his class: Sartre, 'Preface' to A. Gorz, 1959.
70 *Critique*, 1991, vol. 1, p. 679; see also p. 662.
71 Cf Sartre's discussion in 'The Risk of Spontaneity and the Logic of Institution: An interview with Jean-Paul Sartre', *Telos*, no. 4 (1969), pp. 191–205.
72 Sartre, 1985, p. 119.
73 Lévi-Strauss, 1962, trans. 1966.
74 Ibid., p. 254.
75 Ibid., p. 257; and cf p. 254.
76 Jean Rony, 1966, pp. 100–28; the other articles were: A. Gisselbrecht, 'Presentation'; J.-P. Colombel, 'J.-P. Sartre—approches méthodologiques'; F. Hincker, 'J.-P. Sartre et l'histoire'; and C. Glucksmann, 'J.-P. Sartre et le gauchisme esthétique'.

77 A similar criticism was made by another Party intellectual, Roger Garaudy, in an article on Sartre written for a Soviet encyclopedia; see *Filosofskaja enciklopedija*, T.4, M. *'Sov. enciklopedija'*, 1967, p. 557. Quoted in T.J. Blakely, 1968, pp. 122–35, at p. 135.

78 See, for instance, Sartre's articles on Cuba, which deny any importance to the activities of the radical intellectual, Sartre, 1961; *cf* Aronson, 1980, pp. 241–2. See also 'The Purposes of Writing' (1959), in Sartre, 1974. Asked whether he thought his writing had changed anything, his candid reply was, 'Not a thing.'

79 1965a.

80 Ibid., pp. 259–60.

81 'The Burgos Trial' (1971), in 1978, p. 160.

82 Ibid., p. 161.

83 See 'A Friend of the People' (1970), in 1974, p. 297; and 'Justice and the State' (1972) in 1978, pp. 183–4; 'Now, if it was possible to bring the workers and the intellectuals together in at least one area, there could be hope of eventually rebuilding the alliance of the intelligentsia and the proletariat which had been widespread in the nineteenth century and which the Communist Party had broken up.'

84 Worth noting in this context are the reasons he gave for refusing the Nobel Prize. See Contat and Rybalka, 1970, pp. 402–5 (64/410).

85 1974, p. 293 and 227.

86 Ibid., p. 292.

87 Ibid., p. 292. *Cf* 'Justice and the State', in 1978, p. 179: 'if an intellectual chooses the people, he must know that the time for signing manifestoes, for quiet protest meetings, and for publishing articles in 'reformist' newspapers is over. His task is not so much to speak as to try by any means available to him, to *let the people speak for themselves.'*

88 *Cf* Sorel, 1929.

CHAPTER FOUR

1 L. Althusser, 1992a. Boutang, 1992, p. 59.

2 *Cf* Althusser, 1992a, p. 139: 'I was still euphoric over the publication in October of *Pour Marx* et *Lire 'Le Capital'*. But suddenly I was gripped by an unbelievable panic, by the fear that these texts would reveal me naked to a wider public; I would be shown up as a creature of mere artifice and imposture, a philosopher who knew hardly at all the history of philosophy and hardly anything of Marx (whose youthful works I had certainly studied; but by 1964—the year I conducted the seminar which resulted in *Lire 'Le Capital'*—I had only seriously studied Book One of *Capital*).'

3 Boutang, 1992, p. 84; and see p. 128.

4 See H. Hamon and P. Rotman, 1979.

5 Eric Hobsbawm, in a 1966 *TLS* review of *Pour Marx* and *Lire 'Le Capital'* (1965), noted of Althusser: 'His rise has been curiously sudden. Before 1965 he was virtually unknown even to the left-wing public'; reprinted in *Revolutionaries* (London, 1977), p. 145. On the impact of Althusser's work outside France, see, for example: L. Crespo, 1977, pp. 57–63; G. Lock, 1977, pp. 64–72; F. Navarro, 1992, pp. 55–6.

6 Althusser, in Althusser and Balibar, 1979, p. 67.

7 See, for example, P. Dews, 1980b.

8 For a contemporary account which described Althusser's ambition to found a 'science of liberation', *cf* J.-P. Dollé, 1966, pp. 1890–1917, at p. 1917.

9 T. Benton, 1984; see also M. Jay, 1984, p. 387.

10 See G. Elliott, 1987, and *cf* Jay, 1984, pp. 416–17.

11 P. Anderson, 1976, p. 39.

12 Authoritarian dispositions are assumed by, for example, R. Scruton, 1985, and E.P. Thompson, 1978. On his 'sentimentality', see for instance R. Blackburn and G. Stedman Jones, 'Louis Althusser and the Struggle for Marxism', in D. Howard and K.E. Klare (eds), 1972, p. 382.

13 *Cf* ibid.; also P. Anderson, 1976, p. 39.

14 What follows is not intended to be an exposition of the internal mechanisms of Althusser's philosophical construction of Marxism. For such accounts, see G. Elliott, 1987; A. Callinicos, 1976; T. Benton, 1984; S. James, 1984b; A. Schmidt, 1982; M. Jay, 1984; S. Smith, 1984.

15 Jay, 1984, p. 391: 'Oddly, this most tenacious defender of orthodoxy among Western Marxists was also the most promiscuous in allowing non-Marxist influences to affect his ideas'; P. Anderson, 1976, p. 64 and *passim*; and Elliott, 1987, p. 67 *passim*.

16 On this episode, see R.W. Johnson, 1981, p. 38.

17 'Responsabilités de l'intellectuel communiste', *Cahiers du Communisme*, no. 4 (April 1949).

18 *Cf* D. Caute, 1964, p. 55, where he writes of Casanova's instructions to Communist intellectuals that 'Discipline could go no further in a non-communist country.' See also M. Löwy, 1984, p. 174.

19 *Cf Les Cahiers du Communisme*, no. 8 (August 1948), pp. 814–31: 'Dialogue with the Christians is possible, but reciprocal vigilance is necessary.'

20 These links are now covered in detail by Y.M. Boutang, 1992, see chap. 5, esp. 116–39.

21 On this point, Boutang is at times more confident that is perhaps prudent. Some facts which emerge from Althusser's correspondence with Guitton (a correspondence which falls outside the scope of the first volume of Boutang's biography) are worth registering, since they shed light on how Althusser saw his own activity. In a letter dated July 1972, Althusser described his family background, noted that he was not a 'héritier' (i.e. he was a 'scholarship' boy), and expressed gratitude to Guitton for having taught him to see thinking as a kind of 'artisanal' activity, the shaping of material 'objects'. In July 1974, he expressed admiration for Spinoza and Hegel, authors of 'philosophies which have had many effects in history . . . I mean effects outside of philosophy'. In 1978 Althusser travelled to Rome, and on Guitton's introduction had an interview of several hours with Cardinal Garonne, and requested an audience with Pope John Paul II. According to Guitton, Althusser and his wife Hélène at this point believed humanity had entered a decisive phase, a world crisis: 'They saw the salvation of the world as resting in a dialogue between Rome and Moscow.' Althusser never secured his audience with the Pope: shortly after John Paul II agreed to receive him, Althusser fell into a severe depression. In December 1978, he wrote to Guitton, 'My universe of thought has been abolished. I can no longer think. To speak in the language of the *talas* [i.e. Catholic *normaliens*], I ask for your prayers.' See 'Un document Jean Guitton', *Lire* (May 1988). The point of noting these facts is not to suggest some kind of formal homology between Althusser's political beliefs or modes of reasoning and forms of Catholicism (it would any way

be absurd to assume the latter term as designating some unitary body of thought or doctrine), but rather to draw attention to what can only be described as the theological sense Althusser brought to his intellectual work and arguments, the conviction that what lay at stake in these arguments was the conduct of everyday life.

22 Boutang, 1992, p. 245. There is a valuable discussion of Althusser's early *Mémoire* (written under the guidance of G. Bachelard) on 'Content in Hegel's Thought' in Boutang, chap. 7. Boutang brings out Althusser's theological concerns and style here, as well as the increasing difficulty he had in pursuing these within the available forms of Catholic thought; what resulted was, in Boutang's nice phrase, a 'gauchisme théologique'.

23 Boutang speculates that this continued for about four years, until 1952 (p. 237). See also his comments at pp. 242 and 245.

24 1976e, pp. 172 and 173.

25 For an example of attempts to describe Althusser as the Communist Party's official philosopher, see M. Cranston, 1973, pp. 53–60. In fact, reviews of his work which appeared in Party journals were always careful to state that Althusser's views were not those of the Party. See J. Verdès-Leroux, 1987, vol. 2, pp. 283 and 296 *passim*.

26 *Cf* E. Suleiman, 1978. For an historical study of the Ecole Normale between the wars, see J.-F. Sirinelli, 1988.

27 *Cf* H. Hamon and P. Rotman, 1987, vol. 1, p. 258.

28 On Herr, and the political role of the Ecole, see H. Bourgin, 1938; D. Lindenberg and P.-A. Mayer, 1977; Sirinelli, 1988. See also R.J. Smith, 1982.

29 See J.-F. Sirinelli, 1986, pp. 569–88. This represents a con- siderable downward revision of the figure of 25% proposed by Caute, 1964, p. 29, and repeated by Richard Johnson, 1972, p. 33. Nevertheless, Sirinelli's study makes it very clear that the Communists did form the major political grouping at the Ecole Normale.

30 See Sirinelli, 1986, p. 576.

31 See E. Le Roy Ladurie, 1982, p. 108, where he describes his rather attenuated sense of Marx's own texts while at the Ecole Normale. This may have been somewhat less true of the philosophy students, who were most interested in Marxism as an intellectual system. Althusser's influence is highly probable here. According to Michel Foucault, several *normaliens* studying philosophy contributed unsigned articles to the Party journal *La Nouvelle Critique* at this time. There is reasonably founded speculation that Foucault himself was among them; see Sirinelli, 1986, p. 586. The fullest discussion of Foucault's relations with the Communist Party while at the Ecole Normale is D. Eribon, 1989, chap. 3; see also D. Macey, 1993.

32 Figure quoted in *Le Monde*, 17 November 1956.

33 See R. Johnson, 1972. According to Johnson, about 75% of the membership of the UECF was drawn from Parisian institutions.

34 A reference to the Ecole Normale's location at 45 Rue d'Ulm.

35 See, for instance, the highly critical responses to Althusser's reading in Marx in J. Gabel, 1978; H. Lefebvre, 1967b, pp. 3–22 and 1969, pp. 3–25; K. Papaioannou, 1983.

36 See A. Callinicos, 1976; Jay, 1984, p. 394.

37 Althusser, 'To My English Readers', in 1965, trans. 1977, p. 9.

38 'Aujourd'hui', in Althusser, 1965.

39 Althusser was very aware of the need to adduce different arguments to different audiences. Compare his differing analyses of May 1968, for French and Italian readers: Letter to M.A. Macciocchi (15 March 1969), in M.-A. Macciocchi, 1973, pp. 301–20; and Althusser, 1969, pp. 3–14.

40 'Aujourd'hui', 1965, trans. in 1977, p. 21. Further references are in the main text.

41 Ibid., p. 24.

42 For Marx, p. 25; and cf P. Nizan, 1932, trans. 1971, pp. 39–114; esp. pp. 42, 51–2, 100ff.

43 For Marx, p. 25. Cf Althusser's scornful dismissal, 1971, p. 28: 'the French philosophical tradition of the last one hundred and fifty years... must really be a tradition which hardly bears looking at'.

44 See T. Benton, 1984; Elliott, 1987; P. Patton, 1978, pp. 8–18.

45 1974, 1976, p. 132. Spinoza was an important reference for the materialist philosophies of Dietzgen and Plekhanov, both of whose work influenced Lenin's understanding of Marxism.

46 See Althusser's attack on Lacan in a text published without Althusser's permission: 'La Découverte du Dr Freud', 1976a. Althusser's tortured relation to and use of psychoanalysis is clear from his two autobiographical works, which are suffused with—constituted by—psychoanalytic concepts and tropes: his entire adult life was a constant personal engagement with psychoanalysis. See L'Avenir dure longtemps suivi de Les Faits (1992).

47 Althusser and Balibar, 1979, p. 67.

48 Althusser made this claim in the 'Presentation' of the Théorie series he edited for Maspero. See the back cover of Pour Marx (1965).

49 J. Rancière, 1974, p. 58.

50 See R. Garaudy, 1957 and 1959.

51 First published in La Pensée, no. 96 (1961), pp. 3–26; reprinted in 1965, trans. 1977, p. 55.

52 For Marx, pp. 12, 27–8, and 237.

53 J. Rancière, 1974, p. 60.

54 For Marx. Political and historical facts and events had an allusive, ghostly quality throughout Althusser's writing: they are evoked as signs of something else. Compare, for example, his characterization of the 1940s and '50s, in For Marx (p. 22): 'In our political memory this period remains the time of huge strikes and demonstrations... the time when the great hopes aroused by the Resistance faltered and the long and bitter struggle began in which innumerable human hands would push back the shadow of catastrophe into the Cold War horizon.'

55 Reading 'Capital', p. 31. Further references are in the main text.

56 The perhaps unconscious resonance with Durkheim's phrase about socialism need not be seen as purely accidental. There are some notable similarities in the self-conceptions of Durkheim's Sociologist and Althusser's Theorist.

57 Reading 'Capital', p. 58.

58 On this see Verdès-Leroux, 1983.

59 G. Elliott, 1987, p. 111. Althusser was notoriously silent over the details of the 'knowledge effect', a term he suggested to describe the process whereby the 'real' was appropriated in thought. See Reading 'Capital', pp. 66–7.

60 It is worth noting how Althusser saw himself as the founder of a new pedagogic discipline, which one day would become the lingua franca of the new society: only if this is recognized can some of Althusser's more extraordinary comments be understood; cf his

remark in *Reading 'Capital'*, p. 31, that Engels' Preface to *Capital*, vol. 2, 'will become a school text one day'.

61 'Theory, Theoretical Practice and Theoretical Formation: Ideology and Ideological Formation' (April 1965), in L. Althusser, 1990, pp. 3–42, at p. 40.

62 See Althusser's comments in ibid., pp. 16, 30–1, 37 and *passim*, and compare Lenin, *What is to be Done?, Collected Works*, vol. 5 (Moscow, 1961), pp. 373ff.

63 R. Debray, 1977b, p. 267.

64 'Theory, Theoretical Practice, Theoretical Formation', in 1990, p. 16.

65 *Reading 'Capital'*, and 1964, pp. 80–111.

66 *Reading 'Capital'*, p. 141.

67 Althusser defined 'the Communist "morality" of a Communist' as being 'identical with Marxist-Leninist science; which thus makes the content of Communist "moral conscience" identical with a scientific content'. 'Problèmes étudiants', 1964, p. 82.

68 Althusser was quite emphatic about the necessity for individual willed commitment, since 'in the final instance, the ultimate decision about whether or not to fulfil these duties has to do with the individual himself, his own personal liberty' (ibid., p. 82).

69 *Cf* Althusser's letter to Guitton. On the 'héritier/boursier' distinction, see A. Thibaudet, 1927.

70 1964, pp. 94–5.

71 On the changing relationship between the state and the universities, and the development of new quasi-governmental and quasi-academic institutions, see M. Pollak, 1976, pp. 105–21; and A. Drouard, 1982, pp. 55–85.

72 On the importation of new techniques from America, see for example the work of Jean Stoetzel (founder of the IFOP): for in-

stance, 'Sociology in France: An Empiricist View', Stoetzel, 1957. These developments are surveyed in D. Pinto, 1977.

73 M. Crozier, 1964, pp. 602–30. A sociologist, Crozier was associated with the introduction of new management techniques into France.

74 A number of such groups (some with their own journals), appeared during the 1960s, claiming to reflect on 'the problems of French society': for example, *Futuribles* and *Prospectives*. On these groups, see J. Mossuz-Lavau, 1979.

75 See M. Pollak, 1976.

76 *Cf* A. Touraine, 1965.

77 On the rivalry and shifting balance between the disciplines of philosophy and sociology, see P. Bourdieu and J.-C. Passeron, 1967, pp. 162–212.

78 L. Goldmann, 1966, p. 8. The sense that a 'cultural revolution' was taking place was frequently expressed: *cf* for example R. Boudon who spoke (as Althusser had spoken about the need for a science of history) of the need for a 'copernican or galilean revolution' in sociology which would establish it as the new science of society; see R. Boudon, 'La Sociologie de l'an 2000', *Après-Demain*, no. 119 (December 1968), pp. 8–10, reprinted in 1971, p. 45.

79 For an example of how this technocratic vision was underpinned by a neo-evolutionary schema, see P. Bauchet, 1966.

80 A. Gorz, S. Mallet, and P. Belleville were most closely associated with this view of the 'new working class'; see also A. Touraine, 1968. This analysis was adopted by the PSU: see M. Rocard, 1969.

81 These theories of the new working class provoked much controversy and discussion: for a comparative and synoptic account, see A. Giddens, 1973;

and for France, see D. Gallie, 1983. See also G. Ross, 1978, pp. 163–90.

82 On the formation of the Vichyite discourse which described cadres as forming a new third term, crucial to France's progress, and on the continuing presence of this discourse in the postwar period, see L. Boltanski, 1987.

83 *Cf* Boltanski, p. 160; he notes 'the almost obsessional need to protect the working class from bourgeois pollution of any kind, to protect both the "theoretical" purity of the Marxist definition, and the "political" purity of a Party in which the working class played a "leading role"'. For an example of Communist sociology driven by this need, see the study by M. Bouvier-Ajam and G. Mury, 1963, which translates into academic language sound Thorezian theses.

84 See 1990; 'Philosophy as a Revolutionary Weapon' (1968) and 'Lenin and Philosophy' (1968), both in 1971.

85 See 1967b, p. 8; trans. 1990, pp. 74–5.

86 Commentators like Gregory Elliott are right to insist that, after 1967–8, 'the comprehensiveness of his [Althusser's] retreat from the theory of theoretical practice must be highlighted'. *Cf* G. Elliott, 1987, p. 204.

87 See ibid., p. 210 and pp. 198, 209–11, and *passim*.

88 Althusser, 1966, pp. 5–16.

89 Elliott, 1987, p. 211.

90 A. Monchablon, 1983.

91 See R. Johnson, 1972, p. 50.

92 The content of the discussions is well covered in R. Geerlandt, 1978.

93 See, for example, T. Judt, 1986, p. 193.

94 Reprinted in P. Kessel, 1972, vol. 1, pp. 149–61; further references are in the main text.

95 *Cf*, for example, p. 153: 'Le vieil homme aurait-il disparu? Aragon sait-il maintenant ce que "Science" veut dire', and p. 157: 'selon le mot d'Aragon délicieusement poétique... Le verbe haut du poète'.

96 *Cf* Elliott, 1987, p. 194ff.

97 *Cf* L. Kolakowski, 1974, p. 160; E.P. Thompson, 1978. On this point, politically more distant but culturally proximate critics like Aron and J.-F. Revel were more astute. See for example, R. Aron, 1970; see also J. Verdès-Leroux, 1987, pp. 247–9. For a rebuttal of Thompson's charge, see P. Anderson, 1980.

98 Elliott, 1987, p. 252.

99 1967b, trans. 1990, p. 117.

100 Ibid., p. 130.

101 'Philosophie comme arme de la révolution', in 1976d. See pp. 36, 39, 45, 47; trans. as 'Philosophy as a Revolutionary Weapon', in 1971.

102 See *For Marx*, p. 27; and 'Philosophie comme arme de la révolution', 1976d, pp. 36–7, 38, 41.

103 Ibid., p. 37. *Cf* also 'Preface to *Capital* (vol. 1)' (1969), in 1971, p. 74: '[Proletarian wage-labourers] have no ideologico-political difficulty in understanding *Capital* since it is a straightforward discussion of their concrete lives.'

104 Indeed, analogies can be seen between Althusser's shift of position and Lenin's own retreat from his argument in *What is to be Done?* (1903), which stressed the autonomous and specific character of the political, to his position in *State and Revolution* (1917) and other late texts, where he sought to solve problems of controlling the Party and state by arguing for the increased presence of state personnel drawn from the correct social origins, i.e. peasants and workers.

105 See Balibar's discussion in 1979, esp. p. 267. For an attempt to

show that in political practice, Althusser and the Althusserians tended to employ the class categories in a conventional and common way, see R.W. Connell, 1979, pp. 303–45.

106 See 'Reply to John Lewis', in 1976e, pp. 63–4.

107 Cf For Marx, p. 171, note 7.

108 Elliott, 1987, p. 290.

109 Althusser, 1977a, pp. 3–24, at p. 18.

110 Ibid., p. 19.

111 Translation in New Left Review, no. 109 (1978), pp. 19–46.

112 Anderson, 1980, p. 113.

113 Cf Althusser, 1978, pp. 19–46. See p. 25 and passim.

114 Ibid., p. 37.

115 In Britain, journals such as Screen, Theoretical Practice, and Economy and Society sought to develop ideas outlined in Althusser's essay. Cf M. Gane, 1983.

116 The most sustained and incisive internal criticism of Althusser's argument is P. Hirst, 1979. See also P. Anderson, 1980; G. Elliott, 1987.

117 M. Pêcheux, 1982, p. 214.

118 The manuscript, which remains unpublished, was entitled 'De la Superstructure (Droit-Etat-Idéologie)', and was written in 1969; the quotation is taken from G. Elliott, 1987, p. 225.

119 Ibid., p. 231.

120 Elliot has noted of Althusser's account that 'no space is left for oppositional ideology, little efficacy can be assigned the oppositional ideologies Althusser nevertheless posits' (ibid., p. 232).

121 It is possible to read the 'ISA' essay as providing the elements of a theory of nationalism; cf R. Balibar, 1974.

122 Cited in Elliott, 1987, p. 235.

123 Cf E. Hobsbawm, 1973, p. 240, and see A. Touraine, 1968.

124 See M.-A. Macciocchi, 1983, p. 30.

125 V. Gerratana, 1977a, pp. 110–22.

126 See, for example, R. Gombin, 1971; D. and G. Cohn-Bendit, 1968.

127 'Reply to John Lewis (Self-Criticism)' (1973), 1976e; but cf pp. 81 and 83 where Althusser mentions the Trotskyist critique.

128 See P. Anderson, 1980; see also G. Elliott, 1987, who claims that Althusser's attempt to settle accounts within Stalinism fails because he succumbs to the influence of Maoism. Althusser never identified the USSR as a 'Fascist' or 'Fascist-Imperialist' state, a term which was central to the Maoist attack.

129 'Philosophie comme arme de la Révolution', 1976d, pp. 46–7.

130 On the necessity for any serious account of Stalinism to examine the relation between Stalinism and Leninism, see V. Gerratana, 1977b, pp. 59–72; and on Althusser's reluctance to seriously engage with this, see idem., 1977a, pp. 110–22. Charles Bettelheim's The Class Struggles in the USSR (New York, 1976) represents an attempt to produce an 'Althusserian' analysis of the Stalin period: the only—and notable exception—within a general silence.

131 For development of this criticism, see A. Renaut, 'Marxisme et "déviation stalinienne". Rémarques sur l'interprétation althussérienne du stalinisme', in E. Pisier-Kouchner (ed.), 1983.

132 It was precisely this kind of question that intellectuals such as Cornelius Castoriadis were addressing: see 'Marxisme et théorie révolutionnaire', published in successive issues of Socialisme ou barbarie between 1964 and 1965, reprinted in The Imaginary Institution of Society (Cambridge, 1987).

133 'Reply to John Lewis', in 1976e, p. 87.

134 'Unfinished History', Introduction to D. Lecourt, 1977, pp. 14–15.
135 Ibid., p. 15.
136 Ibid., pp. 13–14.
137 Ibid., pp. 15–16.
138 *Cf* G. Elliott, 1987. The explanatory structure of this, the most detailed and comprehensive account of Althusser's project currently available, rests on the claim that Althusser's career was marked by a break, represented by the drift towards Maoism after 1967–8.
139 The suggestion here is not that a different alignment of support would have been more appropriate. The point is that there was little interest in the *content* of the categories themselves (for example, radical students in the 1960s displayed little interest in the internal structure and organization of the Vietnamese FNL): more attention was given to what these terms opposed.
140 See A. Glucksmann's contribution to the collection of articles, 'Nouveau fascisme, nouvelle démocratie' in *Les Temps Modernes*, special issue, no. 310 bis (1972).
141 See M. Pollak, 1976; J. and D. Rancière, 1978, pp. 7–25.

CHAPTER FIVE

1 See the excellent account in J. Hayward, 1986.
2 For the official Party documents relating to the dropping of the concept of the dictatorship of the proletariat, see Parti Communiste Français, 1977; and J. Favre, F. Hincker, L. Sève, 1977. For the criticisms of certain Althusserians, see E. Balibar, 1977.
3 The interest in the work of Popper, Arendt, Hayek and others, was part of this first moment of intellectual *ouverture*.
4 On the electoral campaigns, see J.R. Frears and J.-L. Parodi, 1979.

5 See O. Duhamel and J.-L. Parodi, 1982, pp. 169–80; SOFRES, 1986, pp. 247–51; and J. Rupnik, 1986.
6 J. Michelet, *Pologne et Russie* (Paris, 1852), p. 133. For Voltaire's views, see his *Histoire de l'Empire de Russe*, in *Oèuvres completes*, ed. Morland (Paris, 1877–85). And for Tocqueville's, see *Democracy in America*, (London, 1946), pp. 286–7. Compare J. de Maistre, 1859; Marquis de Custine, *Letters from Russia* (1843), trans. by R. Buss (London, 1991).
   More generally, see A. Lortholary, 1951; D.S. von Mohrenschildt, 1936; and M. Cadot, 1967. For a panoptic survey of European views, D. Groh, 1961, is essential.
7 Librarian of the Ecole Normale Supérieure, Herr exercised a profound influence on several generations of French intellectuals and political figures (including Jaurès and Blum). See C. Andler, 1932, and D. Lindenberg and P.-A. Mayer, 1977.
8 D. Groh, 1961, is a magisterial essay on how it affected such self-conceptions.
9 See D. Caute, 1973; C. Lasch, 1962; R. Arnot Page, 1967.
10 L.A. Allen, 1959, pp. 99–121, at p. 103.
11 A. Kriegel, 1974, pp. 33–53.
12 For a reconstruction of Blum's analysis, see N. Racine, 1971, pp. 281–315; and idem, in E. Pisier-Kouchner (ed.), 1983, pp. 91–107. Blum's analysis was adopted wholesale by Guy Mollet, and with some variations, even by Mitterrand: on these continuities, see N. Racine and O. Duhamel, in L. Marcou (ed.), 1982, pp. 121–53.
13 For the clearest statement of this argument, see Blum's famous pamphlet (first published in 1927 and subsequently reprinted many times), *Bolchevisme et So-*

cialisme (Paris, 1927).

14 There was, however, an informed debate conducted within the SFIO on the consequences and significance of the Soviet Five-Year plans. See, for example, O. Rosenfeld, *Le Plan quinquennal. Examen critique* (Paris, 1931). Critical views were also expressed in the periodicals published by various 'tendencies' within the Party, such as L. Laurat's *Le Combat marxiste*.

15 See J.-M. Cublier, n.d. On the basis of a statistical analysis, Cublier concludes that, as compared with the right-wing press, the left-wing press was significantly less preoccupied with trying to explain the trials: 227 articles on the Trials appeared in the right-wing press, while only 44 were published in the left-wing press (see p. 321). Circulation figures were comparable: around 2,194,000 for the left-wing press, 2,342,000 for the right-wing (p. 304).

16 The experience of Victor Serge was typical. Returning from imprisonment in the Soviet Union, he described the intellectual atmosphere in Paris in the late 1930s thus: 'The Communist cell organization in the Press and the French reviews was admirably complete. The review *Europe*, to which I contributed, was more or less in bond to them. On the *Nouvelle Revue française* they were on close terms with Malraux. The left-wing intellectual's weekly, *Vendredi*, was backed by industrialists doing good business in Russia and so was "on the line". I had to give up my well-paid work on Léon Blum's *Le Populaire* because of pressures influencing the editorial staff' (1984), p. 328.

17 For an early attempt to analyze how holding governmental office affected the Socialists' view of the Soviet Union, see D. Bat-

tistella, 1984.

18 For an excellent survey that suggests some of these contrasts, see P. Hassner, 1979, pp. 113–50.

19 Compare, for instance, André Wurmser's remarks at the opening of the Kravchenko trial in 1948: 'Whoever says he is anti-Soviet indicates in the same words that he is also anti-French', quoted in I. Wall, 1983, p. 94.

20 E. Fajon, *Les Cahiers du Communisme* (1948), p. 927–8, quoted in B. Legendre, 1980, pp. 88–9.

21 In this view, the growth of interest groups, combined with conflict between power élites and technocratic experts, would lead to a greater political pluralism, gradually transforming the Soviet Union into a European polity and society. Both this view, and the belief in convergence, derived from modernization theory: at this time—the latter half of the 1950s—American social science was gaining a foothold in French academic culture. See D. Pinto, 1977. See also J. Hough, 1977.

22 See D. Reynié, 1985, pp. 71–81.

23 A. Solzhenitsyn, *L'Archipel du goulag. Essai d'investigation littéraire 1918–1956*, 2 vols (Paris, 1974).

24 For an account of this filiation, see R. Gombin, 1971.

25 See R. Aron, 'Etats démocratiques et états totalitaires', first given as a lecture in 1939, published by the Société française de philosophie in 1946, and reprinted in *Commentaire*, no. 27 (1984), pp. 701–19. Aron here argued that totalitarian regimes were primarily opposed to democracies, and not to communism. He returned to this theme in *Démocratie et totalitarisme* (Paris, 1966).

26 See *Socialisme ou barbarie* (1949–1965). Although Castoriadis and

Lefort were closely associated in the early part of their career, they split over doctrinal differences in 1958 (only to collaborate once again in the 1970s, on reviews like *Textures* and *Libre*). For expression of these differences, see 'An Interview with C. Castoriadis', trans. B. Grahl and D. Pugh, *Telos*, no. 23 (1975) pp. 131–55; and 'An Interview with C. Lefort', trans. D. Gehrke and B. Singer, *Telos*, no. 30 (1976–77), pp. 173–92.

27 See the articles collected in Castoriadis, 1987.

28 V. Serge, *Les Coulisses d'une sûreté générale: l'Okhrana* (Paris, 1925); *L'An I de la révolution russe* (Paris, 1930); *Destin d'une révolution: URSS, 1917–1937* (Paris, 1937). B. Souvarine, *Staline. Aperçu historique du bolchevisme* (Paris, 1935, reprinted 1985), and *A Contre-courant: Ecrits 1925–1939* (Paris, 1985). S. Weil, 1962. A. Gide, 1937; and compare P. Herbart, 1937: Herbart travelled to the Soviet Union as Gide's secretary, and his book provides a very interesting commentary on some of Gide's observations, which helps to bring out the dissonances between his public and private pronouncements. M. Sperber, *Mémoires*, vol. 2 *Le pont inachevé* (Paris, 1977). P. Pascal, *En communisme* (Paris, 1921) and *Russie* (Paris, 1927). For a useful bibliography of works on the Soviet Union which appeared in France during the 1920s, see V. Victoroff-Toporoff, *Rossica et Sovietica. Bibliographie des ouvrages paru en français de 1917 à 1930 inclus rélatif à la russie et à la L'Urss* (Saint-Cloud, 1931). See also C. Jelen, 1984, who attempts to refute the view that the French Left was simply ignorant about some of the events of the Russian Revolution during the 1920s. On G. Bataille, see for instance his 'Le problème de l'Etat' (1933), pp. 105–7. Bataille helped Souvarine to found *La Critique sociale*, and with J. Monnerot and R. Caillois was responsible for starting the 'Collège de Sociologie' (1937–9); on this influential institution of the intellectual *avant-garde*, see D. Hollier, 1979. Also, J.-M. Besnier, 1988.

29 *Cf* the comments of M. Gauchet, 1974, who was already urging a renewed interest in Castoriadis' work: this 'would finally allow justice to be done to a body of reflection which until now has been generally and scandalously ignored, despite its profound originality and its crucial importance' (p. 908).

30 C. Lefort, 1976; 1978b, pp. 211–46; 1981.

31 During the 1950s and '60s, Tocqueville was very rarely (if ever) read with much attention at the Ecole Normale Supérieure, which at least until 1968 was the central forming ground for French intellectuals. See the forthcoming study by F. Melonio, on the historiography of Tocqueville studies in France.

32 See R. Aron, 1962; 1965; 1968b.

33 R. Aron, 1957. For Aron's response to the Hungarian events of 1956, see R. Colquhoun, *Raymond Aron*, 1986, vol. 2, chap. 2.

34 See D. Pinto, 1977.

35 See R. Aron, 1968a. See also R. Aron, 1983a, pp. 471–98, where he discusses some of the reactions to his book on the May events. For a sympathetic discussion of Aron's attempt to style himself as the Tocqueville of 1968, see A. Renaut, 'La Révolution introuvable?', *Pouvoirs*, no. 39 (1986), pp. 81–9.

36 F. Furet, 'Les intellectuels français et le structuralisme', in 1982, p. 47.

37 For the argument that structuralist theory could be understood as an homology of capitalist and

technocratic society, see Henri Lefébvre, 1967a. For interpretations of the significance of the 'structuralist moment' in France, see E. Tavor Bannet, 1989; F. Dosse, 1991–2; T. Pavel, *Le Mirage Linguistique* (Paris, 1988); and J.G. Merquior, *From Prague to Paris* (London, 1986).

38 M. Gauchet, interview, 20 June 1986. *Cf* Foucault's odd remarks, in M. Foucault, 1981b, trans. 1991, pp. 83–113.

39 On this, see amongst others V. Descombes, 1980. Also helpful is John Heckman, 1973, pp. 128–45.

40 Though whether over a glass of beer or over an apricot cocktail remains in dispute. See A. Cohen-Solal, 1985, p. 139. On balance, Arthur Danto's remark that 'thinking totalistically, apricot cocktails have exactly the right cachet for *normalien* swank' seems judicious; see A. Danto, 1986.

41 For a list of those attending, see R. Aron, 1983a, p. 94; also M.S. Roth, 1985, pp. 293–306; and idem., 1988.

42 See C. Digeon, 1959; and J. Carré, *Ecrivains français et du mirage allemand* (Paris, 1947). Xavier Léon, founder of the *Revue de Métaphysique et de Morale*, (a review representative of the academic mood during the Third Republic) had written scholarly works on Fichte, while historians like Elie Halévy were also writing on German thought. The intellectual relation between Germany and France is very complicated. After the débâcle at Sedan in 1870, the French Left, and Republican thinkers, took a favourable interest in Germany—this was partly to do with an interest in German left-wing politics; the Right, particularly the nationalist Right, were very anti-German. In the 1930s, and during Vichy, these positions were reversed

(although one should not forget complicated cases like that of Marcel Déat, who tried, during the Vichy period, to discover French roots for national socialism, and to detect authoritarian strains in 1789: see his *Pensée française et pensée allemande* (Paris, 1944), and see also D. Lindenberg, 1990, pp. 166–77). Intellectuals like Sartre and Aron were attracted to German philosophy, but rejected German politics. The polemics and debates concerning Heidegger are only the most recent manifestations of this longstanding and fraught connection.

43 The importance of Weber in Aron's thinking is made clear in his first book, *La Sociologie allemande contemporaine* (Paris, 1935).

44 Hegel's importance in postwar French intellectual life derived not only from the formative influence of Kojève's lectures, but also from the renewal of interest in Marxism which occurred after the Bolshevik Revolution: worth remembering here is Lenin's pedagogic injunction that a proper understanding of Marx was impossible without a careful reading of Hegel. See V. Descombes, 1980, pp. 9–16. Also M.S. Roth, 1988; and B. Cooper, 1984.

45 See L. Ferry and A. Renaut, 1985. They trace this radicalization of elements within German philosophy in French thinking through Foucault (Nietzsche), Derrida (Heidegger), Bourdieu (Marxism), and Lacan (Freud). Lacan, however, must be treated separately: his understanding of Freud was mediated through a much deeper reading of Hegel than that of Sartre. This may help to explain some of Sartre's confusions regarding psychoanalysis.

46 For examples of the revival of

neo-Kantian philosophy, combined with a Weberian methodology, see Ferry and Renaut, 1982–5; P. Raynaud, 1987.

47 The national press was at this time going through a curiously weak phase. *Le Monde* had lost some of its credibility as a forum for intellectual opinion because of its studied silence on Solzhenitsyn and the question of Soviet camps: *cf* J. Julliard and J.-N. Jeanneney, 1979, esp. pp. 279–309. Also, A. Besancon, 1974, pp. 137–43.

48 See, for example, R. Aron, 1979, pp. 3–14; and 1980, pp. 349–62.

49 *Les Nouvelles littéraires*, no. 2536 (1976).

50 Interview with A. Glucksmann, translation in *Telos*, no. 33 (1977), p. 99.

51 For typical examples, see J.-C. Guillebaud, 1978; B.-H. Lévy, 1977; J. Paugam (ed.), *Génération perdue* (Paris, 1977).

52 E. Le Roy Ladurie, 1982; Pierre Daix, 1976; Jean Rony, 1978; and compare P. Robrieux, 1977.

53 This view was common across a whole spectrum of studies: see for instance A. Kriegel, 1968; E. Morin, 1957; J. Monnerot, 1949, and idem., 1986, pp. 41–57; and M.-A. Macciocchi, 1977, pp. 22–4, 374–84 and 398, on the 'rétro-spiritualisme' of the New Philosophers. But for a theoretical argument against such forms of explanation, see A. Pizzorno, 1987. There were, however, undoubtedly important and intricate links between Christian elements and some varieties of *gauchisme* (there were for example distinct Christian elements in the UJC (M-L) and in other Maoist groups). On this, see B. Schreiner, 1972, pp. 43–55.

54 J. Benda, 1927; P. Nizan, 1932, 1971. See also D. Schalk, 1979.

55 *Cf* P. Grémion, 1983–4, pp. 767–80, at p. 777; 'Because one could not pardon collaboration between the French intellectual and the Nazi occupier, one could pardon more freely 'collaboration' with Sovietism, particularly since the idea of revolution could be linked to the idea of the nation.' This process was precisely a kind of *antisagoge*, whereby the vicious were punished only in order to reward the virtuous.

56 In France, there was little original historical work done on Nazism or Fascism, nor was there much familiarity with German discussions of totalitarianism: *cf* P. Birnbaum, 'Sur les origines de la domination politique', in 1984, pp. 77–94. Compare also M. Foucault, 'Power and Strategy', in 1977, p. 139: 'The non-analysis of Fascism is one of the important political facts of the past thirty years. It enables Fascism to be used as a floating signifier, whose function is essentially that of denunciation. The procedures of every form of power are suspected of being Fascist, just as the masses are in their desires.' A lonely and monumental exception was J.-P. Faye, 1972.

57 *Cf* D. Desanti, 1975, p. 36: 'No, I would not have believed the *Gulag Archipelago* [in 1946] because no one was willing to renounce hope in the inexorable demonstration of necessity. The USSR remained our saviour, our myth. On the other hand, we had known the Nazis only too well . . .' By the late 1970s, however, the situation was so changed that even the dissident PCF historian Jean Ellenstein could describe the Soviet Union as 'Fascist'; see R.W. Johnson, 1981, p. 243.

58 E. Mounier, 1946, p. 165.

59 See D. Thomson, 1969, 5th edn., pp. 10, 17, 132 and *passim*. On

the instability of parliamentary democracy, and the pressures to which it was subject (including the rise of the anti-parliamentary leagues), see also J.-M. Mayeur, 1984, esp. chaps 11–13, and pp. 290, 297 and 332.

60   For a luminous example of this antipathy, see J.-P. Sartre, 1973a.

61   A. de Jasay, *The State* (Oxford, 1985), may be right to say of the English liberal tradition that it has rarely thought about the state from the point of view of the state itself. But in France, to think about the problem from this angle is standard. For the historical basis for this mode of thinking—which goes much further back than the introduction of Hegelian thought into France—see N. Keohane, 1980, esp. pp. 453–61; T. Judt, 'The Left in France', in 1986; and J. Julliard, 1985, esp. pp. 47–77.

62   A French translation of Rawls' *Theory of Justice* was published in 1987; see J. Rawls, *Théorie de la justice*, trans. by C. Audard (Paris, 1987). For examples of French responses to Rawls, see B. Manin, 1984, pp. 7–25; and the contributions on *Individu et Justice sociale: autour de John Rawls* (Paris, 1988). But see also B. Manin, 1988, pp. 95–101.

63   See A. Werth, 1965, pp. 197–233; also H. Stuart Hughes, 'Gaullism: retrospect and prospect', in E. Mead Earle (ed.), 1951. Demonstrators during 1968 frequently referred in one breath to 'de Gaulle, Franco, Salazar'.

64   For a typical statement of this, see A. Glucksmann, 1968a, chaps 5 and 6 *passim*. The Gaullist and Communist leaderships were described by Glucksmann as forming an 'incestuous couple': 'two powers restrain the revolutionary movement: the power of the state and the Communist leadership'.

65   This is witnessed by the number of very popular biographies that appeared during the 1980s, most of which were couched in the Great Men of History mode. For the most outstanding of these, see J. Lacouture, 1984–6. Lacouture is also the biographer of Léon Blum and Pierre Mendès-France. On the revaluation of de Gaulle, see R. Débray, 1990; and the comments in D. Lindenberg, 1990, p. 13.

66   M. Poster, 1975, p. 361.

67   R. Aron, 1968a. For an early (and still very helpful) attempt to classify the range of interpretations, see P. Bénéton and J. Touchard, 1970, pp. 503–44. See also special issue on 'Mai 68', *Pouvoirs*, no. 39 (1986); and L. Ferry and A. Renaut, 1985. For details of the events themselves, numerous accounts are available. See, for instance: D. Singer, 1970; P. Seale and M. McConville, 1969; D. Caute, 1988.

68   See G. Lipovetsky, 1983. From a quite different political position, Régis Debray also interpreted 1968 as a step in the development of bourgeois individualism, a 'ruse du Capital' which resulted in the opening of 'la voie française vers l'Amérique'; see his *Modeste contribution aux cérémonies officielles du dixième anniversaire* (Paris, 1978), esp. pp. 39 and 41; a partial translation is in 1979a, pp. 45–65.

69   For a fine account of the anti-individualist and holistic emphases of Althusser and the *Annales* historians, see S. James, 1984. For an example of the new interest in individualism (moral, philosophical, methodological, etc.), see the collection of essays (first presented as papers to a colloquium on *L'Individu* held at Royaumont in October 1985, attended by, amongst others, Le Roy Ladurie, Furet,

Dumont, Ricœur, Levinas, Rosanvallon, Rancière, Veyne, Gauchet, Thibaud) published as *L'Individu* (Paris, 1987). This new concern with individualism looms in the work of P. Yonnet, G. Lipovetsky, M. Gauchet, and L. Ferry. See S. Khilnani, 'Individualism and Modern Democratic Culture: Some Recent French Conceptions', *Revue*, no. 2 (1993).

70 Lacan himself of course had little time for the *gauchistes* and *contestaires*; but for evidence of the number of these who were attracted into or by psychoanalysis, see E. Roudenescou, 1986, vol. 2, pp. 483–550.

71 See S. Turkle, 1979, p. 85. See also pp. 60ff and 85–93.

72 See R. Castel and J.-F. Le Cerf, 1980, pp. 22–30.

73 The careers of André Glucksmann and Jean-Claude Miller are exemplary. On the question of why French Maoists did not resort to terrorism, see Antoine Liniers (pseudonym for Olivier Rolin), 'Objections contre une prise d'armes', in F. Furet, A. Liniers, and P. Raynaud, 1985; also M. Wieviorka, 1984, pp. 133–45.

74 Quoted in Turkle, 1979, p. 180.

75 It is of course true that they themselves professed a denial of the possibility of an 'avantgarde'. See, for example, G. Scarpetta, 1979, p. 309: 'It is precisely from the concept of the 'avantgarde' that we must henceforth free ourselves.' Compare also the trajectory, along a different axis, of Jean-François Lyotard.

76 An example of this was Jean Vilar's Théâtre National Populaire.

77 J. Sauvageot *et al*, 1968, pp. 31–2.

78 A. Geismar, S. July, E. Morane, 1969, pp. 22 and 64.

79 A. Glucksmann, 1968b, pp. 67–121, at p. 96.

80 Ibid., pp. 95–6.

81 *La Cause du Peuple* was published by the strongly anti-Leninist Gauche prolétarienne, the most important organized grouping of post-1968 *gauchistes*. This was the product of a fusion between two main groups, drawn from the students of Mouvement du 22 Mars (at the forefront of the student movement) and the Althusserians of the Union des Jeunesses Communistes (Marxistes-Léninistes). For further examples of this type of vocabulary, see: Geismar *et al.*, *Vers la Guerre civile*; special number of *Les Temps Modernes*, 310 bis (1972); *Cahiers de la Gauche Prolétarianne*, no. 1 (1969).

82 Geismar *et al*, 1969, p. 16; and J. Sauvageot, 1968, p. 8.

83 *Cf* A. Glucksmann, 1968, chap. 5: 'The contestation is critique inasmuch as it makes a separation between two types of society; it is aggressive because that separation takes place within bourgeois society. It is the movement through which the forces of production form relations outside the relations of bourgeois production; and it does this not in order to abolish aesthetic, technical or scientific work, but *to destroy those divisions and limitations through which work is adapted to the society in which we live.*'

84 See the account of this experience in R. Linhart, 1978.

85 The foundation of dailies like *Libération* was a direct effect of these concerns.

86 In the context of these divisions, unexpected alliances could be formed. Thus, between 1966 and 1968, professional career academics, the 'mandarins' (who were often members of the Party), joined with those who had turned against (or had never been close to) the Party. This was the time of close links be-

tween *La Nouvelle Critique*, a journal of and for Party intellectuals, and the *gauchistes* of *Tel Quel*.

87 On some ambiguities of the term 'anti-intellectualism', see M. White, 1962, pp. 457–68, and R. Hofstadter, 1964. Hofstadter describes White's notion of anti-intellectualism as 'philosophical anti-rationalism', and saves the term anti-intellectualism to describe social attitudes towards intellectuals. I am not concerned with this latter dimension here: for a vivid and partial account of French social attitudes towards 'intellectuals' and 'intellectual' attributes, see P. Bourdieu, 1986a.

88 *Cahiers prolétariens* (1971), p. 61; quoted in D. and J. Rancière, 1978, pp. 7–25, at p. 16. My comments here are indebted to this analysis.

89 S. de Beauvoir, 1985, p. 25.

90 *Cf* J. Daniel, 1979.

91 *L'Idiot international*, no. 10 (September 1970). See also S. de Beauvoir's discussion of Sartre's interest in Maoism: 1985, pp. 26–7, 29 and *passim*.

92 Sartre was attracted also by the thought that the Maoists seemed to enact the philosophical directives of the *Critique of Dialectical Reason*; see Sartre, 'The Maoists in France' (1972), in 1978, pp. 162–71. Originally published as a Preface to M. Manceaux, 1972.

93 Two editors of *La Cause du Peuple*, Le Dantec and Le Bris, were imprisoned in the spring of 1970, and the journal was banned by government decree on 27 May 1970, though it continued to be published. Alain Geismar was arrested on 25 June 1970, and by summer's end 1970, more than sixty former members of the Gauche Prolétarienne were in prison.

94 This was the time of the dialogues between Sartre and

Maoists like the pseudonymous Pierre Victor; see P. Gavi, J.-P. Sartre, P. Victor, 1974. Foucault also engaged in dialogues with Maoists like Victor: see 'On Popular Justice: a Discussion with Maoists', in M. Foucault, 1980.

95 Recorded on 4 March 1972, the dialogue was published in *L'Arc*, no. 49 (1972), pp. 3–10; translated as 'Intellectuals and Power', in M. Foucault, 1977, pp. 205–17.

96 M. Foucault, 'Revolutionary Action: "Until Now"', in 1977, pp. 223 and 231.

97 Ibid., p. 206.

98 R. Barthes, 'Ecrivains, intellectuels, professeurs, *Tel Quel*, no. 47 (1971); translated as 'Writers, Intellectuals, Teachers', in 1977.

99 M. Foucault, 'Truth and Power', in 1980, p. 118.

100 For Foucault's criticisms of the 'universal' intellectual and his endorsement of the 'specific' intellectual, see 1980, pp. 126–33.

101 *Cf* Foucault and Deleuze, 'Intellectuals and Power', in Foucault, 1977; Foucault, 1980, pp. 126–33.

102 1977, p. 213, and *cf* p. 214.

103 1980, p. 132.

104 Foucault himself played an ambiguous game with the New Philosophers: he seemed to distance himself from them, yet simultaneously he endorsed their political judgements (as in his comments on Glucksmann). See for example his 1977 interview with the *Révoltes logiques* editorial collective, translated as 'Power and Strategies' in 1980, pp. 134–45. Foucault concluded the interview with what was, even for him, unparalleled evasiveness: 'What I have said here is not "what I think", but often rather what I wonder whether one couldn't think' (p. 145).

105 It is worth considering in this

context a work of empirical sociology which attempted to gauge working class militancy: see *L'Ouvrier français en 1970* (Paris, 1972).

106 The 1972 *Programme Commun*, the culmination of moves toward a union of the Left begun in 1962, was in part a consequence of the electoral system put in place by the Fifth Republic, a system which once more introduced sharp polarities into the political arena. In response, the Communist Party. adopted once again its united front strategy of the 1930s: an alliance with the Socialists, representing the middle social groups was seen as a necessary strategy. In terms of content, the *Programme Commun* represented a return to and a revival of a political programme first outlined by the Communists at the time of the Liberation. There are a number of similarities between the 1972 programme and the 1944 programme of the Conseil National de la Résistance (see G. Madjarian, 1980): the working class was the central agent of progressive change. In order to achieve political power electorally, it would have to ally with the middle strata represented by the Socialist Party; governmental power once gained, true (i.e. economic) power would be rendered to the working class through large-scale nationalizations effected by the state. It was a programme that was *ouvrièriste*, statist, and nationalist in its perception of the relevant boundaries of possible economic change. The only concession to altered political circumstances was the replacement of the term 'revolution' by that of 'rupture'. It was in effect, a restatement (in terms of electoral politics) of the traditional idea of revolution as the capture of state power by

the working class. *Cf* G. Ross, 1987, pp. 57–83, who notes that the French Left 'set out on the road to power in the 1970s single-mindedly determined to finish unfinished business from the 1940s' (p. 65).

107 See also Glucksmann's review of Solzhenitsyn's work, 1974, p. 80.

108 See P. Dews, 1979, pp. 127–69; idem, 1980b, pp. 2–11.

109 On the figure of the 'dissident intellectual', see J. Kristeva, 1977, pp. 3–8; and, more analytically, P. Rival, 1979, pp. 219–236.

110 *Projet Socialiste* (Paris, 1980) pp.

111 This development is charted in R. Debray (1979b). To Debray these changes were decisive: 'The new internal composition of the modern intellectual field derives primarily from the new position of the field relative to others' (trans. 1981, p. 80). But his book was precisely a response to the New Philosophers and their saturation of the media: what made it distinctive was its adoption of a sociological approach to the study of France's intellectuals, in the tradition of Thibaudet, Goblot and Bourgin.

112 *Cf* Foucault's comments on this in 1980, pp. 134–45, esp. pp. 142 and 145.

113 The best example from among this large literature is J.-P. Le Dantec, 1978 (Le Dantec was a Maoist who had been involved with Breton regionalist movements). See also J.-C. Guillebaud, 1978.

114 The most adept French example of 'generational' analysis is J.-F. Sirinelli, 1988.

115 *Cf* A. Geismar *et al.*, 1969, p. 231. On contrasting attitudes during the Algerian war, see H. Hamon and P. Rotman, 1979; also, R. Johnson, 1972; for the Vietnam war, see Hamon and Rotman, 1987, vol. 1.

116 On this very French stratification, see A. Touraine, 1977,

pp. 87–91; also R. Debray, 1979b, trans. 1981, pp. 197–204; and J. Julliard, 1977.

117 For a sociological study of Socialist Party supporters that underlines the large role played by teachers, see P. Hardouin, 1978, pp. 220–56. Also M. Dagnaud and D. Mehl, 1981, pp. 372–93.

118 See the interview with Sartre in *Lotta Continua* (15 September 1977).

119 The Union de la Gauche was temporarily patched up in 1978: the Communist Party leadership reversed its earlier attacks on the PS, and struck a short-run deal between the two rounds of the election in March 1978.

120 C. Castoriadis, 1977–8, pp. 49–73, (originally written in July 1977).

121 Ibid., pp. 52, 54 and 60.

122 CERES was the acronym of the Centre d'Etudes, de Recherches, et d'Educations Socialistes, representing the Marxist left-wing of the Socialist Party. On this group, see D. Hanley, 1986.

123 Castoriadis, 1977–8, pp. 71 and 73.

124 C. Lefort, 'L'Impensée de l'Union de la Gauche', in 1981. Written in 1978, but not published until 1981.

125 Ibid., pp. 142–3.

126 This charge was by no means a novel one: it was consonant with de Gaulle's and the RPF's accusations against the Communist Party in the late 1940s and the 1950s; See S. Hoffman, 1974, p. 425.

127 Ibid., p. 140.

128 Worth comparing with these two texts is R. Aron, 1978. Aron too warned that if the Left was returned to power, this would have a drastic effect on political rights; in particular, the programme of nationalization would lead to an expansion of state power: 'The would-be liberal state takes on a crushing burden, and tends to absorb civil and economic society, so moving towards the total state, if not the totalitarian state' (pp. 49–50). Indeed, Jacques Chirac's electoral campaign in 1978 was built around the constant warning that a Left government would lead towards 'l'Etat totalitaire'.

129 The debate was sparked off by a series of articles in *Le Monde*. See M. Gallo, 1983; and P. Boggio, 1983. See also E. Malet, *Socrate et la rose: les intellectuels face au pouvoir socialiste* (Paris, 1983); J.-M. Domenach, 1983; E. Morin, 1983; and J. Baudrillard, 1985.

130 See Furet's discussion of André Glucksmann's *La Cuisinière et le mangeur d'hommes*, in 1975, pp. 52–3, where he dismisses Glucksmann's book as 'un coup de gueule parisien'. But *cf* also Foucault's endorsement of Glucksmann's *Les Maîtres penseurs* in his review, 'La grande colère des faits', *Le Nouvel Observateur* (9 May 1977), pp. 84–6; see also Foucault, 1990, pp. 110–24.

131 See D. Labbé, 1983, esp. pp. 51–9, on the presence of Marxist vocabulary in Mitterrand's speeches and in Socialist Party discourse. References to Marx, and to a revolutionary rupture with capitalism permeate the Socialist Party manifesto, *Projet Socialiste: Pour la France des années 80* (1981), see, for example, p. 10.

132 *Cf* T. Judt, 'French Marxism, 1945–1975', in 1986.

133 Compare Glucksmann's pronouncements on nuclear strategy in *La Force du vertige* (1983) with his populism in *Stratégie et Révolution* (1968) and *La cuisiniere et le mangeur d'hommes* (1975).

134 On the conceptions of power employed by the New Philosophers and by Foucault, see A. Giddens, 'From Marx to Nietzsche?', in 1982. On the influence

upon the New Philosophers of Foucault's attack on Marxism as a science, see Dews, 1979, pp. 127–69, at pp. 154–5; and on Foucault's endorsement of the category of the 'pleb' see Foucault, 1980, pp. 134–45. For an historical argument on the displacement of the struggle for political rights into primarily social terms and language, see the excellent study by J. Donzelot, 1984.

135   P. Clastres, 1974. For a critique of Clastres' conception of the origins of state power, see P. Birnbaum, 'Sur les origines de la domination politique', in 1984. Clastres' was one of a number of studies inflected by anti-statist themes: see P. Legendre's Lacanian *L'Amour de censeur* (1974); and M. Maffesoli, *Logique de la domination* 1976.

136   For an overview of the relations between Marxism and anthropology, see K. Hart, 'The Contribution of Marxism to Economic Anthropology', in S. Ortiz (ed.), *Economic Anthropology: Topics and Theories* (London, 1983). For Clastres' attack on Marxist anthropology, see 1978, pp. 135–49.

137   M. Augé, 1982, p. 11.

138   *Cf* the controversy over David Rousset's book, *Le Procès des camps de concentration soviétiques* (1951). For an example of the kind of attacks drawn by Rousset's claim that the Soviet regime operated labour camps, see the pamphlet by the then Communist, P. Daix, *Pourquoi David Rousset a inventé les camps soviétiques* (1949). Ironically, Daix was later to write the Preface to the French translation of Solzhenitsyn's *One Day in the Life of Ivan Denissovich*, published in France in 1962.

139   But *cf* D. Lecourt, 1978, who argued that the phenomenon of dissidence was in reality a very

recent and limited one, and of no relevance to the fate of the Communist Party.

140   C. Castoriadis, 1986, p. 22.

141   M. Gauchet, 1980, p. 8.

142   P. Hassner, 1979, pp. 113–50.

143   For an account which traces the instabilities of the Communist evaluation, see P. Grémion, 1985.

144   A. Adler *et al.*, 1978.

145   See G. Marchais, 1979, pp. 42–51; and *Le Monde* (24 January 1980), p. 11.

146   *Le Débat*, no. 13 (1981).

147   Quoted in Grémion, 1985, p. 284. For the PS view of the USSR, see *Projet Socialiste pour les années 80*, pp. 64–86.

148   *Projet Socialiste*, pp. 71 and 65. *Cf* also p. 63: 'The west's ideological exploitation of the phenomenon of dissidence is a gigantic effort to demobilize the Left, and to ideologically revive capitalism.'

149   For a statement of how the French intended to celebrate the bicentenary of 1789, see 'Redonner à la France son rôle de conscience universelle (la préparation du bicentenaire de la Révolution)', *Le Monde* (16–17 November) 1986.

150   Compare M. Agulhon, 1981, with President Mitterrand at the Panthéon, 11 May 1981.

151   D. Pinto, 1982, p. 11.

CHAPTER SIX

1   *Cf* G. Rudé, 1961, p. 3: 'no period of history has so frequently been rewritten in the light of current preoccupations or been such a repeated battleground for conflicting ideologies as the French Revolution'. For studies that demonstrate the shaping presence of political interests in the historiography of the Revolution see, for example, S. Mellon, 1958, and P. Farmer, 1944.

2   P. Favre, 1989. The Durkheimian conception of the social sciences—

so closely associated with Republican politics—left no room for political science or political theory: this was encompassed by sociology. Durkheim did not try to capture these disciplines for the Republican Left, but rather to efface them.

3 F. Furet, 1978, trans. 1981, p. 12.

4 *Cf* F. Furet and M. Ozouf (eds), 1989b, p. xvi: 'Historiography occupies a fundamental place in this book—it can be found in nearly all the articles.' See also F. Furet, 1988c, p. 18, where he describes the *Critical Dictionary* (which stands as the symbolic culmination of his project), as 'une sorte de manifeste historiographique'.

5 Tocqueville and Cochin play crucial roles in F. Furet, 1978; Quinet and Michelet are rehabilitated in 1986c. On Michelet, see Furet's essay in F. Furet and M. Ozouf (eds), 1989b, pp. 980–90; also 1981. On Furet's reading of Burke, see 1986a, pp. 56–66.

6 F. Furet, 'Academic History of the Revolution', in Furet and Ozouf (eds), 1989b, p. 883.

7 *Cf* J. McManners, 1965, p. 643: 'What Michelet said in poetry, Aulard said in prose, with scholarly references.' On Aulard's motivations, see also W. Keylor, 1975, p. 69.

8 Aulard, like Ernest Lavisse (1842–1922), 'wished to unite 'the cult of science' with 'the cult of the Fatherland': see P. Nora, 1962, pp. 73–106. For these historians, the potential conflict between patriotism and the claim to scientific and historical universality was circumvented by a 'conviction that France, by virtue of its revolutionary heritage, occupied a special place in the world that rendered its national concerns universal' (Keylor, 1975), p. 94.

9 Barrès' efforts in the 1890s, for example, were a concerted attempt to wrest nationalism away from the Republican Left, and transform it into a right-wing doctrine, and by 1908 the Action Française could launch its journal with the proclamatory masthead, 'Everything that is national is ours'; see E. Weber, 1962a; H. Tint, 1964; W. Keylor, 1975.

10 J. Jaurès, 1969, vol. 1, p. 61.

11 In fact Philippe Sagnac was appointed to succeed Aulard, but was unable to take his chair until 1932; Mathiez's appointment spanned this gap.

12 Furet and Ozouf (eds), 1989b, pp. 885 and 891.

13 Ibid.

14 Ibid., pp. 884–5.

15 Ibid., p. 885.

16 Ibid., p. 885.

17 F. Dosse, 1987, pp. 212–14. See also F. Furet, *Le Débat* (December 1981), pp. 113–14; and D. Caute, 1964, pp. 276–99.

18 *Cf* J. Rancière, 1981, pp. 267–72, which notes that Communist historians, contrary to expectations, showed little interest in French working-class history.

19 On this group, which included René Maublanc, Marcel Cohen, and Georges Friedmann, see P. Laberenne, 1979, pp. 12–25; and D. Caute, 1964, pp. 265–6. See also G. Lefebvre, 1929, reprinted in *Réflexions sur l'histoire* (Paris, 1978), pp. 223–43, at p. 238. Lefebvre himself preferred the expression 'economic interpretation of history', which—in proper rationalist fashion—he felt avoided the 'metaphysical' and 'spiritualist' connotations of the term 'materialism'. *Cf* R. Samuel, 1980, pp. 21–96.

20 M. Dommanget *et al.*, *Babeuf et les problèmes du babouvisme* (Paris, 1963).

21 W. Doyle, 1980, p. 11.

22 See for example Jean Bruhat, 1939, pp. 24–38.

23 As an instance of this forgetting of context, it should be noted that when the English translation of *Quatre-vingt-neuf* was published,

the last paragraph of the book was omitted. The original French edition of the book ended thus: 'Jeunesse de 1939! La Déclaration [of the rights of man] aussi est une tradition et une glorieuse. Entends, en le lisant, la voix des ancêtres qui te parlent, ceux qui ont combattu à Valmy, à Jemappes, à Fleurus, au cri de "Vive la Nation". Ils l'ont faite libre; apprécie la noblesse du présent: dans l'univers, l'homme seul peut l'être. Ils te répétent que ton sort est entre tes mains et que de toi, de toi seul, dépend le sort de la cité. Aperçois le risque: puis'qu'il est un attrait pour toi, il ne fera pas reculer. Mesure la grandeur de la tâche, mais aussi la dignité dont elle te revêt. Renoncerais-tu? Tes anciens ont confiance en toi; tu seras bientôt la Nation: "Vive la Nation!"' (Lefebvre, 1939), pp. 246–7. It is hard to imagine a more fervent statement of the Jacobin revolutionary call to patriotism.

Lefebvre was never a member of the Communist Party, but his political sympathies were evident, and his admiration for Lenin and the USSR was noted by contemporaries; see R. Garmy, 1960, p. 83, who noted that 'he [Lefebvre] never hid his admiration for Lenin, nor his sympathy for the international Communist movement. Like Mathiez, he was led to discover analogies between the French Revolution of 1789–93 and the Russian Revolution of 1917, and to establish illuminating connections, taking into account the differences in situations and periods.' Although Richard Cobb, in his obituary for Lefebvre (*Past and Present*, no. 18 (1960), pp. 52–67, at p. 56), noted that Lefebvre had a low esteem of Soviet scholarship on the Revolution, it is clear that Soviet historians thought highly of his work: see V. Volguine and A. Manfred, 'Hommage des historiens soviétiques à Georges Lefebvre', *Annales historiques de la Révolution française*, vol. 32 (1960), pp. 126–8.

24 From 1954 onwards, Soboul published a series of articles in the *Annales historiques de la Révolution française* and *La Pensée*, which culminated in a major work published in 1958, *Les Sans-culottes parisiens en l'an II*. Appointed to the Sorbonne chair in 1967, he succeeded Lefebvre to the editorship of the *Annales historiques de la Révolution française*.

25 A. Soboul, 1970, p. 6.

26 G. Ellis, 1978, pp. 353–76, at p. 356.

27 For the sterner accusation of contradictions in his views, see O. Bétourné and A. Hartig, 1989, pp. 32–4.

28 F. Furet, 1991a, p. 44.

29 See R. Secher, 1986; also R. Sédillot, 1987.

30 Title of an article by G. Suffert, *Le Figaro Magazine* (11 October 1986), which sought to recruit Furet's arguments for the reactionary Right. Furet himself deplored these efforts: see his comments in 1986b, pp. 90–3; and interview in *Libération* (7 May 1987): 'Today, no doubt because of a shift in the climate to the Right, my works are being used to question the entire revolutionary process. This is an absurdity. The Revolution is the great universal event of French history, it is the birth of democracy.'

31 Furet and Richet, 1965–6. Furet had in fact laid a marker for some of the arguments that appeared here in F. Furet, C. Mazauric, L. Bergeron, 'Les sans-culottes et la Révolution française', *Annales: Economies, Sociétés, Civilisations*, vol. 18 (1963), 1098–1127.

32 D. Guérin, 1946.

33 Soboul published his *Révolution française (1789–99)* in 1951. This did not contain the refutation of Guérin that Soboul, as a leading

Communist historian, had been expected to make. This was the import of J. Poperen's critical review of Soboul's book: see '"La Révolution française (1789–99)" par Albert Soboul', *Cahiers du Communisme*, (February 1952). For Soboul's reply see, 1954.

34 Though of a very different kind from his polemic of the 1960s and after. According to Le Roy Ladurie, in the early 1950s, Furet sided with Poperen in accusing Soboul of conceding too much to Guérin's interpretation of the Revolution. See Le Roy Ladurie, 1982, p. 48.

35 F. Furet, 1963, pp. 1098–1127.

36 C. Mazauric, 'Sur une nouvelle conception de la Révolution', in 1970, p. 59.

37 Ibid., p. 59.

38 Ibid., p. 60: 'an anti-popular bias ... [and] ... finally following from this ... an anti-national bias, which in turn provokes slurs upon the French Revolution's patriotic phase: that is to say, its Jacobin, phase'.

39 Soboul himself, however, did not reply to the revisionist arguments until 1974, when he dismissed Furet and Richet's work in a few pages. He added little to Mazauric's accusations, reiterating that the Revolution must be seen as part of a rationally unfolding process whose causes lay in the social domain, and that the Terror was a merely a necessary if excessive moment that had ensured the defeat of the counterrevolution, and enabled the triumph of the bourgeois revolution. See A. Soboul, 1974, pp. 40–58 in *Comprendre la Révolution* (Paris, 1981), pp. 323–45, see esp. pp. 341–3.

40 After 1968 Braudel handed over the directorship of the journal to three younger historians: the result was a greater emphasis on contemporary history and society, more discussion of methodologies in related disciplines, and the publication of special numbers on historical and interdisciplinary themes; see C. Fink, 1989, p. 338.

41 Introducing in 1974 a special issue on the Revolution, Furet acknowledged that previously the school and its journal 'had never displayed any great curiosity towards the French Revolution'; see 'Ancien Régime et Révolution: Réinterprétations', *Annales: Economies, Sociétés, Civilisations*, vol. 29, no. 1 (1974), p. 3. But from the late 1960s onwards a number of articles on the Revolution was published. In addition to the special issue of 1974 see, for example: D. Richet, 1969; F. Furet, 1970, pp. 434–51; F. Furet, 1971, pp. 255–89; M. Ferro *et al.*, 'Révolution et totalitarisme', *Annales: Economies, Sociétés, Civilisations*, vol. 31, no. 2 (1976), pp. 243–88; 'Sur la Révolution française' (reviews of Furet's *Penser la Révolution française*), *Annales: Economies, Sociétés, Civilisations*, vol. 35, no. 2 (1980), pp. 320–52. This trend was continued during the 1980s.

42 M. Vovelle, 1978, p. 332.

43 C. Mazauric, 1970, p. 15.

44 R. Robin, 1973, pp. 31–54; M. Grenon and R. Robin, 1976, pp. 9–12.

45 In his 1971 essay Furet had referred to and made use of Robin's work, which he claimed had 'the merit of taking Marxism seriously' (p. 120).

46 These themes dominated intellectual reviews in the latter 1970s, which brought together otherwise very dissimilar intellectuals: see, for instance, *Textures*, *Esprit*, *Anti-Mythes*, *Libre*, *Commentaire*, Socialist Party journals like *Faire* and *Dire*, *Les Temps Modernes*, *Tel Quel*, etc.

47 This was certainly how contemporary reviews reacted to the book: see, for example, R. Chartier, 1979, pp. 261–72.

48 The resonances between Furet's

argument and Lévi-Strauss's attack, in *The Savage Mind*, on Sartre and the progressivist account of the French Revolution suggest a conscious allusion.

49 F. Furet, 1978, trans. 1981, p. 10.
50 Ibid., p. 14.
51 Ibid., p. 11.
52 Ibid., p. 12.
53 Ibid., p. 12.
54 F. Furet, *Le Nouvel Observateur* (4 July 1977).
55 Furet, 1978, trans. 1981, p. 12.
56 Ibid., p. 25.
57 Compare the interpretation of Furet in J. Rancière, 1992, pp. 79–88.
58 Ever since the abbé Barruel had seen it in this way, this had become conventional wisdom for those on the Right: see Augustin Barruel, *Mémoires pour servir à l'histoire du jacobinisme* (Hamburg, 1797–9). For an account of Barruel, see J.M. Roberts, 1972.
59 1978, trans. 1981, p. 203.
60 For a contemporary review which made this point, see J.-P. Hirsch, 1980, pp. 320–33.
61 The canonical attitude towards Tocqueville was generally cordial, but little more. See, for instance, Lefebvre's guarded defence of Tocqueville against the criticism of Soviet historians, 1955.
62 In this respect, there was some agreement between Furet's account and R. Palmer's notion of the 'Atlantic Revolutions' (an interpretation which Soubol had dismissed as an instance of Cold–War ideology).
63 *Cf* L. Hunt's review in 1980, pp. 313–23.
64 1978, trans. 1981, p. 48.
65 Ibid., p. 49.
66 F. Furet, 1989c, pp. 264–82, at p. 277.
67 1978, trans. 1981, p. 49.
68 Ibid., p. 50.
69 See M. Foucault, 1980.
70 1978, trans. 1981, p. 51. Nevertheless, in deference to the weight of the historiographic

canon, Furet conceded that there was perhaps some content to the category of 'the people': he spoke of 'the tangible people—a minority of the population to be sure, but very numerous compared to "normal" times' (p. 52).

71 Ibid., p. 49.
72 Ibid., see pp. 52–3.
73 Ibid., p. 56.
74 Ibid., p. 61. See A. Mathiez, 1920b. The centrality of Robespierre continues to be affirmed by this tradition: see M. Vovelle, 1988, pp. 498–506.
75 Furet, 1978, trans. 1981, p. 178. *Cf* M. Foucault, 1979.
76 *Cf* J. Derrida, 1977, p. 296.
77 See the review by A. Bergounioux and B. Manin, 1979, pp. 183–210, which notes this point.
78 'I mean simply that no historical debate about the Revolution involves real political stakes', 1978, trans. 1981, p. 82. Furet was echoing Aron's 'fin des idéologies' claim made in the *Opium of the Intellectuals* and elsewhere.
79 The *Nouvel Observateur* had become one of the instruments of public expression for those intellectuals who had once been Communists, but most of whom had left the Party after 1956. It was also an important medium for a distinct group, of the same generation, but who had never been members of the Party: the intellectuals of the Christian Left, marked by their experience of the Algerian war, and deeply disillusioned both with the PCF and with Mollet's socialism: men like Jacques Julliard, Pierre Nora, Pierre Vidal-Nacquet, and Michel Winock.
80 F. Furet, 1975, pp. 52–3.
81 *Cf* F. Furet, 1986b: 'I am a great admirer of 1789; I think that it is a magnificent event and I do not like historians who try to diminish the dimensions of this event, one of those rare great universal events of history, and which is

also a French event.'
82 Furet, 1988d, p. 142.
83 Ibid., p. 37.
84 F. Furet and M. Ozouf (eds), 1989a; and idem., 1989b.
85 Ibid., p. xviii.
86 Furet, 1991a, p. 44; cf W. Scott, 1991, pp. 147–71, at p. 153.
87 In La Revolution 1770–1880 (1988b), Furet wrote that by the 1880s the Revolution had 'entered port' (p. 517); but elsewhere he also affirmed that it was only in the 1980s that the French Revolution was really brought to a close. See, for instance, Furet, 1988c, pp. 18–20, at p. 19: 'There was a first ending to the Revolution with the Third Republic and the synthesis created by Gambetta and Ferry. And there is a second ending to the Revolution, today.'
88 F. Furet, J. Julliard and P. Rosanvallon, 1988, pp. 52, 54.
89 For the claim that, at the level of public opinion, the French Revolution was no longer politically divisive, see O. Duhamel, 1989, pp. 121–5.
90 Compare M. Agulhon, 1987, pp. 595–610.
91 Cf F. Furet, 1986b, p. 90: 'When I wrote, the Revolution is over, it was a way of expressing both a fact and a wish.'
92 The formulation 'La Révolution française est terminée' was apparently first used in 1791 by Adrain Duport, deputy representing the nobility of Paris, in the Constituent Assembly (17 May 1791). See M.-L. Netter, 1989.
93 For a consideration of this tradition, see J. Hayward, 1991.

EPILOGUE

1 H. James, 1989; L. Colley, 1992.
2 E. Weber, 1976, E. Ritaine, 1983, P. Rosanvallon, 1990.
3 Cf T. Judt, 1992, pp. 300–1; and P. Nora, 1984– , t. 1 La République, 1986, t. 2 La Nation, 3 vols.
4 Cf F. Braudel, 1990; see 'Introduction', vol. 1, esp. at p. 26: '. . . the destiny of France has above all been a sector of the destiny of the world'.
5 The precise ways in which this is so is now better understood as a result of the researches of François Furet, Pierre Rosanvallon, Marcel Gauchet, Lucien Jaume, Bernard Manin, and Pasquale Pasquino.
6 I take it that constitutional representative democracy, in contrast to its rivals, has so far proved itself more able both to maintain the security of its members and to provide them with certain rights of private enjoyment; needless to say, it does not follow that it is in any sense a just form.
7 For elements of such a history, see F. Furet, 1988b; J. Hayward, 1991; P. Rosanvallon, 1992.
8 M. Gauchet, 1989; L. Jaume, 1989; and see T. Judt, 1992, pp. 232–3.
9 Cf J.-M. Le Pen, quoted in P. Rosanvallon, 'Malaise dans la réprésentation', in F. Furet, J. Julliard and P. Rosanvallon, 1988, p. 153.
10 P. Rosanvallon, ibid., p. 159.
11 Cf J. Donzelot, 1984, chap. 4.
12 See, for instance, Club Jean Moulin, 1962; and M. Crozier, 1968. On Crozier's influence on politicians of the liberal Right such as Giscard D'Estaing, cf P. McCarthy (ed.), 1987, p. 3. On the political clubs, see J. Mossuz-Lavau, 1979.
13 For an instance of this shared conception of power, compare M. Foucault, 1979, and 1981a; with M. Crozier and E. Friedberg, L'Acteur et le système (Paris, 1977).
14 See B. Brown, 1982.
15 See J. Rollet, 1982. The notion's fluidity is indicated by the way it was used by quite different political persuasions, including

the Communist Party, CERES, and Mitterrand. For an intellectual celebration of the term, see P. Rosanvallon, 1976, esp. pp. 7–17.

16 Parti Socialiste, 1972, p. 63. Compare K. Marx and F. Engels, *The German Ideology*, in *Collected Works of Marx and Engels*, vol. v (London, 1976), p. 47.

17 M. Rocard, interview in *Libération*, 22 May 1985. *Cf* P. Rosanvallon, *Le Débat*, no. 50 (1988), p. 192: 'The disappearance of the word *autogestion* has been as brutal as its rise was sudden.'

18 Compare P. Rosanvallon, 1979b, p. 8: 'This spectre [social-democracy] paradoxically appears more menacing the more imprecise it is. "Social-democracy", "reformism", "revisionism", "bourgeois socialism", "betrayal": a host of terms that cover very different historical and political realities but which are conflated in order to designate an identical fear and refusal.'

19 *Cf* A. Bergounioux and B. Manin, 1979b, p. 13: 'While the political world continues to use and abuse the epithet 'social democracy', the object itself remains absent from the theoretical arena, no longer given the dignity even of being considered'. On the pressures to maintain doctrinal purity, see T. Judt, 1986, p. 297 and *passim*.

20 See CERES, 1978. For the attitude of CERES towards social-democracy, *cf* D. Hanley, 1986, p. 70: 'At the heart of CERES' project stands the problem of social-democracy. Indeed, its very existence can only be understood as a negative response to this phenomenon.

21 *Cf* M. Rocard, 'La Social-démocratie et nous', in FAIRE, *Qu'est-ce que c'est la Social-Démocratie* (Paris, 1979). It is striking that while the 1970s witnessed an attempt by the Communists to move out of their national cocoon and to link up with other Western Communist Parties (Eurocommunism, another name for one's democratic good intentions), the French Socialists made no such move— there was, for example, an almost complete absence of contact between French Socialists and the German Social Democratic government led by Willy Brandt.

22 For examples of the liberal anti-statist argument in France, see H. Lepage, 1978; J.-F. Revel, 1984; G. Sorman, 1985. In each case, an argument was made for a return to the principle of the market as the way of best ensuring the well-being of the community. To the extent that the State was the target of attack, such arguments converged with those calling for self-management and participatory democracy.

23 *Cf* P. Rosanvallon, 1979a.

24 C. Nicolet, 1982, and 1959.

25 On the crisis of the welfare state see P. Rosanvallon, 1982. On the trade unions, see idem., 1988.

26 *Cf* 'Mitterrand entre le Socialisme et la République', *Intervention* (special issue) (1982), which declared: 'After the eclipse of socialism, the idea of the Republic has resurfaced.' Broadly speaking, *Intervention* was the voice of the Rocardian current in the Socialist Party.

27 *Le Monde* (28 June 1986), emphasis in original. Chévènement's group, CERES, officially changed its name to 'Socialisme et République' in April 1986; see *Le Monde* (22 April 1986). For a reaffirmation of Chévènement's views on the importance of the Republic to 'l'identité de la France', see *Le Monde* (16–17 November 1986), p. 6.

28 *Cf* 'La France?', special issue, *La Quinzaine littéraire*, no. 491 (1987); J.-M. Ferry, 1990, pp. 80–90.

29 Valedictions for the French intellectual have proliferated in recent years: see, for example, P. Ory (ed.), 1990; 'Les grandes causes, ça éxiste encore?', *Le Nouvel Observateur*, no. 1140 (12–18 September 1986), where, with characteristic post-modern self-regard, Pierre Bourdieu writes that 'For my part, I think that if there is a single grand cause today, it is the defense of the intellectuals'; and the comments in J. Sturrock, 'The Last Days of the Intellocrats', *New York Times Book Review* (10 January 1993), p. 1. But see also A. Finkielkraut, 1987a, and 1992.

30 This is evident from the collaborative conferences and volumes on history and political theory organized to commemorate the bicentennial of the French Revolution.

31 *Cf* E. Morin, ''89 Régénéré', *Le Monde* (9 June 1989). See also the opinion poll results in SOFRES, *L'Etat de l'Opinion 1990* (Paris, 1990): 82% of secondary school history teachers rejected Clemenceau's claim that the Revolution had to be understood as 'un bloc', as did 57% of the public.

32 See P. Pasquino, 1987, pp. 214–18; J.-D. Bredin, 1988; M. Gauchet, 1989.

33 See the essays in B. Fontana (ed.), 1993.

34 F. Furet, in Furet, Julliard and Rosanvallon, 1988, p. 54.

Bibliography

Adereth, M. 1967. *Commitment in Modern French Literature*, London.

Adler, A., F. Cohen, M. Décaillot, C. Frioux, and L. Robel. 1978. *L'URSS et nous*, Paris.

Agulhon, M. 1981. *Marianne into Battle*, trans. J. Lloyd, Cambridge.

—— 1984. 'Faut-il avoir peur de 1989?', *Le Débat*, no. 30, pp. 27–37.

—— 1987. 'Conflits et contradictions dans la France d'aujourd'hui', *Annales: Economies, Sociétés, Civilisations*, no. 3, pp. 595–610.

—— 1990. 'Débats actuels sur la Révolution en France', *Annales historiques de la Révolution française*, no. 279, pp. 1–13.

Alain, 1926. *Le Citoyen contre les pouvoirs*, repr. Paris and Geneva, 1979.

Ali, T. (ed.). 1984. *The Stalinist Legacy*, London.

Allen, L.A. 1959. 'The French Left and Soviet Russia: Origins of the Popular Front', *World Affairs Quarterly*, vol. 30, no. 2, pp. 99–121.

Allen, P.A. 1986. 'The Meanings of 'An Intellectual': Nineteenth- and Twentieth-Century English Usage', *University of Toronto Quarterly*, vol. 55, no. 4, pp. 342–58.

Althusser, L. 1964. 'Problèmes étudiants', *La Nouvelle critique*, no. 152, pp. 80–111.

—— 1965. *Pour Marx* (Paris); trans. B. Brewster, *For Marx*, London, 1977.

—— 1966. 'Sur la Révolution culturelle', *Cahiers Marxistes-Leninistes*, no. 14, pp. 5–16.

—— 1967a. 'Letter From Louis Althusser', in R. Debray, *A Critique of Arms*, Harmondsworth, 1977, pp. 258–67.

—— 1967b. *Philosophie et philosophie spontanée des savants*, Paris, 1974.

—— 1968. 'Lénine et la philosophie,' *Bulletin de la Société française de philosophie*, no. 4, pp. 127–61.

—— 1969. 'A propos de l'article de Michel Verret sur Mai étudiant', *La Pensée*, no. 145, pp. 3–14.

—— 1971. *Lenin and Philosophy and Other Essays*, trans. B. Brewster, New York and London.

—— 1974. *Eléments d'Autocritique*, Paris.

—— 1976a. 'La Découverte du Dr. Freud', in L. Chertok (ed.), *Dialogue Franco-Soviétique sur la psychoanalyse*, Toulouse, 1984, pp. 81–97.

—— 1976b. 'Note on the ISAs', *Economy and Society*, vol. 12 (1983), pp. 455–65.

—— 1976c. 'Unfinished History', in D. Lecourt, *Proletarian Science? The Case of Lysenko*, trans. B. Brewster, London, 1977, pp. 7–16.

—— 1976d. *Positions*, Paris.

—— 1976e. *Essays in Self-Criticism*, trans. G. Lock, London.

—— 1977a. 'On the Twenty-second Congress of the French Communist Party', *New Left Review*, no. 104, pp. 3–22.

—— 1977b. 'The Crisis of Marxism', in Il Manifesto, *Power and Opposition in Post-Revolutionary Societies*, London, 1979, pp. 225–37.

—— 1978. 'What Must Change in the Party', *New Left Review*, no. 109, pp. 19–46.

—— 1990. *Philosophy and the Spontaneous Philosophy of the Scientists*, trans. B. Brewster *et al.* and ed. G. Elliott, London.

—— 1992a. *L'Avenir dure longtemps suivi de Les Faits: Autobiographies*, Paris.

—— 1992b. *Journal de Captivité: Stalag XA 1940–1945*, Paris.

—— and E. Balibar. 1979. *Reading 'Capital'*, trans. B. Brewster, London.

—— and E. Balibar, R. Establet, P. Macherey and J. Rancière 1965. *Lire 'Le Capital'*, 2 vols, Paris, repr. 4 vols, Paris, 1970.

Amariglio, J. and B. Norton. 1991. 'Marxist Historians and the Question of Class in the French Revolution', *History and Theory*, vol. 30, no. 1, pp. 37–55.

Anderson, B. 1983. *Imagined Communities. Reflections on the Origin and Spread of Nationalism*, London.

Anderson, P. 1976. *Considerations on Western Marxism*, London.

—— 1980. *Arguments within English Marxism*, London.

—— 1983. *In the Tracks of Historical Materialism*, London.

—— 1992. *A Zone of Engagement*, London.

Anderson, R.D. 1975. *Education in France 1848–70*, Oxford.

Andler, C. 1932. *Lucien Herr*, Paris.

Annan, N. 1955. 'The Intellectual Aristocracy', in J.H. Plumb (ed.), *Studies in Social History*, London.

Ansart, P. 1970. *Naissance de l'anarchisme. Esquisse d'une explication sociologique du proudhonnisme*, Paris.

L'Arc, 1977. 'La Crise dans la tête', special issue on intellectuals, no. 70.

Arguments, 1956–1962, 2 vols, repr., Toulouse, 1983.

Aron, J.-P. 1984. *Les Modernes*, Paris.

Aron, R. 1935. *La Sociologie allemande contemporaine*, Paris.

—— 1945. *L'Age des empires et l'avenir de la France*, Paris.

—— 1955a. 'Les Intellectuals français et l'utopie', *Preuves*, no. 50, pp. 5–14.

—— 1955b. *L'Opium des intellectuels*, Paris; trans. T. Kilmartin, *The Opium of the Intellectuals*, London, 1957.

—— 1956a. *De l'Armistice à l'insurrection nationale*, Paris.

—— 1956b. 'Fascinés par l'Union Soviétique', *La Nef* (March), pp. 213–23.

—— 1957. 'Une Révolution anti-totalitaire', in M. Lasky and F. Bondy (eds), *La Révolution hongroise: Histoire du soulèvement d'octobre*, Paris.

—— 1960. *France Steadfast and Changing: the Fourth to the Fifth Republic*, trans. J. Irwin and L. Einaudi, Cambridge, Mass.

—— 1962. *Dix-huit leçons sur la société industrielle*, (Paris); trans. M. Bottomore, *Lectures on Industrial Society*, London, 1967.

—— 1965. *Démocratie et totalitarisme*, Paris.

—— 1968a. *La Révolution introuvable*, Paris.

—— 1968b. *Progress and Disillusion: The Dialectics of Modern Society*, trans. E.P. Halperin, London.

———— 1970. *Marxismes imaginaires*, Paris.

———— 1972. *Etudes politiques*, Paris.

———— 1975. *History and the Dialectic of Violence. An analysis of Sartre's 'Critique de la raison dialectique'*, trans. B. Cooper, Oxford.

———— 1976. 'Alexander Solzhenitsyn and European "Leftism"', *Survey*, vol. 22, no. 3/4, pp. 233–41.

———— 1978. *Les Elections de mars et la Ve République*, Paris.

———— 1979. 'De l'Impérialisme américain à l'hégémonisme soviétique', *Commentaire*, vol. 2, no. 5, pp. 3–14.

———— 1980. 'L'hégémonisme soviétique: An I', *Commentaire*, vol. 3, no. 11, pp. 349–62.

———— 1983a. *Mémoires: 50 ans de réflexions politiques*, Paris.

———— 1983b. *The Committed Observer: Conversations with Jean-Louis Missika and Dominique Wolton*, trans. by J. and M. McIntosh, Chicago.

———— 1984. 'Etats démocratiques et états totalitaires (Juin 1939)', *Commentaire*, no. 27, pp. 701–19.

———— 1986. *History, Truth, Liberty: Selected Writings of Raymond Aron*, ed. by F. Draus, Chicago.

Aron, Robert. 1967–75. *Histoire de l'épuration*, 3 vols, Paris.

Aronson, R. 1980. *Sartre—Philosophy in the World*, London.

———— 1987. *Sartre's Second Critique*, Chicago.

Assouline, P. 1984. *Gaston Gallimard*, Paris.

———— 1985. *L'Épuration des intellectuels*, Brussels.

Aubral, F. and X. Delcourt, 1977. *Contre la nouvelle philosophie*, Paris.

Augé, M. 1982. *The Anthropological Circle. Symbol, Function, History*, Cambridge.

Aymé, M. 1945. *Le Confort intellectuel*, Paris.

Bacot, P. 1978. 'Le Front de classe', *Revue française de science politique*, vol. 28, no. 2, pp. 277–95.

Baker, K.M. (ed.). 1988. *The Political Culture of the Old Regime*, London.

———— 1990. *Inventing the French Revolution*, Cambridge.

Balassa, B. 1978. 'The French Economy Under the Fifth Republic, 1958–1978', in W.G. Andrews and S. Hoffmann (eds), *The French Fifth Republic at Twenty*, Albany, N.Y.

Balibar, E. 1976. *Sur la dictature du prolétariat*, Paris.

———— 1977. *XXIIme Congrès*, Paris.

———— 1991. *Ecrits pour Althusser*, Paris.

———— et al. 1979. *Ouvrons la fenêtre, camarades*, Paris.

Balibar, R. 1974. *Les Français fictifs: Le rapport des styles littéraires au français national*, Paris.

Bandopadhyay, P. 1972. 'The Many Faces of French Marxism', *Science and Society*, vol. 35, pp. 129–57.

Bannet, E. Tavor, 1989. *Structuralism and the Logic of Dissent*, London.

Bardonnet, D. 1960. *Evolution de la structure du Parti Radical*, Paris.

Barrès, M. 1897. *Les Déracinés*, Paris.

Barthes, R. 1964. *Essais critiques*, Paris.

———— 1977. *Image-Music-Text*, trans. and ed. S. Heath, London.

Bataille, G. 1933. 'Le Problème de l'état', *La Critique Sociale*, no. 9, pp. 105–7.

Battistella, D. 1984. 'La Politique de la France à l'égard de l'Union soviétique depuis 10 Mai 1981', unpublished paper, Institut d'Etudes Politiques, Paris.

Bauchet, P. 1966. *La Plannification française*, Paris.

Baudrillard, J. 1985. *La Gauche divine*, Paris.

Baynac, J. 1978. 'Mai 68: Une hypothèse sur la stratégie, le temps et la révolution', *Libre*, no. 4, pp. 193–205.

Beauvoir, S. de 1982. *The Mandarins*, trans. L. Friedman, London.

——— 1955. 'La Pensée de droite, aujourd'hui', *Les Temps Modernes*, nos. 112–13, pp. 1538–75.

——— 1968. *Force of Circumstance*, trans. R. Howard, London.

——— 1985. *Adieux. A Farewell to Sartre*, trans. P. O'Brian, Harmondsworth.

Becker, J. and F. Knipping (eds), 1986. *Power in Europe? Great Britain, France, Italy and Germany in a Postwar World, 1945–1950*, Berlin and New York.

Bédarida, F. and J.P. Rioux (eds), 1985. *Pierre Mendès–France et le mendèsisme*, Paris.

Bell, D. 1964. *The End of Ideology*, New York.

——— 1976. *The Cultural Contradictions of Capitalism*, London.

Bell, D.S. (ed.). 1982. *Contemporary French Political Parties*, London.

——— and B. Criddle. 1984. *The French Socialist Party: Resurgence and Victory*, Oxford.

Ben-David, J. 1970. 'The Rise and Decline of France as a Scientific Centre', *Minerva*, vol. 8, no. 2, pp. 160–79.

Benda, J. 1927. *La Trahison des clercs*, Paris.

Bénéton, P. 1975. *Histoire de mots: 'culture' et 'civilisation'*, Paris.

——— and J. Touchard. 1970. 'Les Interprétations de la crise de mai-juin 1968', *Revue française de science politique*, vol. 20, no. 3, pp. 503–44.

Bénichou, P. 1973. *Le Sacre de l'écrivain 1750–1830*, Paris.

Benton, T. 1984. *The Rise and Fall of Structural Marxism: Althusser and his Influence*, London.

Berger, S. 1987. 'Liberalism Reborn: the new liberal synthesis in France', in J. Howorth and G. Ross (eds), *Contemporary France*, London.

Bergounioux, A. 1983–4. 'Intellectuels et politique dans l'entre-deux-geurres', *Intervention*, no. 7, pp. 8–18.

——— and G. Grunberg, 1992. *Le Long Remords du pouvoir: Le Parti Socialiste français, 1905–1992*, Paris.

——— and B. Manin, 1979a. 'La Révolution en question (à propos d'un livre de François Furet)', *Libre*, no. 5, pp. 183–210.

——— 1979b. *Le Social-Démocratie ou le compromis*, Paris.

——— 1980. 'L'Exclu de la nation: La Gauche française et son mythe de l'adversaire', *Le Débat*, no. 5, pp. 45–53.

——— 1981. 'L'Option social-démocrate?', *Le Débat*, no. 15, pp. 13–24.

——— 1983. 'La Gauche et 'ses' adversaires', *Intervention*, no. 4, pp. 4–8.

——— 1989. *Le Régime social-démocrate*, Paris.

Berl, E. 1929. *Mort de la morale bourgeoise*, Paris.

Bernard, P. and H. Dubief, 1985. *The Decline of the Third Republic 1914–1938*, trans. A. Forster, Cambridge.

Bersani, J. (ed.). 1976. *Jean Paulhan: Le souterrain*, Paris.

Bernstein, S. 1980, 1982. *Histoire du Parti Radical*, 2 vols, Paris.

——— 1986. 'French Power as seen by the Political Parties after World War II', in J. Becker and F. Knipping (eds), 1986. *Power in Europe?*, Berlin and New York.

Besançon, A. 1974. 'L'Affaire Soljénitsyne', *Contrepoint*, no. 15, pp. 137–43.

———— 1977. *Les Origines intellectuelles du Léninisme*, Paris.

———— 1987. *Une Génération*, Paris.

Besnier, J.-M., 1984. 'De la Terreur jacobine au terrorisme?', *Esprit*, nos 10–11, pp. 157–60.

———— 1988. *La Politique de l'impossible: L'intellectuel entre révolte et engagement*, Paris.

———— and J.-P. Thomas, 1987. *Chronique des idées d'aujourd'hui: éloge de la volonté*, Paris.

Best, G. (ed.). 1988. *The Permanent Revolution: The French Revolution and its Legacy 1789–1989*, London.

Bétourné, O. and A. Hartig, 1989. *Penser l'histoire de la Révolution*, Paris.

Bettelheim, C. 1976. *The Class Struggles in the USSR*, New York.

Birnbaum, P. 1978. 'La Question des élections dans la pensée socialiste', in *Critiques des pratiques politiques*, Paris.

———— 1979. *Le Peuple et les gros. Histoire d'un mythe*, Paris.

———— 1984. *Dimensions du pouvoir*, Paris.

———— (ed.). 1985. *Les Elites socialistes au pouvoir 1981–1985*, Paris.

———— 1988. 'Ideology, collective action and the state: Germany, England, France', in *States and Collective Action: the European Experience*, Cambridge.

Bitoun, P. 1988. *Les Hommes d'Uriage*, Paris.

Blackburn, R. and A. Cockburn (eds), 1969. *Student Power*, London.

Blackmer, D.M. and S. Tarrow (eds), 1975. *Communism in Italy and France*, Princeton.

Blakely, T.J. 1968. 'Sartre's *Critique de la Raison dialectique* and the Opacity of Marxism-Leninism', *Studies in Soviet Thought*, vol. 8, pp. 122–35.

Blanchot, M. 1984. 'Les Intellectuels en question', *Le Débat*, no. 29, pp. 3–28.

Bloch-Lainé, F. and J. Bouvier, 1986. *La France restaurée, 1944–1956*, Paris.

Bluche, F. and S. Rials, 1989. *Les Révolutions françaises*, Paris.

Blum, L. 1927. *Bolchevisme et socialisme*, Paris.

Boas, G. 1925. *French Philosophies of the Romantic Period*, Baltimore.

Bodin, L. 1964. *Les Intellectuels*, Paris.

———— 1966. 'Le PCF dans le Front Populaire' *Esprit*, vol. 24, pp. 436–39.

———— 1973. 'L'Idée de révolution en France de 1920 à 1968', unpublished lecture notes, Fondation Nationale des Sciences Politiques, Paris.

———— and J. Touchard, 1959. 'Les intellectuels dans la société française contemporaine: définitions, statistiques, et problèmes', *Revue francaise de science politique*, vol. 9, no. 4, pp. 835–59.

———— 1961. *Front Populaire 1936*, Paris.

Boggio, P. 'Les Silences des intellectuels de gauche', *Le Monde* (26 and 27 July 1983).

Boillat, G. 1974. *Le Librairie Bernard Grasset et les lettres françaises*, Paris.

Boisdeffre, P. de, 1979. '1929/1979: Crise de l'intelligence?', *Paradoxes*, no. 35, pp. 91–105.

Boltanski, L. 1987. *The Making of a Class: Cadres in French Society*, trans. A. Goldhammer, Cambridge.

Bonnard, A. 1935. *Les Modérés*, Paris.

Boschetti, A. 1985. *Sartre et 'Les Temps Modernes'*, Paris.

Boudon, R. 1971. *La Crise de la sociologie*, Paris and Geneva.

———— 1980. 'The Freudian-Marxist-Structuralist Movement in France', *The Tocqueville Review*, vol. 2, no. 1.

———— 1981. 'L'intellectuel et ses publics: les singularités françaises', in J.-D. Reynaud and Y. Grafmeyer, *Français, Qui-êtes vous?*, Paris.

Bourdieu, P. 1980. 'Sartre', *London Review of Books*, vol. 2, no. 22, p. 10.

———— 1986a. *Distinction. A Social Critique of the Judgement of Taste*, trans. R. Nice, London.

———— 1986b. 'D'abord défendre les intellectuels...', *Le Nouvel Observateur*, no. 1140 (12–18 September).

———— 1986c. 'Interview', *Theory, Culture and Society*, vol. 3, no. 3, pp. 35–51.

———— 1988. *Homo Academicus*, trans. P. Collier, Cambridge.

———— and J.-C. Passeron, 1967. 'Philosophy and Sociology in France since 1945', *Social Research*, vol. 34, pp. 162–212.

Bourgin, H. 1938. *De Jaurès à Léon Blum: L'Ecole Normale et la politique*, Paris.

Bourmeyster, A. (ed.). 1983. *Essais sur le discours soviétique*, Grenoble.

Bourricaud, F. 1980. *Le Bricolage idéologique: Essai sur les intellectuels et les passions démocratiques*, Paris.

———— 1986. *Le Retour de la droite*, Paris.

Boutang, Y.M. 1992. *Louis Althusser: Une biographie*, vol. 1. *La Formation du mythe (1919–1965)*, Paris.

Bouvier-Ajam, M. and G. Mury, 1963. *Les Classes sociales en France*, Paris.

Bowie, M. 1987. *Freud, Proust, Lacan*, Cambridge.

Braudel, F. 1967. *Ecrits sur l'histoire*, Paris.

———— 1988, 1990. *The Identity of France*, 2 vols, trans. S. Reynolds, London.

Bredin, J.-D. 1988. *Sieyès, la clef de la Révolution française*, Paris.

Brenner, J. 1981. 'Dossiers sur les années trente', *Le Matin* (24–30 August).

Brombert, V. 1960. *The Intellectual Hero: Studies in The French Novel 1880–1955*, London.

Brower, D.R. 1968. *The New Jacobins*, Cornell.

Brown, B. 1982. *Socialism of a Different Kind: Reshaping the Left in France*, New York.

Bruhat, J. (pseud. J. Montreau). 1939. 'La Révolution française et la pensée de Marx', *La Pensée*, no. 3, pp. 24–38.

———— 1951. 'Le Coup d'état du 2 December 1851', *Cahiers du Communisme*, vol. 28, no. 12, pp. 1393–1409.

Buci-Glucksmann, C. 1978. 'Mai 68 et le crise du marxisme', *Politique Aujourd'hui*, nos 5–6, pp. 139–47.

Burnier, M.-A. 1966. *Les Existentialistes et la politique*, Paris.

Burrin, P. 1986. *La Dérive fasciste: Doriot, Déat, Bergery*, Paris.

Buthman, W.C. 1939. *The Rise of Integral Nationalism in France*, New York.

Cadot, M. 1967. *La Russie dans la vie intellectuelle française*, Paris.

Cahm, E. 1967. *Péguy et le nationalisme français*, Paris.

Callinicos, A. 1976. *Althusser's Marxism*, London.

Camus, A. 1950–3. *Actuelles. Chroniques 1944–1953*, Paris.

———— 1952. *L'Homme révolté*, Paris.

———— 1965. *Essais*, Paris.

Cannadine, D. 1983. 'The Context, Performance and Meaning of Ritual: the British Monarchy and the 'Invention of Tradition', *c.*1820–1977', in E. Hobsbawm and T. Ranger (eds), *The Invention of Tradition*, Cambridge.

Carr, E.H. 1978. 'The Russian Revolution and the West', *New Left Review*, no. 111, pp. 25–36.

Casanova, L. 1949. 'Responsabilités de l'intellectuel communiste', *Cahiers du Communisme*, vol. 27, no. 4.

―――― et al. 1949. *Le Parti communiste, les intellectuels et la nation*, Paris.

Castel, R. and J.-F. Le Cerf, 1980. 'Le phénomène "psy" et la société française', *Le Débat*, no. 3, pp. 22–30.

Castoriadis, C. 1977–8. 'The French Left', *Telos*, no. 34, pp. 49–73.

―――― 1979. *Le Contenu du socialisme*, Paris.

―――― 1986. *Domaines de l'homme*, Paris.

―――― 1990. *La Société bureaucratique*, Paris.

―――― 1987. *The Imaginary Institution of Society*, trans. K. Blamey, Cambridge.

―――― 1988. *Political and Social Writings*, 2 vols, trans. D.A. Curtis, Minneapolis.

―――― 1992. 'The Crisis of Marxism, the Crisis of Politics', *Dissent* (Spring), pp. 221–25.

Caute, D. 1964. *Communism and the French Intellectuals 1914–1960*, London.

―――― 1973. *The Fellow Travellers. Intellectual Friends of Communism*, 2nd ed., New Haven and London, 1988.

―――― 1988. *Sixty-Eight. The Year of the Barricades*, London.

Cavanaugh, G. 1972. 'The Present State of French Revolutionary Historiography: Alfred Cobban and Beyond', *French Historical Studies*, vol. vii, pp. 587–606.

CERES, 1979. *Un Dessin socialiste pour la France*, Paris.

Cerny, P.G. 1980. *The Politics of Grandeur. Ideological Aspects of de Gaulle's Foreign Policy*, Cambridge.

―――― (ed.). 1984. *Social Movements and Protest in France*, London.

Chambaz, J. et al. 1953. 'Le Marxisme et l'histoire de France', *La Pensée*, no. 51, pp. 109–43.

Charle, C. 1977. 'Champ littéraire et champ du pouvoir: les écrivains et l'affaire Dreyfus', *Annales: Economies, Societies, Civilisations*, no. 2, pp. 240–64.

―――― 1985. 'Naissance des intellectuels contemporains (1860–1898)', in J. Le Goff and B. Kopeczi (eds), *Intellectuels français, intellectuels hongrois. XIIIᵉ–XXᵉ siècle*, Paris.

―――― 1990. *Naissance des 'intellectuels', 1880–1900*, Paris.

Charles, J. et al. 1980. *Le Congrès de Tours. 18e Congrès nationale du Parti Socialiste, texte intégrale*, Paris.

Charlton, D.G. 1959. *Positivist Thought in France during the Second Empire*, Oxford.

―――― 1963. *Secular Religions in France*, Oxford.

Chartier, R. 1979. 'Une Rélecture politique de la Révolution française', *Critique*, no. 382, pp. 261–72.

―――― 1991. *The Cultural Origins of the French Revolution*, trans. L.G. Cochrane, Durham and London.

Châtelet, F. 1979. *Questions-Objections*, Paris.

Chazel, F. 1986. 'Karl Marx et la sociologie américaine contemporaine', *L'Année sociologique*, no. 36, pp. 319–42.

Chebel d'Appollonia, A. 1991. *Histoire politique des intellectuels en France 1944–1954*, 2 vols, Paris.

Chiodi, P. 1976. *Sartre and Marxism*, Hassocks.

Clark, T.N. 1970. 'The Rise and Decline of France as a Scientific Culture', *Minerva*, vol. 8, pp. 599–601.

―――― 1973. *Prophets and Patrons: the French University and the Emergence of the Social Sciences*, Cambridge, Mass.

Clastres, P. 1974. *La Société contre l'état*, Paris.

———— 1978. 'Les Marxistes et leur anthropologie', *Libre*, no. 3, pp. 135–49.

Club Jean Moulin, 1962. *L'Etat et le citoyen*, Paris.

Cochin, A. (1921) 1978. *Les Sociétés de pensée et la démocratie moderne*, Paris.

———— 1979. *L'Esprit du jacobinisme*, Paris.

Cogniot, G. 1950. *Réalité de la nation*, Paris.

Cohen, S. and P. Gourevitch, 1982. *France in the Troubled World Economy*, London.

Cohen-Solal, A. 1985. *Sartre: Une vie*, Paris.

Cohn-Bendit, D. and G. 1968. *Obsolete Communism. The Left-Wing Alternative*, London.

Colley, L. 1992. *Britons: Forging the Nation, 1707–1837*, New Haven and London.

Collignon, J.-G. 1976. 'De l'isolationisme au comparatisme: méthodes et approches anglo-saxonnes pour l'analyse du système politique soviétique', *Revue francaise de science politique*, vol. 26, no. 3, pp. 445–82.

Collignon, J.-G. 1980. 'L'idéologie soviétique devant la soviétologie scientifique française', in L. Dupeux, *Analyse de l'idéologie*, t. 1, Paris.

Collinet, M. 1948. *La Tragédie du Marxisme: de Manifeste Communiste, de la stratégie totalitaire*, Paris.

Collini, S. 1991. *Public Moralists: Political Thought and Intellectual Life in Britain 1850–1930*, Oxford.

Colquhoun, R. 1986. *Raymond Aron*, 2 vols, London.

Comninel, G. 1987. *Re-Thinking The French Revolution: Marxism and the Revisionist Challenge*, London.

Connell, R.W. 1979. 'A Critique of the Althusserian Conception of Class', *Theory and Society*, no. 8, pp. 303–45.

Connolly, W. 1981. *Appearance and Reality in Politics*, Cambridge.

Contat, M. and M. Rybalka, 1970. *Les Ecrits de Sartre*, Paris.

———— 1971. 'Les Ecrits de Sartre de 1969 à 1971', *Le Magazine littéraire*, nos 55–6, pp. 36–47.

———— 1979. 'Les Ecrits de Sartre (1973–1978)', *Obliques*, no. 18, pp. 335–44.

Cooper, B. 1979. *Merleau-Ponty and Marxism: From Terror to Reform*, Toronto.

———— 1984. *The End of History: An Essay on Modern Hegelianism*, Toronto.

Coser, L. 1965. *Men of Ideas. A Sociologist's View*, New York.

Cotten, J.-P. 1979. *La Pensée de Louis Althusser*, Toulouse.

Cotteret, J.-M. and R. Moreau, 1969. *Le Vocabulaire du général de Gaulle*, Paris.

Courtois, S. 1980. *Le PCF dans la guerre*, Paris.

Craipeau, Y. 1971. *Le Mouvement trotskyiste en France: des origines aux enseignements de Mai 68*, Paris.

Cranston, J. 1973. 'Althusser's Ideology', *Problems of Communism*, vol. xxii, no. 2, pp. 53–60.

Crespo, L. 1977. 'Louis Althusser en Espagne (1966–1976)', *Dialectiques*, nos 15–16, pp. 57–63.

Crouzet, M. 1963. 'La Bataille des intellectuels français', *La Nef*, pp. 47–65.

Crozier, M. 1964. 'The Cultural Revolution: Notes on the Change in the Intellectual Climate of France', in S.R. Graubard (ed.), *A New Europe?*, Boston, pp. 602–30.

———— 1968. *La Société bloquée*, Paris.

———— 1979. 'Les Angoisses existentielles des intellectuels français: réflexions sur vingt années de révolution culturelle', *Commentaire*, vol. 2, no. 6, pp. 169–80.

—— 1977 and E. Friedberg. *L'Acteur et le système*, Paris.

Cublier, J.-M. n.d. 'La Presse française et les procès de Moscou', unpublished thesis, Fondation Nationale des Sciences Politiques, Paris.

Curtis, M. *Three Against the Republic: Sorel, Barrès, and Maurras*, Princeton, 1959.

Dagnaud, M. and D. Mehl, 1981. 'Profil de la nouvelle gauche', *Revue française de science politique*, vol. 31, no. 2, pp. 372–93.

Daix, P. 1949. *Pourquoi David Rousset a inventé les camps soviétiques*, Paris.

—— 1976. *J'ai cru au matin*, Paris.

—— 1978. *La Crise du PCF*, Paris.

Daniel, J. 1979. *Le Temps qui reste*, Paris.

Danto, A. 1986. 'A Prodigious Dream of Totality', *Times Literary Supplement*, (11 July).

Davies, H. 1987. *Sartre and 'Les Temps Modernes'*, Cambridge.

Le Débat, 1980. 'De quoi l'avenir intellectuel sera-t-il fait?', special issue, no. 4.

Debray, R. 1977a. 'Marxism and the National Question' (interview), *New Left Review*, no. 105, pp. 25–41.

—— 1977b. *A Critique of Arms*, trans. R. Sheed, Harmondsworth.

—— 1979a. 'A Modest Contribution to the Rites and ceremonies of the Tenth Anniversary', *New Left Review*, no. 115 (1979), pp. 45–65.

—— 1979b. *Le Pouvoir intellectuel en France* (Paris); trans. D. Macey, *Teachers, Writers, Celebrities. The Intellectuals of Modern France*, London, 1981.

—— 1983. *Critique of Political Reason*, trans. D. Macey, London.

—— 1990. *A demain de Gaulle*, Paris.

Delannoi, G. 1982. 'Crise intellectuelle et tentatives de fondation d'une politique de l'homme: *Arguments*, Edgar Morin, J.-P. Sartre', unpublished thesis, Institut d'Etudes Politiques, Paris.

—— 1984. '*Arguments*, 1956–1962 ou la parenthèse de l'ouverture', *Revue française de science politique*, vol. 34, no. 1, pp. 127–45.

—— 1990. *Les Années utopiques, 1968–1978*, Paris.

Delhorbe, C. 1932. *L'Affaire Dreyfus et les écrivains français*, Paris.

Deli, P. 1981. *De Budapest à Prague. Les Sursauts de la gauche française*, Paris.

Delwit, P. and J.-M. Dewaele, 1984. 'The Stalinists of Anti-Communism', *The Socialist Register*, London, pp. 324–48.

Demangeon, A. 1920. *Le Déclin de l'Europe*, Paris.

Derrida, J. 1977. *Of Grammatology*, trans. G. Chakravorty Spivak, London.

Desan, W. 1965. *The Marxism of J.P. Sartre*, New York.

Desanti, D. 1975. *Les Staliniens. Une expérience politique, 1944–1956*, Paris.

Descombes, V. 1980. *Modern French Philosophy*, trans. L. Scott-Fox and J.M. Harding, Cambridge.

—— 1981. Review of Castoriadis, 'La Guerre Prochaine', *Critique*, nos 411–12, pp. 723–43.

—— 1985. 'Les Mots de la tribu', *Critique*, no. 456, pp. 418–44.

—— 1987. 'Je m'en Foucault', *London Review of Books*, (5 March), pp. 20–1.

—— 1989. *Philosophie par gros temps*, Paris.

Dews, P. 1979. 'La Nouvelle Philosophie and Foucault', *Economy and Society*, vol. 8, no. 2, pp. 127–69.

———— 1980a. 'Structuralism and the French Epistemological Tradition', unpublished ms.

———— 1980b. 'The "New Philosophers" and the End of Leftism', *Radical Philosophy*, no. 24, pp. 2–11.

———— 1987. *Logics of Disintegration*, London.

Dialectiques, 1977. Special issue on Althusser, nos 15–16.

Digeon, C. 1959. *La Crise allemande de la pensée française (1870–1914)*, Paris.

Dioujeva, N. and F. George, 1982. *Staline à Paris*, Paris.

Dollé, J.-P. 1966. 'Du gauchisme à "l'humanisme socialiste"', *Les Temps Modernes*, no. 239, pp. 1890–1917.

Domenach, J.-M. 1983. *Lettres à mes ennemis de classe*, Paris.

Dommanget, M. 1969. *L'Introduction du Marxisme en France*, Lausanne.

Donzelot, J. 1984. *L'Invention du social: Essai sur le déclin des passions politiques*, Paris.

Dosse, F. 1987. *L'Histoire en miettes. 'Des "Annales" à la "Nouvelle histoire"'*, Paris.

———— 1991–2. *Histoire du structuralisme*, 2 vols, Paris.

Douglas, K. 1951. 'The French Intellectuals: Situation and Outlook', in E. Mead Earle, *Modern France*, Princeton, pp. 61–80.

Doyle, W. 1980. *The Origins of the French Revolution*, Oxford.

———— 1989. *The Oxford History of the French Revolution*, Oxford.

Drouard, A. 1982. 'Reflexions sur une chronologie: le développement des sciences sociales en France de 1945 à la fin des années soixante', *Revue française de sociologie*, vol. 23, no. 1, pp. 55–85.

Dufrenne, M. 1967. 'La Philosophie du néo-positivisme', *Esprit*, no. 360, pp. 781–800.

Duhamel, O. 1980. *La Gauche et la Ve République*, Paris.

———— 1989. '"La Révolution française est terminée"', *Pouvoirs*, no. 50, pp. 121–5.

———— and J.-L. Parodi, 1982. 'La Dégradation de l'image de Union Soviétique', *Pouvoirs*, no. 21, pp. 169–80.

Dumont, L. 1985. 'Identités collective et idéologie universaliste', *Critique*, no. 456, pp. 507–18.

———— 1986a. *Essays on Individualism: Modern Ideology in Anthropological Perspective*, Chicago.

———— 1986b. 'Are Cultures Living Beings? German Identity in Interaction', *Man*, vol. 21, no. 4, pp. 587–604.

———— 1992. 'Left versus Right in French Political Ideology: A comparative approach', in J.A. Hall and I.C. Jarvie (eds), *Transition to Modernity: Essays on Power, Wealth, and Belief*, Cambridge.

Dunn, J. 1968. 'The Identity of the History of Ideas', *Philosophy*, vol. 43, pp. 85–104.

———— 1984. *The Politics of Socialism*, Cambridge.

———— 1993. 'The Identity of the Bourgeois Liberal Republic', in B. Fontana (ed.), *The Invention of the Modern Republic*, Cambridge.

Durkheim, E. 1898. 'Individualism and the Intellectuals', *Political Studies*, vol. xvii, no. 1 (1969), pp. 14–30.

Duroselle, J.-B. 1963. 'Changes in French Policy since 1945', in S. Hoffmann *et al.*, *France: Change and Tradition*, London.

Duvignaud, J. 1962. 'France: the Neo-Marxists', in L. Labedz (ed.), *Revisionism: Essays on the History of Marxist Ideas*, London.

D'Estaing, G. 1974. *La Démocratie française*, Paris.

Earle, E. Mead, 1951. *Modern France*, Princeton.

Elleinstein, J. 1976. *Le PC*, Paris.

Elliott, G. 1987. *Althusser: The Detour of Theory*, London.

Ellis, G. 1978. 'The "Marxist" Interpretation of the French Revolution', *English Historical Review*, vol. 93, pp. 353–76.

Eribon, D. 1989. *Michel Foucault*, Paris.

Eros, J. 1955. 'The Positivist Generation of French Republicanism', *Sociological Review*, vol. iii, pp. 255–77.

Espace-Temps, 1988. Special issue, 'Concevoir la révolution: '89-'68, confrontations', nos 38–9.

Esprit, 1976. 'Révolution et totalitarisme', no. 460.

———— 1979. 'Les Intellectuels dans la société', nos 9–10.

———— 1983. 'La gauche, expérience faite', no. 12.

———— 1984. 'Traversées du XXe siècle', no. 5.

———— 1986. 'La Passion des idées', nos 8–9.

FAIRE, 1979. *Qu'est-ce que la social-démocratie?*, Paris.

Farmer, P. 1944. *France Reviews its Revolutionary Origins. Social Politics and Historical Opinion in the Third Republic*, New York.

Favre, J., F. Hincker, and L. Sève, 1977. *Les Communistes et l'état*, Paris.

Favre, P. 1989. *Naissances de la science politique en France 1870–1914*, Paris.

Faye, J.-P. 1972. *Langages totalitaires*, Paris.

Fehér, F. 1987. *The Frozen Revolution: An Essay on Jacobinism*, Cambridge.

———— (ed.). 1990. *The French Revolution and the Birth of Modernity*, Chicago.

Fejtö, F. 1987. *The French Communist Party and the Crisis of International Communism*, Cambridge, Mass.

Ferrat, A. 1945. *La République à refaire*, Paris.

Ferry, J.-M. 1985. 'Modernisation et consensus', *Esprit*, no. 5, pp. 13–28.

———— 1990. 'Qu'est–ce qu'une identité postnationale?', *Esprit: La France en Politique 1990*, no. 164, pp. 80–90.

Ferry, L. and A. Renaut 1982–5. *Philosophie politique*, 4 vols, Paris.

———— 1985. *La Pensée 68*, Paris.

Field, T. 1976. 'Vers une nouvelle datation du substantif "intellectuel"', *Travaux de linguistique et de la littérature*, vol. 14, no. 2, pp. 159–67.

Fink, C. 1989. *Marc Bloch: A Life in History*, Cambridge.

Finkielkraut, A. 1987. *La Défaite de la pensée*, Paris.

———— 1992. *Le Mécontemporain*, Paris.

———— *et al.* 1987. 'Changement intellectuel ou changement des intellectuels?', *Le Débat*, no. 45, pp. 40–58.

Fondation Nationale des Sciences Politiques, 1972. *L'Ouvrier français en 1970*, Paris.

Fontana, B. 1991. *Benjamin Constant and the Post-Revolutionary Mind*, New Haven and London.

———— (ed.). 1993. *The Invention of the Modern Republic*, Cambridge.

Foucault, M. 1977. *Language, Counter-Memory, Practice*, ed. and trans. D. Boucher, Oxford.

———— 1979. *Discipline and Punish*, trans. A. Sheridan, Harmondsworth.

———— 1980. *Power/Knowledge*, trans. C. Gordon, L. Marshall, J. Mepham, K. Soper, Brighton.

———— 1981a. *The History of Sexuality*, vol. 1, trans. R. Hurley, Harmondsworth.

———— 1981b. *Remarks on Marx: Conversations with Ducio Trombadori*, trans. R.J. Goldstein and J. Cascaito, New York, 1991.

—— 1988. *Politics, Philosophy and Culture: Interviews and other writings 1977–1984*, ed. L. Kritzman, London.

Frank, R. 1986. 'The French Dilemma: Modernization with Dependence or Independence and Decline?', in J. Becker and F. Knipping (eds), *Power in Europe?*, Berlin and New York.

Fraser, R. 1988. *1968*, London.

Frears, J.R. and J.-L. Parodi, 1979. *War Will Not Take Place: the French Parliamentary Elections, March 1978*, London.

Friedmann, G. 1938. *De la Sainte Russie à l'URSS*, Paris.

Friend, J. 1982. 'Soviet Behaviour and National Responses: the Puzzling Case of the French Communist Party', *Studies in Comparative Communism*, vol. 15, no. 2, pp. 212–35.

Friguglietti, J. 1972. 'Albert Matheiz, an Historian at War', *French Historical Studies*, vol. 7, no. 4, pp. 570–86.

Furet, F. 1963. 'Introduction: Les Sansculottes et la Révolution française', *Annales: Economies, Sociétés, Civilisations*, vol. 18, pp. 1098–127.

—— 1970. 'Tocqueville est-il un historien de la Révolution française?', *Annales: Economies, Sociétés, Civilisations*, vol. 25, no. 2, pp. 255–89.

—— 1971. 'Le catéchisme révolutionnaire', *Annales: Economies, Sociétés, Civilisations*, vol. 26, no. 2, pp. 255–89.

—— 1974. 'La Mort du Roi', *Le Nouvel Observateur*, no. 493 (22 April), p. 76.

—— 1975. 'Faut-il brûler Marx?', *Le Nouvel Observateur*, no. 559 (22 July), pp. 52–3.

—— 1976. 'Au centre de nos représentations politiques', *Esprit*, no. 460, pp. 172–8.

—— 1978. *Penser la Révolution française* (Paris); trans. E. Forster, *Interpreting the French Revolution*, Cambridge, 1981.

—— 1980. 'Le XXe siècle et l'intelligence du politique', *Le Débat*, no. 1, pp. 120–5.

—— 1981. 'La Révolution sans la Terreur? Le Débat des historiens du XIXe siècle', *Le Débat*, no. 13, pp. 40–54.

—— 1982. *L'Atelier de l'histoire*, Paris.

—— 1983a. 'Une polémique thermidorienne', *Passé-Présent*, no. 2, pp. 44–55.

—— 1983b. 'La Révolution dans l'imaginaire politique français', *Le Débat*, no. 26, pp. 173–81.

—— (ed.). 1985. *Jules Ferry. Fondateur de la République* Paris.

—— 1986a. 'Burke ou la fin d'une seule histoire de l'Europe', *Le Débat*, no. 39, pp. 56–65.

—— 1986b. 'Une Révolution sans révolution?' (interview), *Le Nouvel Observateur* (28 February), pp. 90–3.

—— 1986c. *La Gauche et la Révolution française au milieu du XIXe siècle: Edgar Quinet et la question du Jacobinisme (1865–1870)*, Paris.

—— 1986d. 'L'homme retrouvé, *Le Nouvel Observateur* (13 June), pp. 114–50.

—— 1987. 'Preface' to T. Judt, *Le Marxisme et la gauche française*, Paris, pp. i–xix.

—— 1988a. 'Droite, gauche, centre: Sur quelques objections', *Le Débat*, no. 52, pp. 11–14.

—— 1988b. *La Revolution: De Turgot à Jules Ferry 1770–1880*, Paris.

—— 1988c. 'Histoire de l'idée révolutionnaire' (interview), *Magazine littéraire*, no. 258, pp. 18–20.

—— 1988d. *Marx and the French Revolution*, trans. D. Kan Furet, Chicago.

—— 1989a. 'Reflexions sur l'idée de tradition révolutionnaire dans la France du XIXe siècle', *Pouvoirs*, no. 50, pp. 6–13.

—— 1989b. '1789–1917: aller-retour', *Le Débat*, no. 57, pp. 4ff.

——— 1989c. 'The French Revolution Revisited', *Government and Opposition*, vol. 24, no. 3, pp. 264–82.

——— (ed.). 1989d. *L'Héritage de la révolution Française*, Paris.

——— 1990a. 'L'Enigme de la désagrégation communiste', *Le Débat*, no. 62, pp. 166–78.

——— 1990b. *Terminer La Révolution*, Grenoble.

——— 1991a. 'The French Revolution or Pure Democracy' in C. Lucas (ed.), *Rewriting the French Revolution*, Oxford.

——— 1991b. 'The Future of the Left', *Partisan Review*, vol. 57, no. 3, pp. 432–7.

——— and M. Ozouf (eds), 1989a. *The French Revolution and the Creation of Modern Political Culture*, vol. 3 *The Transformation of Political Culture 1789–1848*, Oxford.

——— (eds), 1989b. *A Critical Dictionary of the French Revolution*, trans. A. Goldhammer, Cambridge, Mass.

——— and D. Richet, 1965–6. *La Révolution*, 2 vols, Paris.

——— A. Liniers and P. Raynaud, 1985. *Terrorisme et démocratie*, Paris.

——— J. Julliard and P. Rosanvallon, 1988. *La République du centre: la fin de l'exception française*, Paris.

Gabel. J. 1978. *Idéologies II: Althusserisme et Stalinisme*, 2 vols, Paris.

Gaffney, J. 1987. *Language, Power and the Left in the French Fifth Republic*, London.

Gallie, D. 1983. *Social Inequality and Class Radicalism in France and Britain*, Cambridge.

Gallisot, R. 1981. 'Nation française, nation algérienne en formation. La conception de la nation dans le discours communiste français', in *L'Expérience soviétique et le problème nationale dans le monde (1920–1939)*, Paris.

Gallo, M. 1983. 'Les Intellectuels, la politique et la modernité', *Le Monde* (26 July).

Gane, M. 1983. 'The ISAs Decade', *Economy and Society*, vol. 12, no. 4.

Garandy, R. 1957. *Humanisme marxiste*, Paris.

——— 1959. *Perspectives de l'homme*, Paris.

——— 1966. *Marxism in the Twentieth Century*, trans. R. Hague, London, 1970.

——— 1969. *The Turning Point of Socialism*, trans. P. and B. Ross, London, 1970.

Garmy, R. 1960. 'Georges Lefebvre et l'homme (Souvenirs)', *Annales historiques de la Révolution française*, vol. 32, pp. 80–4.

Garnier, J.-P. and R. Lew, 1984. 'From the Wretched of the Earth to the Defence of the West: An Essay on Left Disenchantment in France', *The Socialist Register*, pp. 299–323.

Gauchet, M. 1974. 'La Logique du politique', *Critique*, vol. 30, no. 329, pp. 907–26.

——— 1980. 'Les Droits de l'homme ne sont pas une politique', *Le Débat*, no. 3, pp. 3–21.

——— 1985. *Le Désenchantement du monde*, Paris.

——— 1989. *La Révolution des droits de l'homme*, Paris.

Gaulle, C. de 1971. *Memoirs of Hope*, London.

Gavi, P., J.-P. Sartre, and P. Victor, 1974. *On a raison de se révolter*, Paris.

Geerlandt, R. 1978. *Garaudy et Althusser. Le débat sur l'humanisme dans le parti communiste français et son enjeu*, Paris.

Geismar, A., S. July, and E. Morane, 1969. *Vers la guerre civile en France*, Paris.

Geras, N. 1977. 'Althusser's Marxism', in G. Stedman Jones. et al. *Western Marxism: A Critical Reader*, London.

Gerratana, V. 1976. 'Sur les difficultés de l'analyse du Stalinisme', *Dialectiques*, nos 15–16, pp. 43–51.

—— 1977a. 'Althusser and Stalintiom', *New Left Review*, nos 101–2, pp. 110–22.

—— 1977b. 'Stalin, Lenin, and "Leninism"', *New Left Review*, no. 103, pp. 59–72.

Giddens, A. 1973. *The Class Structure of the Advanced Societies*, London.

—— 1982. 'From Marx to Nietzsche? Neo-Conservatism, Foucault, and Problems in Contemporary Political Theory', in *Profiles and Critiques in Social Theory*, London.

Gide, A. 1937. *Rétouches à mon retour de l'URSS*, Paris.

Girardet, R. 1958. 'Pour une introduction à l'histoire du nationalisme français', *Revue français de science politique*, vol. 8, no. 3, pp. 505–28.

—— 1973. *L'Idée coloniale en France 1871–1962*, Paris.

—— 1983. 'Du concept de génération à la notion de contemporanéité', *Revue d'histoire moderne et contemporaine*, t. 30, pp. 257–70.

—— 1986. *Mythes et mythologies politiques*, Paris.

Girault, R. 1986. 'The French Decision-Makers and their Perceptions of French Power in 1948', in J. Becker and F. Knipping (eds), *Power in Europe?*, Berlin and New York.

Gleicher, J. 1982. *The Accidental Revolutionary: Essays on the Political Teaching of Sartre*, Washington.

Glucksmann, A. 1967. *Le Discours de la guerre*, Paris.

—— 1968a. *Stratégie et révolution en France 1968*, Paris.

—— 1968b. 'Strategy and Revolution in France 1968', *New Left Review*, no. 52, pp. 67–121.

—— 1969. 'A propos d'Althusser … la pratique Léniniste de la philosophie', *Nouvelle Critique*, no. 23, pp. 39–45.

—— 1972. 'Fascismes: L'Ancien et le nouveau', *Les Temps Modernes*, no. 310 bis, pp. 266–334.

—— 1974. 'Le Marxisme rend sourd', *Le Nouvel Observateur* (4 March), p. 80.

—— 1975. *La Cuisinière et le mangeur d'hommes*, Paris.

—— 1977a. 'A Ventriloquist Structuralism', in G. Stedman Jones *et al.*, *Western Marxism*, London.

—— 1977b. *Les Maîtres penseurs*, Paris.

—— 1983. *La Force du Vertige*, Paris.

—— 1985. *La Bêtise*, Paris.

Godechot, J. 1958. *La Grande Nation*, Paris, 2nd edn., 1983.

Goldmann, L. 1966. *Sciences humaines et philosophie*, Paris.

Goldthorpe, J. 1979. 'Intellectuals and the Working Class in Modern Britain', Fuller Bequest Lecture, University of Essex.

Gombin, R. 1971. *Les Origines du gauchisme*, Paris.

Gorz, A. 1959. *The Traitor*, trans. R. Howard, New York.

—— 1964. *Strategy for Labour*, Boston.

—— 1977. 'Sartre and Marxism', in G. Stedman Jones *et al.*, *Western Marxism*, London.

Graham, B.D. 1947. *The French Socialists and Tripartism 1944–1947*, Canberra.

Graubard, S.R. (ed.). 1964. *A New Europe?*, Boston.

Grémion, P. 1980. 'Crispation et déclin du jacobinisme', in H. Mendras (ed.),

242   BIBLIOGRAPHY

La Sagesse et la désordre: France 1980, Paris.

———— 1983–4. 'Le rouge et le gris: les intellectuels français et le monde soviétique', *Commentaire*, no. 24, pp. 767–80.

———— 1985. *Paris-Prague*, Paris.

———— 1992. 'Michel Crozier's Long March: the making of *The Bureaucratic Phenomenon*', *Political Studies*, vol. xl, pp. 5–20.

Grenon, M. and R. Robin 1976. 'A propos de la polémique sur l'Ancien régime et la Révolution: pour une problématique de la transition', *La Pensée*, no. 187, pp. 9–12.

Gröh, D. 1961. *Russland und des Selbstverständnis Europas: Ein Beitrag zur europaischen Geistesgeschichte*, Neuwid-am-Rhein.

Guérin, D. 1946. *La Lutte des classes sous la Première République (1793–97)*, 2 vols, Paris.

———— 1965. 'D'Une nouvelle interprétation de la Révolution française', *Annales: Economies, Sociétés, Civilisations*, vol. 20, pp. 84–94.

———— 1968. *La Révolution française et nous*, Brussels.

Guibal, F. 1980. 'Cornelius Castoriadis: un appel à une lucidité active', *Etudes*, no. 723, pp. 761–78.

Guillaume, M. 1986. *L'Etat des sciences sociales en France*, Paris.

Guillebaud, J.-C. 1978. *Les Années orphélines*, Paris.

Guitton, J. 1988. 'Althusser reste mon ami', *Lire* (May), pp. 81–9.

Guizot, F. 1828. *Histoire de la civilisation en Europe*, Paris.

Habermas, J. 1987. *The Philosophical Discourse of Modernity*, Cambridge.

Hamon, H. and P. Rotman 1979. *Les Porteurs de valises*, Paris.

———— 1981. *Les Intellocrates*, Brussels.

———— 1987, 1988. *Génération*: vol. 1, *Les années de rêve*; vol. 2, *Les années de poudre*, Paris.

Hanley, D. 1986. *Keeping Left? CERES and the French Socialist Party*, Manchester.

Hanley, D. and A.P. Kerr (eds), 1989. *May '68*, London.

Hardouin, P. 1978. 'Les Caractéristiques sociologiques du Parti Socialiste', *Revue française de science politique*, vol. 28, no. 2, pp. 220–56.

Harmel, C. 1980. *Le Parti Socialiste. Courants et conflits*, Paris.

Hassner, P. 1979. 'Western European Perceptions of the USSR', *Daedalus*, vol. 108, no. 1, pp. 113–50.

Hassner, P. 1984. 'Le totalitarisme vue de l'Ouest', in G. Hermet *et al.*, *Totalitarismes*, Paris.

Haupt, G. 1987. *Aspects of International Communism*, Cambridge.

Hawthorn, G. 1987. *Enlightenment and Despair. A History of Social Theory*, Cambridge.

Hayes, C.J.H. 1930. *France, a Nation of Patriots*, New York.

Hayward, J. 'Solidarism', *International Review of Social History*, vol. iv, no. 2 (1959), pp. 261–84; vol. vi, no. 1 (1961), pp. 19–48; and vol. viii, no. 1 (1963), pp. 1–17.

———— 1981. *Surreptitious Factionalism in the French PC*, Hull.

———— 1983. *Governing France: The One and Indivisible Republic*, London.

———— 1986. *The State and the Market Economy. Industrial Patriotism and Economic Intervention in France*, New York.

———— 1991. *After the French Revolution: Six Critics of Democracy and Nationalism*, Hemel Hempstead.

Hazareesingh, S. 1991. *Intellectuals and the French Communist Party*, Oxford.

Heckman, J. 1973. 'Hyppolite and the Hegel Revival in France', *Telos*, no. 16, pp. 128–45.

Hellman, J. 1981. *Emmanuel Mounier and the New Catholic Left, 1930–1950*, Toronto and London.

Herbart, P. 1937. *En URSS 1936*, Paris.

Hermet, G. *et al.*, 1984. *Totalitarismes*, Paris.

Hess, R. 1973a. 'Le Maoisme, l'analyse et les analyseurs', *L'Homme et la Société*, nos 29–30, pp. 35–44.

——— 1973b. 'Maoisme français et autogestion', *Autogestion et socialisme*, nos 22–3, pp. 165–88

——— 1988. *Henri Lefebvre et l'aventure du siècle*, Paris.

Higonnet, P. 1986. 'Le Sens de la Terreur dans la Révolution française', *Commentaire*, no. 35, pp. 436–45.

Hirsch, J.-P. 1980. 'Pensons la Révolution française', *Annales: Economies, Sociétés, Civilisations*, no. 35, pp. 320–33.

Hirsh, A. 1981. *The French New Left*, Boston.

Hirst, P. 1979. *On Law and Ideology*, London.

Hobsbawm, E. 1977. *Revolutionaries*, London.

——— 1990. *Echoes of the Marseillaise*, London.

——— and T. Ranger (eds), 1984. *The Invention of Tradition*, Cambridge.

Hoffmann, S. 1961. 'The Effects of World War II on French Society and Politics', *French Historical Studies*, vol. 2, no. 1, pp. 28–63.

——— *et al.* 1963. *France: Change and Tradition*, London.

——— 1974. *Decline or Renewal? France since the 1930s*, New York.

——— 1987. 'France and Europe: the dichotomy of autonomy and co-operation', in J. Howorth and G. Ross (eds), *Contemporary France*, London, pp. 46–54.

Hofstadter, R. 1964. *Anti-Intellectualism in American Life*, London.

Hollier, D. 1979. *Le Collège de sociologie*, Paris.

Hough, J.F. 1977. *The Soviet Union and Social Science Theory*, Cambridge, Mass.

Howard, D. and K.E. Klare (eds), 1972. *The Unknown Dimension: European Marxism since Lenin*, New York.

Howorth, J. and G. Ross (eds), 1987. *Contemporary France: A Review of Interdisciplinary Studies*, London.

Hughes, H. Stuart. 1969. *The Obstructed Path. French Social Thought in the Years of Desperation 1930–1960*, New York.

Hunt, L. 1981. 'Review of F. Furet, *Penser la Révolution française*', *History and Theory*, vol. 20, no. 3, pp. 313–23.

——— 1984. *Politics, Culture and Class in the French Revolution*, Berkeley.

Hutton, P. 1991. 'The Role of Memory in the Historiography of the French Revolution', *History and Theory*, vol. 30, no. 1, pp. 56–69.

Invitto, G. 1971. *Merleau-Ponty politico: L'eresia programmatica*, Rome.

Irvine, W.D. 1974. 'French Conservatives and the "New Right" during the 1930s', *French Historical Studies*, no. 4, pp. 534–62.

Jackson, J. 1988. *The Popular Front in France*, Cambridge.

James, H. 1989. *A German Identity 1770–1990*, London.

James, S. 1984a. *The Content of Social Explanation*, Cambridge.

——— 1984b. 'Louis Althusser' in Q. Skinner (ed.), *The Return of Grand Theory in the Human Sciences*, Cambridge.

Jameson, F. 1971. *Marxism and Form*, Princeton.

Janover, L. 1980. *Les Intellectuels face à l'histoire*, Paris.

Jaume, L. 1989. *Le Discours jacobin et la démocratie*, Paris.

Jaurès, J. 1969. *Histoire socialiste de la Révolution française* 7 vols, ed. A. Soboul, Paris.

Jay, M. 1984. *Marxism and Totality: The adventures of a concept from Lukács to Habermas*, Cambridge.

Jeanneney, J.-N. 1977. *Leçon d'histoire pour une gauche au pouvoir. La Faillite du Cartel 1924–1926*, Paris.

Jelen, C. 1984. *L'Aveuglement. Les Socialistes et la naissance du mythe soviétique*, Paris.

Jenkins, B. 1990. *Nationalism in France: Class and Nation since 1789*, London.

Johnson, R. 1972. *The French Communist Party versus the Students: Revolutionary Politics in May–June 1968*, New Haven.

Johnson, R.W. 1981. *The Long March of the French Left*, London.

Judt, T. 1976. *La Réconstruction du Parti Socialiste 1921–1926*, Paris.

——— 1982. '"Une historiographie pas comme les autres": The French Communists and their History', *European Studies Review*, vol. 12, pp. 445–78.

——— 1985. '"The Spreading Notion of the Town": Some recent writings on French and Italian Communism', *The Historical Journal*, vol. 28, no. 4, pp. 1011–21.

——— 1986. *Marxism and the French Left*, Oxford.

——— 1992. *Past Imperfect: French Intellectuals, 1944–1956*, Berkeley.

——— (ed.). 1989. *Resistance and Revolution in Mediterranean Europe 1939–1948*, London.

Julliard, J. 1977. *Contre la politique professionelle*, Paris.

——— 1985. *La Faute à Rousseau*, Paris.

——— 1988. 'Droite, centre, gauche', *Le Debat*, no. 52, pp. 4–10.

——— and J.-N. Jeanneney, 1979. '*Le Monde' de Beuve-Méry ou le métier d'Alceste*, Paris.

Kahn, J.-F. 1982. *La Guerre civile: essai sur les Stalinismes de droite et de gauche*, Paris.

Kail, M. 1986. 'Les Droits de l'homme, philosophie indépassable de notre temps?', *Les Temps Modernes*, no. 476, pp. 161–82.

Kaisergruber, D. 1978. 'Les Ruses linguistiques de l'histoire: analyse de la réponse à John Lewis de Louis Althusser', *Dialectiques*, no. 20, pp. 59–73.

Karz, S. 1974. *Théorie et politique: Louis Althusser*, Paris.

Kedward, H.R. 1978. *Resistance in Vichy France*, Oxford.

——— 1982. 'Patriots and Patriotism in Vichy France', *Transactions of the Royal Historical Society*, 5th series, no. 32, pp. 175–92.

Kelly, M. 1982. *Modern French Marxism*, Oxford.

Keohane, N. 1980. *Philosophy and the State in France*, Princeton.

Kessel, P. 1972. *Le Mouvement 'maoiste' en France*, 2 vols, Paris.

Keylor, W. 1975. *Academy and Community: The Foundation of the French Historical Profession*, Cambridge, Mass.

——— 1979. *Jacques Bainville and the Renaissance of Royalist history in Twentieth-Century France*, Baton Rouge.

Kogan, N. 1973. 'The French Communists—and their Italian Comrades', *Studies in Comparative Communism*, vol. 6, nos 1–2.

Kojève, A. 1969. *Introduction to the Reading of Hegel: Lectures on the Phenomenology of Spirit*, ed. A. Bloom and trans. J.H. Nichols, Ithaca and London.

Kolakowski, L. 1974. *L'Esprit révolutionnaire*, Brussels.

Koselleck, R. 1988. *Critique and Crisis. Enlightenment and the Parthogenesis of Modern Society*, Oxford.

Kriegel, A. 1964a. *Aux origines du communisme français 1914–1920*, 2 vols, Paris.

—— 1964b. *Le Congrès de Tours. Naissance du Parti Communiste Français*, Paris.

—— 1968. *Les Communistes français*, Paris.

—— 1972. 'Consistent Misapprehension: European Views of America and their Logic', *Daedalus*, pp. 87–102.

—— 1974. *Communismes au miroir français*, Paris.

Kristeva, J. 1977. 'Un Nouveau type d'intellectuel: le dissident', *Tel Quel*, no. 77, pp. 3–8.

—— 1988. *Etrangers à nous-mêmes*, Paris.

Kuisel, R. 1981. *Capitalism and the State in Modern France*, Cambridge.

Kupferman, F. 1979. *Au Pays des Soviets*, Paris.

Labbé, D. 1977. *Le Discours communiste*, Paris.

—— 1983. *François Mitterrand; Essai sur le discours*, Paris.

Laberenne, P. 1979. '"Le Cercle de la Russie Neuve" (1928–1936) et "l'Association pour l'etude de la culture soviétique"', *La Pensée*, no. 205, pp. 12–25.

Lacorne, D. 1973. 'Analyse et "reconstruction" de stereotypes: communistes et socialistes face au socialisme soviétique', *Revue française de science politique*, vol. 23, no. 6, pp. 1171–1201.

—— J. Rupnik, and M.-F. Toinet (eds), 1990. *The Rise and Fall of Anti-Americanism: A Century of French Perception*, trans. G. Turner, London.

Lacouture, J. 1975. *André Malraux*, London.

—— 1984–6. *De Gaulle*, 3 vols (Paris), trans. in 2 vols: vol. 1 *The Rebel: 1890–1944*, trans. P. O'Brian, London, 1990; vol. 2 *The Ruler: 1945–1970*, trans. A. Sheridan, London, 1991.

Landau-Aldonov, M.-A. 1921. *Deux révolutions. La Révolution française et la Révolution russe*, Paris.

Lapointe, F. 1975. *Jean-Paul Sartre and his Critics. An International Bibliography 1938–1974*, Ohio.

Laponce, J.A. 1981. *Left and Right. The Topography of Political Perception*, Toronto.

Lardreau, G. and C. Jambet, 1976. *L'Ange*, Paris.

—— 1977. *Ontologie de la Révolution*, Paris.

Lasch, C. 1962. *The American Liberals and the Russian Revolution*, New York.

Lauber, V. 1983. *The Political Economy of France. From Pompidou to Mitterrand*, New York.

Lavau, G. 1965. 'Les Clubs devant l'action politique', *Revue française de science politique*, vol. 15, no. 3, pp. 555–69.

—— 1975. 'The PCF, the State, and the Revolution: an Analysis of Party Policies, Communications, and Popular Culture', in D. Blackmer and S. Tarrow (eds), *Communism in Italy and France*, Princeton.

—— 1978. 'The Effects of Twenty Years of Gaullism on the Parties of the Left', in W.G. Andrews and S. Hoffmann (eds), *The Fifth Republic at Twenty*, Albany, NY.

—— 1981. *A quoi sert le Parti Communiste Français?*, Paris, 1981.

—— 1982. 'L'URSS et eux...(Le Parti Communiste français et le socialisme existant, 1964–1981)', in L. Marcou (ed.), *L'URSS vue de gauche*, Paris.

Lazar, M. 1990. 'Damné de la terre et homme de marbre: L'ouvrier dans l'imaginaire du PCF du milieu des années trente à la fin des années cinquante', *Annales: Economies, Sociétés, Civilisations*, vol. 45, no. 5, pp. 1071–96.

Lecourt, D. 1977. *Proletarian Science? The Case of Lysenko*, trans. B. Brewster, London.

———— 1978. *Dissidence ou révolution?*, Paris.

Le Dantec, J.-P. 1978. *Les Dangers du Soliel*, Paris.

Leenhardt, J. 1982. *La Force des mots: le rôle des intellectuels*, Paris.

Lefebvre, G. 1929. 'Les historiens de la Révolution française', repr. in *Réflexions sur l'histoire*, Paris, 1978.

———— 1939. *Quatre-vingt-neuf*, Paris.

———— 1954. *Etudes sur la Révolution française*, Paris.

———— 1955. 'A propos de Tocqueville', repr. in *Réflexions sur l'histoire*, Paris, 1978.

Lefebvre, H. 1937. *Le Nationalisme contre les nations*, Paris.

———— 1940. *Dialectical Materialism*, trans. J. Sturrock, London, 1968.

———— 1957. 'Le Marxisme et la pensée française', *Les Temps Modernes*, nos 137–8 , pp. 104–37.

———— 1959. *La Somme et le reste*, 2 vols, Paris.

———— 1961. 'Marxisme et politique: le Marxisme a-t-il une théorie politique?', *Revue française de science politique*, vol. 11, no. 2, pp. 338–63.

———— 1967a. *Position: Contre les technocrates*, Paris.

———— 1967b. 'Sur une interpretation de marxisme: Louis Althusser', *L'Homme et la société*, no. 4, pp. 3–22.

———— 1968. *The Explosion. Marxism and the French Upheaval*, trans. A. Ehrenfeld, New York, 1969.

———— 1969. 'Les Paradoxes d'Althusser', *L'Homme et la société*, no. 13, pp. 3–25.

Lefort, C. 1953. 'Le Marxisme et Sartre', *Les Temps Modernes*, vol. 8, no. 89, pp. 1541–70.

———— 1958. 'La Méthode des intellectuels progressistes', repr. in *Eléments d'une critique de la bureaucratie*, Geneva, 1971.

———— 1976. *Un Homme en trop. Réflexions sur 'l'Archipel du Goulag'*, Paris.

———— 1978a. *Sur une colonne absente*, Paris.

———— 1978b. 'De l'Egalité à la Libertè', *Libre*, no. 3, pp. 211–46.

———— 1980. Review of F. Furet, *Penser la Révolution française*, in *Annales: Economies, Sociétés, Civilisations*, vol. 35, no. 2, pp. 334–52.

———— 1981. *L'Invention démocratique*, Paris.

———— 1983. 'La Terreur révolutionnaire', *Passé-Présent*, no. 2, pp. 11–43.

———— 1986. *The Political Forms of Modern Society*, ed. J.B. Thompson, Cambridge.

———— 1988. *Democracy and Political Theory*, trans. D. Macey, Cambridge.

Lefranc, G. 1963. *Le Mouvement socialiste sous la troisième république (1875–1940)*, Paris.

Legendre, B. 1980. *Le Stalinisme français: Qui a dit quoi? (1944–56)*, Paris.

Legendre, P. 1974. *L'Amour de censeur*, Paris.

Le Goff, J. and B. Kopeczi (eds), 1985. *Intellectuels français, intellectuels hongrois. XIIIᵉ–XXᵉ siècles*, Paris.

Lemert, C. (ed.). 1981. *French Sociology: Rupture and Renewal Since 1968*, New York.

Lepage, H. 1978. *Demain le libéralisme*, Paris.

Le Roy Ladurie, E. 1982. *Paris-Montpellier. PC-PSU 1945–1963*, Paris.

—— 1983. 'Sur la révolution française: les révisions d'Alfred Cobban', *Commentaire*, no. 27, pp. 834–7.

Lévi-Strauss, C. 1962. *The Savage Mind*, London, 1966.

Lévy, B.-H. 1977a. *La Barbarie à visage humain*, Paris.

—— 1977b. Power and Sex: an Interview with Michel Foucault', *Telos*, 32, pp. 152–61.

—— 1987. *Eloge des intellectuels*, Paris.

—— 1991. *Les Aventures de la liberté*, Paris.

Lichtheim, G. 1961. *Marxism*, London.

—— 1966. *Marxism in Modern France*, New York.

Lindenberg, D. 1975. *Le Marxisme introuvable*, Paris.

—— 1982. 'Adieux à l'intelligentsia?', *Le Débat*, no. 18, pp. 11–15.

—— 1990. *Les Années souterraines 1937–1947*, Paris.

—— and P.-A. Mayer, 1977. *Lucien Herr: Le Socialisme et son destin*, Paris.

Linhart, R. 1978. *L'Etabli*, Paris.

Lipovetsky. G. 1983. *L'Ere du vide. Essai sur l'individualisme contemporain*, Paris.

Lipset, S.M. 1963a. *Political Man*, New York.

—— 1963b. *The First New Nations*, New York.

Lochore, R.A. 1935. *History of the Idea of Civilization in France (1830–1870)*, Bonn.

Lock, G. 1977. 'Althusser en Angleterre', *Dialectiques*, nos 15–16, pp. 64–72.

Lorthalory, A. 1951. *Le Mirage russe en France au XVIIIe siècle*, Paris.

Lottman, H. 1980. *Albert Camus: A Biography*, New York.

—— 1982. *The Left Bank*, London.

—— 1985. *The People's Anger. Justice and Revenge in Post–Liberation France*, London, 1985.

Loubère, L. 1959. 'The Intellectual Origins of French Jacobin Socialism', *International Review of Social History*, no. 4, pp. 415–31.

Loubet del Bayle, J.-L. 1969. *Les Nonconformistes des années trente*, Paris.

Lough, J. 1978. *Writer and Public in France: From the Middle Ages to the Present Day*, Oxford.

Löwy, M. 1979. *Georg Lukács—From Romanticism to Bolshevism*, trans. P. Camiller, London.

—— 1984. 'Stalinist Ideology and Science', in T. Ali (ed.), *The Stalinist Legacy*, London.

Lucas, C. (ed.). 1991. *Rewriting the French Revolution*, Oxford.

Lukes, S. 1985. *Marxism and Morality*, Oxford.

Lüthy, H. 1955. *France Against Herself*, New York.

—— 1960. 'The French Intellectuals', in G.B. de Huszar (ed.), *The Intellectuals: a Controversial Portrait*, Glencoe.

Lyotard, J.-F. 1983. *Derive à partir de Marx et Freud*, Paris.

—— 1984. *Tombeau de l'intellectuel et autres papiers*, Paris.

—— 1988. *The Differend: Phrases in Dispute*, trans. G. van den Abbeele, Manchester.

Macciocchi, M.-A. 1973. *Letters from Inside the Italian Communist Party to Louis Althusser*, London.

—— 1974. *Pour Gramsci*, Paris.

—— 1977. *De la France*, Paris.

—— 1983. *Deux milles ans de bonheur*, Paris.

Macey, D. 1993. *The Lives of Michel Foucault*, London.

Madjarian, G. 1980. *Conflits, pouvoirs et société à la Libération*, Paris.

Maffesoli, M. 1976. *Logique de la domination*, Paris.

Magazine Littéraire, 1987. Special issue on 'Idéologies: le grand chambardement', nos 239–40.

—— 1988. Special issue on 'La Révolution Française', no. 258.

Maistre, J. de. 1859. *Quatre chapitres inédits sur la Russie*, Paris.

Mallet, S. 1963. *La Nouvelle classe ouvrière*, Paris.

Malraux, A. 1952. 'Le Gaullisme sans de Gaulle et les républicains sans république', *Carrefours*, no. 384 (23 January).

—— 1972. *Fallen Oaks: Conversations with de Gaulle*, trans. I. Clephane, London.

—— and J. Burnham, 1948. *The Case for de Gaulle*, trans. S. Byard, New York.

Manceaux, M. 1972. *Les Maos en France*, Paris.

Manent, P. 1981. 'Démocratie et totalitarisme: A propos de Claude Lefort', *Commentaire*, vol. 4, no. 16, pp. 574–83.

—— 1982. *Tocqueville et la nature de la démocratie*, Paris.

—— 1987. *Histoire intellectuelle du libéralisme: dix leçons*, Paris.

Manin, B. 1984. 'Pourquoi la République?' *Intervention*, no. 10, pp. 7–25.

—— 1988. 'Tristesse de la social-démocratie? (la réception de John Rawls en France)', *Esprit: La France en politique 1988*, Paris.

Marchais, G. 1979. 'Pour une avancée démocratique', *Cahiers du Communisme*, vol. 56, no. 6 (June–July), pp. 42–51.

—— 1980a. *Les Intellectuels, la culture et la révolution*, Paris.

—— 1980b. *Le Monde* (24 January), p. 11.

Marcou, L. 1977. *Le Kominform, le communisme et la guerre froide*, Paris.

—— (ed.). 1982. *L'URSS vue de gauche*, Paris.

Marcus, J.T. 1958. *Neutralism and Nationalism in France*, New York.

Mascolo, D. 1955. 'Sur le sens et l'usage du mot "gauche"', *Les Temps Modernes*, nos 112–13, pp. 1679–97.

Mathiez, A. 1917a. 'La Chute de Kerenski', *Le Petit Comtois* (10 November).

—— 1917b. 'Vive la Russie', *Le Petit Comtois* (17 March).

—— 1920a. *Le Bolchevisme et le jacobinisme*, Paris.

—— 1920b. 'Pourquoi nous sommes Robespierristes', repr. in *Etudes sur Robespierre*, Paris, 1958.

Maublanc, R. 1936. 'Le Rayonnement du marxisme', *Cahiers du Bolchevisme*, nos 1–2, pp. 85–94.

Mauriac, F. 1944. *Le Cahier noir*, London.

—— 1953. 'L'Engagement de l'écrivain', *Le Figaro* (8 April).

—— 1969. *Mémoires politiques*, Paris.

Mayer, D. 1968. *Les Socialistes dans la Résistance*, Paris.

Mayer, J.P. 1949. *Political Thought in France: From the Revolution to the Fourth Republic*, London.

Mayeur, J.-M. 1984. *La Vie politique sous la Troisième République*, Paris.

Mazauric, C. 1970. *Sur la Révolution française*, Paris.

—— 1984. *Jacobinisme et Révolution: autour du bicentenaire de la Révolution*, Paris.

McBride, W. 1970. *Fundamental Change in Law and Society: Hart and Sartre on Revolution*, The Hague.

—— 1991. *Sartre's Political Theory*, Bloomington and Indianapolis.

McCarthy, P. 1979. *The French Socialists*, Bologna.

—— (ed.). 1987. *The Socialists in Power 1981–1986*, London.

McManners, J. 1965. 'The Historiography of the French Revolution', in A. Goodwin (ed.), *The New Cambridge Modern History*, Cambridge.

Mellon, S. 1958. *The Political Uses of History*, Stanford.

Mer, J. 1977. *Le Parti de M. Thorez ou le bonheur communiste français*, Paris.

Merleau-Ponty, M. 1947. *Humanisme et Terreur*, Paris, 1980 edn.

—— 1948. *Sens et non-sens* (Paris); trans. As *Sense and Non-Sense*, H.L. and P.A. Dreyfus, Evanston, 1964.

—— 1953. *Eloge de la philosophie et autres essais* (Paris); trans. as *In Praise of Philosophy*, J. Wild and J. Edie, Evanston, 1963.

—— 1955. *Les Adventures de la dialectique* (Paris); trans. as *Adventures of the Dialectic*, J. Bien, Evanston, 1973.

—— 1960. *Signes* (Paris); trans. as *Signs*, R.C. McCleary, Evanston, 1964.

Merquior, J.G. 1985. *Foucault*, London.

—— 1986. *From Prague to Paris*, London.

—— 1987. 'The Renaissance of French Political Theory', *Government and Opposition*, vol. 22, no. 1, pp. 101–14.

Michelet, J. 1846. *Le Peuple*, Paris.

Miller, J. 1993. *The Passion of Michel Foucault*, London.

Mohrenschildt, D.S. von, 1936. *Russia in the Intellectual Life of Eighteenth-Century France*, New York.

Monchablon, A. 1983. *Histoire de l'UNEF de 1956 à 1968*, Paris.

Mongin, O. 1977. 'D'une vulgate à l'autre: à propos de la nouvelle philosophie', *Esprit*, no. 12, pp. 62–78.

—— 1985. 'Dégénérescence intellectuelle ou regénération?' *Esprit*, nos 8–9, pp. 109–19.

Monnerot, J. 1949. *La Sociologie du communisme*, Paris.

—— 1986. 'Du pouvoir intellectuelle de la gauche', *Contrepoint*, nos 52–3, pp. 41–57.

Morin, E. 1957. *Autocritique*, Paris.

—— 1960. 'Intellectuels: critique du mythe et mythe de la critique', *Arguments*, vol. 4, no. 20.

—— 1983. *La Rose et le noir*, Paris.

—— 1986. 'Ce qui a changé dans la vie intellectuelle française', *Le Débat*, no. 40, pp. 72–84.

—— C. Lefort, and C. Castoriadis. 1988. *Mai 68: La brèche* suivi de *Vingt ans après*, Paris.

Mossuz-Lavau, J. 1982. *André Malraux et le gaullisme*, Paris.

—— 1979. *Les Clubs politiques*, Paris.

Mouchard, C. 1980. 'Claude Lefort: une pensée politique', *Critique*, vol. 36, no. 403, pp. 1111–23.

Mounier, E. 1946. 'Débat à haute voix', *Esprit*, no. 2, pp. 164–90.

—— 1961–3. *Oèuvres complètes*, 4 vols, Paris.

Mourin, M. 1967. *Les Rélations franco-soviétiques, 1917–1967*, Paris.

Mury, G. 1947. *Les Intellectuels devant l'action*, Paris.

Navarro, F. 1992. 'La Réception en Amérique latine', special issue on Louis Althusser, *Magazine littéraire*, no. 304, pp. 55–6.

Naville, P. 1975. *La Révolution et les intellectuels*, Paris.

La Nef, 1972. 'Les "gauchistes"', special issue, no. 48.

Negroni, F. de, 1985. *Le Savoir-vivre intellectuel*, Paris.

Netter, M.-L. 1989. *La Révolution française n'est pas terminée*, Paris.

Nettl, J.P. 1970. 'Ideas, Intellectuals, and Structures of Dissent', in P. Rieff (ed.), *On Intellectuals*, Garden City, New York.

Nettlebeck, C. 1989. 'Getting the Story Right: Narratives of the Second World War in Post-1968 France', in G. Hirschfield and P. Marsh (eds), *Collaboration in France*, Oxford.

Nicolet, C. 1957. *Le Radicalisme*, Paris.

—— 1959. *Pierre Mendès-France ou le métier du Cassandre*, Paris.

—— 1982. *L'Idée républicaine en France: Essai d'histoire critique*, Paris.

Nizan, P. 1932. *Les Chiens du garde* (Paris); trans. P. Fittinghof as *The Watch Dogs*, New York, 1971.

Nora, P. 1962. 'Ernest Lavisse: son rôle dans la formation du sentiment national', *Revue historique*, no. 228, pp. 73–104.

—— 1980. 'Que peuvent les intellectuels?', *Le Débat*, no. 1 pp. 3–19.

—— (ed.). 1984–. *Les Lieux de mémoire*, 7 vols, Paris.

Ory, P. 1986. 'Introduction to an Era of Doubt. Cultural Reflections of 'French Power', around the year 1948', in J. Becker and F. Knipping (eds), *Power in Europe? Great Britain, France, Italy and Germany in a Postwar World, 1945–1950*, Berlin and New York.

—— (ed.). 1990. *Dernières questions aux intellectuels*, Paris.

—— and J.-F. Sirinelli, 1986. *Les Intellectuels en France de l'Affaire Dreyfus à nos jours*, Paris.

Ozouf, M. 1981. 'Jacobinisme: fortunes et infortunes d'un mot', *Le Débat*, no. 13, pp. 38–9.

—— 1984. *La Fête révolutionnaire*, Paris.

—— 1989. *L'Homme régénéré: Essais sur la Révolution française*, Paris.

Pacquot, T. 1980. *Les Faiseurs de nuage: essai sur la genèse des marxismes français 1880–1914*, Paris.

Page, R. Arnot, 1967. *The Impact of the Russian Revolution in Britain*, London.

Pages, R. 1970. 'Lignes de Force (et de faiblesse) du gauchisme en Mai 1970', *L'Homme et la Société*, no. 16, pp. 137–48.

Papaioannou, K. 1967. *L'Idéologie froide: Essai sur le dépérissement du marxisme*, Paris.

—— 1983. *De Marx et du Marxisme*, Paris.

Parti Communiste Français, 1977. *Le Socialisme pour la France*, Paris.

Parti Socialiste, 1972. *Changer la Vie. Programme de gouvernement du Parti Socialiste*, Paris 1972.

Parti Socialiste, 1978. *Le Programme Commun de gouvernement de la Gauche*, Paris.

—— 1981. *Pour la France des années '80*, Paris.

Pasquino, P. 1987. 'Emmanuel Sieyès , Benjamin Constant et le "Gouvernement des Modernes": Contribution à l'histoire du concept de réprésentation politique', *Revue française de science politique*, vol. 37, no. 2, pp. 214–28.

—— 1989. 'Le Concept de nation et les fondements du droit public de la Révolution: E.J. Sieyès', in F. Furet (ed.), *L'Héritage de la Révolution française*, Paris, pp. 309–33.

Patton, P. 1978. 'Althusser's Epistemology: the limits of the Theory of Theoretical Practice', *Radical Philosophy*, no. 19 (Spring), pp. 8–18.

Paulhan, J. 1948. *De la Paille et du grain*, Paris.

—— 1952. *Lettre aux directeurs de la Résistance*, Paris.

Pavel, T. 1988. *Le Mirage linguistique: Essai sur la modernisation intellectuelle*, Paris.

—— 1990. 'Empire et paradigmes', *Le Débat*, no. 58, pp. 170–81.

Paxton, R. 1972. *Vichy France: Old Guard and New Order 1940–44*, London.

Pêcheux, M. 1982. *Language, Semantics and Ideology*, London.

Petot, J. 1989. 'La Tradition républicaine en France', *Jahrbuch des Offentlichen Rechts der Gegenwart*, no. 38, Tübingen, pp. 77–108.

Pierce, R. 1966. *Contemporary French Political Thought*, Oxford.

Pinto, D. 1977. 'Sociology as a Cultural Phenomenon in France and Italy: 1950–1972', unpublished Ph. D. thesis, Harvard University.

—— 1982. 'Le Socialisme et les intellectuels: le conflit caché', *Le Débat*, no. 18, pp. 4–10.

—— 1983–4. 'Italie: aux origines de la culture communiste', *Intervention*, no. 7, pp. 26–34.

Pinto, L. 1984. *L'Intelligence en action: Le Nouvel Observateur*, Paris.

Pisier, E. and P. Bouretz, 1985. 'Camus et le Marxisme', *Revue française de science politique*, vol. 36, no. 6, pp. 1047–63.

Pisier-Kouchner, E. (ed.). 1983. *Les Interprétations du stalinisme*, Paris.

Plamenatz, J. 1973. 'Two Types of Nationalism' in E. Kamenka (ed.), *Nationalism*, London.

Pizzorno, A. 1987. 'Politics Unbound', in C. Maier (ed.), *The Changing Boundaries of the Political*, Cambridge.

Pollak, M. 1976. 'Le Plannification des sciences sociales', *Actes de la recherches en sciences sociales*, nos 2–3, pp. 105–21.

Poperen, J. 1952. '"La Révolution française (1789–99)" par Albert Soboul', *Cahiers du Communisme* (February).

Portelli, H. 1980. *Le Socialisme français tel qu'il est*, Paris.

Posner, C. (ed.). 1970. *Reflections on the Revolution in France: 1968*, Harmondsworth.

Poster, M. 1973. 'The Hegel Renaissance', *Telos*, no. 16, pp. 109–27.

—— 1975. *Existential Marxism in Postwar France*, Princeton.

—— 1979. *Sartre's Marxism*, London.

Poulantzas, N. 1973. *Political Power and Social Classes*, London.

Pouvoirs, 1987. 'La Tradition politique', no. 42.

—— 1988. 'Mai 68', no. 39.

Quadrupanni, S. 1983. *Catalogue à prêt-à-porter penser français depuis 1968*, Paris.

Racine, N. 1971. 'Le Parti Socialiste (SFIO) devant le bolchevisme et la Russie soviétique, 1921–1924', *Revue française de science politique*, vol. 21, no. 2, pp. 281–315.

—— 1983. 'Les Socialistes français devant le régime soviétique (1920–1939)' in E. Pisier-Kouchner (ed.), *Les Interprétations du stalinisme*, Paris.

—— and O. Duhamel, 1982. 'Léon Blum, les socialistes français et l'Union soviétique' in L. Marcou (ed.), *L'URSS vue de gauche*, Paris.

Rancière, J. 1974. *La Leçon d'Althusser*, Paris.

—— 1981. '"Le Social": The Lost Tradition in French Labour History' in R. Samuel (ed.), *People's History and Socialist Theory*, London.

—— 1983. 'La Répresentation de l'ouvrier ou la classe impossible', in J. Rogozinski *et al.*, *Le Retrait du politique*, Paris.

—— 1983. *Le Philosophe et ses pauvres*, Paris.

—— 1985. 'On the Theory of Ideology—Althusser's Politics', in R. Edgley and R. Osborne (eds), *Radical Philosophy Reader*, London.

———— 1992. *Les Mots de l'histoire: Essai de poétique du savoir*, Paris.

———— and D. Rancière, 1978. 'La Légende des philosophes: les intellectuels et la traversée du gauchisme', *Les Révoltes logiques*, no. 25, pp. 7–25.

Ranger, J. 1986. 'Le déclin du Parti Communiste français', *Revue français de science politique*, vol. 36, no. 1, pp. 46–63.

Raynaud, R. 1987. *Max Weber et les dilemmes de la raison moderne*, Paris.

Reader, K. 1987. *Intellectuals and the Left in France since 1968*, London.

Rémond, R. 1959. 'Les Intellectuals et la politique', *Revue française de science politique*, vol. 9, no. 4, pp. 860–80.

———— 1966. *The Right Wing in France: From 1815 to de Gaulle*, trans. J.M. Laux, Philadelphia.

———— 1976. 'Les Problèmes politiques au lendemain de la Libération', in CNRS Symposium on *La Libération de la France*, Paris, pp. 815–34.

Renan, E. 1871. *La Réforme intellectuelle et morale*, Paris.

———— 1882. *Qu'est-ce qu'une nation?*, Paris.

Resch, R.P. 1992. *Althusser and the Renewal of Marxist Social Theory*, Berkeley.

Revault, d'Allones, M. 1989. *D'une morte à l'autre. Précipices de la Révolution*, Paris.

———— 1988. 'En finir avec la Révolution?', *Esprit: La France en politique 1988*, Paris, pp. 197–206.

Revel, J.-F. 1984. *Le Rejet de l'état*, Paris.

Reynié, D. 1985. 'La Question russe', *Intervention*, no. 13, pp. 71–81.

Richet, 1969. 'Autour des origines idéologiques lointaines de la Révolution française: élites et despotisme', *Annales: Economies, Sociétés, Civilisations*, vol. 24, no. 1, pp. 1–23.

Ricœur, P. 1980. *The Contribution of French Historiography to the Theory of History*, The Zaharoff Lecture, Oxford.

Rieber, A. 1964. *Stalin and the French Communist Party 1941–1947*, New York.

Rieff, P. (ed.). 1970. *On Intellectuals*, New York.

Rioux, J.-P. 1987. *The Fourth Republic*, trans. G. Rodgers, Cambridge.

Ritaine, E. 1983. *Les Stratèges de la culture*, Paris.

Rival, P. 1979. 'L'Etat, les intellectuels et le mouvement: de l'engagement à la dissidence', *L'Homme et la société*, nos 51–4, pp. 219–36.

Roberts, J.M. 1972. *The Mythology of the Secret Societies*, London.

Robin, R. 1973. 'La Nature de l'état à la fin de l'ancien régime: formation sociale, état et transition', *Dialectiques*, nos 1–2, pp. 31–54.

Robrieux, P. 1977. *Notre génération communiste*, Paris.

———— 1978. 'Le Rôle de l'UNEF et de l'UEC dans la préhistoire de '68', *Politique Aujourd'hui*, nos 5–6, pp. 3–6.

———— 1980–4. *Histoire intérieure du Parti Communiste*, 4 vols, Paris.

Rocard, M. 1969. *Le PSU*, Paris.

Rollet, J. 1982. 'Le Parti Socialiste et l'autogestion 1971–1978', unpublished thesis, Institut d'Etudes Politiques, Paris.

Rollin, H. 1931. *La Révolution russe*, 2 vols, Paris.

Roman, J. 1990. 'La fin du modèle républicain', *Esprit: La France en Politique 1990*, pp. 67–79.

Rony, J. 1966. 'J.-P. Sartre et le politique', *La Nouvelle Critique*, nos 173–4, pp. 100–28.

———— 1978. *Trente ans de parti: Un communiste s'interroge*, Paris.

Rorty, R. 1984. 'The Historiography of Philosophy: Four Genres' in R. Rorty,

J.B. Schneewind and Q. Skinner (eds), *Philosophy in History*, Cambridge.

Rosanvallon, P. 1976. *L'Age de l'auto-gestion*, Paris.

——— 1979a. *Le Capitalisme utopique: Critique de l'idéologie économique*, Paris.

——— 1979b. 'Le socialisme français et la peur de la social-démocratie', in FAIRE, *Qu'est-ce que c'est la Social-Démocratie?*, Paris.

——— 1982. *La Crise de l'état providence*, Paris.

——— 1984. 'Mais où est passé l'autogestion?' *Passé-Présent*, no. 4, pp. 186–94.

——— 1985. *Le Moment Guizot*, Paris.

——— 1988. *La Question syndicale*, Paris.

——— 1990. *L'Etat en France de 1789 à nos jours*, Paris.

——— 1992. *Le Sacre du citoyen: Histoire du suffrage universel en France*, Paris.

Rose, M. 1987. 'Economic Nationalism and the Unions: the Decline of the Solution Franco-Française' in G. Ross and J. Howorth (eds), *Contemporary France: A Review of Interdisciplinary Studies*, London.

Rosen, L. 1971. 'Language, History, and the Logic of Inquiry in Lévi-Strauss and Sartre', *History and Theory*, vol. 10, pp. 269–94.

Ross, G. 1978. 'Marxism and the New Middle Classes: French Critiques', *Theory and Society*, vol. 5, no. 2, pp. 163–90.

——— 1987. 'Adieu vieilles idées: the middle strata and the decline of Resistance-Left discourse in France', in J. Howorth and G. Ross (eds), *Contemporary France: A Review of Interdisciplinary Studies*, London.

——— 1990. 'Intellectuals against the Left: the case of France', *The Socialist Register*, London.

——— and J. Jenson, 1985. 'Pluralism and the Decline of Left Hegemony: the French Left in Power', *Politics and Society*, vol. 14, no. 2, pp. 115–46.

——— 1988. 'The Tragedy of the French Left', *New Left Review*, no. 171, pp. 5–44.

Roth, M.S. 1985. 'A Problem of Recognition: Alexandre Kojève and the End of History', *History and Theory*, vol. 24, no. 3, pp. 293–306.

——— 1988. *Knowing and History: Appropriations of Hegel in Twentieth Century France*, Ithaca.

Roy, C. 1976. *Somme Toute*, Paris.

Roudenescou, E. 1982, 1986. *Histoire de la psychoanalyse en France*, 2 vols, Paris.

Rousset, D. 1951. *Le Procès des camps de concentration soviétiques*, Paris.

Rudé, G. 1961. *Interpretations of the French Revolution* Historical Association Pamphlets (General Series), no. 47, London.

Rudelle, O. 1982. *La République absolue: Aux origines de l'instabilité constitutionelle de la France républicaine, 1870–1889*, Paris.

Rupnik, J. 1986. 'L'Opinion publique française et l'Union Soviétique', *L'Autre Europe*, no. 5.

Rustin, M. 1980. 'The New Left and the Present Crisis', *New Left Review*, no. 121, pp. 63–89.

Ryan, W.F. 1982. 'France: the Return of the Revolutionary Tradition', *Current History*, vol. 81, no. 479, pp. 422–5.

Sadoun, M. 1978. 'Les Facteurs de la conversion au socialisme collaborateur', *Revue française de science politique*, vol. 28, no. 2, pp. 459–87.

——— 1982. *Les Socialistes sous l'occupation*, Paris.

Salomon, J.-J. 1973. *Science and Politics*, London.

Salmon, J.-M. 1973. 'Le Désir du 22 mars', *L'Homme et la Société*, nos 29–30, pp. 3–20.

Samuel, R. 1980. 'British Marxist Historians 1880–1980', *New Left Review*, no. 120, pp. 21–96.

Sartre, J.-P. 1947–76. *Situations*, vols I–X, Paris.

———— 1948. 'Qu'est-ce que la littérature', in *Situations* II (Paris); trans. as *What is Literature?* B. Frechtman, London, 1967.

———— 1952–4. 'Les Communistes et la paix', repr. in *Situations* VI, Paris, 1964; trans. as *The Communists and Peace*, I. Clephane, London, 1969.

———— 1955. *Literary and Philosophical Essays*, trans. A. Michelson, New York.

———— 1960. *Critique de la raison dialectique*, vol. 1 (Paris); trans. as *Critique of Dialectical Reason*, vol. 1, A. Sheridan, London, rev. edn., 1991.

———— 1961. *Sartre on Cuba*, New York.

———— 1965a. 'A Plea for Intellectuals', in *Between Existentialism and Marxism*, pp. 227–85.

———— 1965b. *The Spectre of Stalin*, trans. I. Clephane, London, 1969.

———— 1968. *Search for a Method*, trans. H. Barnes, New York.

———— 1969a. 'France: Masses, Spontaneity, Party', in *Between Existentialism and Marxism*, pp. 118–37.

———— 1969b. 'Itinerary of a Thought', in *Between Existentialism and Marxism*, pp. 33–64.

———— 1970. 'A Friend of the People', in *Between Existentialism and Marxism*, pp. 286–98.

———— 1973a. 'Elections, pièges à cons', *Les Temps Modernes*, no. 318, pp. 1099–1108.

———— 1973b. *Politics and Literature*, trans. J.A. Underwood, London, 1973.

———— 1974. *Between Existentialism and Marxism*, trans. J. Matthews, London.

———— 1978. *Sartre in the Seventies*, trans. P. Auster and L. Davis, London.

———— 1984. 'Pourquoi des philosophes?', *Le Débat*, no. 29, pp. 29–42.

———— 1985. *Critique de la raison dialectique*, vol. 2, *L'Intelligibilité de l'Histoire*, Paris.

———— D. Rousset and G. Rosenthal, 1949. *Entretiens sur la politique*, Paris.

Sauvageot, J. et al., 1968. *La Révolte étudiante*, Paris.

Sawer, M. 1978. 'The Soviet Image of the Commune: Lenin and Beyond', in J. Leith (ed.), *Images of the Commune*, Montreal.

Scarpetta, G. 1979. *Brecht, ou le soldat mort*, Paris.

Schalk, D. 1979. *The Spectrum of Political Engagement*, Princeton.

Scheinman, L. 1969. 'The Politics of Nationalism in Contemporary France', *International Organization*, vol. 23, no. 4, pp. 834–58.

Schmidt, A. 1982. *History and Structure*, Boston.

Schreiner, B. 1972. 'L'Extrême gauche du Christ', *La Nef*, no. 48, pp. 43–55.

Scott, J.C. 1951. *Republican Ideas and the Liberal Tradition in France 1870–1914*, New York.

Scott, W. 1991. 'François Furet and Democracy in France', *The Historical Journal*, vol. 34, no. 1, pp. 147–71.

Scruton, R. 1985. *Thinkers of the New Left*, Harlow.

Seale, P. and M. McConville. 1969. *French Revolution 1968*, Harmondsworth.

Sécher, R. 1986. *Le Génocide franco-français: La Vendée-Vengé*, Paris.

Sédillot, R. 1987. *Le Coût de la Révolution*, Paris.

Seigel, J. 1986. *Bohemian Paris: Culture, Politics and the Boundaries of Bourgeois Life 1830–1930*, New York.

———— 1990. 'La Mort du sujet: origines d'un thème', *Le Débat* no. 58, pp. 160–9.

Serge, V. 1984. *Memoirs of a Revolutionary*, trans. P. Sedgewick, London.

Seton-Watson, H. 1955. 'The Russian Intellectuals', *Encounter* (September), pp. 43–50.

Sewell, W. 1980. *Work and Revolution in France. The Language of Labour from the Old Regime to 1848*, Cambridge.

Shennan, A. 1989. *Rethinking France: Plans for Renewal 1940–1946*, Oxford.

Short, R. 1966. 'The Politics of Surrealism 1920–1936', *Journal of Contemporary History*, no. 2, pp. 3–25.

Siegfried, A. 1956. *De la IIIe République à la IVe République*, Paris.

Signoret, S. 1975. *La Nostalgie n'est plus ce qu'elle était*, Paris.

Singer, D. 1970. *Prelude to Revolution. France in May 1968*, London.

Sirinelli, J.-F. 1986. 'Les Normaliens de la Rue d'Ulm après 1945: une génération communiste?', *Revue d'Histoire moderne et contemporaine*, t. 32, pp. 569–88.

———— 1988. *Génération intellectuelle: Khâgneux et normaliens dans l'entre-deux-guerres*, Paris.

———— 1990. *Intellectuels et passions françaises: manifestes et pétitions au XXᵉ siècle*, Paris.

Skinner, Q. 1969. 'Meaning and Understanding in the History of Ideas', *History and Theory*, vol. vii, no. 1, pp. 3–53.

———— 1974. 'The Principles and Practice of Opposition: the Case of Bolingbroke versus Walpole', in N. McKendrick, *Historical Perspectives: Studies in English Thought and Society in Honour of J.H. Plumb*, London.

Smith, R.J. 1982. *The Ecole Normale Supérieure and the Third Republic*, Albany.

Smith, S. 1984. *Reading Althusser*, Ithaca and London.

Soboul, A. 1951. *La Révolution française (1789–99)*, Paris.

———— 1954. 'Classes et luttes de classes sous la Révolution française', *La Pensée*, no. 53, repr. in *Comprendre la Révolution*, Paris, 1981.

———— 1958. *Les Sans-culottes parisiens en l'an II*, Paris.

———— 1970. 'Preface' to C. Mazauric, *Sur la Révolution française*, Paris.

———— 1974. 'Historiographie révolutionnaire classique et tentatives révisionistes', repr. in *Comprendre la Révolution*, Paris, 1981.

SOFRES, 1969. *Sondages*, nos 1–2, Paris.

———— 1976. *Sondages*, nos 3–4, Paris.

———— 1986. *L'Opinion publique*, Paris.

Sorel, G. 1929. *Matériaux d'une théorie de prolétariat*, Paris.

Sorman, G. 1985. *L'Etat minimum*, Paris.

Sorum, P.C. 1977. *Intellectuals and Decolonization in France*, Chapel Hill.

Stedman Jones, G. 1983. *Languages of Class*, Cambridge.

Sternhell, Z. 1972. *Maurice Barrès et le nationalisme français*, Paris.

———— 1986. *Neither Left nor Right. Fascist ideology in France*, trans. D. Maisel, Berkeley.

Stiefbold, A.E. 1977. *The French Communist Party in Transition: PCF-CPSU Relations and the Challenge to Soviet Authority*, New York.

Stoekl, A. 1992. *Agonies of the Intellectual: Commitment, Subjectivity, and the Performative in the Twentieth-Century French Tradition*, Lincoln, Nebraska, and London.

Stoetzel, J. 1957. 'Sociology in France: An empiricist view', in H. Becker and

H. Boskoff (eds), *Modern Sociological Theory*, New York.

Strauss, D. 1978. *Menace in the West: the Rise of French Anti-Americanism in Modern Times*, Westport, Conn.

Sturrock, J. (ed.). 1979. *Structuralism and Since: From Lévi-Strauss to Derrida*, Oxford.

Suleiman, E. 1978. *Elites in France. The Politics of Survival*, Princeton.

Swaart, K. 1964. *The Sense of Decadence in Nineteenth–Century France*, The Hague.

Taine, H. 1889. *Les Origines de la France contemporaine*, Paris.

Talmon, J. 1952. *The Origins of Totalitarian Democracy*, London.

Tarr, F. de 1961. *The French Radical Party from Herriot to Mendès-France*, Oxford.

Tarrow, S. 1975. 'Communism in Italy and France: Adaptation and Change', in D. Blackmer and S. Tarrow (eds), *Communism in Italy and France*, Princeton.

Tartakowsky, D. 1979. 'Le Marxisme et les intellectuels: 1920–1935', *La Pensée*, no. 205, pp. 30–40.

Taylor, L. 1989. 'The Parti Communiste Français and the French Resistance in the Second World War', in T Judt (ed.), *Resistance and Revolution in Mediterranean Europe*, London, pp. 53–79.

Terray, E. 1970a. 'Le Maoisme de la gauche prolétarienne et la pensée de Mao-tse-toung', *Que Faire?*, no. 1.

———— 1970b. 'La Révolution Culturelle et nous', *Que Faire?*, no. 5.

Thévenot, L. 1977. 'Les Catégories sociales en 1975', *Economie et statistique*, no. 91, pp. 3–31.

Thibaud, P. 1987. 'Les français et leur état', *Esprit*, no. 3, pp. 15–22.

Thibaudet, A. 1927. *La République des professeurs*, Paris.

———— 1932. 'Pour l'histoire du parti intellectuel', *La Nouvelle Revue française*, pp. 265–72.

Thirion, A. 1975. *Revolutionaries without Revolution*, trans. J. Neugroschel, London.

Thompson, E.P. 1978. *The Poverty of Theory*, London.

Thomson, D. 1969. *Democracy in France since 1870*, 5th edn., Oxford.

Tiersky, R. 1973. *Le Mouvement communiste en France 1920–1970*, Paris.

Tint, H. 1964. *The Decline of French Patriotism 1870–1914*, London.

Tocqueville, A. de 1963. *Democracy in America*, 2 vols, trans. H. Reeve, New York.

Tocqueville, A. de 1980. *L'Ancien régime et la Révolution*, ed. by A. Jardin, Paris.

Todorov, T. 1989a. *The Deflection of the Enlightenment*, Stanford.

———— 1989b. *Nous et les autres: la réflexion française sur la diversité humaine*, Paris.

Touchard, J. 1977. *La Gauche en France depuis 1900*, Paris.

———— 1978. *Le Gaullisme 1940–1969*, Paris.

Touraine, A. 1965. *Sociologie de l'action*, Paris.

———— 1968. *Le Mouvement de Mai ou le communisme utopique*, Paris.

———— 1969. *La Société post-industrielle*, Paris.

———— 1977. 'Intellectuels d'en haut et intellectuels d'en bas', *L'Arc*, no. 70, pp. 87–91.

———— 1980. *l'Après-Socialisme*, Paris.

Travis, D. 1989. 'Communism and Resistance in Italy, 1943–48', in T. Judt (ed.), *Resistance and Revolution in Mediterranean Europe*, London.

Tully, J. (ed.). 1988. *Meaning and Context. Quentin Skinner and his Critics*, Cambridge.

Turkle, S. 1979. *Psychoanalytic Politics: Freud's French Revolution*, London. .

Vaughan, M. 1986. 'Intellectual Power and the Powerlessness of Intellectuals', *Theory, Culture and Society*, vol. 3, no. 3, pp. 93–103.

Verdès-Leroux, J. 1983, 1987. *Le Parti Communiste, les intellectuels et la culture*, 2 vols. vol. 1: *Au service du Parti (1944–56)*; vol. 2: *le Réveil des somnambules (1956–85)*, Paris.

Victoroff-Toporoff, V. 1931. *Rossica et Sovietica. Bibliographie des ouvrages paru en français de 1917 à 1930 inclus rélatifs à la russie et à l'Urss*, Saint-Cloud.

Vidal-Naquet, P. and A. Schnapp. 1968. *Journal de la Commune étudiante*, Paris.

Vincent, J.-M. *et al.*, 1974. *Contre Althusser*, Paris.

Voltaire, 1877–85. *Oèuvres complètes*, ed. L.E.D. Morland, Paris.

Vovelle, M. 1978. 'La Longue durée', in J. Le Goff, R. Chartier, J. Revel (eds), *La Nouvelle Histoire*, Paris.

——— 1988. 'Pourquoi nous sommes encore Robespierristes', *Annales historiques de la Révolution française*, no. 274, pp. 498–506.

Wall, I. 1983. *French Communism in the Era of Stalinism*, Westport, Conn.

Wahl, J. 1932. *Vers le concret*, Paris.

Weber, E. 1962a. *Action française. Royalism and Reaction in Twentieth-Century France*, Stanford.

——— 1962b. 'Nationalism, Socialism, and National-Socialism', *French Historical Studies*, vol. 2, no. 3, pp. 273–307.

——— 1976. *Peasants into Frenchmen*, Stanford.

Weber, H. 1988. *Vingt ans après*, Paris.

Webster, P. and N. Powell. 1984. *Saint-Germain-des-Prés*, London.

Weil, S. 1962. *Selected Essays, 1934–1943*, trans. R. Rees, Oxford.

Werner, E. 1972. *De la violence au totalitarisme. Essai sur la pensée de Camus et Sartre*, Paris.

Werth, A. 1965. *De Gaulle*, Harmondsworth.

——— 1966. *France 1940–1955*, rev. edn., Boston.

White, M. 1962. 'Reflections on Anti-intellectualism', *Daedalus*, vol. 91, no. 3, pp. 457–68.

Whiteside, K. 1988. *Merleau-Ponty and the Foundation of Existential Politics*, Princeton.

Whitford, M. 1982. *Merleau-Ponty's Critique of Sartre's Philosophy*, Lexington.

Wieviorka, M. 1984. 'Les Maoistes françaises et l'hypothèse terroriste', *Esprit*, nos 10–11, pp. 133–45.

Wilkinson, J. 1981. *The Intellectual Resistance in Europe*, Cambridge, Mass.

Williams, S. (ed.). 1983. *Socialism in France: From Jaurès to Mitterrand*, London.

Wilson, E. 1968. *To the Finland Station*, London and Glasgow.

Winock, M. 1975. *Histoire politique de la revue 'Esprit', 1930–1950*, Paris.

——— 1984. 'Les Intellectuels dans le siècle', *Vingtième siècle*, no. 2, pp. 3–14.

Wohl, R. 1966. *French Communism in the Making 1914–1924*, Stanford.

Wolf, D. 1969. *Doriot. Du Communisme à la Collaboration*, trans. G. Châtenet, Paris.

Woloch, I. 1990. 'On the Latent Illiberalism of the French Revolution', *American Historical Review*, vol. 95, no. 5, pp. 1452–70.

Wood, E.M. 1986. *The Retreat from Class: a New 'True' Socialism*, London.

Zeldin, T. 1979. *Politics and Anger*, Oxford.

——— 1980. *Intellect and Pride*, Oxford.

Index

DATE DUE

JUN 0 4 2012		

Demco, Inc. 38-293